American Drama

Jacqueline Foertsch

American Drama

In Dialogue, 1714–Present

First published 2017 by
PALGRAVE

Palgrave in the UK is an imprint of Macmillan Publishers Limited, registered in England, company number 785998, of 4 Crinan Street, London, N1 9XW.

Palgrave® and Macmillan® are registered trademarks in the United States, the United Kingdom, Europe and other countries.

ISBN 978–1–137–60528–3 hardback
ISBN 978–1–137–60527–6 paperback

This book is printed on paper suitable for recycling and made from fully managed and sustained forest sources. Logging, pulping and manufacturing processes are expected to conform to the environmental regulations of the country of origin.

A catalogue record for this book is available from the British Library.

A catalog record for this book is available from the Library of Congress.

Contents

Preface

American Drama: In Dialogue, 1714–Present has been designed on behalf of undergraduates seeking an introduction to major American plays since early national inception, specifically as these are "in dialogue," with key texts and traditions from abroad and with noted predecessors in their own national canon. As America is a nation profoundly influenced by transatlantic traditions across the cultural spectrum, it is not surprising that key dramatic works and the literary movements they represent have fostered responses from US playwrights that frequently mix pronounced citation with what is uniquely native to the American experience. Thus, each part of this text begins with examination of a Transatlantic Touchstone, representing a phase in the modern dramatic tradition (e.g., expressionism, realism, Theater of the Absurd). American plays from the same period are then analyzed via individual notes, and Drama in Dialogue discussions appear throughout, comparing two works with a shared theme and/or shared influence by a Transatlantic Touchstone. Further resources, including scripts of some of the earlier plays, are available to you at www.palgravehighered.com/americandrama.

A Note Regarding Plays Selected: Because the list of plays meriting the American drama student's attention is ultimately longer than any single text can include, the decision was made to limit reference to those written by American-born authors (with the necessary exceptions of Hunter and Boucicault), receiving full-scale debut productions on an American stage (Hunter's closet drama again an exception), and devoted to native topics. Thus several canonical early works on foreign themes, indicating early America's widespread interest in classical subject matter and exotically set romantic tragedy, have been excluded. Among these are Thomas Godfrey's *The Prince of Parthia* (1765), Robert Montgomery Bird's *The Gladiator* (1831) and *The Broker of Bogota* (1834), Robert T. Conrad's *Jack Cade* (1835 [as *Aylmere*], 1841), Nathaniel P. Willis's *Tortessa, or the Usurer Matched* (1839), and George Henry Boker's widely acclaimed *Francesca da Rimini* (1853). Though many of these foreign-themed plays have fascinating American subtexts, they are yet somewhat naturally disqualified from consideration in a collection such as this, due to the marvelous array of dramas that directly and thus more deeply and diversely treat questions of vital importance to American audiences then and today.

Jacqueline Foertsch

Denton, TX, USA

Acknowledgements

I wish to thank the editors, readers, and staff at Palgrave Macmillan for their invaluable assistance with this work, including my gracious and incisive anonymous reviewers and especially Rachel Bridgewater and her predecessors in the Commissioning Editor's role, whose interest in this book has more or less called it into being. Thanks also to Production Editors Robin Moul and Elizabeth Holmes and especially to Integra Project Manager Deepakraj Murugaiyan, for keeping me and this project always on-track. I also thank the staff at the University of North Texas's Willis Library, especially its Interlibrary Loan specialists and ILL Borrowing Supervisor Lynne Wright, Remote Services Supervisor James Flowers, and Head of Access Services Mary Ann Venner, for their essential assistance in procuring on-hand, far-flung, and otherwise unavailable vital materials. To Ashley Balcazar, who indispensably assisted with the indexing of this text, I am greatly indebted. My thanks also to dear colleagues in UNT's English Department, especially Alexander Pettit, who has been a source of information and inspiration in all matters American-dramatic and who has encouraged this project at every turn. Thanks finally to my family, whose loving support is eternally appreciated, especially brother-in-law and talented Hudson Valley stage presence Michael McKee, for sharing my excitement for American drama from its earliest days. As always, this work is dedicated to Aurora McKee and Solana McKee, my bright angels, and to Terence Donovan, my ever-love.

Part I

Un-American Origins (1714–1798)

In many remarkable respects, "American drama" is an oxymoronic concept whose terms have repelled and attracted each other since national inception. Foremost among the cultural institutions fled by the Puritans in their early-seventeenth-century sojourn in the New World was the English theater, where immoral behaviors proliferated, including offenses as specific as pickpocketing and prostitution and as generally questionable as relaxation and merrymaking. Worse yet was the stage's obvious emphasis on the mystification, deception, sensationalism, and lavish display all long associated with Puritanism's theological arch-nemesis, Catholicism, and all threatening to steal thunder from the performative qualities (dare we say the entertainment value?) of the Puritan minister's own sermonizing (see also Davis, "Plays and Playwrights," 220–21). As the English Lord Protector Oliver Cromwell created strict laws to rein in the popularity of the English theater, so the Protestant factions controlling various regions in the New World made life difficult to impossible for its budding theater troupes: the earliest known staged theatrical in the colonies, *Ye Bare and Ye Cubbe* (1665), comes down to us not in the play itself, now long lost, but in the legal transcripts describing the grounds on which its cast of players were hauled into court. And in his remarkable *History of the American Theater* (1832), William Dunlap notes the religious proclivities of various colonies of the mid-eighteenth century: landing among the Episcopalians of Williamsburg, Virginia, in June 1752, Lewis Hallam's London (later American) Company thrived. As Arthur Hornblow reports, Williamsburg happily welcomed acting companies as early as 1716 (23), and players found an equally warm welcome in the southern provinces of Richmond, Charleston, and later French-Catholic New Orleans. Meanwhile, the doors of Puritan Boston remained officially closed to theater until 1793, and in Philadelphia, the Quakers, notably opposed

1

to "scenic representations" (Dunlap, *History*, 13), gave thespians more trouble than did the Puritans.

Yet as Jeffrey H. Richards has observed, "it was not only Puritans who objected to the stage…. Theater was the province of the enemy, the British" (xii), a distinction carried forward in the present-day dominance of the American theater scene by New York, "the one American city of note held by the British for the entirety of the [Revolutionary] war" (J. Richards, xii.) The earliest extant play published (though never performed) on US soil was *Androboros* (Gr. "Man-Eater," c. 1714), a satire of the colonists' misguided attempts to do away with their "plaguey Keeper[s]," including the royal governor of New York, Robert Hunter, who wrote the piece for the amusement of friends back home in England. Meanwhile, the earliest works by an American playwright—Benjamin Coleman's *Gustavas Vasa*, performed by a group of Harvard students in 1690, and Thomas Godfrey's *The Prince of Parthia* (1767), performed by Hallam's company four years after the playwright's death—were historical tragedies dealing only analogically, if even, with American themes. They were broadly indebted to numerous better-renowned dramas by the Bard himself (e.g., *Richard III, Macbeth, The Merchant of Venice*) and romantic tragedies like Thomas Otway's *Venice Preserved* (1682) and Joseph Addison's *Cato* (1712). During the war British soldiers amused themselves with amateur theatricals, and General John Burgoyne, who wrote the historical drama *The Blockade of Boston*, was only one of several English wits who used the stage (or the printed satiric dialogue) to mock the American upstart's strategic missteps during the war. The January 8, 1776, production of Burgoyne's *Blockade* was famously interrupted when a British soldier ran onstage to announce a Yankee attack on a royalist stronghold. The audience of redcoats, under the impression that the messenger was part of the cast, needed several minutes to respond to the actual call of battle.

Notably, Dunlap, who happily attended the theater from an early age, wrote numerous plays (most memorably *André* [1798]) and adaptations, and for several years managed the American Company, himself belonged to a family of staunch royalists; though he might contest the assertion, Dunlap, in his *History*, recorded the Pennsylvania legislature's Dr. Logan as saying that "theatres were only fit for monarchies" (56), that they were weapons wielded by kings to "subvert the republic" (56) and weaken democratic feelings wherever they occurred. General Wayne's canny counterclaim, that the Republic might have won the war with more ease had it made use of this same "tool" (57), is an early indication of the powerful and thus controversial effects—artistic, social, and political—of popular media such as drama in American culture.

Thus although this text focuses on "Drama in Dialogue" for reasons in evidence throughout, we might just as well have foregrounded "Dramatic Debates," "Drama's Dilemmas," or even "Dramatic Destruction!" and still be telling at least half the story. Yet we will consider the more flexible form of the dramatized conversation—sometimes harmonious, sometimes heated to riotous degrees—between the American dramatic experiment and its numerous transatlantic touchstones, its changing historical contexts, and its ever-expanding canon of works. Specifically, American drama has been influenced—if in fatefully oedipal fashion—by the forms and contents successful since the Renaissance in its parent culture of Great Britain, as well as by melodrama from France, realism from Scandinavia and Russia, and expressionism and absurdism from diverse European originators of these forms. All the while, American dramatists, managers, and critics struggled to encourage a native style that indeed became visible almost immediately—but almost always in dialogue with or, as early American playwright Royall Tyler would put it, in "contrast" to the European influences that were equally ever present. Each section of this text, therefore, opens by discussing one of the transatlantic touchstones integral to the development of American drama.

Despite both the religious intolerance and the patriot loyalism broadly in play during the Revolutionary era, both publically staged and private, at-home theatricals were a popular pastime. Even in Puritan-dominated Boston, subscriptions filled immediately to build a theater in 1796, a mere three years following repeal of a 40-year law banning public performance (Dunlap, *History*, 140). Again, ironically, the dramatic subject was almost always English or European—Shakespeare, Sheridan, English translations of the French Molière or the German Kotzebue—as were the theater staff and players. With unstinting regularity, managers sailed back across the Atlantic to recruit their actors, and the "theatrically vigorous community" of Jamaica (Williams, 304) was a regular resting ground whenever theater became too controversial in the colonies or yellow fever raged too close to the stage door (see also Williams, 305).[1] The aristocratic husband of one of America's original sweethearts—the lovely and talented Mrs. Ann Merry—would have been scandalized to let his wife cavort onstage before home audiences (Dunlap, *History*, 175–76; see also Hornblow, 214). In the far-flung, socially meaningless provinces of the New World, however, she was allowed to ply her trade with success, and Americans took it for granted that all of their favorite stage actors hailed from the land of their recent mortal enemy. Even several of early American theater's most

---

[1] To explain the discrepancy, Francis Wemyss suggested in 1852 that "the stage seems to have been overlooked as a means of livelihood, and it was only as the children of the English actors (born in the United States) became men and women, and adopted the Profession of their parents, that native talent was brought into requisition" (116–17).

popular "stage Yankees"—naïve yet forthright comical characters espousing the homespun views of American backwoodsmen, foot-soldiers, and green-horns—were British born, including Thomas Wignell, Joseph Jefferson I, and Charles Mathews.

Thus in the decades of our origin as a nation, to write for, act in, build stages for, attend, or enjoy dramatic production was declared (and often felt) to be spiritually, politically, and artistically un-American. Well into the nineteenth century, American theater was a notably lopsided proposi-tion: evermore-stately theaters on US soil, packed to the rafters with eager, native-born playgoers imbibing a mainly foreign import of English plays presented by English players. As Hornblow explains, British and European dramas dominated partly for economic reasons: the lack of copyright pro-tection for published works with proven success abroad made these works attractive and affordable (often free for the taking). There prevailed the largely unquestioned sentiment (due no doubt to the centrality of Shakespeare to the dramatic endeavor throughout the West at this point) that any play worth seeing would have "lately played in London." Who better to interpret these favorite English or translated Continental narratives than Englishmen themselves? And as Hornblow's helpful transcription of several early playbills indicates, an rather narrow spectrum of English favorites could and often did provide a lifetime's entertainment: one was hardly bored, in fact, from one's 15th viewing of Shakespeare's *Macbeth* or Sheridan's *School for Scandal*, as the point was not to be surprised by the plot, but transported by the unique staging and performance from one presentation to the next. Finally, American drama—plays by native-born authors most often on American themes—comprised the slenderest portion of American theater as it was received in this country for almost a century. Two famous early examples of such—Royall Tyler's *The Contrast* (1787) and Anna Cora Mowatt's *Fashion* (1845)—are comedies of manners obviously derived from their English pre-decessors by the likes of Congreve, Goldsmith, and Sheridan, despite their clear attempts to differentiate uniquely American virtue from superannuated European vice.

American theater's enthrallment to the English tradition takes on a remark-able cast in the example of William Alexander Brown's African Company, which fought admirably and even profitably for existence throughout the early 1820s. Himself a British subject from the West Indies, Brown estab-lished a successful lower-Manhattan pleasure garden, the African Grove, for his fellow citizens of color, in a style coincident with sophisticated, rooftop entertainment venues of the period that catered to whites only. When the Grove was disbanded, Brown recruited actors, singers, and dancers from his entertainment staff for a troupe, then opened a theater with a full slate of English favorites including Shakespeare's *Richard III* and *Othello* and Sheridan's *Pizarro*. Bruce McConachie adds, "So many white New Yorkers began to attend his productions that Brown was pulling patrons away from the nearby Park Theater" (144).

If the entire American theater scene might be accused in this period of over-indebtedness to a non-native tradition, the African Company's "imitations" of the English classics struck the white theatrical establishment as beyond the pale: the manager of the high-tone Park Theater, Stephen Price, chased Brown's company out of its own Park Row venue when it dared to stage *Richard III* shortly after the Park had presented the same; Price's henchmen broke up Brown's production and then followed the cast downtown, where they destroyed scenery and costumes and brutalized Brown himself (see also McConachie, 144). Later the English comedian Charles Mathews returned to England after a convivial meeting with Brown's leading man, James Hewlett, only to "parod[y] the black company as incompetent would-be Shakespearians" (Hill, "The African Theater," 36). According to Errol G. Hill, who provides all of the details in this account, "Hewlett addressed a public letter to Mathews denouncing his actions, then traveled to England in the fall of 1824 to challenge Mathews, but the two never met. Hewlett came home bitterly disappointed" ("The African Theater," 36; see also Toll, 26–27).

Notably, the versatile Hewlett was American-born, yet his penchant for English "imitation" went beyond the typical early nineteenth-century American actor's reliance on Shakespeare and his brethren for major roles. Hewlett impersonated not only famous tragic figures but also actors themselves, including the uncivil Charles Matthews, the great Edmund Kean, the new American star Edwin Forrest, and "some thirty actors and singers, male and female" (Hill, "The African Theater," 36). When, in their venue across from the Park, Brown announced that the African Company would imitate the Park by playing *Richard III* and that Hewlett would present his Richard "in imitation of Mr. Kean" (qtd. in Hill, "The African Theater," 29), this must have struck the likes of Stephen Price as the last straw. Brown was himself an Englishman, with, one could argue, more rights to and affinities with the Bard's canon than the average American-born theater manager of the day. But all other encounters between Shakespeare and blackness in early America involved the mediations of burnt cork and (except in the case of *Othello*) the comic mode, specifically the Shakespeare travesties that comprised the afterpiece of many minstrel shows. There was simply no room in the 1820s white imaginary for African Americans to get Shakespeare right, as evidenced by the writing of "editor Mordecai Noah of the *National*

Advocate [who] found it necessary to advise readers that his criticism of the African Theater's staging of *Richard III* was not a satiric fable, but that the production actually took place" (Hill, "The African Theater," 26).

Thus Hewlett's "Kean" imitations of white acting styles implicitly shone a spotlight on white American actors' imitations of an English tradition not their own; likewise, it reverse-mimicked white minstrels' imitations of black faces and forms of expression in equal measures of admiration and mockery (or as Eric Lott has phrased it, "love and theft"), the turned tables of which white audiences simply would not countenance. The African Company was disbanded by 1824, yet, despite his foreign origins, Brown is credited with having written the first African American drama produced in the United States, the non-extant *Drama of King Shotaway* (1822), based on Caribbean historical events (see Hill, "The African Theater," 32–33). It is likely that the great black Shakespearean Ira Aldridge, who spent most of his illustrious career abroad, got his start with Brown's African Company as well. Loften Mitchell observes, "With the destruction of the African Company, [Aldridge] felt there was little opportunity for a black actor on these shores.... It is a comment on the era in which he lived that, while he was sailing for England, white British actors were sailing for America" (25).

In this section, led off with discussion of Sheridan's key text, the styles most popular across the Atlantic in this period—satiric dialogues, manners comedies, and verse tragedies—are exemplified, yet Americanized, in the plays of Hunter, Tyler, and Dunlap.

A Transatlantic Touchstone: *The School for Scandal* (1777)

Richard Brinsley Sheridan (1751–1816)

Early American playgoers enjoyed the dramatic output of eighteenth-century English playwrights almost as often as they did Shakespeare. From available records, their favorites included George Farquhar's *The Beaux Stratagem* (1707), Oliver Goldsmith's *She Stoops to Conquer* (1773), and this masterpiece from Sheridan, *The School for Scandal*. It is this play that Royall Tyler saw performed when he visited the theater for the first time in New York, on military business in March 1787, and this play that the naïve Yankee Jonathan fails to realize he has witnessed during his night of adventure in Tyler's American answer to Sheridan, *The Contrast*. The original Jonathan, played by the great comic mainstay of Lewis Hallam's Old America Company,

Thomas Wignell, even remarks, in a moment of meta-theatric high comedy, on his special enjoyment of the performance of a "cute … little fellow … with red hair" (35) by the name of Darby Wagall. (Darby was the name of a comic character from John O'Keefe's musical comedy *The Poor Soldier* [1783], played by Wignell with great success. Arthur H. Nethercot suggests that this would have been the afterpiece viewed by Tyler on the night he saw *School for Scandal* performed.) In Sheridan's play, Wignell played the lead spoiler, Joseph Surface, although Sir Peter Teazle and Lady Teazle have always been audience favorites, regarded as comic tours de force to be enjoyed from their favorite romantic leads. It was especially the role of the coquettish, gossipy, grasping, but ultimately chastened, loving, and heroic Lady Teazle that was prized by sweethearts of the early American stage; the nineteenth-century theater critic William Winter remarked in 1874 that beloved Lady Teazles to date included Fanny Kemble in the 1830s, Anna Cora Mowatt (see discussion of her play *Fashion* later in this text), and Lillie Langtry in the late nineteenth century. Since its first performance in New York (believed to be in 1785), *The School for Scandal* "has been performed in every considerable theater in the United States, and often it has enlisted the talent of remarkably brilliant groups of actors" (Winter, 10).

As Winter also suggests, Sheridan embodied the legacy of English manners comedy in place for the preceding 80 years; he claimed the likes of Congreve, Wycherley, and Farquhar as literary ancestors but modernized their themes for his late eighteenth-century audiences. Per Winter, Sheridan "came upon the scene at a period when English fine society was in an extremely artificial state" (3) and satirized the backbiting, hypocrisy, and subterfuge of his own social milieu; "the piece transcends locality and epoch…. The inhabitant of yesterday, to-day, and to-morrow, can perceive the meaning, feel the power, and enjoy the sparkling gaiety of 'The School for Scandal'" (5). Though some regard Sheridan, with his blending of manners and sentimental comic forms, to have softened the bitter edges of work from earlier playwrights, Winter, who wrote from the rather tightly wound Victorian age, considers that Sheridan in his own life succumbed to some of his age's worst vices, specifically "profligate associations (with the Prince Regent and his shameless set) and most of all [to] intemperance" (6). Sheridan's play "rebukes vice by depicting it," but "there is no considerable comedy in our language … that stands further off from the simplicity of nature [or] moves in a more garish light…. [His play] contains no person on whom the imagination can dwell with delight or to whom the heart can become devoted" (Winter, 4–5). Notably, this review appears on the occasion of an adaptation of Sheridan's play by the late nineteenth-century playwright Augustin Daly; Winter defends Daly's revision against the charge of "Bowdlerism," claiming instead, "There is much gold in the Old English Comedy [including *The School for Scandal*]; but the dirt that is in it should be cast aside" (12).[2]

The School for Scandal updates the ancient comedy ensuing from the marriage of a foolish old man and a flirtatious young woman, giving these traditional stock characters the dimensions, intelligence, and integrity to recognize finally their own shortcomings and their actual love for each other (see also Havens, 28). Instead of being hustled offstage with a horns on his head as the curtain falls, Sir Peter enters the charmed circle of marital felicity, seeming to meet the woman of his dreams for the first time as Lady Teazle transforms from scheming scandalmonger into the loving wife he deserves. Joining them are Charles Surface and his beloved Maria, the former a fun-loving but goodhearted libertine. He grows into the role of husband just in time to save Maria from the predations of his elder brother Joseph (favored by Maria's misguided uncle Sir Peter) and the inauthentic intentions of foppish Benjamin Backbite. Even the conniving Joseph is pledged to troublemaking Lady Sneerwell—enjoined to "marry her" (219) by wise old Sir Oliver as Joseph dashes after her when their plot is foiled. As Sheridan's great-grandson, the second Marquess of Dufferin and Ava, remarked in a 1902 edition of Sheridan's plays, Joseph is one of Sheridan's many complex characters; to retain our sympathies for Lady Teazle, who would plummet in our estimation should she be caught dallying with "a mere vulgar hypocrite," Sir Joseph "ought to be rendered sufficiently attractive" (ix) to account for her momentary diversion. The hard-drinking spendthrift Charles seems equally difficult to measure by any traditional moral yardstick.

Notably, therefore, Sheridan does not reserve a happy ending only for the Dudley Do-Rights and blushing virgins of his cast; many are redeemed by pairing off, with the suggestion that true love can either improve or simply withstand improvident but typical human behaviors. By contrast, Royall Tyler's conscientious imitation *The Contrast* (with even its own heroine named Maria with her own cantankerous guardian pushing her into the wrong marriage) banishes everyone from the charmed circle except the rather drippy Colonel Manly and Maria. The sparkling coquette Charlotte has reformed by play's end, just as does Sheridan's Lady Teazle, but remains stage-right to sparkle on unattended, as her main prospect, Dimple, combining the two

---

[2] The most striking aspect of Daly's version is the massive rearrangement of scene order from Sheridan's original. Daly has in fact cut "scenes" altogether, extending each act into one lengthy session, perhaps to reduce the number of sets required, and likely to drastically reduce the number of scene changes. With these streamlining shifts, there are also some cuts, and there is an overall galloping quality to Daly's rendition. In general he seems to have spared his late-nineteenth-century audience from whatever seemed excessive in Sheridan's original by having there be less of it.

imperfect Surface brothers into one perfectly odious villain, has been pushed offstage in Tyler's somewhat prudish and moralistic (i.e., American) update (see also Seibert, 9; and Havens, 19–22).

Androboros (c. 1714)

Robert Hunter (1666–1734) with Lewis Morris (1671–1746)

This early American document—the earliest extant play—precedes by many decades Sheridan's manners comedy from a more sentimental age and belongs instead to two genres popular in that same century: the political satire and the comic farce. Author Robert Hunter (royal governor of New York) and his likely coauthor Lewis Morris (Hunter's close friend and anticorruption ally, later governor of New Jersey) may have started the play as a comment on the absurd "vestment scandal" that rocked lower Manhattan, when unidentified intruders entered the vestryroom of Trinity Church in February 1714 and smeared prayer books and clerical vestments with excrement. The offended Rev. William Vesey had been embroiled with Hunter since his arrival in 1710 over land and parish jurisdiction disputes; as Hunter searched out the culprit of the desecration, he took the occasion to insinuate that Vesey had done the smearing himself in an effort to impugn Hunter's administration. In *Androboros*, Hunter casts Vesey as the scheming cleric Fizle, who indeed perpetrates the scandal just to cause trouble. Androboros figures Gen. Francis Nicholson, known for his vicious temper and vindictive ways, who was on his way to investigate the vestry scandal when *Androboros* appeared. (Nicholson never arrived and was later recalled from his supervisory role.) At the end of Hunter's play, Androboros, Fizle, and Flip (Francis Philips, a dissipated minister from Connecticut whom Vesey supported during his own scandals) go through a trapdoor designed to remove "Keeper" (Hunter himself); as might be suggested by this name, an insane asylum is the setting where the state legislature and related merchants and litigators convene. As Peter A. Davis remarks in his recent full-length book on this play, "[S]hort, crude and often bawdy plays [like *Androboros*], written by anonymous authors and passed from hand to hand, were rarely acted due to their severe and inflammatory lampoonery. Nevertheless, they provided an opportunity for disgruntled colonists (and at least one royal governor) to vent their grievances and promote their ideas to fellow citizens …" (*From Androboros*, xv).

Keeper is assisted by wise Aesop (Hunter's good friend and advisor David Jamison) and Solemn (coauthor Morris). Aesop forever tries to rein in the power-crazed assemblymen with pertinent animal fables, and Solemn ring-leads a plot to drive Androboros to distraction by pretending that he has died and can no longer be seen or heard or do any harm. In addition to the Shakespearian-style "walking ghost" (Richardson, *American Drama*, 10) and "vestment" farces, the play satirizes the infantile machinations of the inmates, who persist in deluding themselves regarding their consequentiality. Establishing rules in an early scene, they declare that "to prevent Confusion, not above three or four at most are permitted to speak at Once" (3) and agree to protest the quality and quantity of food provided. Coxcomb (Daniel Coxe, a detracting assemblyman who later complained directly to the Crown regarding Hunter's administration) keeps interjecting, "Damn all rules! Let's proceed to business," (4), but it is ultimately decided "that neither this House, or they whom we represent are bound by any Laws, Rules, or Customs, ... that this House disclaims all Powers, Preeminencies [*sic*], and Authoritys [*sic*] except it's [*sic*] own" (4). The assemblymen use high-flown, nonsensical rhetoric to enlarge their persecuted status, including, "Our Grievances being innumerable, I shall Enumerate them" (2). Arguing about how to broadcast the vestment scandal, the dimwitted Mulligrub (Samuel Mulford, who led Long Island's campaign to secede from New York) thinks the ministers are complaining about "odours," some of which are "sweet ... as well as sower."

FLIP: Slid; tis *Ordure*, (and not *Odour*) which is but another name for T—d.
MULLIGR: Write it down so then, for a T—d is a T—d the world over.
AESOP: And the more you stir it, the more 'twill stink. But go on. (12)

It is ironic that America's earliest surviving play is so vigorously anti-American; a blogger for "the Archivist's Mailbag" on *Trinity Wall Street*'s website notes that in *Androboros*, "The conflict between England and the colonies that would erupt into Revolutionary War 60 years later is apparent," and Hunter mocks the very claims to "Liberty" soon to be central to the patriot cause. Yet Hunter is congratulated by historians for his anticorruption campaigns (of which this play is considered especially effective);[3] his native "wit and intelligence"

---

[3] Meserve, posits that with *Androboros* "Hunter silenced his opposition, turned the people to his point of view, and ... could report by 1717 political Harmony in New York (40). Richardson emphasizes the play's accessibility and credits it with "ha[ving] the desired effect: ... Nicholson's appointment [was] revoked, and Hunter had reached a *rapprochement* with the colonial assembly" (*American Drama*, 10). Richardson also points out that the many comic action sequences suggest that Hunter had envisioned a staged production, yet all agree that the play never received fame in Hunter's lifetime, that it was received as a closet drama and circulated mainly among Hunter's allies (see, e.g., Davis, *From Androboros*, 53). How well this play was known, and how it managed to effect such change despite its closet status, remain, therefore, questions of interesting debate.

and his "rational approach to the teachings of the Church" that clashed with Vesey's "narrow interpretation" (Meserve, 39); and his administration's overall "earnestness, fairness, and competency" (Davis, *From Androboros*, 51). Hunter died as colonial governor of Jamaica in 1734, leaving for New York lawmakers an example of good governance—and effective political satire—to emulate during their own rule in later decades.

The Contrast (1787)

Royall Tyler (1757–1826)

Royall Tyler wrote the first comedy—and the first drama of any kind on an explicitly American theme—performed by a professional company in the United States. It was a success by early American standards, yet Tyler was notably removed from the theatrical world for much of his life: he was trained at Harvard for the legal profession and spent most of his career in his native Massachusetts and later in Vermont as a lawyer and a judge, even a justice of the Vermont Supreme Court. He may have taken part in forbidden student theatricals while in college and was surely exposed to classical and contemporary dramas in that student role. But as a citizen of the most Puritan state in the union it was all but guaranteed that his experience with live theater would be nil up until the day, March 21, 1787, when, while on a military junket to New York, he entered the John Street Theater and watched the Hallam-Henry-Wignell Old America Company perform Sheridan's *The School for Scandal*. Immediately inspired to write his own play in the Sheridan mode, Tyler completed the draft in three weeks and presented it to the John Street managers for approval; instantly the low-comic genius Wignell identified for himself an opportunity in the bumpkin Jonathan, the original stage Yankee and one of *The Contrast*'s most enduring contributions. Other types in his company—the strapping John Henry as Colonel Manly, the "well-formed" Mrs. Morris as Charlotte—were soon cast, and *The Contrast* debuted on April 16, 1787, playing to great acclaim up and down the colonies until 1804 (Meserve, 97). Thenceforward, Tyler wrote a half-dozen other plays of minor note, one novel, and sundry essays and poems; he later suffered professional and personal setbacks, losing his judgeship, ending his life in relative poverty, and suffering greatly from the facial cancer that ended his life in 1826. Though he was a well-known, widely admired jurist in his day, he is remembered mainly for *The Contrast*, a pinnacle achievement for all involved.

Hailed at its debut and ever since as an essential document in national identity formation, *The Contrast* arrived on the scene at a moment rife with economic, political, and cultural upheaval. Shays's Rebellion (1786–1787), an insurrection of impoverished farmers against pro-mercantile government policy, had been put down just months earlier (due at least minimally to the efforts of Tyler himself); the country was in the depths of a postwar depression; and Tyler's satire waded into the debate between elites and populists that carries on in the United States to this day. As several critics have pointed out, *The Contrast* would have all of it both ways, such that a more accurate name for the play might have been *The Conflict, The Contradiction, The Confusion,* or even *The Complexities of Context.* What is most clearly distinguished, however, is some form of honest Americanism against shameless and shameful Anglophilia. Because none of the characters is actually English, those who obsessively quote the famous English womanizer Chesterfield and, even more obnoxiously, refer to him as "my lord" violate core American values with respect to democracy and equality: per Gary A. Richardson, "Dimple's willingness to adopt an English moral and social model suggests the precariousness of the identity that flowed from national independence.... British social attitudes and values, long admired by Americans, still held many captive" (*American Drama,* 48).

The main contrast, therefore, is between Colonel Manly (with his "waiter," Jonathan) and Billy Dimple (with his servant, Jessamy), while the various females are up for grabs: fought fought over by the men from both factions or subject to improvement by the proper circumstances, in which all fortuitously find themselves at the final curtain. The sentimental heroine, Maria, is rescued by the shining example of Manly from her loveless attachment to the dissipated and duplicitous Dimple (and the misplaced preference bestowed on him by Maria's doting father),[4] Charlotte is also rescued by Manly (her brother) from dishonorable advances once more from the conniving Dimple, and Jessamy pretends to attach Jonathan to Jenny only to win her for himself. But as the contrast develops in the play's early scenes, "Charlotte, Letitia,

---

[4] Tyler's biographers, Ada Lou and Herbert L. Carson, report the remarkable background to this triangle: as a young man, Tyler himself was regarded as the Dimple character in his budding romance with Nabby Adams, daughter of the second president. In 1782, Abigail Adams wrote her husband while he represented the United States in London that Tyler "had a very pretty patrimony left to him, possessing a sprightly fancy, ... [but] he was rather negligent in his business ... and dissipated two or 3 years of his Life and too much of his fortune for to reflect upon with pleasure" (qtd. in Carson and Carson, 18). John Adams separated the couple by taking his daughter for a year's sojourn with him in London; Tyler was so distraught that he failed to keep up his communications with Nabby, who eventually met and

and Dimple all constantly speak in asides, signaling their duplicity…. Only Maria, Manly and Van Rough [Maria's father] soliloquize: only they say what they mean and mean what they say" (Rinehart, 36). Thus the play's success may be best explained by what Richardson refers to as its "artistic jingoism" (*American Drama*, 48)—its foregrounding of the opposition that had unified the various patriot classes during the war: no sooner had the redcoats marched back to their boats than the infighting began, but at least Americans could agree about the originality and worth of their native enterprise.

Everywhere else in *The Contrast* such distinctions shimmer and dissolve. Even in scenes designed to point up the difference between Jonathan and Jessamy, for instance, it is evident that both servants resemble their masters: Jonathan regards Jessamy as dressed so "topping" that he mistakes him for his master, the critique here against servants dissatisfied with their station in life. Yet Jonathan quickly insists on the term "waiter," as "servant" is too servile for a "true blue son of liberty," whose "father has as good a farm as the colonel" (464). We certainly could not admire Colonel Manly if he lorded it over the humble Jonathan, yet Dimple and Jessamy enjoy their own classless fraternity in their shared love of Chesterfield and their equal skills with the flirtation, gossip, and misbehavior that occupy the *bon ton*. Jessamy is so slick that the reader may forget that he is not destined for one of the coquettes (Charlotte or Letitia), but must set his cap for the crude and lowborn Jenny, per his actual social station. Thus even as it targets the issue of social class—and the inborn sense of honor and integrity frequently described as "class" today—*The Contrast* slips on the slippery slope that is class identification in the US context.

As several readers of this play have also noted, Colonel Manly is almost as difficult to like as the sugary Dimple; Richardson regards him as "more than a bit pompous" (*American Drama*, 49), though as early as 1889, theater historian George Seilhamer described Manly as "an insufferable prig" (qtd. in Pressman, 96), and somewhat later Walter J. Meserve could only note that he was "a stiff and sentimental bore, but a patriotic bore" (98). Though admirable in his

---

married a very "Manly" type of character, Colonel William Smith, described by Abigail as "a Gentleman of unblemished reputation" (qtd. in Carson and Carson, 19–20). As irony would have it, Adams eventually rued the day when he pushed these two together, declaring, in June 1786, Smith to have disgraced him more than any other person ever had: "His pay will not feed his dogs; and his dogs must be fed if his children starve. What a folly!" (qtd. in Carson and Carson, 50). Within the year, Tyler was busy with his career in Boston and had evidently recovered enough to satirize the event in his play; compounding the irony, Mrs. Adams saw it performed and thought that Dimple had been written to satirize Colonel Smith (Carson and Carson, 33).

threadbare soldier's coat and his efforts to locate funding for his ailing fellow veterans, Manly never met the man (or woman) he would not sermonize on patriotic themes. (In Manly's defense Daniel F. Havens observes that Tyler wrote in an age taken with the high-flown rhetoric of heroic drama and as the product of a college experience saturated with "the high political and patriotic oratory of his day" [11]). Mid-story Manly counters Dimple's inquiries regarding his travels with the indeed priggish "Therefore I do not wish to see [the sites of Europe]. For I can never esteem that knowledge valuable which tends to give me a distaste for my native country" (486). Yet earlier that day, Jonathan exhibited the same cultural myopia—due to moralistic fears of the playhouse as the "devil's drawing room"—when he comically relates an inadvertent trip to the theater the night before, mistaking the actors onstage for a family behind a removable wall in the house next door. As Sarah E. Chinn remarks, "[W]here Manly's lack of experience of the world outside the United States is represented as a virtue, Jonathan's naiveté about the sophisticated urban world he has just entered is played for laughs" (110; see also Richardson, *American Drama*, 50; and Havens, 11). In general, the play's more debatable points are regarded as something of a draw; per Richard S. Pressman, "Tyler's strategy is to place himself and the audience *between* Dimple and Manly, though closer to the latter" (98), and per Donald T. Seibert Jr., "the often extremely staid sentiments, though clearly threatened by the element of laughter, are not finally undercut" (5).

Yet the other contests staged in the play—between country and city, agrarianism and mercantilism, populism and elitism—are synthesized in the marriage of Manly and Maria in favor of the already well-formed ruling class, represented by Maria's father, whose mantra is to "mind the main chance": "Through its modeling of Henry Manly, who merges republican and self-interested theatricality in his settling of the American cultural future, *The Contrast* theatrically enacts post-revolutionary American identity as adjustment to the marketplace" (Evelev, 84). And "the marriage, then, represents the union of physiocrat and Federalist, country and city, agrarian and mercantile—but under the locus of the mercantilist class" (Pressman, 100).

André (1798)

William Dunlap (1766–1839)

As noted in the introduction, theater during the Revolutionary Era was the provenance of the occupying British army, at the same time flying in the face of numerous Puritan and Quaker phobias regarding "representations" unique to the New England context. As New York City grew eventually into the epicenter for dramatic production in the United States, due to its nonstop occupation by the British in this period, so the American-but-loyalist-born William Dunlap came into his love of theater partly through his exposure to productions staged by occupying soldiers in 1770s New York. Notably, Major John André was not only a talented featured player in such companies, well loved by audiences of both loyalist and patriot stripes, but he was also infamously involved in Benedict Arnold's attempt to hand over West Point to the royal military, and hanged by General Washington as a spy in a climate of great ambivalence and controversy. André had petitioned for the gentleman-soldier's death by firing squad and was resolutely consigned by Washington to the ignominy of hanging, and those who bore witness to these events were as mixed regarding the death of this beloved local figure as they were regarding the severing of ties to a noble culture that had only recently been their own (see also Richardson, *American Drama*, 57).

With regard to how enmeshed the warring parties were in this period, General Arnold was married to a staunch loyalist who may have been André's mistress, and the three militiamen responsible for André's capture certainly could not identify his enemy status by a "foreign accent" or any manner of dress or comportment. Only when they searched his person and located incriminating documents from Arnold did they know who André was, and one of the captors was himself dressed in the coat of a Hessian mercenary to the British cause, causing André to mistake them for Tories and ask them for safe passage. In other words, the only way to distinguish oneself as an American patriot or a sworn enemy at this inaugural national moment was to purposely *enact* the identity in question. There was no inherent way to claim either one or the other, and André was captured, tried, and executed because he failed to maintain his spy's role—to act the part of a patriotic American—in desperate circumstances. As Jeffrey H. Richards notes, André "might have been released [by the three militiamen] with a pass had he not, under Arnold's urging, disguised himself (60) and been found with a passport for one 'Mr. Anderson'" (Philbrick, 104). Ironically, André was caught because he was costumed as an American peasant instead of as the British military officer he was, and hanged like a common felon because his act of disguise guaranteed to his prosecutors that he was not simply an enemy officer caught off-post, but a nefarious spy. Celebrated during the war as a talented presence on the New York stage, André was caught and executed for a fatally flawed performance.

André develops the thesis that both treachery and patriotism are "acts" put on with duplicity or valor in desperate circumstances such as war and its aftermath; "honor" and "virtue" (gained, lost, and debated everywhere in this play) are only maintained by staunch adherence to one's designated role. Equally prevalent is the contest between "fame" (the immortal reputation attending noble deeds in battle and/or an honorable soldier's death) and "infamy" (diversely construed as spying itself, basing decisions on emotion or influence, emotional outbursts, and the death by hanging so piteously feared by, yet so inevitably awaiting, the otherwise brave and stoical André). General Washington's advisor M'Donald and the young officer, Bland, stage an intractable debate between reason and passion as André moves closer to his execution hour. M'Donald, named by Richardson as "the author's surrogate" (*American Drama*, 56) insists that even the "gratitude" Bland feels for André (who had years earlier saved his life) is a self-interested motivation for loyalty and admiration: "These things prove gossamer, and balance air:/Perversion monstrous of man's moral sense." (Dunlap, *André*, 545). Representing sentiment and idealism, Bland critiques "[c]old-blooded reasoners, such as thee, [who] would blast/All warm affection, asunder sever/every social tie of humanized man" (Dunlap, *André*, 546). Ultimately, the General earns "fame" in the hearts of a grateful nation by sticking to his guns (or noose, as the case may be); even Bland's mother, whose husband will be killed by the British in retaliation if André is executed, reveres him as a paragon of Enlightenment rationality. Bland's own father nobly echoes Washington's honor-boundedness when he posts from his site of capture that, under all circumstances, the General must "do [his] duty" (Dunlap, *André*, 541). Despite his sticking with the unpopular choice, the General portrays "the touch of sweet humanity" (Dunlap, *André*, 554) when he hears the pleas of André's fiancée and weeps openly. If anything, the General is in greater agony over the impending execution than is André himself; his longest speech opens: "O, what struggles must I undergo!/Unbless'd estate!" (Dunlap, *André*, 557). Overall, a generation gap develops throughout the story—between young, impetuous romantics (Bland, André, and fiancée, Honoria) whose desires are foiled, and sadder, wiser elders whose decisions carry the day (see also Canary, 95).

The modern reader might well regard the André-mania enabling this original American tragedy as only the founding example of the American cult of celebrity worship that to this day excuses all manner of bad behavior so long as the perpetrator is attractive, glamorous, talented, or wealthy. Surely, Dunlap's original audience would have sent countless less charming war criminals to their deaths without a tear shed. Yet *André* works to redeem its title character by drawing him not as a good actor or as a crafty spy, but as an honorable ("true") man who finally humbly accepts his sentence. Per the record, the historic André walked arm in arm with his executioners to the gallows and slipped the noose around his own neck (Thacher, 228) and deserves our best estimation because of this noble death if nothing else. Although it is possible that such magnanimity at one's own execution was just the final "act" of a talented player who on the inside trembled with cowardly fear or mocked his gullible American admirers, it becomes impossible to extricate the fabrication from the actuality when the chips are down this far—when the "trapdoor" that opens at the last moment is not a means of escape to the green room, but to his actual demise.

As complicated as was the reaction to André's execution in its original moment and for the characters reenacting this reaction in Dunlap's play, the audience for *André* (a fair number of whom were surely veterans and their families) spent their hisses on the prospect of the excitable Bland ripping the cockade (a badge denoting officer's rank) from his helmet in a gesture of rebuke to the executioner Washington: "Thus from my helm/I tear, what once I proudly thought, the badge/of virtuous fellowship" (535). Whether the play valorized such statement making as speaking truth to power in defense of a noble friend, or whether it condemned Bland's unpatriotic act by giving Washington the final word, remains forever indeterminate; as Norman Philbrick observes, "Dunlap … attempted to keep a balance [between conservative, English-identified Federalist and revolutionary, French-identified Republican sentiments], but his own prejudice in favor of Federalism colors the play. More importantly … a point of view which gave both sides fairly would have satisfied no one, so intensely partisan was the political climate" (111; see also Canary, 96). Such artistic quandaries suggest the confusion, contentiousness, and general dangerousness of political life in the decades following the American Revolution.

Either the offensive business with the cockade or intrinsic deficiencies elsewhere caused attendance to fall sharply after one night and the play to close after three, and Dunlap's rather awkward attempt to smooth ruffled feathers —by inserting dialogue restoring Bland's badge after a proper display of remorse—came too late for the staged production and even the print version, as it had to be appended in a last-minute Preface. Though General Washington would have never caved in to popular sentiment thus, Dunlap five years later repurposed the gist of his story into the overtly patriotic *The Glory of Columbia—Her Yeomanry!* This version enjoyed "fame" as a Fourth of July pageant for years afterward, though "infamy" among modern readers, such as biographer Robert H. Canary, who describes it as "execrable but [once] profitable" (99) for sacrificing the complex challenges presented in the original tragic rendition. Dunlap was serving time in this period as the beleaguered manager of the Park Theater, so knew better than any simply aspirational playwright the bitter truths regarding the need to please the public in order to keep the candles lit. *The Glory of Columbia* was one of several insipid pageants penned by Dunlap to maintain his theater's solvency and his own, and his several translations of early melodramas by the German August von Kotzebue were instantly, tremendously preferred to the artistic and political challenge presented by the likes of *André*.

Drama in Dialogue: *The Contrast* and *André*

These original American dramas, though closely modeled on genres inherited from the English tradition, take nevertheless as their shared subject a thorough exploration of the newly minted American character. For both, this character is largely reducible to a single historical figure—George Washington, whose values are shown to represent the American at his best in the heady throes of a righteous victory against the English king. Were Washington not a married man throughout the lives of the plays in question, Tyler might have imported him directly into the boots of the eminently honorable, stoical, sensible, and ultimately marriageable Colonel Manly (see also Seibert, 9; and Evelev, 80) while he plays a major role as himself in Dunlap's tragedy. Washington was, notably, an enthusiastic playgoer whenever his circumstances allowed and headed the list of subscribers to the print edition of Tyler's play (see, e.g., Rinehart, 34).

Of course, the Washington figure is much less representative (i.e., typical) than unique in even his various Revolutionary-era contexts. In both plays, he stands surrounded by heedless, emotional, treacherous, *interested* parties; in the comedy, he locates one woman deserving of his attentions and in the last minute converts a host of self-absorbed schemers whose resolve cannot but be questioned in its remarkable speed and serendipity. In the tragedy, Washington remains alone, without his wife to comfort him and with the upshot of threatening or ruining the happiness of the play's several females. As Sarah E. Chinn observers, in *André* Washington is held up "as a desirable, though possibly inaccessible, model" (108). Dunlap was in fact inspired by Tyler's success to try his own hand at playwriting, but his *The Modest Soldier; or, Love in New York* was never staged because of its lack of a part for the tall, strapping lead actor John Henry (Moses, "William Dunlap," 503). Henry, who had happily inhabited the role of Manly for Tyler's play, must have felt alienated from some aspect of a "modest" solider in what seemed to have been a piece as patriotic and lighthearted as Tyler's, causing Dunlap to try his hand at verse tragedy instead. (Notably, Henry had no part in the original production of *André* either, with another America Company owner/lead actor Lewis Hallam as the original Washington.) Tyler's play was a hit at various theaters in multiple cities for several years, but Dunlap's closed after three nights, likely not only because of audiences' traditional preference for smiles over tears: whereas Tyler staged "the contrast" that left no question as to the superiority of American homespun over European silk, Dunlap's text (reflecting his own sentiments in that era) might have been named "The Ambivalence," challenging as it does any easy distinction between the American hero Washington and the English traitor André.

Though audiences hissed the act of disavowal performed by the American Capitan Bland, they knew that many among them regarded the execution of the talented and charming André as little less than the original national tragedy—the death that American identity formed in part in response to. As Gary A. Richardson observes, André's "destruction allows Dunlap the opportunity to portray that death's pathos and to suggest the moral and political complexities that arise in the ostensibly unambiguous arena of war" (*American Drama*, 56), and audiences may have resented the playwright's putting the situation in these terms. Ironically, André was admired in Revolutionary-era New York and revered in the play for his personal charms and exquisite manners—the very forms and protocols that are satirized by Tyler in his more acerbic and jovial mood. Because the contrast is so much narrower—almost incidental, contrived, perfunctory—in Dunlap's play, André's excellent comportment and Washington's profound sense of honor are read as fitting complements or close competitors difficult to choose between. Tyler's is thus the more American play, both in its flag-waving preference for an easily distinguished American hero and in its attempt to make black-and-white a theme that had been productively grayed by the more English-influenced writer, Dunlap.

Part II

The Rise of Melodrama (1798–1870)

It was not the American Revolution of the 1770s, but the French Revolution of the 1790s, that finally disrupted the dominance of the English classics—and the elite dramatic tendency toward highborn characters speaking in clever aphorisms or blank verse—on the American stage. In his 1843 introduction to some collected works by the revolutionary French dramatist René-Charles Guilbert de Pixérécourt, Charles Nodier describes Pixérécourt's new genre, the "melodrame," as "the only popular tragedy befitting the period in which we live" (xi) and as purposefully staging "the morality of the revolution." Specifically, melodrama featured the plights of common persons, intensifying its moods of pathos, danger, or tragedy with emotion-laden musical cues and assuredly delivering its virtuous hero/ine from the clutches of evil by the final curtain. Notably, melodrama was identified by Nodier as little less than a modern religious experience, a uniquely edifying influence on newly liberated French peasants who had never been "better behaved morally" and among whom "crime has never been more rare" (xii), thanks to melodrama's resounding assertion that it simply does not pay. From the Puritans' fear of theaters as dens of vice and depravity, we shift to Nodier's declaration that "[e]vil-doers would not have dared to show themselves in a place of amusement where everything spoke to them of harrowing remorse and inevitable punishments" (xii); it was exactly melodrama's tendency, however sensationalized, toward moral uplift that American managers such as P. T. Barnum, profit-motivated showman extraordinaire, latched onto in their efforts to market theatrical entertainment among the religiously or otherwise moralistically oriented middle classes as the nineteenth century wore on. For Nodier, post-revolutionary theater enabled a decidedly post-Christian populace to renewed communion with the traditional values of sexual continence, honesty, humility, and nonviolence, and the melodramatic form itself "lends a skillful and powerful helping hand to providence by demonstrating its working through facts!" (xv).

Quickly adopting this French format, American plays of a notably excitable but instructively topical variety dominated American theatrical output throughout the nineteenth century; their hallmarks were overwrought emotions, starkly polarized villains and heroes, sentimentalized death scenes, and late-arriving letters, wills, deeds, identities, and marriage partners too convenient to be plausible but welcomed by all nevertheless. Theater historian Dunlap, ever the Anglophile and the intellectual, thus complained in his *History* against two American populations dominant during his lifetime: those religious and cultural fanatics of the mid- to late eighteenth century who phobically turned their backs on what theater offered, and those lowbrow masses of the early nineteenth century who loved it almost to ruination. Many (e.g., Dunlap, *History*, 302–03) have described the ambience of levity and mayhem that accompanied even dramatic or tragic renditions on stage in the early decades of the Republic—loud hecklers standing on the benches of the main floor, pounding their boots; seated patrons chatting indifferently across the boxes during the performance; and the illicit bargains struck between prostitutes and their customers in the notorious third tier. It was not until the mid-nineteenth century that advances in gaslight technology enabled theater owners to darken the auditorium, which for centuries had been as brightly lit as the stage and thus a competing "scene" for every dramatic performance.

Nodier's boosterism notwithstanding, Dunlap rued the sensationalism and artistic degradation boded in the rampant vogue for melodrama, suggesting a resemblance between the whoring transpiring in the theater's upper balcony and the selling-out perpetrated on the stage below: to attract and retain large audiences, stage managers and casts found themselves pandering to the lowest tastes with their sensational tales of drunkenness, financial ruin, late-revealed identities, and incredible reversals of fortune. As the increasing popularity of theatergoing necessitated ever larger (and more over-decorated) venues, so the vocal intonations, stage gestures, and crisis-point scenic effects had to get louder, broader, and more overplayed—in short, more egregiously melodramatic—to reach the easily distracted denizens of the cheap seats. In return, audiences pelted actors and orchestra members with rotten vegetables whenever they disfavored a dramatic interpretation or musical interlude; high emotions led to theater riots throughout the period, and the flickering safety standards of nineteenth-century lighting, heating, and pyrotechnic technologies made for numerous fires that reduced wooden playhouses to cinders. Dunlap thus regards the early nineteenth-century theaters as "marts of vice and portals of destruction" (403); he argued throughout his *History* for generous subsidization of a decent and intelligent national theater. That the United States has never supported theater in this manner has led to a stage history often beleaguered with monetary need but importantly reflective of popular taste in all of its nobility, absurdity, and historical contingency.

Dunlap's lamentations aside, the era of American melodrama was in fact a terrifically active time for the invention of uniquely native styles and themes (see also Richardson, "Plays and Playwrights," 258). Melodrama's simplified moral universe and mood-enhancing soundtrack eventually gave rise to the quintessentially American entertainments of the minstrel show (incomplete without its musical interludes and racist sentimentalism), vaudeville and burlesque, the earliest silent films, the radio plays and sketch comedy of the early twentieth century, and most of the television and Hollywood film that Americans view today. In its thirst for topical themes to attract an audience, nineteenth-century melodrama functions today as an archive of issues deemed most significant at the time: the Indian question and settlement of the West, racial discord and slavery, temperance, and women's equality. Among these, slavery, sectional discord, and race relations were so pressing as to dominate the scene, such that, ironically, America came into its dramatic own only when it undertook to shine a spotlight on its most shameful past and present episodes.

Exemplary in this case is John Augustus Stone's *Metamora, or the Last of the Wampanoags* (1829), the first play to win an annual contest sponsored for more than a decade by America's first theatrical "star," Edwin Forrest. Forrest was a riveting presence on the stages of early nineteenth-century America, known for his muscular physique, booming voice, and ranting declamatory style ideal to both the melodramatic form and the growing national interest in heroic figures cut from the Jacksonian, common man's cloth. As audiences during this time were overwhelmingly male, Forrest appealed to masculine tastes in theatrics, with an emphasis on dramatic action and honorable, unavoidable death, although the role he played in fomenting the notorious Astor Place Riot of May 10, 1849, can hardly be described as honorable. Forrest had an infantile pride in his talent and a sensitivity to critique bordering on paranoia. His main rival during the era was the renowned English actor William Charles Macready, whose lower-key style and authentic ties to the Shakespearian canon made him a favorite with elite American theatergoers. Misperceiving that naysaying from Macready had led to a lukewarm reception during his second visit to the United Kingdom, Forrest attended Macready's *Hamlet* in Edinburgh and loudly hissed the actor's performance. On Macready's next and final visit to the States, his *Macbeth* at the Astor Place Opera House was disrupted on May 7, 1849, and resulted in large-scale rioting on May 10: hecklers in the third tier bombarded the stage with rotten eggs, potatoes, and shoes, with some 20 or 30 killed and dozens injured in the melee outside. As historians have noted, the rivalry between Forrest and Macready was little more than an "excuse" (Mason, 39) for American audiences to express an anti-British sentiment that had only grown since the Revolution and that ruined the future prospects of Macready—and even damaged the once-universal popularity of Shakespeare (see Cliff)—on US shores thenceforward. More specifically, the Astor Place Riot was a staging of the class war that had developed throughout the nineteenth century and had at last invaded the once socioeconomically diverse haunts of America's leading theater district. In the words of David Grimstead, "The Astor Place Riot intimated that this union was no longer possible. The country had grown, and grown apart.... One roof, housing a vast miscellany of entertainment each evening, could no longer cover a people growing intellectually and financially more disparate" (75).

Despite Forrest's shameful role in these proceedings, his playwriting contests are to be credited, as Hornblow points out, with inaugurating the compensation of playwrights beyond the traditional nominal sum, thus fostering an incentive for native-born dramatists to develop a canon of texts on uniquely American themes. Specifically, Stone's *Metamora* was born from Forrest's stipulation, published in his friend William Leggett's *Critic* on November 28, 1828, that the prize-winning play would be "the best tragedy in five acts, of which the hero or principal character, shall be an aboriginal of this country" (qtd. in Page, 4); *Metamora* was one of the most successful in a long string of "Indian plays," a vogue only mildly dampened by mid-century burlesques such as John Brougham's *Metamora; Or the Last of Pollywogs* (1847), which poked fun at the excesses of the trend itself. Finally, the most "American" aspects of *Metamora* might be the capitalist transactions that shaped its birth, life, and untimely death (or at least the playwright's own): though Forrest's award of $500 and half-proceeds from the third night were unprecedented remuneration at that point, it was but a patch on the profits reaped by Forrest himself in the thousands of performances over the next several decades that he gave in the role (see also Kippola, 68). As he would be accused of bargaining in bad faith by another contest winner and personal friend, Robert Montgomery Bird, whose *Gladiator* and *Broker of Bogota* won yet more grossly lopsided profits for Forrest himself, so Stone unsuccessfully pressed for a fairer settlement in the months and years following *Metamora*'s debut and drowned himself in the Schuykill River at the age of 34. Even the epitaph engraved on the monument erected by his grieving but tight-fisted benefactor shifted the spotlight away from the playwright, onto the star himself: "To the Memory of John August Stone, Author of Metamora, by his friend Edwin Forrest" (qtd. in Page, 5). The perceived unimportance of playwrights relative to theater managers and later actors, which led playwrights for decades to such impoverished and even tragic ends—or as in the case of Tyler and Bird to abandon the unprofitable American stage altogether—led the popular nineteenth-century playwright Dion Boucicault to successfully press for the first American copyright protections in 1856.

The popularity of slavery melodrama in this era is even more mystifying, so controversial had the topic become. In fact, as Jeffrey Mason points out, the Fugitive Slave Act of 1850 required even abolition-minded northerners to aid whenever possible in the restoration of runaway slaves to "claimant" masters (94–95), thus remaking the citizenry into a national network of overseers. As with the Indian plays, white actors impersonated African Americans in stage makeup while white audiences helped themselves to the heroism, drama, and tragedy belonging uniquely to the slave's experience—as well as the moods of lightheartedness and humor in popular depictions of black song and dance. One of the most consummately American entertainment forms in theater history—equal parts African American cultural particularity and white racist appropriation—was the minstrel show, famously originated in 1828 by stage humorist Thomas Dartmouth Rice, who one night comically imitated the song-and-dance style of a partially lame African American stable hand "jumping Jim Crow."

Rice's well-received impersonations inspired yet more imitators—the likes of Dan Emmett, E. P. Christy, and later Lew Dockstader (who gave Al Jolson his start), who developed blackface music and humor into a full evening's entertainment. Played out in three parts, the minstrel show's opening segment included song and dance and humorous banter between a well-spoken white-face interlocutor and two uneducated "end men," seated at the ends of the semicircle of performers and known as Tambo (for playing the tambourine) and Bones (for playing the bone castanets). Their comedy emerged from the botched encounter between the educated straight man and the unschooled fool whose roots go back at least as far as the clowns miscommunicating with the gentlefolk in Shakespearian comedies. With the notable exception of Benjamin A. Baker's lowborn but loveably heroic New York local "Mose" the Fireman, portrayed during the 1840s in a series of misadventures by the popular Frank S. Chanfrau, comic figures in nineteenth-century American comedy were almost always visibly, audibly "other" to the white mainstream: heavily accented, often hard-drinking immigrants; unattractive and/or over-sexed women; naïve rubes on trips to the city; or jolly plantation negroes such as Tambo and Bones (see also Toll, 14–15).

The second part of the minstrel show, known as the "olio," was in the variety format inspiring to the vaudeville and American burlesque forms that soon followed (see Sobel, 33)—more song and dance, as well as various tumbling, balancing, and novelty performances. This segment usually featured a faux lecture by one of the comically unschooled characters, holding forth on a high-minded subject and generating laughs with his copious malapropisms and misinformation. This "stump speech" was a verbal tour de force for the seemingly simpleminded comic in the role. The final act was either a plantation skit or, as noted above, a burlesque of a popular Shakespeare or other elite play, the comedy once more originating from the collision of high and low cultures with the obvious racist undertones of mocking black ignorance and pretentiousness. The skit included rousing song-and-dance routines, and to be sure music was as integral as comedy to each segment of the performance. Most of the main characters took their names from musical references or song titles, including Tambo and Bones as above, Jim Crow, Zip Coon, and Nelly (a wench character played in blackface drag) from Stephen Foster's "Nelly was a Lady." Foster, widely credited as the "Father of American Music," wrote numerous hits for Christy's Minstrels, including "Camptown Races" (1850), "Nelly Bly" (1850), "The Old Folks at Home" (1851), "My Old Kentucky Home" (1853), and "Jeannie with the Light Brown Hair" (1854). Minstrel performer Dan Emmett was another prolific songwriter and lyricist, with "Old Dan Tucker" (1843), "I'm Going Home to Dixie" (1861), and numerous jigs to his credit. As per the indication in Emmett's "Going Home to Dixie," a measure of maudlin sentiment was added to many performances, based on slave-characters' putative homesickness for the Deep South or grief over the death of beloved masters. As Robert C. Toll trenchantly observes, the minstrel form "became a major vehicle through which Northern whites conceptualized and coped with many of their problems" (33)—the "negro problem" first and foremost, but in the war years and beyond, also their anxieties regarding displacement by immigrant labor, the Civil War soldier's plight, technological innovation, and the oppressive upper classes.

Beyond the bounds of such variety entertainments, white actors in blackface provided comic relief in English-styled manners comedies such as Mowatt's *Fashion*, yet their featured presence in American melodramas confronted audiences with an artistic and moral challenge. Notably Frank Queen, the influential publisher of the New York *Clipper* (established in 1853 and absorbed in 1924 into the *Variety* trade magazine in circulation today) championed the unique American art form of the minstrel show (see e.g., "City Summary" [1860], "City Summary" [1868], and "Introductory" [1878]) while inveighing against the dignity conferred on black characters in tragedies such as George L. Aiken's adaptation of Harriet Beecher Stowe's *Uncle Tom's Cabin* (1852) and Dion Boucicault's *The Octoroon* (1859). In one editorial,

Queen called *Uncle Tom* the minister's "excuse," lambasting the sham of anti-theatrical preaching and the pseudo-moralism of Aiken's "nigger drama" ("Amusements"). If such regrettable views are at all representative, it was New York's educated class who sneered at serious depictions of the black experience in America, whereas the theater-loving masses leapt at *Uncle Tom*'s enthralling melodramatic bait: per William Lloyd Garrison's review in his abolitionist *Liberator*, "O, it was a sight worth seeing, those ragged, coatless men and boys in the pit (the very *material* of which mobs are made) cheering the strongest and the sublimest anti-slavery sentiment! The whole audience was at times melted to tears, and I own that I was no exception" (qtd. in Birdoff, 77). If Stone's *Metamora* ultimately served not at all to save indigenous peoples from their dire fate, American melodramas featuring centrally the horrors of slavery were key to the personal and political resolve (on both sides of the Mason-Dixon line) leading eventually to the Civil War.

With Pixérécourt's emotion-laden *Coelina* setting the tone, this section includes richly melodramatic renderings of the temperance, Indian, and slave crises confronting American audiences of the period, as well as Mowatt's sprightly reprise of the earlier manners-comedy tradition in *Fashion*.

A Transatlantic Touchstone: *Coelina, or the Child of Mystery* (1800)

René-Charles Guilbert de Pixérécourt (1773–1844)

Born in 1773 into a family of provincial noblemen, René-Charles de Pixérécourt arrived in Paris at the age of 21 as Robespierre's Reign of Terror caused the streets to run with clerical and aristocratic blood. Miraculously, he survived the siege in the employ of Lazare Carnot, a mathematician with a flair for military strategizing who ran the war ministry for Revolutionary France's egregiously misnamed Committee of Public Safety; Pixérécourt maintained his day job as a government inspector for the next 30 years. As things quieted down post-Reign, he also turned dramatist, gladly adopting the populist stance that was now a national mandate and joining the commoner's theatrical "drame" tradition by coining a music-augmented variation, the "melodrame." As he wrote somewhat defensively in his essay "Melodrama" of 1832, when the intellectual merit of such entertainments had come into question, "If I like to be moved, if I am gratified by seeing well painted stage sets, costumes that are accurate and new, well designed ballets connected to a reasonable action written in a natural study ... and all of that at a modest price ...; what right has anyone to compel me to pay a high price for the tedious performances of masterpieces?" (312).

Notably, Pixérécourt includes in this list of praiseworthy traits both melodrama's ability to "move" an audience (connecting it to the sentimental and gothic traditions that exemplified Romanticism's reaction to the hyper-rationalism of the Enlightenment era) *and* its basis in unassailable "reason." Elsewhere in that same essay, he underscores his work's indebtedness to Enlightenment thinking—at least in his own mind—when he distinguishes between "classic" and "romantic" melodrama and declares that he will "speak ... only about the former [and] abandon romanticism to its frenetic admirers" ("Melodrama," 311). Pixérécourt deplored the "modern" (i.e., romantic) offshoot to the "classic" form he had invented, with its "diffuse and florid" language (315) and reliance on lurid reenactments of true crime. Yet as he himself admitted the year before he died—blind, stroke-ridden, impoverished, and largely forgotten in his home region of Nancy in 1844—he was by the end of his career collaborating with writers on just such plays ("Final Reflections on Melodrama," 317). An example is his well-made thriller *Alice* (1829), based on the notorious case of two gravediggers supplying the lucrative black market in cadavers for early-nineteenth-century medical students. Eventually these real-life felons bypassed the graveyard and simply began creating their own inventory (see Gerould and Carlson, 230–31). Finally, the classic-romantic distinction that Pixérécourt insisted on is largely lost on modern readers; his earliest success, *Coelina, or the Child of Mystery* (1800) models all the marvelous emotional and situational excess that he assigned to the Romanticist dregs of the canon.

Based on the 1798 sentimental novel of the same name by Francois Guillaume Ducray-Duminil, Pixérécourt's melodrama displays the hallmarks of the genre whose moral absolutism is a staple in popular formats to this day: a virtuous heroine whose life (or, worse, said virtue) is threatened by a thoroughgoing villain when a benign but aging or otherwise weakened protector fails in his parental mission. A dashing young hero must then arrive onstage with the necessary paperwork, backstory, or even just a fast-enough horse to save the day. Sentiment inheres in the pathetic situation of the heroine herself; she is typically orphaned and poor, dealing with her own or a loved one's disability (often blindness or muteness romanticized in its lack of a physical cause or disfiguring effect) and the tear-drenched discovery of a missing relative, which Lynn Hunt identifies as "the scene of recognition" (183). In Pixérécourt's play, Coelina is an orphan facing a dreadful marriage, and the muteness of a dignified beggar has occurred by his tongue having been rather unromantically ripped from its root. Per the observations of Phyllis Hartnoll and Peter Found, Pixérécourt's "work typifies the mixture of ferocity and idealism of the French Revolution, when blood and tears were shed with equal facility." The kindly mute beggar triggers the recognition scene as well, when it is discovered that he is Coelina's long-lost father. When our translator writes in a stage direction that the beggar "opens his arms" and the heroine "falls on his neck" (23), he has encapsulated the emotional import of a narrative whose ability to move audiences to tears has entered its third century. *Coelina* emphasizes its moral dimension (and gothic undertones) by subjecting the spoiler, evil Count Romaldi, to hallucinations of assault by fiends and of being covered in his victim Francisco's blood; he is likewise "haunted" by this very victim who did not wind up dying in the bloody tongue-ectomy perpetrated before the curtain rose. Clearly, Pixérécourt insisted on melodrama's heavy-handed moral instruction as its chief contribution to political and cultural life.

Following the success of this play, and succeeded by dozens like it, Pixérécourt was dubbed "the Corneille of the Boulevards"; he is famously quoted as having said in response to elite theater critics, "I write for those who cannot read" (see Hunt, 181–84). Meanwhile, melodrama's earliest examples also reveal their gothic inflections through intense preoccupation with class distinction and the tendency to equate virtue with noble birth. Although often it is an evil count or duke generating the story's mayhem, the well-mannered beggars and orphans foiling their plots are also frequently rewarded with restoration to noble lineage. As Hunt observes, "Melodramas such as *Victor* [Pixérécourt's first play] played on anxiety about lineage, father-son relationships, incest, and social mobility and then resolved it, again and again" (188).

Pixérécourt's English translator was a dramatist in his own right, Thomas Holcroft (1745–1809), skilled in French and German and thus responsible for introducing numerous Continental works of the period to the English— and American—stage. *Coelina* was the first melodrama presented in both England (in 1802) and New York (in 1803); Holcroft changed the title—to *A Tale of Mystery*—and Anglicized all of the characters' names but retained the original's moral polarities, sweeping scenic effects, and emotionally manipulative musical cues. Holcroft was notably a sympathizer with the ideals of the French Revolution; his novel *Anna St. Ives* (1792) has been described as the first English Jacobin novel (Jacobins being the radical faction that fomented the French Revolution). Ironically, although Pixérécourt escaped persecution during his tenure in Reign-of-Terror Paris, Holcroft was accused of high treason and confined to Newgate Prison (before eventual release) in 1794 for his membership in London's agitating Society for Constitutional Information. The fraught political careers of both Pixérécourt and Holcroft thus emphasize the work done by melodrama to explain and justify the Revolution engulfing France (and all Europe) at that time, as well as to warm the democratic sentiments of those in both England and America, just a few decades past its own Revolutionary inception.

The Indian Princess (1808)

James Nelson Barker (1784–1858)

James Nelson Barker was the son of Philadelphia politician who served various roles as an elected Democrat and ascended to the office of mayor in 1808, the year that Barker himself enjoyed his first theatrical success with the play discussed here. Barker's play was not only a personal first but also a benchmark in the wider history of American drama, being the first play by an American to transfer to London after its American premiere and the earliest extant "Indian play" by an American-born author to have been performed professionally. Not only does Barker's script survive, but so does John Bray's original light-operatic score, without which in the wry estimation of music historian H. Wiley Hitchcock, "the drama would be virtually unplayable" (375). Compliments to the music aside, *The Indian Princess* is still well worth the read, if for no other reason than the many cultural influences on view therein.

Specifically, Barker's text, named on its original title page as an "operatic melodrame," not only intersperses its more serious action with light-hearted ballads and novelty songs but also seems to borrow directly from the example of Pixérécourt's *Coelina*, a hit in Philadelphia only four years earlier (see Hitchcock, 378). Pixérécourt's play, and soon many others like it, used background music throughout the dramatic sequences to modulate the audience's emotional response. In addition, Pocahontas is one of America's original melodramatic sweethearts, finding herself in a situation identical to that of Pixérécourt's Coelina—reluctantly betrothed to an unsavory suitor, loved but not sufficiently protected by a weak father (history's Chief Powhatan), and finding rescue from a kindly older man (history's Captain John Smith) who blazes the trail to her more suitable love interest (history's Lieutenant John Rolfe). Like Coelina, Pocahontas's pathetic situation is intensified by her lack of a mother and the aggressions of her intended—in this case, Miami, aided by the scheming Grimosco.

As it establishes a melodramatic character configuration within a centuries-old historical narrative, *The Indian Princess* borrows even more heavily from a dramatic mode contemporaneous with the story of Smith's founding of Jamestown—Shakespeare's, mainly his comedies, with a brief echo of Iago poisoning the ear of Othello in a key scene between Chief Powhatan and the nefarious Grimosco. In Eugene H. Jones's estimation, *The Indian Princess* "is a sort of American *As You Like It* with a serious center and frivolous edges" (53). In Shakespearian mode, the European wives and girlfriends of several of Barker's characters flout the historic record by arriving on the next ship, disguising themselves as pages, and making general mischief while testing their lovers' loyalty. High- and low-born characters interact to comic effect, and a clear line is drawn between the two by the shift from prose to blank verse, emblematic of the Shakespearian and broader early modern style.

As several scholars of this play have remarked, Pocahontas enjoys an upgrade to blank verse once she becomes sufficiently civilized by Rolfe's loving instruction. Per Jones, "The whiter [her] speech and the fairer [her] skin, the less offensive … was the taboo of miscegenation" (59). She and her brother Nantaquas are singled out as "noble" characters, not "because they are 'noble savages' but because they are potential Europeans" (Crowley, 367). Per Jeffrey H. Richards's assessment, Barker makes it plain that "[t]he only good Indian is a whitened, acculturated one" (111). The troublemaking natives are dispatched by the end of the play, and Powhatan is welcomed back to the circle due to his advanced age (i.e., the short-term obstruction to white enterprise that he represents) and his contrite heart. Thus Barker uses his marriage comedy to suggest the felicity of white conquest for all willing to accept its terms (see also J. Richards, 110), although the twenty-first-century reader understands—as perhaps even his early-nineteenth-century audience did—that it is only within the resplendent mythology of convivial first contact that Barker's version of the Pocahontas story holds together.

Barker's Preface for publication has received almost as much critical attention as the play itself, as in it the playwright cannily melodramatizes the traditional plea for a receptive audience and lenient critical response. Describing his work as "one … of those unfortunate children of the American drama, who, in the brief space that lies between their birth and death, are doomed to wander, without house or home unknown or unregarded," Barker casts it as a piteous orphan under dire threat from "some critic beadle to receive the usual treatment of vagrants" (575). With the withering orphan and cruel father figure in place, Barker now calls upon a sympathizing savior—"the ladies" in his audience who are asked to plume their maternal instincts and protect his play from critical assault by their steady attendance and vigorous applause. If the gambit seems risky from a professional standpoint because theater audiences in this era remained overwhelmingly male, it at least echoes the action of the play itself, as Pocahontas plays the beleaguered child for much of the time but switches into heroic-mother mode at a key moment: in her rescue of John Smith from the vengeance of her own tribe, she gives birth to the invader nation whose story Barker now stages.

Shakespeare's *The Tempest*, with its famous lines from Prospero regarding all the world being a stage, was surely inspired by exploration narratives like Capt. Smith's own (whence Barker also gets his information). So also Smith in Barker's play is very much a Prospero figure, fending off threats to his infant colony and benignly presiding over the many couples that form or reunite in the course of the story. His early speech echoes Prospero's and suggests the riveting drama that has constituted the national narrative since inception:

> Gallant gentlemen,
> We have a noble stage, on which to act
> A noble drama; let us sustain
> Our sev'ral parts with credit and with honor. (580)

Having written ten plays (original and adapted), with the manners comedy *Tears and Smiles* (1806), *The Indian Princess*, and the Puritan drama *Superstition* (1824) the best regarded among these, Barker spent his later years emulating his father's example of civil service. He enlisted in the War of 1812, seeing action at the Canadian border, and was himself elected Mayor of Philadelphia, 1819–1820. Later he was a port administrator and First Controller of the Treasury in the Van Buren administration (see Moses, "James Nelson Barker," 565–68). John W. Crowley points helpfully to the year 1817, when Barker was researching the life of inventor Robert Fulton, who himself started as an artist (an oil painter) and gave up his creative vocation to make a more important mark on civilization. Barker saw the parallel to his own life and "concluded that he could better serve the 'convenience of society' in Washington than on the Philadelphia stage" (Crowley, 365). In Crowley's apt summation, "Barker [later] viewed his plays with detachment, even distaste, as the frivolous diversions of youth…. As he might have wished, the posthumous tributes in Washington newspapers ignored his plays; he was praised solely for his long service in the military and in the government. Ironically, only in the role that he repudiated is he at all remembered now" (365–66).

Metamora, or the Last of the Wampanoags (1829)

John Augustus Stone (1801–1834)

Like his tragic hero Metamora, Stone was exploited and deceived by a power-ful patron whose favor Stone had no choice but to court, but whose contin-ued indifference to the artist's plight resulted in an early, self-inflicted death. If Forrest's audience could only love an Indian when he sacrificed himself to white onslaught, Stone's suicide is something of a just deserts for Forrest, who would lose both Stone and another extremely useful wordsmith (and per-sonal friend), Robert Montgomery Bird, who turned to more lucrative, less aggravating professions (novel writing, journalism and medicine) following similar shortchanging from Forrest over his hugely popular epic tragedy, *The Gladiator* (1831). Yet even Bird, according to biographer Christopher Looby, may have "suffered a breakdown of his health, possibly including mental dis-order," due to his "literary labors" (xxiv), such that those who wrote Forrest's contest-winning plays achieved small fortunes early on but came to resent the curtailing of compensation when their plays continued to be profitably produced. (As will be noted in discussion of *The Octoroon*, Bird assisted play-wright Dion Boucicault in the campaign that led to the first American copy-right protections for dramatists.)

Like James Nelson Barker's *Indian Princess* from 20 years previous, and to be sure like many native dramas from this period, *Metamora* is a generic mash-up of Shakespearian rhythms, characters, and situations, and the plot conventions much more recently imported from French melodrama. One extant variant, Lord Chamberlain's copy from 1845, "shifts from prose to poetic lines" (Moody, 405), although notably one high-born villain is consigned to prose, along with the tramps and Indians, for being so evil in his intentions. In an 1866 version from a production in the Western states, all of the lines are in prose format, although one does not even need to read them aloud to pick up the heavy iambic beat that Stone pursued throughout:

> **OCEANA:**   This place—the hour—the day—heavens! 'tis my moth-er's birthday, and her grave undecked with flowers. O my mother, my dear mother! Perhaps her angel spirit hovers here, o'er her lone daughter's steps, a guardian still. Ah, what flower is this? "Forgetmenot!" (10)

Later,

ERRINGTON: 'Tis news that asks from us most speedy action. Heaven has in sounds most audible and strange, in sights, too, that amazed the lookers-on, forewarned our people of their peril. 'Tis time to lift the arm so long supine, and with one blow cut off this heathen race. (20)

These speeches by Oceana (a dramatic descendent of Miranda from Shakespeare's *The Tempest*, born on the waves and left with only her father) and the Puritan elder Errington (his name a delightful poke at his extreme religious hypocrisy) exemplify the action mash-up that characterizes this play as well: Oceana is the pathetic, motherless heroine of melodrama, whose scheming father Mordaunt seeks to marry her off to repulsive Lord Fitz-Arnold while Errington, along with Metamora, anchor the tragic historical narrative. Oceana's true love is the poor orphan, Walter, who, again per melodramatic convention, wins the hand of his lady once Fitz-Arnold is dispatched (done in by Metamora for lunging after Oceana's virtue) and once Walter himself is restored to his noble identity (he is the long-lost son of his erstwhile patron, Sir Arthur Vaughn). Walter opens the play in literally the same boat as many of Forrest's newly emigrated, nigh-penniless audience members—"the wretched ship boy who could trace existence no further than the wreck from which you plucked him" (13)—and at some point in the production history, his plain American name had been changed from the fussy, Shakespearean-sounding Horatio. Yet Walter embodies the same contradictions as heroes of the earliest French melodramas: to satisfy Jacobean audiences, these were always of the humblest sort, and yet, old habits dying hard, they were also always restored to aristocratic lineage as a veritable precondition for the happy ending awaiting them.

In Stone's play Metamora intervenes in the romance/melodrama as both a father figure morally superior to the conniving Mordaunt and, through his rescue of Oceana, a stand-in lover until Walter returns from his own delay. Notably, the play takes care to protect the main couple from any entanglement with the slaughter raging around them; Oceana bonds with Nahmeokee, Metamora's queen, following her kidnap by white war agents, and Walter's only word on the subject early on is that Metamora is too noble and innocent for this white, wicked world. Thus the love plot trips in and around the Indian tragedy that gets larger, noisier, and bloodier as the story progresses, as if the two were being staged on separate nights. Each more or less ignores the other except through the sentimental ties formed in the first scene between Metamora and Oceana and renewed at various crisis moments.

This same obliviousness characterizes treatment of the Indian problem in plays throughout the period; Sally L. Jones observes "the almost schizophrenic view of native peoples" by playgoers and citizens alike, "as the loss of such savage majesty was bewailed, on the one hand, and the removal of the existing descendants of that legacy was condoned, on the other" (16). As noted above, the beloved stage idol Forrest would not have played the part of Metamora were it not shot through with dauntless nobility, yet as a hated, fated Indian, Metamora also had to display the deviousness and cowardice often accorded the stereotype: in an early speech, he warmly invites Walter and Oceana to "Come to my wigwam" for "sweet fish of the lake," then bestows on Oceana a white feather as protection "when the startling whoop is heard and the war hatchet gleams in the red blaze" (12). He astonishingly concludes this speech by renewing the dinner invitation, though again, it is less Metamora's duplicity than the play's own irresolvable ambivalence that puts such contradictory statements into the same breath. Throughout, the native and white characters debate whether to love or hate each other, the mood shifting from one speech to the next.

Metamora utters radically anti-white statements: that the white man will only "spare us" (16) when the last Indian is dead, that the Bible is useless to Indians who treat each other with goodness without written orders to do so (21), and that he deplores his condition as "a wretch who comes for plunder and for prey" (25) in his own land. But such challenges are undermined by the unintentional comedy arising from several encounter moments, the invitation to the young couple being one of these. In another early scene, Metamora has been summoned to the Council chambers, but when he arrives, the general reaction is shock and gun brandishing, and Metamora has to remind the fools that they summoned him there: "You sent for me and I am come. Humph! If you have nothing to say, I will go back" (20). More ridiculous yet are his several departures; although the stage business is described variously as "rushing out" (23), "escap[ing] the swift flight of the white man's bullet" (24), and "exit[ing] hastily" (29), in fact all Metamora does on each occasion is run away, as the most cowardly villain is wont to do. As his real-life analogues were then being vigorously hustled "stage left" (to the American West), so Metamora is rarely allowed to hold his ground until he proudly insists that he "lives to defy you" (38) in the minute before he is gunned down for good. At his lowest moment, Metamora sneaks away from the accusation that he killed Sasamond, one of the whites' most trusted snitches. After proudly laying claim to the deed, he is confronted with another turncoat, Annawandah, who accuses him before the Council and is inexplicably stabbed by his chief for having "uttered a lie" (23). If the effect created here is less careless than intentional, this is yet another artless dodge on Metamora's part—heroic in its bluster, but insupportable in its twisted logic and murderous hypocrisy.

Finally, the audience must be ready to face the death of Metamora with equanimity, even satisfaction; as B. Donald Grose observes, "Forrest as Metamora continually reaffirmed to white audiences the irrefutable inevitability of white progress and Indian extinction" (185). In a similar vein, Eugene H. Jones argues that the play's message "is double, as if Stone had set out at first to needle the conscience of the whites but also to show the necessity for the Indians' demise" (68).

Critics have drawn attention to the marked overlap, both chronological and ideological, in the careers of Edwin Forrest, who "authored" *Metamora* in ways rare among actors then or now, and Andrew Jackson, whose Indian Removal Act of 1830 must be read as inextricably bound up with Forrest's performance. Indian removal was a national theme—if not a national mania—at that point, and Forrest's broadly known allegiance to Jackson's Democratic Party had mutually enlarging effects. Per Mark E. Mallett, "Forrest's goal was an image like the Democrats' image of Jackson, one that combined his common-roots audience identification with an idealized stage persona"; in return, "Democrats identified themselves with a call for native arts and artists" (37) just as Forrest did in his call for contest-winning plays. The ironies abound in our understanding that in this era one of the most effective ways to present oneself as a "native artist" was to stage a play overrun with acts of removal, land theft, and wholesale execution of actual natives, that the most authentically American move Forrest could make was to lead an original drama to its conclusion in these very same acts of theft and destruction.

Despite the discomforts elicited in white audiences encountering this tragedy, our first clue to its huge popularity may be found in the title itself: only in being the very "last" of his kind—and in dying grandiosely in the play's final moments—can a proud, powerful, radically anti-white Indian be received as heroic—ironically as a sort of ultimate American hero who makes the ultimate sacrifice on behalf of the nation forming furiously at his heel (see also Toll, 168). Just as Forrest climbed into his red-face makeup and chieftain's garb each night without a second thought, so his largely white male working-class audience claimed the death of Metamora and the millions he represented as their own "national" tragedy, without a qualm regarding their personal implication, as directly descended from the villains of the piece. Indeed, the story takes pains to create distance between the audience per se and the double-dealing, trigger-happy, largely dishonorable whites who saddle Metamora (historically, Metacomet, second son of Massasoit) with a false name; per the play's own view, he consistently denied the Anglicized moniker "King Philip." Much worse, the whites lie regarding their intentions for peace, kidnap his wife, murder his son, and cold-bloodedly gun down the chief himself in grossly unsportsmanlike fashion. As with many historical reen-actments that present openly, even admiringly, one's ancestors' most blood-thirsty doings, the situating of this narrative in the remote, irretrievable past implicitly excuses those confined to the more innocent-because-irreversible present day (see also Mason, 46). As well, most of the whites in the story are notably, obnoxiously English: several have titles; one is a regicide-in-hiding; and the worst of the lot cannot wait to sail for home (see also Jones, 17). As Jace Weaver observes across the trend of Indian plays, "Others commit-ted atrocities but not Americans" (95). As was clear in the example of the Astor Place Riots (see the introduction to this section), the Americans of Stone and Forrest's early nineteenth century were as busily disowning their English heritage as they were removing indigenous persons to the west of the Mississippi, if not to simple oblivion. Anticipating his leading role in the Riots twenty years hence, Forrest plays the resolutely "good American" in this story, yet ironically an American covered in red makeup and at the last drenched in the blood of his wife and himself. "Only by appropriating Indianness did Forrest most effectively distinguish himself from all that was English" (Lepore, 200), and in its remarkable themes and circumstances, *Metamora* is thus an important ur-text in American dramatic history, if for no other reasons than the grievous ironies that made it so uniquely American.

Drama in Dialogue: *The Indian Princess* and *Metamora*

Written only twenty years apart, Barker's and Stone's heavily revised histo-ries of the Indian in America divide between them the full range of American attitudes toward their aboriginal predecessors from John Smith's first contact in 1607 to President Andrew Jackson's Indian Removal Act of 1830. Despite their generic differences—Barker's play being a Shakespeare-infused comedy and Stone's a melodramatic tragedy—both were received (save by a rather sensitive group in Augusta, Georgia [see Grose, 190–91; and Lepore, 203–04]) as fundamentally anti-Indian, or in 1820s parlance, pro-removal. Both did the difficult cultural work of excusing heinous past (and present) action to their complacent white audiences, and with their drastically different moods, plots, and soundtracks, each drew from the two veins of cultural stereotype assigned most often to native persons in that period—the "noble savage" and the "red devil." Per the analysis of B. Donald Grose, "the noble savage exemplifies the Indian as a creature of physical beauty and natural grace, ... stoic, and totally loyal to friends, family, and loved ones" (186). By contrast, the "red devil ... is viewed as a sub-human animal who thrives in an environment of rape, murder, violence, torture, and trickery toward well-meaning whites" (Grose, 187).

Barker's play, despite its heavy debt to Shakespeare, has its own melodramatic framework and thus starkly polarizes the good Indians (epitomized by the angelic Pocahontas and her brother Nantaquas) and the bad Indians (epitomized by Pocahontas's bloodthirsty suitor, Miami, and his evil advisor, Grimosco). Meanwhile, Stone's is surely the more complex treatment because its tragic mode—not to mention the considerable range of its sponsor and original lead, Edwin Forrest—provides both "noble savage" and "red devil" tendencies within the same heroic figure: being a vehicle for Forrest, America's first star, the character of Metamora is loaded down with noble sentiments (his loyalty to the white heroine Oceana and his love of wife and child), brave intentions (his willingness to go to war when his tribe fears white power), and visionary insight. Yet on several occasions, Metamora dashes offstage in a moment of panic, dissembles to white interlocutors when the truth would impugn previous statements or actions (see also Grose, 189), and tragically fails to protect tribe, family, and self from white onslaught.

Pocahontas and Metamora are both likened to children early in their respective plays, and the education and assimilation through marriage of the lovely squaw Pocahontas is one of Barker's main themes. For Metamora, however, assimilation is never an option, as Oceana's plea that her lover Walter "make [Metamora] like to us" is rejected outright: "'T'would cost him half his native virtues.... his [heathen] worship though untaught and rude flows from his heart, and Heaven alone must judge of it" (12). Although pegged as tragically uneducable from the first scene, in fact Metamora's wisdom and eloquence regarding the dying gasp of his ancient culture are his most engrossing dramatic traits. By contrast, Pocahontas's "heart of perfect simplicity" (Barker, 599) is so preposterously naive that, though a grown woman, she does not even recognize the physiological stirrings of sexual attraction during her first meetings with John Rolfe. Remarkably, speeches Barker assigns his villains—the scheming Miami and his advisor Grimosco—are nearly identical to the sentiments of Stone's tragic hero; in the Edenic garden cultivated by Pocahontas, her generous father Powhatan, and their charming white invaders, it is only the spoiler Grimosco who has the foresight to "beware the white man. He has fixed his serpent eye upon you, and like the charmed bird, you flutter each moment nearer to the jaw of death" (614). As Grimosco compares Smith and his crew to "the deadly adder that lurks in his covert," so earlier in the story, Smith slithers into the presence of Powhatan and his court and, echoing Milton's Satan, promises that

> Had not your people first beset me, king,
> I would have prov'd a friend and brother to them;
> Arts I'd have taught, that should have made them gods. (594)

Barker's Native American Eve gladly eats from Smith's tree of knowledge, and Grimosco's warning seems paranoid among this small, convivial gathering. It is Metamora's observation 70 years after Smith's landing, however, that bears Grimosco out: "When the great stream of the mountains first springs up it is very weak, and I can stand up against its waters, but when the great rain descends, it is swift and swollen, death dwells in its white bosom and it will not spare" (Stone, 410).[1] Where Barker's villain Miami stabs himself to death in a cowardly escape from white trial and punishment, Stone's hero stabs his wife to protect her from the same fate, then stands bravely for his own immediate death by English musket.

Americans in the Jacksonian era regarded the extermination of the Indian with heavyhearted pathos but as fated, inevitable, and already largely accomplished (see also Lepore, 211–12). Grose observes that though the removal question was hotly debated in the very midst of Forrest's premiere of Stone's work, contemporaries such as William Cullen Bryant, America's leading poet and a key judge in the play contest that brought *Metamora* to Forrest's attention, depicted Native Americans as all but vanished in poems such as "The Disinterred Warrior" and the portentously titled "Prairies" (Grose, 184). Therein, the speaker sees only "verdant waste" and "high rank grass" where, self-fulfilling prophecy-style,

> the red man, too,
> has left the blooming fields he ranged so long
> and nearer to the Rocky Mountains, sought
> a wilder hunting-ground.

Per the observations of Jace Weaver, Indians then and to this day "must be stereotyped, relegated to the fabulous nineteenth century, seen as an extinct breed. This is necessary if the myth of the frontier, upon which so much of

---

[1] The page numbering to Eugene Page's widely available edition of this play is erratic since Act IV, whence comes this quote, was recovered by Richard Moody in an archive years after the earlier acts of the play were found. It was therefore published at the end of volume 14 in the *America's Lost Plays* series, whereas the rest of the play appeared at the beginning of volume 13.

American self-image is based, is to survive intact" (93). In Jill Lepore's estimation, "*Metamora*'s debut and Jackson's [initial Indian Removal] address, separated by seven short days in December 1829, intensified and accelerated two developments: the popularity of Indian plays and the pursuit of Indian removal. Two developments? Or were they one?" (192–93).

Barker's and Stone's plays are among the earliest in the canon of Indian plays that eventually numbered in the many-dozens and drew huge audiences throughout the first half of the nineteenth century. Notable variations include Charlotte M.S. Barnes's somewhat feminist, pro-Indian treatment of the Pocahontas story, *The Forest Princess; or, Two Centuries Ago* (1844) and John Brougham's burlesque of the Indian drama fad, *Metamora, or the Last of the Pollywogs* (1847). Per Gary A. Richardson, Barnes's play "minimizes the romance" and is "noteworthy for its respectful treatment of Native Americans" ("Plays and Playwrights," 275; see also Jaroff). In Lepore's analysis, Brougham's parody "resist[ed] the vanishing-Indian theme prevalent in nineteenth-century Indian drama by simply refusing to kill off his protagonist…. [It] acknowledged the cultural importance of the dead stage Indian in placating whites' fears of real-life Indians. But while *Last of the Pollywogs* mocked the conventions of early Indian drama, it also expressed bitter scorn for Indian people, an attitude that was becoming increasingly widespread at mid-century" (221–22).

The Drunkard; or, The Fallen Saved: A Moral Domestic Drama in Five Acts (1844)

William Henry Smith (1806–1872)

Smith's classic melodrama, originated in Boston with himself (a reformed drinker in real life) in the title role, stands at a remarkable intersection in American drama; it was one of the first plays whose theme was an issue of such urgency that "people who had never before entered a theater … saw no harm in attending a lesson in morality" (Frick, 127). Historians credit the play with intensifying the impact of the temperance message that in mid-nineteenth-century America was everywhere—and necessarily so because alcoholism had been a rampant and under-analyzed problem since national inception (see Rorabaugh). Yet temperance was just as good for the theater as theater was for temperance; through their desire to endorse the importance of "taking the pledge," those who had hesitated at the theater steps for decades—especially Evangelical Christians and the respectable middle classes of all stripes—gave in to the temptation to partake of the theater experience and never looked back.

The Drunkard was indeed marketed as a "lesson in morality" in 1844 by Moses Kimball at his Boston Museum and in 1850 in New York by P. T. Barnum in his American Museum, who "selected *The Drunkard* as the inaugural drama for his [newly renovated and modernized] Moral Lecture Room" (Frick, 119). Kimball, Barnum, and other dime museum operators were early "infotainment" entrepreneurs who opened theater doors to unprecedented numbers by blending prurient interest with moral uplift; one sees the convergence of these impulses in the phenomenon of the "curiosity," a seemingly benign habit of mind that leads to life-learning but that often translated into voyeuristic gawking at the biological novelties and physically or racially non-normative humans—named "curiosities" themselves—housed elsewhere in these museums. In similar fashion, museum visitors gazed on the sensational doings displayed in *The Drunkard*—especially the famous "DTs" scene in which the protagonist evokes a fit of alcohol withdrawal—with the idea that they did so for righteous understanding instead of vicarious thrills. As the play grew in popularity at Barnum's museum, C. W. "Drunkard" Clarke made a career out of the title role (see Frick, 135), and his execution of the DTs scene was a universal crowd-pleaser. In this period, audiences turned *The Drunkard* and contemporaneous temperance melodramas such as *Little Katy, the Hot Corn Girl*, adapted from journalist Solon Robinson's 1853 tenement exposé, and the dramatization of T. S. Arthur's novel *Ten Nights in a Bar-room* (1858) into long-running hits. Like the great moral drama that would debut in 1852, *Uncle Tom's Cabin*, these temperance dramas played to appreciative crowds in multiple New York theaters, and in the hinterlands for years after; John W. Frick calls *Hot Corn* an "arch-rival" of *Uncle Tom's Cabin* in terms of this broad appeal, though to the degree that there were ticket sales high enough for all of these mid-century reform pieces, "*The Drunkard* [did] more than any other play, with the possible exception of *Uncle Tom*, to legitimize the theater in the eyes of respectable Americans" (Frick, 127). Interestingly, G. C. Germon, who made US theater history by portraying Uncle Tom as a noble hero instead of a minstrel caricature (see entry on *Uncle Tom's Cabin* below), was *The Drunkard*'s original Andrew Rencelaw, the millionaire who saves the day.

Though many have read Barnum as a genius of great cynicism and manipulative skill, Frick points out that Barnum was himself a recovering alcoholic who, in his remodeled American Museum "banished the conventional theater bar from his establishment and refused to readmit patrons who had snuck out to neighborhood taverns at intermission" (120). As theaters and drinking establishments were frequently one and the same since the nation's earliest days, Barnum's renovations constituted true reform; he even gave matinees for children and the elderly, creating a family environment that has characterized much American theater ever since. Historian Howard Becker calls Barnum a "moral entrepreneur [who] operates with an absolute ethic" (qtd. in Frick, 120) but who had in the process "discovered the commercial value of decency" (Frick, 120) in ways that made him one of the most successful showmen in US history.

The coauthor of *The Drunkard* is widely assumed to be the Boston Unitarian minister and vigorous temperance advocate Rev. John Pierpont. Described in the Author's Preface as a "scholar and a gentleman" who had developed a "story in dialogue" (250), drastically in need of perking up by a skilled dramatist, Pierpont boldly used both his pulpit and his pen (he was known in other circles as the "temperance poet" [Frick, 118]) to castigate the evils of drink. His likely coauthorship illuminates another important intersection for this play—between the enlarging of religious instruction through inspiring drama and the already dramatic elements of Evangelical preaching, temperance sermonizing per se, and the "experience speeches" that formed the centerpieces of numerous temperance rallies in the period. The experience speech was a secular-style testimonial; the reformed drinker narrated his slide into drunkenness and dissipation, his crimes committed against family and society, and his movement back into the light of communal acceptance through embraced sobriety. Jeffrey D. Mason describes the experience meeting as "unintentionally theatrical" and "resembling a revival" (65). The dramatic impact of the conversion itself was enlarged by the presence of "guardian angels" such as *The Drunkard*'s philanthropist Rencelaw, a figuration of real-life crusaders who, at the behest of reform groups such as the Washingtonians, "ventured nightly into the city's 'mean streets' to seek drunkards for reclamation" (Frick, 126). As Mason observes, "the antebellum temperance movement … seems virtually to invite melodrama, for its essential concerns were the sanctity of family life and the preservation of the middle class, and its vision of the human condition encompassed by heroes, victims, and villains" (61).

In this testimonial vein, Smith's Preface swears to the "terribly real" nature of his play, its "representation [of] … a powerful and living picture" and the acclaim by "all that saw it, felt it, for IT WAS TRUE" (3). Notably, Smith lapses into some deception even as he promotes *The Drunkard*'s veracity, referring to himself in this originally anonymous text in the third person. The unnamed Author hails "Smith's" aesthetically and psychologically informed "personation of Edward, evidently the result of accurate and laborious study, and deep knowledge of human frailty" (3). Here Smith obscures the fact that

"Smith's" fine acting is not at all the fruit of "laborious study," but the natural results of lived experience. Whether it was modesty or shame that kept Smith from owning the whole truth regarding the origins of this play, there is no denying that its hard-hitting themes treated with near deadly seriousness would have shaken its first audiences from their complacency regarding the dangers of alcoholism (which had mainly ever been treated comically onstage before; see J. Richards, 243) and their tendency to regard the theater as an avenue of escape, with little bearing in either tragic or comic modes on the depressing features of their own lives.

That said, it is ultimately impossible for the twenty-first-century student of this maudlin and preposterous narrative to locate realism (let alone reality) anywhere within its pages. Per the dictates of melodrama as a genre, the plot develops its highs and lows from the most emotionally fraught, logistically implausible circumstances. Following Edward Middleton's succumbing to temptation at the hands of the wicked Lawyer Cribbs, Edward's long-suffering wife, Mary, loses her beloved mother to a broken heart over her son-in-law's dissolution, endures near-starvation and humiliation as an exploited piece-worker in her miserable New York City hovel, and enters a misery contest with her pathetic daughter regarding who is the colder and hungrier:

JULIA:	[*goes to sleep murmuring—MARY puts the shawl on herself, waits till the child slumbers, and then places it over JULIA, and returns to work*]
MARY:	[*Taking bread from the table … Looking eagerly at it.*] I am hungry—horribly hungry. I shall have money in the morning. [*Pause.*] No, no, my child will wake and find her treasure gone. I will not rob my darling….
JULIA:	[*awakes noiselessly, perceiving shawl, rises and places it over her mother's shoulders.*] Dear mother, you are cold. Ah, you tried to cheat your darling.
MARY:	[*On her knees.*] Now heaven be praised. I did not eat that bread. (48)

As in all melodramas, the fallen are saved through equally preposterous means—here, the recovery of Agnes, a local "maniac" (Smith, 2), to her senses and her subsequent location of a will restoring Edward's property. As in all melodramas, the protagonist's happy ending coincides perfectly with his restoration to the wealthy or noble class, and this play is notable for its explicit equation of the recovery of sobriety with that of fortune: the Christlike philanthropist Rencelaw has as much wealth as goodness, and Edward's moral recovery is part and parcel of the economic improvement he enjoys due to

Rencelaw's beneficence. In this way, wealth becomes the substitute high that enables Edward's weaning from alcohol (see also Mason, 71).

Also particular to this melodrama is its assignment of hero and victim roles. In standard format, the charming and well-to-do Edward plays the saving angel when he spares charming Mary and her saintly mother from homelessness and rescues the younger woman from the lascivious clutches of Cribbs by immediately falling in love with and marrying her. Once demon brandy enters the fray, however, Edward is forced into the victim's role. Per the findings of Frick and other temperance historians, crusaders of the period tended much more often to blame the bartender and liquor manufacturer than the drinker himself; Mason calls these "regenerative narratives" (71) and notes that American playwrights specialized in these, while British playwrights produced "censorious narrative" (76), which blamed the drinker himself. But as Edward is spared the worst accusations of moral turpitude, so he is denied an active, heroic stance after Act I. He is so passive a receiver of ill- and good-will that Mary is soon redundant;[2] she likewise has no power to dissuade her husband from drinking, and her dogged devotion would read into the category of enabling today.

As both Edward and Mary shoehorn themselves into the victim's role, so Rencelaw (who does not arrive until Act IV) shares the rescuer's task with Edward's foster-brother William. A reincarnation of the beloved cranky Yankee from theatricals since the late eighteenth-century, loyal William deals harshly with Edward's detractors, insulting the elderly and comically misspoken Miss Spindle, who would have Edward for herself, and throwing Cribbs down a flight of stairs. Most implausible of all, William is simply everywhere when he needs to be, running onstage to save a distressed damsel, break up a fight, or supply necessary information no fewer than seven times in five acts. When Mary asks William from her hovel in New York, "How came you here so opportunely?" (51), the audience has begun to grow suspicious as well.

---

[2] Notably, a 1964 musical adaptation with music and lyrics by Barry Manilow, and first staged off-Broadway in the 1970s, provides Mary and her daughter with more active roles. Rencelaw is excised, and Mary and William rescue Edward in the last act. Even Carrie A. Nation, famed temperance crusader who once played a featured role in *Ten Nights in a Bar-room* (see Frick, 135), shows up in Act II. Despite these more active female characters, a recent reviewer criticized the portrayal of Nation: "a real-life hero of the temperance movement who made a career of single-handedly destroying taverns with rocks, bricks, hatchets, and brute strength ... [Nation] was six feet tall and reportedly could rip cash registers out and heave them across a room. Unfortunately, *The Drunkard*'s Nation is a mere Bible thumper. She implores a crowd of barflies to stop drinking ... and gets shouted down" (Shaw).

Equally implausible are the arrival of Miss Spindle, who hates the city and has no business there, and Lawyer Cribbs, who certainly has cause to trail Edward through New York, but who is also extremely fortunate in always locating this floundering needle in the dynamic urban haystack. In other words, all that most of the characters need do is "enter" to intensify *The Drunkard*'s implausibility quotient for the reader of this play; its many arrivals, rescues, and redemptions can only be chalked up to "Providence," which in its infinite goodness oversaw the reclamation of lost sheep like Edward and explained *The Drunkard*'s melodramatic excesses in one swoop.

Fashion (1845)

Anna Cora Mowatt (1819–1870)

Among the brawling drunkards and sentimentalized Indians of the era's middlebrow fare, Anna Cora Mowatt's sparkling social satire *Fashion* may seem like a throwback to the manners comedies of the previous century but actually simply continued a tradition that had never died out among New York's theatergoing elite. In the cultured environment of the Park Theater, actors from London were welcomed with the snob's preference for "the real thing," despite the growing animosity toward imported talent in other venues, and a standard roster of classics—Shakespeare, Sheridan, and sumptuous romantic tragedies such as *The Lady of Lyons* (Bulwer-Lynton, 1838) and an adaptation of Sir Walter Scott's *The Bride of Lammermoor*—engaged the audience on a nightly basis. Not at all surprisingly, the smartly educated daughter of a prominent New Yorker would write an upscale manners comedy, and her distinction as an American writer for a serious American stage still dominated by works new and old from London and the Continent, as well as her unique distinction as America's first successful female playwright, add to the instructive, representative properties of Mowatt's play.

For all the culture, intelligence, and breeding of its author, it is yet ironic that *Fashion*, as with every other facet of Mowatt's illustrious career, was undertaken to stave off the pauperism presented by her once-successful husband's encounter with debilitating blindness, then permanent financial collapse. To contend with the first crisis, Mowatt began performing staged readings, which met with great success; to fend off the ill effects of the much longer-term business downturn, Mowatt wrote her enduring comedy and then—in the face of vigorous protest from this same well-born constituency regarding the scandal of women onstage—became an actor of great renown. Mowatt's memoir,

Autobiography of an Actress: Eight Years on the Stage (1854), is valued by feminist scholars for its sharp delineation of both the prejudice against female actors
within polite society and the exhaustion they faced keeping the lightning pace
of professional theater in this period. Mowatt describes a comic incident in
which she "personates" Lady Teazle from Sheridan's *School for Scandal* and
must wait a quarter of an hour behind a screen before her entrance. In those
quiet moments of abeyance one night, Mowatt collapsed into deep slumber
and was awakened by the hysterical prompter just as her fellow actor moved to
reveal her. Despite the humor in this anecdote, the bigger picture of Mowatt's
own frail physical health and the toll taken in the learning of numerous roles
in rapid succession speak critically, if not radically, of women's work lives in
that period. As Myron Matlaw sums up Mowatt's contribution: "Her unex-
ceptionable behavior as an actress, both onstage and off, as well as her energy,
dignity, beauty, and charm were all effective in raising and making respectable
the status of what was still considered a fairly disreputable profession" (29).

The *Autobiography* is overall a marvelous recapture of the stage experience
in this period that any actor can appreciate today:

> The tinkling bell of warning rang, and the curtain slowly ascended, disclosing
> first the footlights, then the ocean of heads beyond them in the pit, then the
> brilliant array of ladies in the boxes, tier after tier, then the thronged galleries. I
> found those footlights an invaluable aid to the necessary illusion. They formed
> a dazzling barrier that separated the spectator from the ideal world in which
> the actor dwelt. Their glare prevented the eye from being distracted by objects
> without the precincts of that luminous semicircle. (225)

At the end of her triumphant debut as Pauline in *The Lady of Lyons*, "It would
be impossible to describe my sensations of relief as I watched that welcome
screen of coarse green baize slowly unrolling itself and dropping between the
audience and the stage. Then came the call before the curtain, Mr. C____
led me out. The whole house rose, even the ladies—a compliment seldom
paid. I think it *rained* flowers" (227). Biographer Eric Wollencott Barnes
credits the elegant, socially prominent Mowatt in this triumphant debut as
importantly responsible for legitimizing life on the stage: "After 1850 the
actor ceased to be a social and moral vagabond, and the drama as one of the
arts of the devil. This was largely the doing of Anna Cora Mowatt, who in
addition to genius possessed boundless courage, an uncompromising moral
sense, and—superlatively—what the modern world calls glamor" (xi).

Elsewhere Mowatt relates the time-honored right of audiences, no matter
how elegant the atmosphere, to hiss an unpopular actor from the stage. As
Mowatt brought her Pauline to the Walnut Street in Philadelphia, she realized

that Mr. C____ was receiving increased disfavor for having muscled out the local favorite and, as she later learned, for acting his part that night in a drunken stupor. As Mowatt recalls,

> Claude [acted by Mr. C____] enters; and with the first words he uttered came that sound, more fearful than all others to an actor's ears—a hiss—a faint one, still a hiss! … As the act advanced, the hisses were repeated whenever he spoke. A succession of false notes in a concert could not have had a more jarring effect upon the nerves. I could scarcely remember a line of my part, and, immediately after the curtain fell, had not the slightest recollection how the act ended. (229)

Notably, the audience warmly applauded Mowatt's own every entrance and well-scored "point" but increased their indignant reaction to Mr. C____ until Mowatt finally broke character and implored the audience to behave itself.

Early in her acting career, a stage manager asked Mowatt to take a part in her own play, clearly mindful of the winning advantage of such a combination. Sure enough, her turn in the role of the ingénue Gertrude was a success, yet as far as the author herself were concerned, "The character affords no opportunities for the display of dramatic abilities, and I reluctantly consented" (*Autobiography*, 232). To be sure, the fools and scoundrels have most of the fun in *Fashion*; the beloved Yankee character, Adam Trueman, spouts the play's moral wisdom but is as comically uncouth as his dramatic forebear, the utterlynaïve Jonathan from Royall Tyler's *The Contrast* (1787). The other comic standouts are Mrs. Tiffany, the "ow-daciously" extravagant and vulgar, mode-obsessed wife of a nouveau riche financier; Count Jolimatre, the conniving imposter of French nobility who is actually a jack-of-all-trades (and general ne'er-do-well) of American origin; Millenette, the clever French maid who knows Jolimatre's humble past and schemes to use this leverage to regain his love; and her fellow-servant Zeke, straight from the regrettable minstrel tradition in his malapropisms, heavy dialect, and social pretensions, but an arch commentator on the shenanigans of the social climbers nonetheless (see also J. Richards, 368). When Mrs. Tiffany's beleaguered husband finds himself caught between a blackmailing villain and his free-spending wife, the couple engage in a debate about reining in spending that anticipates the marital/monetary crisis in Ibsen's *A Doll's House*.

Rounding out the cast is the Tiffanys' coquette daughter, various hangers-on in the drawing room, and the tutor Gertrude, who, per Mowatt's estimation, really is something of a drip. Dressed in white, white flowers in her hair, she is required to anchor the play's equation between moral upright-ness and outer beauty. She indeed winds up with the handsome officer while the coquette Seraphina goes home with her mother, but she has little fun compared to almost everyone else onstage, engaged as they are in constant rounds of trading insults, fighting with sticks, hiding in closets, blackmailing, and general mayhem making. The one time she tries to get in on the act—disguising herself as Millenette to catch Jolimatre in the act of cheating on Seraphina—it blows up in her face; as those about to expose her ruse come bounding up the stairs, she resorts to melodrama's favorite exclamation—"Ruined, ruined!" (43)– when Sheridan or Tyler might have sent her out the side door with a wink and a flounce.

Mowatt's title takes us well into her story's thematic thrust; on its surface, the gorgeously attired men, women, and rooms are a visual delight even as they are objects of satire. And as overbearing and blustery as Mrs. Tiffany may be, she is so fashion-obsessed that she literally answers to her French maid, taking (and comically failing) instruction in the French idiom and constantly adjusting her social protocols to conform to whatever is "all the rage in the bow-monde!" (41). More broadly, "fashion" is little more than a fashionable term for "falsification" or "lying"; every character in the play—even the upright Gertrude and (surprise! her grandfather) Trueman—has a secret to keep, a buried identity, and a scheme or con that is exposed before the story ends. Although Mowatt presents such dissembling as a universal human condition, she diagnoses Americans in particular as succumbing to "fashion" whenever they try too hard to copy habits from abroad. In this period, American audiences craved a popular drama that delineated both native themes and native types, and despite its debt to Sheridan's "school for social satire," *Fashion* delighted audiences (even London audiences) with its promotion of homespun American values. Famously, Edgar Allan Poe reviewed this play for *The Broadway Journal* and condemned its "imitations" of an outdated style from the last century; just as famously, he retracted his critique some three weeks later: "having attended every performance of *Fashion* 'since its first production,' he now judged it to be 'one of the clearest indications of the revival of American drama'" (Hutchisson, 248). Although the plot unravels with the gentlest tug, "[i]t is rather the sureness and vivacity of the comic touch which is perceptible in even the portrayal of the minor and the stock characters" (Matlaw, 28) that make this play an enduring contribution to American manners comedy.

Uncle Tom's Cabin (1852)

George L. Aiken (1830–1876)

The themes, sentiment, and political challenge embodied in Stowe's original narrative properly earned Stowe the designation (popularly, if only allegedly, bestowed by Lincoln himself) as the "little woman who wrote the book that made this Great War." The countless dramatized versions of her text only exponentially intensified the reach and significance of her original message. As Harry Birdoff suggests in his essential history of "Tom shows" in nineteenth- and early twentieth-century America, although many millions read Stowe's novel, many millions more encountered the narrative onstage; Thomas F. Gossett reports "approximately five hundred companies producing Tommer shows" (371) at the height of their popularity in the 1890s. And because Stowe's pronounced abolitionism got repackaged into so many different views that even the most rabid racists found a version to satisfy them, there was eventually an *Uncle Tom's Cabin* for every theatergoer.

To be sure, Stowe's original novel contained the seeds of what pro-slavery dramatists and minstrel showman could turn to their own purposes as soon as it was published. Her stoical Uncle Tom is a model of Christian fortitude whose great reward is a sentimentalized death in his prime (although most dramatic versions cast Tom as a declining, older man) and reunion in heaven with the patronizing whites who had betrayed him on earth; a favorite tableau from Aiken's version, "The Apotheosis of Little Eva," presents the child in heaven, mounted on the back of a giant dove, her hands extended in bene- diction toward her kneeling (now dead) father and Uncle Tom. The young slave girl Topsy was stereotypically wild, thieving, and work avoidant; her comic presence reliably introduced minstrel themes into every production. As all of the slave characters were products of Stowe's well-meaning but limited white outlook, so they were portrayed onstage for many decades by actors in blackface. The romanticized mulatto characters, George and Eliza Harris, were easily portrayed by white actors; their anti-slavery heroics were accept- able even to racially insensitive audiences due to the implicitly felt "injustice" of their "single drop" of black blood. The devoutly Protestant, anti-theatrical Stowe never gave her blessing to a single staged version of her story, yet neither did she need to, as copyright protections were nonexistent until 1856, and no one, not even the author herself, questioned the unfathomable financial loss incurred by securing no rights to the phenomenally profitable stage ver- sions. Later in life, she attended a few productions, was confused by many of them and left at least one "in disgust" (Birdoff, 87), so politically and artisti- cally strident were the numerous adaptations to which her original story was subjected.

Meanwhile, one of the earliest, most faithful, and most influential dram- atizations of Stowe's novel was George L. Aiken's six-act version, written at the behest of his cousin G. C. Howard, a theatrical manager in Troy, New York. Howard was fresh from his own success in the title role of Smith's *The Drunkard*, and in search of a meaty role for his four-year-old prodigy of a daughter, Cordelia, who had played Julia in Smith's play. She was the ideal incarnation of Stowe's Little Eva, while Howard himself played Eva's father, St. Clare, and Mrs. Howard "blacked up" for the role of Topsy to wide critical acclaim—including, one remarkable evening, from Stowe herself—for years to come. Aiken, himself a busy actor when not writing plays, originated the roles of the militant mulatto George Harris and Uncle Tom's original owner, George Shelby, while the talented G. C. Germon at first resisted the role of Uncle Tom, on the assumption that blackface "delineation" was comic nonsense beneath the dignity of his serious aspirations. Per Birdoff's reenactment of the conversation between himself and Howard, "'But Uncle Tom is a new type,' insisted the manager, 'a type that will bring out the leading man's genius…. If you could only submerge yourself in the straight interpretation of the Negro,' pleaded Howard, 'there is no telling to what heights you will reach'" (42). If the lore is reliable, it was Germon's moving performance in a "straight" portrayal of African American tragedy and moral triumph that transformed New York's masses from a population noted for its "hatred of the Negro" (Birdoff, 64–65) into those weeping, cheering "Bowery B'hoys" described by Garrison in the introduction to Section II. As Birdoff narrates,

> [a] good actor had the part of Tom, and his very first words were … spoken so earnestly that the first laugh died away into deep silence…. At the end of the scene, the women in the boxes fluttered white cambric handkerchiefs, surreptitiously removing all traces of emotion; the gentleman, shifting their position, commented in audible tones. The coldest listeners in the gallery had shown the closest attention to the plot…. (69)

Notably, the rowdy clientele of lower Manhattan's National Theater, where the Howard production enjoyed its New York run, soon had to share its rough-hewn benches with the classes more likely spotted at the elegant Park Theater uptown or Henry Ward Beecher's theater-avoidant Plymouth Church in Brooklyn. If incidents such as the Astor Place Riots forced the separation of classes into their respective venues and entertainments, Stowe/Aiken's great American drama, anchored by the earnest performances of Germon and the Howards, brought New Yorkers from diverse classes back under the same theatrical roof, at any rate for the duration of *Uncle Tom*'s historic original run. Its several iconic moments—Eliza's escape from slave catchers across the frozen Ohio River, Tom's rescue of Little Eva when she tumbles from the riverboat and their subsequent blossoming friendship, the death of Little Eva, and finally the death of Uncle Tom at the hands of dastardly Simon Legree—were not just visually riveting but politically inspiring with regard to the humanity of slaves and the devilishness of slavery. This play is also credited with modernizing theater format into the shape it takes today: due to its lengthy production time, as well as its arresting thematic significance, theaters presenting *Uncle Tom's Cabin* did only that, dispensing with the musical interludes and farcical afterpieces that had traditionally kept audiences in their seats until midnight; theaters nationwide soon followed, regardless of the play in question.

Another version of *Uncle Tom*, penned by H. C. Conway and staged at Barnum's American Museum, a few blocks from the National, was both a monetary and ideological competitor: although it stole admissions from the Howards' show with its sophisticated "panoramic" scenes, it also swayed conservative theater patrons with its downplayed versions of white cruelty and black suffering (see Birdoff, 86–89). From that point forward, every conceivable variation on Stowe's plot and politics made some kind of debut: in minstrel versions, Tom discovers freedom and laments the loss of his carefree days on the plantation; in others, neither Tom nor Eva dies; in yet others, whole sections of Stowe's admittedly long and unwieldy novel are dropped, whereas characters (such as the Yankee con artist Gumption Cute of Aiken's play) are added for comic relief.

Birdoff, who speaks from the notably less enlightened era of the late 1940s, expresses his preference for the Conway version (89–90), although not for its soft-pedaling of white culpability, but for its closer adherence to the dictates of melodramatic form: per the conventions established by Pixérécourt, the moral paragon (in this case, Uncle Tom) is preserved from fatal harm and restored to a central place in the family circle. To be sure, American dramatists followed this rule in many of their own works, for instance Smith's *The Drunkard* (1844), wherein even weak-willed, abusive Edward Middleton is spared his somewhat well-earned consignment to the flames. At the climax of Augustin Daly's sensational *Under the Gaslight* (1867), Snorkey, the stouthearted Civil War veteran amputee, is rescued from the train track he is tied to, just as a speeding locomotive approaches, by the plucky heroine, Laura Courtland, herself dramatically delivered from ignominy and destitution by story's end. (We will likely recognize this train-track scenario as a cliffhanger restaged ad nauseam—with the speeding train replaced by the racing buzz saw just often enough—throughout the silent film era, though with the gender roles of rescuer and rescuee always assuredly reversed.) Uncle Tom, like his aboriginal forebear Metamora, and his tragic mulatta sister, Zoe (from Boucicault's hugely successful slave tragedy *The Octoroon*, discussed below), all violate melodramatic convention by dying in the final scene while the oppressors causing their demise maintain the stage in perfect health, bury the dead hero(ine)'s memory, and move on.[3]

A rather obvious pattern emerges here, involving melodramatic leads who hail from nonwhite ethnic groups and must therefore seek their reward, with dismaying regularity, in the world beyond. Especially Metamora and Zoe (who dies tragically in the midst of an untenable love affair with a white planter) are implicitly blamed for the trouble caused by their very existence and therefore must be permanently removed in order for white society to close ranks and go forward. Tom's death, meanwhile, causes the most persistent moral quandary for melodrama's white audience: as no threat whatsoever to the white system that controls him, there is no implicit ideological need for his removal yet no dramatically satisfying way to end his story otherwise. Despite Birdoff's preference for the more forgiving, generically obedient *Uncle Tom* of Conway's design, Aiken's much more successful, truly tragic rendering broke dramatic rules, disturbed audiences, and changed the course of US history in ways that Stone's *Metamora* or Boucicault's *The Octoroon* never did.

The Octoroon; Or, Life in Louisiana (1859)

Dion Boucicault (1820–1890)

As the curtain rises on Dion Boucicault's landmark melodrama, the setting is charming Plantation Terrebonne, complete with a wrap-around veranda and the Mississippi River winding its way through the background. When "GRACE, discovered sitting at breakfast-table with CHILDREN" (3) completes this tableau of elegance and ease, few would assume that Grace is any other than the lady of the manor, presiding "at table" over her charming offspring in the dignified manner connoted by this elevated language. Moments later, however, the reader is surprised to discover that Grace is a plainspoken slave whose seated charges are not the master's own, but a group of young bondschildren who have lingered too long over their "bananas and rolls." Grace's first words are "Hee! Ha—git out!" (3), and her first action is to pick

---

[3] Richard Fawkes tells the story of *The Octoroon* at the Adelphi Theater in 1861; as at the 1859 debut, Boucicault's wife, Agnes Robertson, was in the title role, and so beloved a stage figure had she become that the audience booed loudly at her death. When a week later Boucicault announced "a new last act, 'composed by the audience and edited by the author'" (Fawkes, 128), his audience immediately hated the depiction of interracial nuptials and caused the show to close a few months later.

up a flyswatter and shoo the kids away. That Grace is therefore not an especially gracious example of Southern womanhood completes our confusion, and yet we must assume that the playwright selected her name on purpose and that every element of this character and scene has meaning for the larger story. In fact, Grace all but disappears shortly after this comic business with the flyswatter; her main contribution to the dramatic action therefore is her discovery at table: instead of being "caught in the act" of both sitting and eating on her master's porch, Grace seems instead discovered in the course of her normal day, and the convivial, indeed familial, democracy that is Plantation Terrebonne is established thereby.

Dionysus Lardner Boucicault is easily the most important American dramatist ever to be born abroad—in Dublin to a poor but dishonest mother and, very possibly, her young lodger, Dionysus Lardner, who gave Boucicault his first and middle names and financial support throughout his youth (see Hogan, *Dion Boucicault*, 17–23). His first successful play, at Covent Garden in 1841, was *London Assurance*, a comedy of manners channeling the verbal wit, quick pacing, and comic subterfuge of Sheridan and Goldsmith (see Stierstorfer, xx). His keen talent for gauging public taste led to a hit with the swashbuckling romance *The Corsican Brothers*, adapted from the Dumas novel in 1852; a year later he crossed the Atlantic with his English bride, Agnes Robertson, and downshifted once more: *The Poor of New York* (1857) drips with the maudlin melodrama of its French predecessor, *Les Pauvres de Paris* (1856), which Boucicault conscientiously Americanized with respect to character (e.g., Puffy the Baker) and setting (e.g., New York's Five Points Neighborhood). A year earlier, he had successfully campaigned, along with fellow dramatists Robert Montgomery Bird and George Henry Boker, for the copyright protections of 1856 and was thus poised with his hit play about New York's destitute to secure for himself great wealth.[4] All of Boucicault's later American hits were melodramas, even those—*The Colleen Bawn* (1860), *Arrah-Na-Pogue* (1864), and *The Shaughraun* (1874)—that drew on Boucicault's native Irish culture for their themes and characters. For all his work done to patent his theatrical output, Boucicault was an inveterate "adaptor" of others' work—though whether he ever paid royalties for these texts is unknown—for the vast majority of his plays. As Robert Hogan reports, *The Octoroon* was based on Captain Mayne Reid's novel *The*

---

[4] Regarding *The Poor of New York* and his other potboilers, Boucicault remarked, "I can spin out these rough-and-tumble dramas as a hen lays eggs. It's a degrading occupation but more money has been made out of guano then out of poetry" (qtd. in Hogan, *Dion Boucicault*, 67).

Octoroon (1856), and even the intrigue with the camera (see below) was borrowed from Albany Fonblanque's *The Filibuster* (1862) (see Hogan, *Dion Boucicault*, 73).

Because he sought always to both shape and respond to public taste, Boucicault knew as he sat down to pen *The Octoroon* in the late 1850s that slavery was a hot topic, yet also a subject fraught with the controversy that could cause his efforts to close out of town. Whereas dramatizations of Stowe's *Uncle Tom's Cabin* shifted drastically from pro- to anti-slavery sentiment with each new adaptation, Boucicault sought to appeal to audiences on both sides of the question and, as an outsider to American sectionalism, perhaps felt himself ideally suited to do so. He once wrote to the *Times* of London that he regarded the slaves he had encountered as "a happy, gentle, kindly treated population" (qtd. in J. Richards, 446); meanwhile, as Richard Fawkes observes, he concluded this letter by remarking that "there are features in slavery far more objectionable than any hitherto held up to human execration" (qtd. in Fawkes, 109), and Fawkes points to Boucicault's background as an Irishman, himself thus "a member of a subjugated nation" (109), as grounds for his disapproval. Yet in its largely successful effort to have it both ways, the play overall redeems the South's peculiar institution as a basis for strong interracial family feeling—at least when a plantation is run by the genteel likes of the Peytons—hence the oddly ascendant placement of Grace the slave in the opening scene. Boucicault likewise locates the evil-minded tendencies of slave holding in the northern-born overseer M'Closky, a mustache-twirling villain of the first order. If readers (and even viewers to some extent) begin their experience of *The Octoroon* thoroughly confused regarding who is the master and who the slave at Plantation Terrebonne, this confusion is only richly thematized over the course of the play; masters and slaves weep over their shared and respective fates when the plantation must be sold, and the romantic hero George Peyton fails to recognize the mixed-race heritage of his beloved Zoe, which dooms their courtship until she realizes this doom for him in her own dramatic finale.

Boucicault often changed up the traditional sex assignments of melodrama's romantic triangle; in *The Poor of New York*, the social-climbing Alida preys on for the hapless Mark Livingstone, and in *The Octoroon*, the coquette Dora Sunnyside goes after George Peyton, who considers prostituting himself to her wealth, just as Zoe will soon have to climb the auction block to save the plantation. When Zoe emerges as Dora's romantic rival, Boucicault maximizes the melodrama of racial discovery in the short exclamations ideal for musical underscoring from the da-da-DA! school of shocking sensation:

DORA:	Here! Since you arrived! Impossible: you have seen no one, whom can you mean?
ZOE [advancing]:	Me.
GEORGE:	Zoe!
DORA:	You! (22)

When Boucicault was not thrilling his audience with such revelations, he set a paddleboat afire using his day's latest pyrotechnics and shifted focus from slave tragedy to murder mystery whose solution involves another recent technological breakthrough—a daguerreotype camera—perfectly aimed to capture the perpetrator in the act. If the diverse cast of northern and southern whites, adult and youth characters, heavily accented slaves and lovely octoroons were not crowded enough, Boucicault threw in a stage Indian to round out the spectacle; until they walked out at the end of their first week at the Winter Garden (see Fawkes, 111), he himself played the monosyllabic Wahnotee, regrettably though not surprisingly, for laughs, while his charming wife acted the tragic Zoe. Though of few words, Wahnotee saves the day by fingering M'Closky as the murderer of his young slave friend, Paul; the overseer's removal saves Zoe from his evil grasp, and the plantation itself is redeemed by the requisite late-arriving deed. For *The Octoroon*'s London debut, Boucicault felt free to resuscitate his heroine—cured from her suicide attempt and altar bound—but knew that he would have to present a tragic ending to his American audience. As noted above, Zoe's death violates the dictates of melodrama, wherein the lovely and the good are always to be saved, because prohibitions against interracial marriage trumped dramatic convention, and audiences were left to wrestle with the contradiction between their prevailing politics and their most popular theatrical format.

Drama in Dialogue: *Uncle Tom's Cabin* and *The Octoroon*

Despite the comic business that opens Dion Boucicault's *The Octoroon*—young slaves dashing about stealing breakfast items, with their elders, Grace and Solon, chasing them merrily off to the fields—this drama is every bit as tragic and thus controversial as George L. Aiken's adaptation of Harriet Beecher Stowe's *Uncle Tom's Cabin*. Both include the racist murder of a black male character—the saintly Uncle Tom under the whip of Simon Legree as the tragic highpoint in Aiken's drama, and young Paul at the hands of the white overseer M'Closky early in Boucicault's play. Both dramas confront complacent audiences with heart-wrenching scenes of black families separated when white owners break up plantations due to financial exigency (or monetary mishandling or simple greed), and both suggest that suicide is the preferred escape when a virtuous mixed-race heroine is challenged by white society: in Aiken's play, Cassie and Emmaline fear the lecherous reach of Legree, and Boucicault's Zoe dies for love of her devoted planter, George Peyton. Forever forbidden from honorable marriage to a beloved white man, Zoe, like Cassie and Emmaline, faces constantly the threat of rape from a white man much less honorable. In each play, white characters are largely impugned for serving self-interest over the more legitimate needs of slave dependents; in diverse contexts they "sell down the river" those whom they had promised freedom or at least stability in less desperate times, or they look with outright cunning upon the bondspersons' market value and move to auction with no sympathy.

Each text is radical in its own way: Aiken/Stowe's with its opening scenes of cruel family separation and outright rebellion on the parts of George and Liza Harris, not to mention the vital assistance of white pacifists who proudly serve as "race-traitors" in scenes written to elicit audience approval. The most challenging aspect of Boucicault's play is the undeniable allure of its mixed-race heroine, doomed to suffer tragically for failing the nineteenth-century South's "one drop" rule, which equated the least element of black ancestry with permanent stigma. As white theatergoers may have found themselves cheering (or weeping) against their own interests throughout *Uncle Tom's Cabin*, so they likely found themselves uncomfortably attracted to (or in identification with) the lovely Zoe. Very likely Zoe's original impersonator, the popular ingénue Agnes Robertson, was associated by antebellum audiences with her several other, often Irish roles, and would have worn little to no darkening makeup to suggest a slave heritage. Per the dictates of her excellent breeding, Zoe would have been dressed and coiffed as any of the play's "white" women, with no trace of dialect or other unschooled speech pattern to mark her vocal delivery. There seems no way to consider the reception of Robertson's performance but to assume at least an inkling regarding the ridiculous charade of racial difference embodied in her performance. It is one (already absurd) thing to perform racial difference by donning heavy cork makeup; it is simply too many layers of irony to process when a white actor plays a hated, excluded black slave in the guise of her own white self. Once more, the entire Harris family from Aiken's play, including their son Harry, would have likely been played by white actors in little if any makeup, and Cassie and Emmaline would present just as whitely in their own scenes. Although Zoe is surrounded by her fellow whites for much of the play, the mulatto characters in Aiken's play associate closely with the very darkly made up Uncle Tom and Aunt Chloe, a jarring—and confusing—scene of race mixing in each instance.

As suggested above, Zoe and Tom are mid-nineteenth-century descendants of the early-nineteenth-century Pocahontas (from J.N. Barker's *The Indian Princess*) and Metamora (from J.A. Stone's *The Last of the Wampanoags*). With respect to the lovely young female characters, each is "whitened" to the maximum, made over with respect to costume and diction and matched with the story's white romantic lead. The main reason Pocahontas is allowed to survive and even gain a husband through her encounter with the white race in *The Indian Princess* is because history dictates that she did so, and because a fair amount of such intermarrying was typical, thus noncontroversial. Interracial marriages between white men and black women were far less common, so the scheme of Zoe's suicide is introduced to remove her from the narrative and to spare her lover the moral taint of having to brush her aside. Neither Metamora nor Uncle Tom are any sort of intermarriage prospect (or threat), both being of at least middle age and happily married to women of their own race, but again the black character is singled out for special mistreatment: Metamora, although noble and brave, is ultimately a mortal threat to the white characters and a moral liability to the dramatic equation, necessitating his doom. Tom, as noted earlier in this text, violates melodramatic convention by being utterly good but suffering a villain's fate; in the same way the good Pocahontas marries and thrives, but the equally good Zoe is sent to an early grave. Notably both Pocahontas and Metamora are "historical" through and through—both based on actual figures and, colloquially, "history," having lived—and died—many centuries before. By contrast, Tom and Zoe, though entirely fictional, were all too real: representative of living inhabitants of nineteenth-century American soil, whose tragic lives could only be solved by white audiences with dramatically inexplicable tragic deaths.

Part III

An Explosion of Entertainments—and the Emergence of Realism (1870–1916)

Following the Civil War, various versions of *Uncle Tom's Cabin* cast black actors in the role of Uncle Tom or employed them as extras in the "double mammoth" productions that took to the highways and byways of rural America. Closely resembling their lowbrow siblings the circus and the revival meeting—including a lavish parade that heralded their arrival in town and big-top tent settings during the summer months—the traveling Tom show trafficked in the evermore outsized and over-produced; African American actors and musicians built up the ranks of these traveling troupes—dozens in the parade marching bands and sometimes hundreds in the production numbers that enlivened each outdoor scene in the play. Ironically, this mass inclusion of African American performers into American theater history came at the expense of whatever historical accuracy and political integrity the original dramatizations once sought after: even the play's most lugubrious moments, including the sale of Tom at auction and his arrival at the plantation of dreadful Simon Legree, were kicked off with rousing song-and-dance routines by a large body of more or less choreographed black actors. The play's more and more prominent backdrop of happy slaves conflicted disorientingly with the tragic violence that remained an emotional staple at other points in the production; only during the death of Little Eva, when distraught slaves crowded the stage behind her deathbed in reverent silence, did the mood coincide with the business at hand, though again it perpetuated the notion—embodied always most forcefully by Tom himself—that white lives and deaths mattered more to nineteenth-century African Americans than their own ever could. Near the turn of the twentieth century, it became more common for an African American to be cast as Uncle Tom, but the minor or comic roles of Aunt Chloe, Cassy, Emmeline, and of course Topsy remained the purview of white actors in various tints of dark makeup. Some of the more noted African American actors who played Tom include John Beecher, who played with Terry's Uncle Tom's Cabin Company for 25 years, beginning in 1903; prizefighter Peter Jackson, who fought and acted during the 1920s; and Sam Lucas, who played Uncle Tom for the World Producing Corp.'s silent film of 1914—clips of this film and many other enlightening archival materials are preserved on the University of Virginia's valuable website, Uncle Tom's Cabin *and American Culture*.

The circus-like feel of the traveling Tom shows epitomizes the style of much theatrical entertainment of the postbellum period. Ever-improving roads and railways made large-scale touring companies possible, and one way to compete with other traveling shows was to present increasingly elaborate casts, sets, and effects. If one Tom, Eva, and Topsy added up to a fine evening's entertainment, then two Toms, Topsys, and/or Lawyer Markses playing off each other or reciting lines together could only mean ten times the fun. If one or two sleepy bloodhounds had to be coaxed into chasing Eliza across the frozen Ohio River in the original Tom plays, "Six Mammoth Hounds" in an 1888 production in Ottumwa, Iowa, not to mention "the Funniest Donkey in Existence … and The Only Trick Alligator Ever Introduced on Any Stage" (Birdoff, 268–69) only reflected the expansive, excited mood of the late nineteenth century to an ever more profitable degree. The circus–Tom connection is confirmed when Harry Birdoff remarks, "When two circus magnates, P.T. Barnum and J.A. Bailey, combined shows in 1881, offering … twice as many clowns, twice as many performers, twice as many animals, the consolidation intrigued their closest competitors, the Tom shows" (309).

As indicated, circuses themselves were hugely popular in this era (emphasis on whatever was "huge" or "mammoth" in their offerings), and "human curiosities" were widely in demand for the sideshows, dime museums, lecture halls, and vaudeville entertainments attended into the twentieth century. Even Haverly's United Mastodon Minstrels of the late 1870s cashed in on the plus-size craze by staffing productions with 100 players, and the remarkably successful African American ensemble known as the Hyers Sisters Combination staged an interracial *Uncle Tom's Cabin* in the 1880s that included the popular Sam Lucas as Tom and during which "Anna Madah [Hyers] played Eliza and sometimes a second Topsy" (Hill, "The Civil War," 73; see also Hill, "The Hyers Sisters"). In 1883, the sisters enlarged their production to maximum proportions by including "the two separate Callender's Minstrel Festival Companies (one Black, the other White) to combine their actors in a spectacular production of the play in San Francisco" (Hill, "The Civil War," 73).

Burlesque acts of the 1870s and 1880s presented dozens of scantily clad, almost always blond, buxom-to-rotund dancing girls for male audience members to fantasize choosing from. They paved the way for the densely populated, identically dressed, coiffed, and made-up chorus lines of Busby Berkeley's early-film extravaganzas, as well as the Radio City Rockette, Miss America, and Dallas Cowboy Cheerleader pageantry of today. Inaugurating this genre in America was the extravagant musical spectacle *The Black Crook* (1866), which made a huge splash in New York and stayed on as a tourist favorite for years. It is regarded as both America's original musical comedy and first girly show; light on both artistic merit and original plot, the audience came and stayed (for more than five hours) instead for the lavish displays of lighting, sets, and costumes—or lack thereof. The beautiful ballet dancers' flesh-colored tights struck the uninitiated audience as sheer nudity and paved the way for actual occasions of flesh baring in the burlesque (and later striptease) productions that scandalized the theater scene into the middle twentieth century. *The Black Crook* told a melodramatic story, in which the hero defeats two villains—a Faustian tempter and his romantic rival—to win his soul and his heart's desire. Per historian Myron Matlaw, "Almost every scene gives ample scope for theater magic: displays of water, fire, transformations of all sorts, phantasmagorias of horror, caverns, grottos, necromancy, and conjury, and most important of all the [scantily clad] ballet extravaganzas" (320). The show was reviewed excitedly by the major drama critics of the period, many of which commented on "the large number of female legs" (qtd. in Allen, 111).

The scandalous but solid success of *The Black Crook* set the scene for the next "British invasion" of the American theater, that by Lydia Thompson and her witty, attractive troupe of "English Blondes" whose cross-dressed send-ups of classical narratives such as *Ixion, The Forty Thieves*, and *Sinbad* had as much in common with the literate travesties of John Brougham (of *Pollywog* fame) as with the mindless feminine spectacle that was *The Black Crook*. Still, the Blondes' shockingly exposed legs and bosoms garnered most of the attention and came to characterize burlesque entertainment in its American format, as it hit the road in well-organized "wheels" or circuits, along with the Tom shows, minstrel extravaganzas, circuses, carnivals, freak shows, medicine shows, and Wild West shows, that enthralled the American everyman in the 1870s and 1880s. The lovelies sang and shimmied together, then took part in ribald comedy routines featuring acerbic male wits, many of whom went on to noted careers in radio, film, and television. Robert C. Allen lists Phil Silvers, Abbott and Costello, Jackie Gleason, Red Skelton, and Red Buttons as famous early twentieth-century burlesque alumni but notes that "burlesque produced no female stars who enjoyed equivalent success in other branches of show business" (258). In its final days, the *New Yorker*'s theater critic Gilbert W. Gabriel lamented the dancers on the runway: "Their *glutei maximi* heave in and out of sparse frills, and they pour a shrill, utterly intelligible sing-song through the spigots of their nostrils…. The smallish auditorium is a bog of damp faces, flowered with cigar ends. The smoke looks like an oily canopy, except where some drunken electric fans above the boxes suck and snort to unravel the edges of it" (qtd. in Ochsner). As Allen concludes, by the time of burlesque's demise in the early twentieth century, the female burlesquer had descended from the role of empowered producer to silenced sex object, in a long era during which the sexphobic middle classes wielded tremendous spending power and dictated tastes in leisure entertainment: "Variety [racy working-class shows staged in saloons and beer halls] became incorporated into bourgeois theater as vaudeville at the same time and as a part of the same process that resulted in the excorporation of burlesque" (Allen 179).

To be sure, there remained an alternative to this post-bellum explosion of sensationalized entertainment in serious American drama, wherein a promising trend in realism, imported from European dramatists such as Strindberg, Ibsen, and Shaw, and zealously encouraged by the American editor and dramatist William Dean Howells, boosted the intellectualism of traditional melodramatic fare. Despite the sensationalist effects of *Under the Gaslight*, Augustin Daly sought after gritty realism in this and other plays, through emphasis on common persons and detailed scenery. As a theater manager, Daly is credited with encouraging the American realism of Bronson Howard, whose markedly successful *Saratoga* (1870) "was a notable event in the history of our theater [for changing] … the attitude of managers toward the native-made play" (Hornblow, 247). Although he specialized in leading roles (e.g., Hamlet, Richelieu) in international classics, late-nineteenth-century superstar Edwin Booth abetted the new American trend toward dramatic realism by working in a refined and understated manner that gave audiences an alternative to Edwin Forrest's histrionics; per Karl M. Kippola's helpful contextualization, historical "circumstance required the masculine transition from Jackson to Lincoln, and the journey from Forrest to Booth followed a similar path" (159). Booth's style came to characterize acting styles during the late nineteenth century, even unto the present day.

David Belasco was a playwright of some note and, like Daly, a hugely successful theater manager, famed for the detailed realism he brought to the sets of his productions—down to actual eggs frying in a pan and the installation of an entire room from a rundown boardinghouse, wallpaper and all. William Gillette was a dashing leading man and talented playwright who starred in his own well-made thrillers such as *Secret Service* (1895) and *Sherlock Holmes* (1899); according to Matlaw, "Gillette stressed the realism of his characters' actions and thoughts by inserting a profusion of details in his stage directions" (21).

Edward Sheldon's radical melodrama *The Nigger* (1909) tells the story of a race-baiting southern governor who eventually confesses his own mixed-race heritage and repudiates his former ways. The play was hailed by Loften Mitchell for bringing "drama about the American Negro to searing heights.... [Sheldon] said things the American theater had never heard before" (39; see also Bryan, 8). Sheldon's other realist dramas include *Salvation Nell* (1909) and *The Boss* (1911).

Augustus Thomas wrote on distinctly American subjects, including *Alabama* (1891), *In Mizzoura* (1893), and *Arizona* (1899), and Bronson Howard wrote the Civil War–themed *Shenandoah* (1889). Likely inspired by the European realists' focus on the predicaments of modern women (e.g., in Ibsen's *A Doll's House* [1879] and *Hedda Gabler* [1890], Strindberg's *Miss Julie* [1888], Shaw's *Mrs. Warren's Profession* [1895] and *Candida* [1897]), Howard also was one of many in this period to feature female main characters, as in his *The Young Mrs. Winthrop* (1899). Other women-centered dramas of the period include Steele MacKaye's popular and sentimental *Hazel Kirke* (1880)—Matlaw reports "fourteen *Hazel Kirke* road companies" by 1882–83 (23); Belasco's *The Wife* (1887, cowritten with Henry C. DeMille) and *The Girl of the Golden West* (1905); the hugely successful but tragically short-lived Clyde Fitch's *Barbara Frietchie* (1899), *The Girl with the Green Eyes* (1902) and *The Climbers* (1906); William Vaughn Moody's frontier romance, *The Great Divide* (1906); Langdon Mitchell's arch look at divorcing socialites, *The New York Idea* (1906); Rachel Crothers's feminist frontier drama, *The Three of Us* (1906); Eugene Walter's riches-to-rags prostitution story, *The Easiest Way* (1908); and most enduring (though in its day most controversial) of all, James A. Herne's *Margaret Fleming* (1890). As above, these playwrights introduced realistic scenery and low-key dialogue even as melodramatic plot elements (villains and victims, reversals of fortune, the pathos of blindness or other disability) remained staples in their work.

By the turn of the twentieth century, with mega-hits like *Uncle Tom's Cabin* and *The Black Crook* setting the pace, a vast array of live entertainments reached into every corner of the nation and its territories, with its lavish, garish spectacles of fantasy and excess—the triumph of theater for the masses or the realization of William Dunlap's worst nightmare, depending on one's perspective. It was a theatrical "bubble" stretched to its breaking point before the advent of radio and silent film burst it for good. Indeed, cinema's earliest venue was the vaudeville stage (see also Postlewait, 163), where short features (of bodies in motion or filmed enactments of vaudeville skits themselves) took their place on the evening's bill alongside the animal acts, jugglers, sword swallowers, recitation givers, singers, dancers, mimes, and instrument virtuosos who made up a typical night at a vaudeville palace. But by the late 1920s, the entertainment-seeking masses had vacated these and other live-performance venues en masse, for the nickelodeons and then, after radio, the coziest chairs in the parlor, permanently changing the character and purpose of the American dramatic enterprise (see also Savran, "Haunted Houses," 118). Although it is common to identify Eugene O'Neill as the first dramatist since national inception worth referring to with pride—and exporting to the wider world—one could also argue that a Eugene O'Neill (or who knows how many O'Neills before him?) would have simply never succeeded in the American decades during which theaters were little more than circuses with speech. Perhaps it is only when lowbrow theatergoers embraced the glittering promise of the silver screen that the American stage was cleared for a native American dramatic intellectualism that has prevailed on the ever less well attended but ever more serious minded boards to this day (see also Downer, 41; and Savran, "Making Middlebrow Theater," 21–22). Although the high-concept, high-dollar musical-comedy format continues, to be sure, to attract a long train of average-American, Broadway-bound pilgrims each theatrical season, the American musical itself underwent a remarkable upgrade by the mid-century, such that it and its higher-brow sister tradition of legitimate American drama may be read as equally the result of native genius and the technological innovations that gave birth to radio and silent film, clearing the way for same.

With the exception of Jack's heedless, brainless, and surely topless extravaganza *Beauty in Dreamland*, the plays in this section take up the challenge posed by Ibsen's realist masterwork, *A Doll's House*. Though still inflected with the trappings of melodrama, early explorations by Herne and Walter of middle-class hypocrisy and the sexual double standard (notably, just as burlesque completed its shift from witty satire to tawdry girlie show) pave the way for even sharper critiques of these themes in American plays since that time.

A Transatlantic Touchstone: *A Doll's House* (1879)

Henrik Ibsen (1828–1906)

This landmark in dramatic realism tells the morally complex story of Nora Helmer, a grown woman living a doll's life due to mishandled finances in the early years of her marriage to a domineering man. Every aspect of this play would have shocked original audiences—from its thorough excavation of a bad marriage and the deeply flawed characters of husband and wife to its willingness to look sharply at women in poverty, social hypocrisies, and a general shattering of middle-class assumptions at every turn. Fluttering about her well-appointed home, chirping about a lavish Christmas in the offing, and squirreling into her pocket the macaroons her husband does not want her to eat, Nora is repeatedly likened to a helpless but charming forest creature and most especially to a child—to the lovely but naïve dolly that her husband can dress and set in motion however he pleases. Conflict builds when Nora reveals to her visiting friend, Kristine Linde, that she in fact has been acting like a man: in a previous year, she had obtained a loan to save her husband's life, with a medically necessary trip to southern Europe, and has been doing paid work to reduce the debt ever since.

Though these particulars alone would suffice to send her arrogant husband, Torvald, into a rage, it is revealed soon that Nora's pretensions to the man's role were only pretenses after all: she faked her father's cosignature on the loan papers, plunging herself and her husband into legal risk, and she has only a vague idea regarding how difficult it will be to pay the principle plus interest on her own. Finally, Nora has only a child's understanding of financial matters and a child's access to the wealth necessary to do actual good. She brags about having saved her husband's life but without "her father" cosigning for the loan and without her husband's impending raise, which she plans to siphon off to close it out, she could have done nothing at all.

The subplots involve the Helmers' various visitors, as the entire play is set within the "doll's house" itself—the Helmers' main living area—which suggests that Nora, although she comes and goes a bit throughout, is very much caged inside the domestic setting. Kristine is an early arrival, whom Nora does not recognize at first, so worn down has this old friend become due to the trials of supporting an aging mother and two younger brothers on a widow's salary. Nora's failure to know Kristine also comments on the heroine's tendency to deny the realities of female oppression as well as to myopically focus on her own family, future doings, and prospects for increased wealth and happiness in narcissistic fashion. Immediately, the audience prefers Kristine's well-grounded sensibility to Nora's flighty selfishness and hopes that Kristine's request—that Nora influence her husband to employ Kristine at the bank where he serves in upper management—succeeds. Ironically, another employee at the bank is both Kristine's former intended *and* the desperate climber who has made Nora the loan, and he begins to threaten blackmail to secure his own promotion under Torvald. Deaf to his wife's pleas to keep him on at the bank, Torvald fires Krogstad and replaces him with Kristine. After an argument between Krogstad and Kristine over this matter, they are resolved to reunite and work together.

The third visitor is the family friend Dr. Rank, whom Nora considers turning to for help with the loan when Krogstad starts pressing in. When Dr. Rank reads Nora's unspecified call for aid as a come-on to consummate the affair that he himself has always dreamed of, she must turn him away, ruing the loss of financial assistance a good deal more than loss of honor threatened by his advances. For better or worse, Dr. Rank will not be around to pursue his cause much longer, for he is a dying man who spends most of his time bitterly protesting the profligate appetites of his father, which have led to his own weakened state:

> NORA: I suppose you mean that he was too fond of asparagus and Strasbourg pâté, wasn't he?
> RANK: Yes; and truffles.
> NORA: Yes, truffles, to be sure. And oysters, I believe? ... It is sad that all of these good things should attack the spine....
> RANK: Especially when the luckless spine attacked never had any good of them. (110–11)

This nonsensical theory about the nature of hereditary illness had some currency in the late nineteenth century and huge thematic significance for Ibsen: in *Ghosts* (1881), he treats the topic of inherited syphilis and other sins of a father visited upon the head of an unfortunate son. When not complaining about his own sorry state, Dr. Rank criticizes lax modern attitudes, mocking Kristine's compassion for the downtrodden as "that notion that makes society a hospital" (50). Not surprisingly, his good friend Torvald shares his strident views; thinking that he is criticizing only Krogstad, Torvald informs Nora that "a man with [forgery and cover-up] on his conscience must always be lying and canting and shamming." And "such a dust-cloud of lies poisons and contaminates the whole air of home. Every breath the children draw contains some germ of evil" (65). Immediately, Nora fears she is poisoning her own dear children and banishes them pitifully from her presence.

A Doll's House is perhaps most modern in its relentless focus on the meaning of work—not swashbuckling or empire building, but holding an ordinary office job that keeps the employee solvent, respectable, marriageable, and fulfilled. As obsessed as Torvald is with maintaining his own position of authority at the bank, Ibsen takes the radical step of suggesting that women are just as capable and just as deserving of rewarding work; Nora whispers daringly regarding the clerical work she has taken on the sly to pay back her loan, and Kristine regrets her past history of under-compensated employment but enthusiastically anticipates a more lucrative post at the bank. Her reunion scene with Krogstad is one of the oddest declaration scenes ever staged; note how often the idea of work is substituted for that of love:

MRS. LINDE: What do you think brought me to town?

KROGSTAD: Had you any thought of me?

MRS. LINDE: I must have work or I can't bear to live. All my life, as long as I can remember, I have worked; work has been my one great joy. Now I stand quite alone in the world…. Nils, give me somebody and something to work for….

KROGSTAD: Kristine, do you know what you are doing? … Have you the courage then—?

MRS. LINDE: I need some one to be a mother to, and your children need a mother….

KROGSTAD: I was never so happy in all my life![1] (*Exits.*)

MRS. LINDE: What a change! What a change! To have someone to work for, to live for—a home to make happy! (147–51)

Throughout this exchange, the two propose *to each other* as a way to regain the respectability that each has lost in bruising episodes from their recent past. It is especially Krogstad who will gain in stature simply by having a wife to demonstrate her faith in him. Specifically, this faith will manifest in placing Krogstad in the employer's role; Kristine rejoices in the prospect of "working for" him and spends the duration of this love scene enumerating her abilities—especially in the mothering of his children—as if interviewing for a job. Perhaps Ibsen was the first playwright to recognize the modern truism, that the greatest cause of marital discord is financial crisis, and that, in reverse, the strongest love bonds form when two people regard each other as mutual opportunities for social and professional gain. The equal partners Krogstad and Kristine, rooted in the financial realities of their modern day, enjoy Ibsen's happy ending, whereas the fairytale couple in their polarized romance roles see their pretensions to love and happiness destroyed.

Not surprisingly, the ending of this play caused tremendous controversy in its own day and continues to foment debate now. Nora's view, that she must leave both husband and children to find herself, is realized in her resolute exit; as Ibsen's biographer Michael Meyer phrases it, "[t]he terrible offstage slamming of that front door … resounded through more apartments than Torvald Helmer's" (328), and drama critic F. L. Lucas remarked that "the door

---

[1] Another widely available translation is even more suggestive of the couple's monetary motives: "I have never had such an amazing piece of good fortune in my life!"

slammed by Nora shook Europe" (qtd. in Quigley, 91). Theater critics divided in their reception of the play's debut at the Royal Theater in Copenhagen in December 1879: many applauded Ibsen's progressive views, but the anonymous writer for *Faedrelandet* took indignant issue with his attempt to show marriage as "an arrangement ... which corrupts [individuals], and which they therefore have a moral right to immediately dissolve, as soon as it no longer satisfies them." M. V. Brun, in *Folkets Avis*, regretted that Ibsen, evidently no longer satisfied with swinging "the whip of satire" throughout the likes of *The League of Youth* and *Peer Gynt*, must now "throw himself into the mishmash of bourgeois realism," succeeding so well that "all of the enjoyment he offers us in the first acts [of *A Doll's House*] evaporates in the third." The first actress to portray Nora in Germany refused the part as written, so intensely did she fear it would reflect upon her own role as a loving mother, and Ibsen rewrote the final moments himself, lest the attempt be made by some hack with no copyrights preventing him. In the new (almost as depressing) ending Torvald drags Nora into the children's room, and she sinks to the floor in tears—of salvation? defeat?—at her realization that she cannot leave them "mutterlos!" Ibsen himself "described this alteration to my translator as a 'barbaric act of violence'" ("Alternative Ending"), and fortunately it was reviled by audiences even during the initial run by the German actress, who then played Nora as originally written.

An odd melodramatization by Henry Arthur Jones and Henry Herman, retitled *Breaking a Butterfly*, was the first English-language version of the play; it debuted at London's Prince's Theater in March 1884 and included four male parts of vague attachment to their originals; the versatile character actor Herbert Beerbohm Tree played "Dunkley, a melodramatic villain who took the place of Krogstad" (Archer, 16), and Dr. Rank got reprocessed (if not disappeared entirely) into "a useful young man" played by Mr. Anson and "an impecunious clerk" played by Mr. Maclean ("Breaking a Butterfly"). When Ibsen's own version arrived in London in 1889, it was no more warmly embraced by critics there than it was in Denmark. Clement Scott for the *Daily Telegraph* wrote a mocking appraisal of the play's contents, including Dr. Rank "enlarg[ing] on the virtues of oysters and truffles," which is not exactly the case, and "the spoiled baby" Nora "miraculously developed into a thinking woman [who] leaves her home, breaks her marriage oath ... abandons her innocent children, and becomes absolutely inhuman, simply because she discovers her husband is an egotist." Many reviewers who loathed Nora's final exit took issue with her dubiously quick shift from naïf to revolutionary, although Nora was based on a real-life associate of Ibsen's, Laura Kieler. She had asked Ibsen for an introduction to a publisher when Kieler sought to sell her book to pay for her own neurotically proud husband's tuberculosis cure. Ibsen refused his assistance because of the rushed and mediocre nature of the manuscript, and Kieler forged a check to pay back the loan originally taken. When discovered, Kieler's husband had her committed to an insane asylum; although she was released a month later, grudgingly reinstated to her family, and later became a renowned author in her own right, Ibsen began *A Doll's House* within weeks of learning the tragic upshot of Kieler's story (see Meyer, 318–20). Although Meyer regards the play as "an admiring vindication of [Kieler's] conduct" (330), it is equally readable as Ibsen's meager attempt to atone for his betrayal of his fellow writer and to fend off an egregious and unavoidable irony—that while fresh from having ruined the prospects of Kieler's *novel*—and arguing vociferously for women's right to selfhood in other contexts—Ibsen yet instantly lit upon the value of Kieler's *story* and felt free to establish his reputation as a modern master on its ruins. In the United States, *A Doll's House* premiered in Louisville, Kentucky, in 1883, produced by and starring the respected Polish-born Shakespearian Helena Modjeska, and debuted in New York at Palmer's theater in late December 1889, exactly ten years after the play's original Copenhagen run.

Beauty in Dreamland, or The Pearls of the Orient (1889)

Sam T. Jack (1852–1899)

Sam T. Jack was a successful manager of variety and burlesque entertainments throughout the late nineteenth century; of all the plays discussed in this text, his *Beauty in Dreamland* is most clearly the one penned by a producer instead of a playwright—that is, written as sheer entertainment with zero artistic aspiration, but with maximized box office receipts in mind. Hailing from Pennsylvania's oil country and (if a glowing biography from the period can be trusted) serving the Union forces during the Civil War, Jack's first adult line of work was oil speculator, then manager of an opera house in an oil boomtown. Soon he was operating several "gaiety," light opera, and variety companies—eventually and most successfully on the lightly policed streets of Chicago—including the Lilly Clay Colossal Gaiety Company through which he mostly likely produced *Beauty in Dreamland*. Even more famously, Jack established the Creole Company, celebrated for its pioneering presentation of African American beauty and talent without the blackface exaggeration typically on display. Vaudeville historian D. Travis Stewart (who publishes under the penname Trav S. D.) remarked in his blog that Jack "was instrumental in the metamorphosis of the minstrel show into the girlie show"; Orrin Clayton Suthern II, adds that "[i]n 1890, the first successful departure from original Minstrelsy was launched by Sam T. Jack, who managed a burlesque unit. He conceived the idea of putting on an all-Negro show, immediately different.... Among the men whom Jack contacted was Sam Lucas (the composer) [of *Uncle Tom's Cabin* fame and numerous accomplishments in this period] and sixteen of the prettiest girls he could find who could sing and dance" (79). Jack was famous in death for the odd terms of his will, wherein he requested that his wife, former burlesque star Emma Ward, marry his brother before receiving her inheritance. In a write-up in the *New York Times*, Jack's widow averred that Jack's brother himself had unduly influenced the dying Jack to add in the marriage clause, as well as to cede his brother a large portion of his estate ("Sam T. Jack's Will Probated"). Jack's widow later remarried, to some other man ("Sam T. Jack's Widow to Marry").

Ever indebted to Lydia Thompson and her sharp-witted Imported British Blondes, Jack and other burlesque operators of the period plied their own brand of backhanded feminism by giving women more stage "exposure" than ever before, as in the shift from male to female minstrel performers, and, as he boasted in quoted material in his promotional biography, paying them better salaries than the servants of tightfisted anti-smut crusaders like the Women's Christian Temperance Union (O'Neill, 261–62). Burlesque historians describe Jack as the most successful and most boundary-pushing of the nineteenth-century managers; per Frank Cullen et al., "Jack was an unapologetic producer of ever-rawer burlesque, reaching a level of lascivious display heretofore only attempted by the fly-by-night *turkey-show* troupes" (164). Later, "Jack's Chicago house had an adjoining bar, through which all the girls in the show needed to pass, and nudity was unabashedly displayed onstage" (557). Bernard Sobel regards Jack as having given burlesque its "early ill-repute," and in the bar attached to his Chicago house, "they got away with murder" (61).

Biographer M. J. O'Neill presents Jack as a globe-trotting folk hero who once saved a man from drowning in the Allegheny River, rescued a woman from a predator on the docks in Santiago, and piloted a drunk friend's hot air balloon "in a far western town" (O'Neill, 144), among numerous other acts of derring-do. He is most brightly glorified by O'Neill as an intrepid explorer of far-flung corners in search of feminine delights to present to American audiences; Jack famously booked the "hooch" dancer Little Egypt, fresh from her scandalous appearance at the 1893 Chicago Colombian Exposition, but whether the international origins of this or any of his other performers went beyond their stage names is open to question. Jack even claims to have brought back from Egypt a band of eunuchs to guard the virtue of his female performers as they traveled the rails in their circuit days: "They are big, strapping, good-natured fellows, and my ladies are perfectly safe under their care" (qtd. in O'Neill, 71–72).

Jack's reputed taste for brown-skinned beauties from exotic locales, from New Orleans to Brazil, to Egypt, is on display in *Beauty in Dreamland*, set in a harem run by Islam, "shah of Persia!" The lush setting would have given Jack's designers opportunity to clothe the stage lavishly while dressing the girls as scantily as possible; "Tulip Tint" and "Mossrose" are featured female characters, surrounded by almost too many wisecracking male retainers to keep track of: Gin Sour, the shah's chief officer; Boulanger Jim, "commanding general of the Persian army!"; Flipflop the eunuch; Legs, "a Persian dude!," and other named male roles. Bevies of slave and dancing girls provide the visual attraction, as do of course the seminude women posed in various "artistic" attitudes each time Shah Islam calls for another "tableau!" The plot is nearly nonexistent; one or two male servants challenge the shah's authority, and the singing skills of others are heartily mocked by all. As the characters speak in rhymed couplets of flickering musicality throughout—

GIN SOUR:	To enjoy anything good they will not refuse.
ISLAM:	Good! And while they're on—
	The bowstring waits for anyone who takes a snooze.

—it is possible that the entire show was sung, in the comic-opera tradition epitomized by Gilbert and Sullivan. Their influence is felt even in lowbrow American entertainments like *Beauty in Dreamland*, and one traces the influence of both light opera and Jack-style burlesque to the clever lyrics and crowded choruses of the Marx Brothers film comedies, the Marx Brothers being famed vaudevillians in the early twentieth century. In the original handwritten script, Jack designates four solo "Song" interludes, actual lyrics and score to be added later or perhaps simply borrowed from the popular songbook, and five tableaux, also without further specification, of what we can only assume would be the typically titillating variety. Despite the tawdry proceedings thus far—and despite the Persian designation of setting, characters, and references from the first moment—Shah Islam assures us that

[t]he final tableau, I am sure, will meet your approbation!
In it will be introduced the flag of every nation!
Concluding with the greatest flag yet made!
Of Uncle Sam! Of no other flag afraid!

This 11th-hour lunge toward the patriotic, with ranks of topless or barely dressed women saluting the American flag, was likely meant to send skeptical (or guilt-ridden) audiences into the cold with warm feelings regarding the righteousness of an evening spent in Sam T. Jack's house of burlesque. It is yet another remarkable example of the inextricable weave of the high and low in American popular entertainments of the period.

Margaret Fleming (1890)

James A. Herne (1839–1901)

The son of an Irish immigrant from upstate New York, James A. Herne was a fairly well sought-after actor and manager in the postbellum period, in the theaters of Washington, DC; Baltimore; San Francisco (where he met his beloved second wife and lifelong collaborator Katherine Corcoran); and occasionally New York City. But it is not surprising that Herne was required to seek an audience for his own daring masterwork *Margaret Fleming*, deeply inspired by Ibsen's *A Doll's House* (1879), among the intelligentsia of greater Boston, the burgeoning late-nineteenth-century epicenter of American literary realism. Williams Dean Howells, editor of *The Atlantic Monthly*, "dean of American letters," and champion of realism in all genres, and his disciple Hamlin Garland were early promoters of Herne's work. In May 1891, Howells famously referred to *Margaret Fleming* as "epoch-marking," and his early review raved: "The power of the story, as presented by Mr. Herne's every-day phrase, and in the naked simplicity of Mrs. Herne's acting of the wife's part was terrific. It clutched the heart. It was pitilessly plain; it was ugly; but it was true, and it was irresistible" (qtd. in Perry, 160). Garland, who saw Herne's naturalistic *Drifting Apart* in early 1889 and shortly thereafter befriended the Hernes for life, persuaded Boston's leading thinkers to sign publicity materials and talked up the play among important theater critics.

Ironically, *Margaret Fleming*'s original three-show run in Lynn, Massachusetts, in an oversized, unconvivial barn of a theater in July 1890, received warm support from the critics, whereas its three-week stay in May 1891 in Boston's convivial Chickering Hall, which Herne rented and remodeled to suit the play's quiet conversations and low-key revelations, met with universal disdain. As several Herne scholars have observed, *Margaret Fleming* was taken to the bosom of Boston's educated circles, but there were only so many liberals and intellectuals to attend plays and write reviews even in

Boston; as *Margaret Fleming*'s run wore on, reviews turned rancorous and ticket sales flagged. In the always more commercially minded New York theater districts, *Margaret Fleming* eventually attracted the wary interests of Klaw and Erlanger, the most successful theatrical syndicate owners of their age, and later the Broadway magnate A. M. Palmer. Each attempted a brief run, in October 1891 back at Chickering Hall and in December 1891 at Palmer's Broadway theater, but each withdrew support when the show met immediately with yet more press vilification and public indifference.

Critics sneered at the footbath taken by Margaret's husband, Philip, in an early scene; shrieked at the Act III curtain when Margaret opens her blouse to breastfeed Philip's illegitimate child; and quaked in fear of the final moments, when Margaret refuses to forgive her husband despite his swearing off both other women and, of late, drinking to the point of delirium tremens. As recorded by Herne's superb biographer John Perry, Thomas Russell Sullivan, who walked out after the breastfeeding scene, "thought the play thin and commonplace, dull beyond description, and badly acted" (156). A critic for the *Boston Morning Journal* vigorously objected to the tossing about of "the third commandment" (qtd. in Perry, 157), and Herne's lifelong nemesis William Winter lambasted the play when it reached New York as "a long conversation interrupted from time to time by the falling of the curtain" (qtd. in Perry, 170). Herne and his plays, especially *Margaret Fleming*, were a generation ahead of their time; it was only in a brief but triumphant run at Chicago's New Theater, six years after Herne's death, that *Margaret Fleming*, directed by Herne's widow and with Herne's daughter Chrystal in the title role, received widespread critical acclaim.

The story opens in the notably ordinary environs of Philip's factory office; there he meets, in a comic relief exchange too early to relieve much of anything, his perpetually luckless old friend Joe Fletcher (played from 1891 forward by Herne himself, who specialized in warmhearted sages of the Stage Yankee tradition). Joe tells a sob story about the cruel wife who threw him out and tries to sell Philip an item from his peddler's pack. That same morning, Philip hears from a disgruntled shop foreman, whose main function seems to be to signal Philip's mediocre handling of business affairs, and then from the intensely moralistic Dr. Larkin, cut sharply from the same cloth as Ibsen's Dr. Rank. If Dr. Rank was a sneering cynic, Dr. Larkin is a haranguing scold; he castigates Philip for having impregnated an immigrant millworker, taking breaks from his campaign throughout the play only to shower Margaret with paternalistic coddling. Philip insouciantly insists that he tried to get his mistress to abort the child, but Dr. Larkin excoriates Philip's insensitivity, his betrayal of his role as member of the cultured middle class. Soon after, Margaret enters as a paragon of wife- and motherhood, a patient sponsor of her sharp-tongued, middle-aged maid, Maria, and a sympathetic listener to Maria's own sob story of her sister Lena, lying on her deathbed following the birth of her illegitimate child. Not only is this child Philip's, but Maria is the cruel wife of Joe's recent regaling; when he sneaks around to the Fleming house in an attempt to sell more wares, Joe is recognized by Maria, who was in fact abandoned by Joe instead of the reverse, and who grabs him by the lapels and "throws him through the French window" (488). It is on her visit to the dying Lena that Margaret learns the truth of Philip's infidelity, goes blind due to the trauma as Dr. Larkin had warned she would, and takes the little bastard to her breast in a moving testimony to her indefatigable maternity.

The play's final act has a remarkable history; it survives in the original in summary only, thanks to Garland's July 8, 1890, review for the *Boston Evening Transcript* (see Perry, 143–44). Here we learn that in the original fourth act, four years have passed, and Philip is now a drunken bum, perhaps opening the scene with a display of the DTs frequently referred to and roundly condemned by critics. Joe Fletcher, reunited with Maria, runs a shop whose counter is attended by five-year-old Lucy, the Flemings' long-lost legitimate daughter. Margaret enters the shop, tapping her cane, is reunited with her daughter, and exits; Joe comes in with Philip, who is seen by Maria and informed out of lasting spite that she has just sold away his child. In the final scene at the police station (evidently to look into the kidnapping charge), Philip and Margaret meet but do not reconcile. Margaret utters her wonderfully poignant line, "The wife-heart has gone out of me" (qtd. in Garland, 557) and although she agonizes over the decision, she leaves Philip for good. The stage gradually darkens, signifying Margaret's permanent future of principled solitude—a condition identical to Ibsen's Nora's—as Philip departs.

When the play received a receptive welcome from Joseph McVickers, who presented *Margaret Fleming* at his Chicago theater in summer 1892, Herne consented to a heavily revised final act that attaches to the play to this day. (Notably, this entire version was lost as well, when a fire at the Hernes' Long Island home destroyed numerous important papers in 1909. It was reconstructed from memory by Herne's widow in 1914 and is largely regarded as a worthy estimation of the edition acted from 1892 forward.) Now the final action takes place days following the end of Act III in the Flemings' living room. Although Margaret is still blind and still bereft of her wife-heart, the alcoholism is no longer an issue, and prospects for an eventual reunion are much improved. Margaret insists, echoing Torvald Helmer in the last moments of *A Doll's House*, that she and Philip will stay married in name only—no more physical relations between them—but that "I will help you—we will fight [the assault on Philip's personal and professional reputation] together" (508). When Philip takes comfort in Margaret's support and his own exuberant return "to work" (509), he directly echoes the hopeful upshot for *A Doll's House*'s second couple, the discredited Krogstad and his helpmeet, Kristine, who will both find personal fulfillment and social redemption by returning to work. Margaret then "gives a long sigh of relief and contentment" with "serene joy illuminat[ing] her face" while "Philip steps buoyantly into the garden" (510). Regrettably, these major concessions to public sentiment did little to improve the play's durability. Even its successful revival in 1907 was short-lived due to Chrystal's other obligations, and the play was forgotten until much later in the century.

Though it is well worth regarding Herne as ahead of his time in his own day, it is likewise impossible to encounter *Margaret Fleming* now and not be struck by the melodramatic and farcical elements—the implausible coincidence of Philip's mistress and Margaret's maid being sisters, Margaret's pathetic and equally implausible attack of blindness due to shock, the hokey slapstick between Maria and Joe—that mark this work as much more a transition from melodrama to realism than as the clear breakthrough it was originally considered to be. Herne's inspiration, *A Doll's House*, endures as an example of modern drama at its best, whereas *Margaret Fleming* enjoys a much dimmer reputation, perhaps because "Garland and Howells ... were stronger influences upon [Herne] than Ibsen" (Edwards and Herne, 53). And in a statement that might have been uttered by either of them, Garland took pains to distinguish American dramatic realism from Ibsenism per se: "[T]here is a strain of morbid psychology in [Ibsen's] characters which I do not value.... Ibsen has helped us in our war against conventionalisms, but he must not dominate us.... Our drama must be more human, more wholesome, and more humorous" (qtd. in Edwards and Herne, 52).

Dated in its dogged Americanness though it may be, *Margaret Fleming* is worth our continued consideration; its author was a maverick in several spheres—as an early advocate for an actors' union and as a method actor years before the advent of Stanislavsky—and its short stay at Chickering Hall with its 100-member audience was an early example of "little theater" in its exciting formative stage (see Julie A. Herne, xix; and Perry, 185, 194). Though we might flinch at the inclusion of a "DTs" episode in the 1890–1891 version, reminiscent of the crisis moment from William Henry Smith's egregiously melodramatic *The Drunkard* (1844), it is certainly possible that Herne cited such business for the express purpose of doing it as it has never been done, in the revolutionary guise of understated realism. As Brenda Murphy observes, Herne was a vital bridge between the literary realism that reigned in that era and its dramatic aspect, still decades away from broad acceptance: "*Margaret Fleming* ... made realism a force for the theater to contend with. It alerted playwrights, critics, and public alike that a change was on the horizon" (*American Realism*, 85). In an important essay on the dramatist's craft, Herne averred that "[a]rt for art's sake may be likened to the exquisite decoration of some noble building; while art for truth's sake might be the building itself" (Herne, 362). He proudly staked his claim in this newer, truer vein, "because it perpetuates the everyday life of its time, because it develops the latent beauty of the so-called commonplaces of life, because it dignifies labor and reveals the divinity of the common man" (Herne, 369). Notably, Arthur Miller would celebrate just such a glorification of the common man in his own manifesto 50 momentous years following Herne's. Perhaps it is Herne's detailed anticipation of the master of modern American drama that best confirms his reputation as a founding father of this tradition.

The Easiest Way (1908)

Eugene Walter (1874–1941)

In this remarkably forthright, Ibsen-inspired reaction to the New Woman of the early twentieth century, heroine Laura Murdock accepts the strings-attached sponsorship of a Broadway producer in order to maintain her career onstage while awaiting the professional success of her fiancé, John Madison, out West. When John returns to discover Laura's unorthodox sexual/business arrangement in New York, he leaves her stranded, as does the producer Will Brockton, and Laura faces the prospects of utter "depravity" (i.e., prostitution) in order to survive. As in *A Doll's House*, stark realities regarding women's financial solvency are plumbed to the depths in *The Easiest Way*. Laura is prevented by the powerful producer from receiving any acting jobs without returning to the live-in arrangement she had with him as the play began, and the fiancé absents himself entirely in the course of his long and finally successful attempt to make a fortune prospecting in the mines. In this way, Walter depicts both Brockton and John as human equivalents of a money faucet: in their respective orbits, Laura swims in well-fed luxury; in the absence of both, she is plunged instantly into desperate poverty, and Walter is likely guilty of overselling the point but effectively stresses the crisis.

Notably, Laura's career, as opposed to the office work specialized in by Ibsen's Mrs. Linde, is stage acting. If talent were understood in Walter's day as an inborn trait that women as well as men might exploit with great financial success, there was yet the prevailing sense that actresses were closely akin to prostitutes to begin with, such that Laura rather asks for her fate by choosing theater life (see also Gottlieb, 86). Contemporary reviewers (e.g., Clark, 278) compared Laura to the title characters of A. W. Pinero's *Iris* (1902) and Shaw's *Mrs. Warren's Profession* (1902). The equation was underscored by the playwright himself, who described Laura as "a type not uncommon in the theatrical life of New York, and one which has grown … since the business of giving public entertainments has been so reduced to a commercial basis" (qtd. in "The Easiest Way," 73). In other words, even whatever talent Laura may have is "prostituted" in this cynically mercenary Broadway environment, and Laura is presented as not especially committed to her craft anyway, only hanging on in the profession until John succeeds. In this light, it is just a cruel twist of fate that his fortune does not pay out in time to rescue Laura from a return to the stage, which is simultaneous with her reinstatement of the illicit living arrangement with Brockton. As Katie Johnson observes, however, almost all reviews of the play—and in separate comments by both playwright Walter and producer David Belasco—condemned Laura herself for her weak-willed, morally insupportable ways. The reaction is explained in part by fears of "*single* working women [who] transgressed the conceptual framework of the patriarchal leisure class in not only working but also in consuming commodities" (Johnson, 74).

Walter also Americanizes his response to Ibsen's work in the heavy gunplay at crisis moments. As the Western theme trended heavily in this period—in both plays and early film texts (see Ludwig, 110–11)—Walter's play starts on a peaceful ranch at the foot of the Rocky Mountains, where Laura is resting from her work out East and falls for the straight-shooting prospector. As Ronald Wainscott observes, Laura "falls in love with the beauty and apparent purity of the unspoiled West and finds her ideal mate, 'a real man'" (271). If disputes are naturally settled with a showdown in this lawless environment, the handshake between Brockton and John that strangely concludes their confrontation in Act I is indeed replaced by gun bearing in the last act: John threatens Brockton with his Colt revolver, then puts it back in its holster when Laura begs him not to shoot. With Brockton gone and John on the way out, Laura grabs her own gun from her trunk and threatens suicide; Nora Helmer contemplated tossing herself into the icy water, and both women poignantly lack the courage to go through with their desperate threat.

Laura's floozy girlfriend, Elfie St. Claire, is an inspired minor character—an American version of Kristine Linde, who enters the heroine's premises and confronts her with hard fact. Before reestablishing her connection to Brockton, Laura admits that she has kept the truth of her financial desperation from John because she was ashamed to pressure him into supporting her before he was able to do so. Facing the predicament, as Laura will not, Elfie insists that John be told the truth: "Well, what does he think you're to live on—asphalt croquettes with conversation sauce?" (765). When it is determined that he is simply unable to step into the husband's role, Elfie sends Laura back to the producer. It is sell out or starve, and yet both men—and finally, to a certain extent, the playwright himself—hold this impossible choice against her. As Lois C. Gottlieb observes, "Ultimately, *The Easiest Way* portrays woman's freedom as a catalyst of her own destruction and as a barrier to honorable relations between men" (85).

Another key minor figure is the servant Annie, played originally in blackface to both comic and menacing effect. Upon her final expulsion from Brockton's home, Annie follows Laura to the rundown boarding house—that was famously reproduced from a downtown original, wallpaper and all, by the master of vérité set design David Belasco—where she meets her fate. The servant is closely associated with Laura's trunk full of "finery," helping to dress the actress for her final performance, which is clearly understood as a rapid slide into perdition. As Annie cheerfully sings a song coming up from a hurdy-gurdy player on the sidewalk outside, she is the harbinger of ironic tragedy, of the indifference and scorn of a cruel outside world now that a man's love and a man's protecting arm have been withdrawn.

Drama in Dialogue: *Margaret Fleming* and *The Easiest Way*

At the turn of the twentieth century, the emergence of the New Woman opened a Pandora's box of controversy and backlash that perfectly coincided with the broader turn toward realism and its focus on social problems and psychological truth in fiction and drama. In both *A Doll's House* (1879) and *Ghosts* (1881), Ibsen notoriously eviscerated the sanctity of marriage and the cult of parenthood, exposing the lies, betrayals, and irreversible conditions that he suggested contaminated the most upstanding households in early Industrial Europe, and throughout the West. In the wake of these and related terrifically "popular" (widely discussed even if roundly vilified) theatrical premieres, American playwrights obsessed over "the woman question" and positioned transgressive women center-stage. Both Herne's *Margaret Fleming* and Walter's *The Easiest Way* react to Ibsen's example—portraying strong, modern women taking command of their crumbling lives yet receiving consequences in accordance with the melodramatic moralism that still controlled the American dramatic context that Ibsen's Nora Helmer had been provisionally allowed to escape. If proto-feminism is on display in *A Doll's House*, many American audiences received staged versions of the New Woman—regardless of the playwright's own intentions—as fearfully as they might a hatchet-wielding Indian or an escaped slave.

In Herne's drama, the eponymous heroine is a virtuous woman married (as in Ibsen's *Ghosts*) to an unreconstructed two-timer; she created scandal for her original audience by daring to visit the bedside of the slattern who seduced her husband and is only foiled in the attempt by the woman's death. Adding insult to injury, she brings home the bastard child of her husband's affair and breastfeeds it onstage with the milk generated on behalf of her legitimately born daughter. Meanwhile, Margaret more than atones for her several sins of generosity by losing both her sight (due to excessive stress) and her "wife-heart" by story's end: in terms almost identical to those exchanged between Nora and Torvald as their marriage dissolves, Margaret states simply that she no longer loves her husband, but that if he would do right by her, he would return to their home and maintain a respectable semblance for the sake of the children—both of them.

To be sure, the 20 years separating Herne's and Walter's plays mean that the women on view in *The Easiest Way* (in case the title itself did not indicate as much) are much "newer" as dramatic heroines than the traditionally construed females who populate Herne's ultimately quaint, regionalist drama. Herne's more traditional story chooses a respectable, devoted wife as its heroine and assigns Philip's mistress both a marginalized role—she never appears but is only referred to—and an early death. By contrast, Walter's Laura Murdock is a consternating combination of lady and whore—the romanticized beloved of the story's straight arrow out West and the loose-living "working girl" who only succeeds in her acting career back East by simultaneously joining the world's oldest profession. Ironically, Herne's much tamer New Woman was met with much greater opprobrium due to her shocking novelty. Two eventful decades later, the much racier situation in Walter's play was greeted favorably by its unfazed "first night audience," says Montrose J. Moses, as "one of the most direct pieces of work the American stage had thus far produced—disagreeably realistic but purging—and that is the test of an effective play—by the very poignancy of the tragic forces closing in around the heroine" ("Eugene Walter," 707). Notably, Walter was not only an experienced newsman, therefore familiar with (and surely responsible for) copious coverage of life's seamy underbelly, but a former theatrical advance man with thus firsthand knowledge of the impoverished life that many actors (not to mention advance men) led: in a noted recounting of the genesis of his play, Walter admits that "the need of money caused me to write [the] one-act piece" (Moses, "Eugene Walter," 709) that became *The Easiest Way*.

When one of the producers almost turned down the show because the minimally talented "*Laura* was kept out of work in order to be compelled to yield herself to *Brockton*" (Moses, "Eugene Walter," 709), Walter could have easily excised the contrivance of Laura's mediocrity: even into the early twentieth century the association of theater women of all calibers with moral laxity was widely held; the corrosive influences of work and independence on women's inherent frailty broadly assumed and the overabundance of talented actresses necessitating moral selling out for success readily understood. Walter's implicit point is easily taken to be that it is only the rare (i.e., truly great or exceptionally lucky) actress who does *not* have to prostitute herself to catch the attention of Broadway's powerful men; the very system Walter's enthusiastic first-night audience patronized is responsible for the moral demise of Laura and those many she represents, and such an acknowledgement brings Walter's work dangerously close to the proto-feminism of Ibsen. Laura's final swaggering line, "Yes, I'm going to Rector's to make a hit, and to hell with the rest" (Walter, 814) indeed rings upon the twenty-first-century ear with admirable bravura. Although Katie Johnson points out that Rector's was a notorious pickup joint in the Broadway district of the era (73), it is notable that Walter frames Laura's impending venture as "making a hit": she will succeed according to the same terms used by producers who score with a popular Broadway play, and her performance—as happy hooker, as successful woman—will bring her the same personal gratification and financial compensation that all deserving actresses receive.

Yet the reader must stay on for Walter's heavy-handed final stage direction, whereby the actor playing Laura is required to hear some evocative music on the street below and exhibit her understanding of "the panorama of inevitable depravity that awaits her. She is torn from every ideal that she so weakly endeavored to grasp, and is thrown into the mire and slime at the very moment when her emancipation seems most assured" (Walter, 814; see also Peirce, 119). If ultimately neither Herne's nor Walter's play is readable as pro–New Woman in any defensible regard, the remaining interpretive lens is melodrama, which held on strongly throughout the early twentieth century, despite certain scenic, situational, and characterologic innovations courtesy of the new realism. Although Ibsen's Nora makes her daring break with tradition more or less unscathed, to teach herself some vital life lessons as she does, middle-class American audiences relied on Margaret and especially Laura to end their stories alone and unhappy to reestablish the reliability of the audience's own traditional moral compass.

Part IV

O'Neill, His Cohort, and the Legitimate Stage between the Wars (1916–1945)

The advent of modern American drama coincides not surprisingly with the predominance of the literary, artistic, and performative modernism that defined the cultural experience in Europe and America between the World Wars. In the words of David Krasner, "To be a modern American dramatist was to be an experimenter … [and Eugene] O'Neill often became immersed in the modernist movements of his time" ("Eugene O'Neill," 145). O'Neill famously incorporated expressionist effects (in *The Emperor Jones* [1920] and *The Hairy Ape* [1922]); Jungian masks (in *All God's Chillun Got Wings* [1924], *The Great God Brown* [1926], and *Lazarus Laughed* [1928]); Nietzschean philosophy (again, in *The Great God Brown*); Freudian-style voiceovers speaking the conflicted subconscious (in *Strange Interlude* [1928]); and neoclassical revivalism shaped along Freudian-Oedipal lines (in *Mourning Becomes Electra* [1931]). And yet interspersed among (and even within) these more experimental works is a gritty, daring realism that was itself a bracing departure from the merely "mechanical" (Downer, 41) or scenic realism of Augustin Daly or David Belasco. As Allan Lewis notes, such organic realism shocked early twentieth-century audiences with "hard language, brutal violence, and psychological truth. The Los Angeles company [of O'Neill's *Desire Under the Elms* (1925)] was hauled off to jail on charges of lewdness and immorality" (21). Beyond the initial shock value of O'Neill's subject matter and word choice, what is most enduringly modern about his oeuvre is the "richness of detail and psychological depth rarely seen before in American drama. His dialogue was sensitive to regional and ethnic vernacular, and his three-dimensional characterizations have rarely been equaled" (Krasner, "Eugene O'Neill," 142). As Alan S. Downer has noted, "After 1915 … the American drama is filled with characters memorable in themselves, characters who have survived the actors who first impersonated them…. The sailors of O'Neill's Provincetown plays … are drawn from his own observation and understanding of such men, and not from a gallery of theatrical types" (44).

O'Neill famously attached himself to a group of radical thinkers in the artists' colony of Provincetown, Massachusetts, in 1916. There he arrived with his "trunk full of plays" at the doorstep of Susan Glaspell and George Cram Cook, key figures in a group of bohemian actors, writers, and journalists who formed themselves into the Provincetown Players for the express purpose of performing plays unaccountable to the commercial dictates of Broadway (see, e.g., Ben-Zvi, *Susan Glaspell*, 177). On a memorable night in July of that year, the Players staged O'Neill's one-act tragedy (culled from O'Neill's own brief but eye-opening career as a merchant seaman) of a sailor who dies in his sordid bunk, *Bound East for Cardiff*, in a falling-down shack on the Provincetown Wharf. With the waves rolling beneath them and the fog drifting through the cracks, the Players electrified the small but engaged audience, who knew they were bearing witness to the very dawn of the legitimate American stage. The Players knew as well that they had found their vocation—in Glaspell's words, on reading O'Neill's play, "[W]e knew what we were for" (qtd. in Murphy, "Plays," 291)—and soon relocated to a storefront theater on Macdougal Street in New York's Greenwich Village, now much closer to America's theatrical epicenter but resolutely removed from the atmosphere of glitz and pandering that characterized Broadway itself. Notably, O'Neill's father, the late nineteenth-century matinee idol James O'Neill, had made his fortune but ruined his artistic reputation in this very atmosphere, having bought the rights to the stage adaptation of Dumas's *The Count of Monte Cristo* and did nothing but play the lead—more than 6000 times—for the remaining 25 years of his career.

Despite deep discord between the two, James O'Neill's professional standing enabled his son to a Broadway opening for *Beyond the Horizon* (1918), the realistically told story of a swaggering older brother, a dreamy and sensitive younger brother, and the woman who impulsively chooses the youth and then regrets the decision for the rest of her life. The show was a striking success, running for 111 performances, winning the Pulitzer Prize, and alerting the wider theatrical world that a new and important addition to the modern dramatic canon had arrived. O'Neill soon returned to the Provincetown group with his more experimental *The Emperor Jones* and *The Hairy Ape*. Both are structured as expressionist-style "station plays" (Murphy, "Plays," 294; see also Beard, 60) in which the main character moves from scene to scene in a regressive journey back to his primal roots in vintage Darwinist/Freudian fashion. Brutus Jones is a murdering con artist hiding out among the natives in the West Indies; at first, they crown him king but then tire of his dictatorial ways, plotting assassination to the beat and an ever-accelerating drum as Jones flees through the forest and back through elemental time. Traumatized by hallucinations of his crimes in the States, the horrors of slavery, and his tribal-ancestral past, Jones circles back to the waiting natives and is gunned down by them as the drum/pulse beat immediately ceases.

The *New York Tribune*'s influential critic Heywood Broun complained about the long wait times between scenes at the tiny Provincetown theater—each a "vulture which preys upon the attention"—but raved about the performance of the actor in the lead role: "[I]f the Emperor Jones were taken elsewhere, we have little doubt that the manager would engage a white man with a piece of burnt cork to play Brutus Jones.... [I]n Macdougal Street ... [t]he emperor is played by a negro actor named Charles S. Gilpin, who gives the most thrilling performance we have seen any place this season" (8). We should recall that a hundred years earlier, only a few blocks from the Provincetown Playhouse's Macdougal Street address, the Africa Company's William Alexander Brown was beaten by thugs from the Park Theater for his attempt to play Shakespeare uptown, and his downtown venue ransacked for good measure. Though important barriers had been broken by Gilpin's performance, the journey to a truly democratized American stage was (and remains) far from complete: even a competing review of O'Neill's play, Alexander Woollcott's own favorable report for the *New York Times*, still uses the term "darky" to refer to Jones (88), and Gilpin himself eventually broke with O'Neill over O'Neill's refusal to remove several uses of the word "nigger" from the play. The following March, Gilpin was one of ten honorees by the Drama League but was almost barred from the ceremony because of the discriminatory policies of the hotel where it occurred.[1]

The Hairy Ape is another tale of a rough-hewn but proudly vigorous sailor who is thrown into a crisis of self-loathing when a wealthy shipping heiress visits his stokehole and shrieks hysterically regarding his unnerving resemblance to a hairy ape. As with Jones's journey through his archetypal past, Yank makes a regressive journey through various expressionistically rendered New York scenes, arriving at last in the gorilla cage at the Bronx Zoo, where he is bludgeoned to death by his hostile cousin. When, remarkably, both of these artistically challenging plays were welcomed uptown following their Playhouse debuts, it was clear that Broadway itself—though its emphasis on commercial entertainment would never wane—had modernized sufficiently to bring its audience a dramatic depth and intelligence that they in turn embraced. In

---

[1] The happy upshot to this narrative: "At the banquet, Gilpin's acceptance speech was met with an outbreak of cheering and applause, which continued until Gilpin rose to speak a second time" (Bechtel, 138).

other words, O'Neill's regular visits to the Great White Way did not consti-tute a knuckling under to Broadway standards, but a stretching of aesthetic boundaries and an increase in intellectual expectations on Broadway's own stages to accommodate O'Neill's grand vision (see also A. Lewis, 34).

From 1916 until 1931, O'Neill's star rose meteorically, with the striking success of his art theater days, his daring experimentalism lauded by critics and audiences alike, and the sheer number and diversity of hit plays—often two in one year, with seven productions in his watershed year of 1924 (see Murphy, "Plays," 289). The crowning achievement during O'Neill's own life-time was his nine-hour, 14-act trilogy, *Mourning Becomes Electra* (1931), a retelling of the *Oresteia* by Aeschylus, now set in Civil War–era New England, where, as with both *Beyond the Horizon* and *Desire Under the Elms*, a pre-vailing theme is the crumbling stone of Puritan repression and hypocrisy. Remarkably, this draining theatrical experience engaged audiences during 150 performances and, though rarely staged in full today, is regarded as one of O'Neill's most important works.

In 1936, O'Neill won the Nobel Prize in Literature, the only American playwright ever to do so, yet the award seemed something of a "final tribute" (if not a kiss of death): at this time a hazily understood "family illness" char-acterized by hand tremors seriously diminished and at last permanently cur-tailed O'Neill's ability to write in longhand, with typing and dictation both being impossible conduits for him. All but two elements of a lengthy history cycle (*A Touch of the Poet* [1942] and *More Stately Mansions* [1935–41]) were destroyed by O'Neill's wife at his behest when he realized he would never finish the cycle. And ironically his three autobiographically informed master-works—*The Iceman Cometh* (1939), *Long Day's Journey into Night* (1941), and *A Moon for the Misbegotten* (1941)—written in the last years that O'Neill was physically able to do so, received only one mishandled staging, of *The Iceman Cometh*, directed by Eddie Dowling 1946, before O'Neill died, discredited and largely forgotten, in 1953. It is little short of tragic that *Iceman* did not receive until three years after his death the production it deserved—by José Quintero at Circle in the Square, with Jason Robards in the role of Hickey—and that immediately returned the American theatergoing public to its long-held, never truly forgotten understanding of O'Neill's unmatched greatness. In the four-act story, a gang of barflies awaits their annual visit from the trav-eling salesman Hickey, who springs for lavish rounds of drinks and inflates his fellows' sense of self-worth with his magnanimous, affirming ways. On this occasion, Hickey arrives much changed, insidiously undermining the "pipe dreams" of each denizen of Harry Hope's saloon and giving each an enlight-ening confrontation with his own irreversible self-betrayal. Yet the play's larger thesis is that such pipe dreams are essential to fallible humans' ability to cope with the disappointments and failures of their lives: as arresting officers approach, Hickey reveals that he has killed his wife, due to the permanent shattering of his own pipe dreams, and the young Parritt rushes off to commit suicide, to escape the guilt of having sent his mother to prison. The Quintero production had 565 performances and, according to Brenda Murphy, was "largely responsible for the revival of O'Neill's reputation" ("Plays," 303).

As noted above, O'Neill's original artistic home was the Provincetown Players, one of the more prominent "little," experimental, and university theaters that sprang up in major cities throughout the United States in the early twentieth century. In 1912, the wealthy philanthropist sisters Alice and Irene Lewisohn established the Neighborhood Playhouse for the edification of the impoverished, dislocated immigrants of New York's Henry Street Settlement (see Fearnow, 349–52). At the height of the Harlem Renaissance, more than a dozen art theaters launched, including W.E.B. DuBois's Krigwa Players (1925–1928), Langston Hughes's Harlem Suitcase Theater (1938), and the American Negro Theater (1944), whose production of *Anna Lucasta* moved to Broadway, thereby regrettably ending this group's existence (see also Mitchell, 113–14; Bigsby, *A Critical Introduction*, 249, 253; Bean, 94). New York–based leftist theater groups also proliferated in this period, notably the American Laboratory Theater, where Lee Strasburg got his start; ARTEF/Worker's Theater Alliance, a politicized offshoot of the Yiddish Art Theater; and Orson Welles and John Houseman's Mercury Theater, whose heyday was 1937 to 1939 (see Fearnow, 364–65).

The Washington Square Players, founded in 1914, sprang from the gatherings at an intellectuals' watering hole on Macdougal Street, called the Liberal Club. As did most proponents of the Little Theater movement, the Washington Square Players opposed the "commercially oriented, artificial and vapid world of Broadway" (Bigsby, *A Critical Introduction*, 9). Yet their ultimately more mainstream tastes led them to reject Cook and Glaspell's Freudian satire, *Suppressed Desires*, at which point the couple inaugurated their Provincetown collective to stage the play themselves. An important debut for the Provincetowners was Glaspell's own feminist classic *Trifles* (1916), in which a demoralized farm wife takes the life of her taciturn, brutish husband and is rescued from legal consequences by the wives of investigating officials. In addition to the work of O'Neill, they staged plays by communist firebrand John Reed, journalist Louise Bryant, and poet Edna St. Vincent Millay. Both Washington Square and Provincetown had successful initial seasons, although the advent of World War I distracted the average art theater patron from attendance and absorbed several of these groups' male players into the armed forces.

The Provincetowners' post-WWI success with *The Emperor Jones* was both their pinnacle achievement and the beginning of their undoing. Regarding *Jones*'s move uptown as an artistic sellout, Cook and Glaspell decamped for Greece; the group hung on through the mid-1920s, fueled largely by the plays and production support of O'Neill, but never regained its original force.

The Washington Square Players were disbanded by World War I and reconstituted themselves as the Theater Guild the moment it ended, in December 1918. They included several alumni of Harvard Professor George Pierce Baker's Workshop 47 for playwrights and maintained a well-organized professionalism that boded well for long-term success. Yet as Mark Fearnow observes, the Guild did not present a bill of majority-American plays until its 15th season; its view was that "Strindberg, Tolstoy, Molnár, Shaw ... offered a kind of school for the degraded American authors whose only exposure had been to a crass commercial stage" (358; see also Savran, "Making Middlebrow Theater," 31). As in the days of William Charles Macready being chased from the stage of the Astor Place Opera House, a founding member of the Theater Guild went on the defensive thus:

> [T]hey [the Guild] could not experiment with undeveloped native work, however promising, as an amateur group [a dig at the Provincetown Players?] could do, because they were definitely pledged to the subscribers to produce finished entertainment.... Accordingly the Guild had to endure more or less in silence the frequent charges that they were "un-American" and to go ahead proving that good drama, written with distinction and intellectual point, would pay in America, and especially pay in their theatre.... (qtd. in Bigsby, *A Critical Introduction*, 120–21)

Despite this demurral, the Guild presented numerous important American plays of the early twentieth century: Percy MacKaye's *The Antick* (1915); Zoë Akins's *Magical City* (1916); Zona Gale's *Neighbors* (1917); Elmer Rice's expressionistic *The Adding Machine* (1923); John Howard Lawson's also-expressionistic *Processional* (1925) and melodramatic critique of capitalist excess, *Success Story* (produced by the Guild's offshoot Group Theater in 1932); S. N. Behrman's comically staged debate between idealism and cynicism, *The Second Man* (1927); Philip Barry's *Hotel Universe* (1930) and hugely successful manners comedy, *The Philadelphia Story* (1939); Robert Sherwood's farcical *Reunion in Vienna* (1931) and pacifist tragicomedy, *Idiot's Delight* (1936), which won the Pulitzer Prize in 1936; the verse dramatist Maxwell Anderson's "prose political lampoon" (Fletcher, 120) *Both Your Houses* (1933), which won the Pulitzer Prize in 1933; and William Saroyan's *My Heart's in the Highlands* (produced by the Group in 1939). For the Guild, Saroyan wrote the widely acclaimed *The Time of Your Life* (1939), termed by Christopher Bigsby as "a comic counterpart to O'Neill's *The Iceman Cometh*" (*A Critical Introduction*, 136). As in *Iceman*, the setting is a bar occupied by a gang of regulars, although this time the mood is largely comic-optimistic, which Bigsby deems "evasive" (*A Critical Introduction*, 137) and inappropriate on the eve of war.

Many of these playwrights enjoyed careers beyond (though surely helped by their early dealings with) the Guild: Akins won the Pulitzer for *The Old Maid* in 1935, as did Zona Gale in 1920 for *Ms. Lulu Bett*, also about an old maid living meagerly with her sister's family as their unpaid servant but eventually finding happiness through love and marriage. Rice's naturalistic *Street Scene* (1929) enjoyed a run of more than 600 performances and yet again won that year's Pulitzer in drama. Behrman and Barry specialized in comic plays featuring society characters, although where Barry sharply critiqued the materialism of his native upper class, "Behrman's plays maintaine[d] a noncommittal position between two extremes, usually a self-interested and hypocritical Left and a vacuously materialistic and power-hungry Right" (Murphy, "Plays," 320). As World War II approached, Sherwood wrote *Abe Lincoln in Illinois* (1939) about an American hero reluctantly realizing his national duty, winning his second Pulitzer, and *There Shall Be No Night* the following year, also on the theme of patriotic duty. During the war, he was president of the Dramatists Guild and a speechwriter for FDR. Anderson's verse drama *Winterset* (1935) critiqued the injustice of the Sacco and Vanzetti executions, and his *Key Largo* argued against cynicism and for commitment to a cause, this time the Spanish Civil War.

As mentioned above, the Guild gave birth to the Group Theater, an actor/director-centered collective founded by Guild actors Harold Clurman and Lee Strasberg, Guild casting director Cheryl Crawford, and actor Stella Adler in 1931. A year later, they formally separated from Guild auspices and found their most talented spokesman in an erstwhile undistinguished member of the acting company, Clifford Odets. His *Waiting for Lefty* (January 1935) was an agitprop melodrama about a union leader murdered offstage, inspiring both cast and audience to erupt into cries of "Strike! Strike!" at the final curtain. The play inaugurated the Group's finest hour, and Odets's follow-up family drama *Awake and Sing!* (February 1935) was equally successful. As Odets's star rose and fell, so did the Group's: their failed debut of his *Paradise Lost* (December 1935) dealt the company a spiritual and financial setback; in subsequent years, Hollywood siphoned off much of the Group's writing and acting talent, and "[t]hough 'the Group' would resurrect itself under the leadership of Clurman and [*Lefty* lead-actor Elia] Kazan, for the production of Odets's [largely successful] *Golden Boy* in 1937, the productions from that point until the Group's final dissolution in 1940 included numerous non-Group actors" (Fearnow, 373). Although the Group disbanded without achieving its rather elevated goal of revolutionizing theater's purpose in American culture, various members were instrumental in forming the Actors Studio in 1947, run by Strasberg from 1951 until his death in 1982. In the post-WWII era, the Studio instructed and inspired iconic figures such as Marlon Brando, James Dean, and Marilyn Monroe, and trains aspiring actors, many of them remarkably successful, to this day.

In this period, and less affiliated with any particular "Players" groups, emerged a number of critically acclaimed and/or commercially successful playwrights, including Angelina Weld Grimké, who is credited with the first African American protest play, *Rachel* (1916). It was written in rebuke to D. W. Griffith's *The Birth of a Nation*, released the year before, and tells the story of a talented brother and sister who are reduced to servant roles as they enter the job force in Washington, DC. Her colleague at DC's Dunbar High School was Mary Burrill, who wrote *They Sit in Darkness* (1919), about a young woman's dashed hopes due to the death of her exhausted mother, and *Aftermath*, addressing issues of black military service and lynching. Alice Dunbar-Nelson's *Mine Eyes Have Seen* (1918) shared those themes (see Bean, 99–101). Rachel Carothers's most noted works—*A Man's World* (1910) and *He and She* (1920)—surprised audiences with their frank investigation of the New Woman's dilemma regarding marriage versus career. The earlier play was famously rejoindered by Augustus Thomas, whose heyday was in the preceding century, with *As a Man Thinks* (1911), which "reflected the generally held views regarding the role of women in the household and the acceptability of the double standard" (Shafer, 19). Later in her career, Crothers's satire of American faith fads, *Susan and God* (1939), enjoyed a successful Broadway run and film adaptation the following year. She directed many of her plays herself, was active in the American Theater Wing's relief efforts in World War II, and never married, evidently taking to heart the modernist edict that family life threatened if not prevented the New Woman's professional fulfillment. In this same era, Sophie Treadwell's feminist-expressionist courtroom drama, *Machinal* (1928), told the story of a beleaguered office worker who kills the brutish boss forcing her into marriage and is executed for her crime. *Machinal* was acclaimed in its day and is regarded now as "arguably the finest example of American expressionist drama" (Beard, 67).

Edna Ferber, a contemporary of these women, had an early play, *The Eldest* (1918), produced by the Provincetown Players but is mainly remembered for her hugely successful collaborations with George S. Kaufman on the mainstream commercial stage: among others, *Old Man Minnick* (1924), which was selected by theater critic Burns Mantle for inclusion in his influential "ten best" edition for the 1924–25 season; *The Royal Family* (1927), satirizing the grandiosity of a Broadway acting dynasty, widely recognized as the Barrymores; *Dinner at Eight* (1932), a darkly comic view of seemingly gay socialites, each with a sorrowful or guilty secret; and *Stage Door* (1936), set in a boarding house for aspiring actresses and described by Yvonne Shafer as "a bouquet to the live theater. It is essentially about the joy and anguish of the acting profession" (95). Ferber saw many of her plays translated into film and is also one of the most financially successful female playwrights in American history, mostly due to dramatic and film adaptations of her novel *Showboat* (1926) and film adaptation of her novel *Giant* (1958).

Kaufman was also famous for his collaborations; in addition to his work with Ferber, he cowrote with Marc Connelly a "genial satire" (Murphy, "Plays," 323) about a ditzy housewife called *Dulcy* (1921) and an expressionistic comedy about art versus wealth, *Beggar on Horseback* (1924); his election satire *Of Thee I Sing* (1932), with Morrie Ryskind and with music by George Gershwin, won the Pulitzer Prize, the first musical comedy ever to do so. His most successful partnership was with Moss Hart; together they invented or perfected such middlebrow American comedy staples as sight gags, slapstick, wisecracks, and unabashed sentimentalism. Kaufman and Hart's two most successful and oft-revived hits are *You Can't Take It With You* (1937), which won the Pulitzer Prize the year it premiered, enjoyed a lengthy initial Broadway run, and was made into an Academy Award–winning film by Frank Capra in 1938; and *The Man Who Came to Dinner* (1939), whose egregiously rude visitor of the title, Sheridan Whiteside, is based on the famously acerbic culture critic and Algonquin Roundtable member, Alexander Woollcott, who once visited Hart's country estate and comported himself horribly the entire time. As the joke between Hart and Kaufman in the aftermath involved relief that Woollcott had not broken a leg and been stranded there long term, Whiteside, of the play, slips on the walkway to the home of an Ohio businessman, then runs roughshod over family and house staff in his convalescence. *You Can't Take It With You*, likely Kaufman and Hart's best-remembered play, involves a zany family of eccentrics, headed by Grandpa, who years earlier had determined that the rat race was bad for his well-being. In the years intervening, he has simply enjoyed life in diverse ways, as have his daughter and son-in-law, two granddaughters, and their various visitors, tutors, and hangers-on. One granddaughter, Alice, loves the son of a stuffy Wall Street magnate, and when the son, Tony, purposely brings his parents to dinner on the wrong night, the uptight capitalists learn a lesson about what is worth most in life. The engaging cast, daffy action (ballet dancing, oil painting, xylophone playing), pyrotechnics (fireworks set off in Act II), fast pace, and gentle wisdom of Grandpa have drawn raves from audiences who appreciate, according to Bernard F. Dukore, this fine example of Depression-era "American escapism" (76) but that Anne Fletcher reads as one of those important 1930s comedies that "emphasized cultural engagement and Depression-era conditions" (109).

Also from the depths of the Depression emerged the New Deal's Federal Theater Project, led by Hallie Flanagan, a director at Vassar College, and employing thousands of out-of-work actors, directors, playwrights, and stage crews in the four years of its existence, 1935 to 1939. The FTP sponsored diverse programming units, including Negro, Yiddish, children's, and puppet theater; most popular were its Living Newspaper docudramas, styled on *March of Time* newsreels preceding American movie showings in the period. Especially successful was *One Third of a Nation* (about the nation's poor), but it staged smaller (and often more controversial) productions such as *Ethiopia* (about Mussolini's invasion threat), *Triple A Plowed Under* (about the Supreme Court's ruling against FDR's Agricultural Adjustment Act), and *Spirochete* (about venereal disease). As Christopher Bigsby observes, "Where previously the American theater had been largely bifurcated between the commercial theaters and the often-arcane Little Theater movement, now, for the first time, experimentation could be conducted on a large scale" (*A Critical Introduction*, 213; and see Chapter 6).

Willis Richardson was an important African American folk dramatist and anthology editor of the Harlem Renaissance, whose *The Chip Woman's Fortune* (1923) was the first black-authored drama ever produced on Broadway. He widely influenced the folk-drama tradition in this context and wrote, as Annemarie Bean asserts, "in direct response to what he perceived as misguided interpretations of black life" (97) written by O'Neill, Dubose Heyward (author of *Porgy*), and others. Langston Hughes penned several important plays in this period, including *Scottsboro Limited* (1932), which narrates the dramatic story of the Scottsboro Nine, falsely accused of raping two white women in a train car, and most famously *Mulatto* (1935), which dramatizes the tragic dilemma of its mixed-race hero and which Bigsby describes as a "brutal play" (*A Critical Introduction*, 244) that nevertheless enjoyed an initial Broadway run of 373 performances. For his own Suitcase Theater group, Hughes wrote parodies of white-authored texts such as *The Em-Fuehrer Jones, Colonel Tom's Cabin*, and *Limitations of Life* (a lampoon of Fannie Hurst's novel). In the early 1930s, Hughes and Zora Neale Hurston cowrote the folk comedy *Mule Bone*, involving a love triangle between a woman and two men, whose contest for the lady involves the weapon of the title. Due to the dissolution of the friendship between Hughes and Hurston while writing the play, it was not staged until 1991 (see Shafer, 404, 407).

Despite the commercial and/or critical acclaim enjoyed by these many playwrights of the early twentieth century, American drama, even as it approached the Second World War, boasted as of yet only one world-class practitioner on par with the Ibsens and Shaws of his day—Eugene O'Neill. Yet many position two war-era playwrights of great achievement, Thornton Wilder and Lillian Hellman, in the second and third chairs behind O'Neill. Both of their canons are comparatively slim—Wilder wrote several one-acts and three widely remembered full-length dramas; and Hellman, eight original plays (although numerous screenplays and adaptations)—and yet the best works of each are universally regarded as truly excellent and (especially in the case of Wilder) unabashedly yet unsentimentally American.

Like O'Neill, Wilder was an experimentalist, calling attention in provocative fashion to theatrical convention; in postmodern terms, his work was often meta-theatrical, manipulating time and place in nonrealistic ways and infusing his work with a universal, archetypal quality through sparsely furnished or empty stages. He blended themes gently humorous with those somber or even ominous, challenging audiences to confront the unnerving proximity of great human happiness with ever-present prospects of loss and death. In *The Long Christmas Dinner* (1931), characters enter from a fruit- and flower-festooned doorway on one side of the stage (signifying birth) and exit through a velvet-draped portal (signifying death) on the opposite side. The eldest family members make reference to nineteenth- and early twentieth-century America; younger ones move the family and national history forward to the present day; and the play ends with the death of the last surviving family member. *Pullman Car Hiawatha* (1931) contains themes of death and insanity, and *The Happy Journey to Trenton and Camden* (1931) is also a visit to a daughter whose infant has just died. As Dukore points out, even in Wilder's most realistic, thematically accessible play, *The Merchant of Yonkers* (1938; revised into *The Matchmaker* [1954] and later adapted as the Broadway musical *Hello, Dolly!* [1964]), "three major characters are widowed" (123).

In his farcical and widely acclaimed *The Skin of Our Teeth* (1942), the Family Antrobus (a take on "anthropos," or "human") survive the Ice Age, the Great Flood, and a cataclysmic war by the teeth-skin of the play's title; each scene mixes the modern with the ancient, the local with the far-flung, and profound philosophical questions with absurd comedy. The play's most striking "meta" moments involve the Antrobus's maid Sabina, who breaks the "fourth wall" to provide the audience with her low estimation of the proceedings. In an early address, "I hate this play. I don't understand a single word of it, anyway." Amidst the unrelenting daffiness, the play addresses serious questions about surviving catastrophe and rebuilding a better world; it enjoyed 359 performances in its original run, won the Pulitzer Prize in drama in 1943, and has been revived numerous times on New York and regional stages since then.

Our Town (1938) is Wilder's masterwork, presenting all of his major themes and pioneering elements of stagecraft. In Bigsby's estimation, "*Our Town* is simply one of the most effective and affective American plays" (*A Critical Introduction*, 260). On a dark, empty stage, a kindly and plainspoken Stage Manager guides the audience into the story, introduces the Webb and Gibbs families of Grovers Corners, New Hampshire, and various other townsfolk, including a young man killed in World War I on the eve of his matriculation to MIT and the despairing, alcoholic choirmaster who commits suicide in the course of the play. Despite the specific place and character names, the town is presented as an archetypal "Everywhere USA," and the characters are shaped by the moments of love, fear, regret, loss, and longing that are universal to human existence. As Allan Lewis observes, Wilder's bare stage not only helped "put an end to the Belasco era" (69) but "avoid[ed] all pretense [whereby] greater illusion was achieved" (68). At young Emily Gibbs's suggestion (or insistence), George Webb gives up his trip to college to stay home and marry her; giving birth to their child, Emily dies, and the Stage Manager, commenting on each event with an equanimity bordering on indifference, assumes a god-like guise that is equal parts good shepherd and death's harbinger. As observed by Dukore,

> *Our Town* is immensely theatrical. Actors planted in the audience ask questions about the town…. In her white wedding gown Emily walks down a theater aisle to the stage. The dead who appear in Act III sit quietly and patiently on three rows of ordinary chairs. Large black umbrellas that virtually conceal mourners indicate a funeral; from behind this mass of black, Emily appears in a white dress to join the dead. (137–38)

Our Town also won the Pulitzer in 1938, ran originally for 336 nights, and has been constantly revived since then.

Hellman is appreciated for her war-themed dramas *Watch on the Rhine* (1941) and *The Searching Wind* (1944), but remembered best for her first play, *The Children's Hour* (1934), and for *The Little Foxes* (1939), both of which treat themes of deception and betrayal so intense as to produce fatal outcomes and destroy the lives of the survivors. *The Children's Hour* tells the story of a spiteful girl attending the boarding school of Martha Wright and Karen Dobie, whom the child accuses of being lesbian lovers. The child's grandmother and parents of other children conduct a witch hunt against the women, leading to the ruin of their school, the dissolution of Karen's engagement, and the suicide of Martha, who discovers actual lesbian feelings toward Karen and is too overcome with self-loathing to go on. The play's context of paranoia and false accusation (and likely to some degree career-ruining homophobia) inspired a successful revival in 1952, directed by Hellman herself, at the height of the McCarthy era (see Shafer, 126). Bigsby regards it as in many ways Hellman's "best play" (*A Critical Introduction*, 275). Notably, this play was passed over for a Pulitzer Prize in 1935, due to its controversial subject matter; the theater community was so outraged by the slight, and by the commercially-influenced direction taken by the Pulitzer committee in general, that the Drama Critics Circle Award was inaugurated soon after (see Shafer, 124; and dramacritics.org).

The Little Foxes is set in Hellman's native South and tells the story of a corrupted, capitalist-minded aristocratic family, content to sell off their region's land, resources, and values to the highest bidder from the industrial North. Regina Giddens and her two brothers scheme to maximize their positions of wealth and power and let nothing stand in the way of a lucrative business deal with a northern industrialist—including allowing Regina's reluctant husband to die of a heart attack instead of fetching his life-saving medications. By the end, Regina has gotten away with murder and secured her personal fortune but is disowned by her good-hearted daughter, Alexandra. Dukore reads the play as an allegory of contemporary affairs: "[T]he foxes [are] the fascists who had begun to devour the earth, ... the defeated Birdie [wife of one of the brothers], decayed European aristocracy, ... the dying banker Horace [Giddens], European capitalism too weak to intervene effectively, and ... young Alexandra, hope that America would fight" (153). Critics have admired Hellman's later original works, the Chekhovian *The Autumn Garden* (1951) and especially *Toys in the Attic* (1960), both again set in the South (see Shafer, 145). The later play tells once more of greed, lies, and intrigue within an extended family; in a career that had come "full circle," it won the Drama Critics Circle Award for 1960, and Bigsby, who regarded *The Children's Hour* as Hellman's best in several respects, likes *Toys in the Attic* even more: "Lillian Hellman, whose career began with a good play, ended with a better" (*A Critical Introduction*, 293).

With the influential example by Kaiser setting the scene, this section includes canonical feminist, expressionist, and agitprop texts from the modernist era, a sampling of O'Neill in realist mode, and the masterpieces of Hellman and Wilder.

A Transatlantic Touchstone: *From Morn to Midnight* (1912, 1917)

Georg Kaiser (1878–1945)

Widely credited as the first expressionist drama, Georg Kaiser's *From Morn to Midnight* was written in 1912, but not performed until 1917, when the playwright's challenging views of soulless bureaucratic society found a more receptive audience among the jaded survivors of the First World War. It was first staged in the United States by the Theater Guild in 1922. Per the conventions of the genre, the expressionist effects in Kaiser's play include repetitive, mechanical movements and speeches; generically designated characters (e.g., The Cashier, the Salvation Lass); and shadowy, skewed, dreamlike scenes and set designs that connote reality as received by a disturbed mind. In the words of Montrose J. Moses, "The expressionistic play is a reality and a phantasmagoria…. It is a kinetic series of scenes in which the tangible is interpreted from the angle of the intangible" ("Expressionism," 133). Later, "Beyond its disjointed story [is] the brooding thunder of social revolution, the menace of capital, the stir of the Mob" ("Expressionism," 134). Let us recall that in the realist context of Ibsen's *A Doll's House*, characters stumble over each other in their attempt to gain or maintain jobs as bureaucrats in a bank. Once the Industrial Revolution began to lose its shine, these same office jobs took on a nightmarish cast in this modern offshoot of the romantic tradition (which has always looked askance at the workaday), expressionism. To borrow a term from a contemporaneous literary style, such "Kafkaesque" characters will also slouch through the halls of impersonal corporations in the offerings of Rice and Treadwell, discussed later in this section.

The structure of this expressionist play, as with many, is the *Stationendramen*, or station play, whereby the protagonist, the Cashier, undergoes a journey "from morn to midnight" that takes him from his dreary, mindless role as a bank employee and an unfulfilled father, husband, and son to that of a rebel quester who uses 60,000 DM stolen from his employer to search out spiritual renewal among a large crowd of sports enthusiasts at a velodrome, among courtesans at a cabaret, and finally among a group of penitent sinners at a Salvation Army hall. When the last inquiry ends in disillusionment, the Cashier strikes a Christlike pose—"arms outstretched"—and utters famous words from the Passion (and Nietzsche), "Ecce Homo" (165), shooting and killing himself.

Per the station-play format, major characters such as the Italian Lady and the Cashier's wife, each of whom importantly motivate the Cashier on his journey, drop away in the early scenes, and new characters emerge; the

Salvation Army Lass presents as the soulmate to complete the Cashier's search but ends by betraying him to the police in order to claim the reward for his capture. She is one of several characters who is not what she seems; as Robert J. Cardullo observers, "What was originally meant to be a carefree outing with a lady of easy virtue—the Italian Lady—turns into a nightmarish journey where nothing is as it seems to be" ("Appearance," 172), and the Cashier is done in as badly by his failed romantic prospects as he is by the behemoth of bureaucracy.

The play is broadly influenced by Nietzsche's ethos of the Superman—he who breaks decisively with demoralizing routine and must be congratulated in his attempt to revolutionize society, even if criminal activity (e.g., theft and, in the American examples by Rice and Treadwell, murder) is involved. As Cardullo remarks, "It could be said that Kaiser, in fact, created the figure of the 'New Man' who will always be associated with expressionistic drama; he was also the first to realize that this figure might be nothing more than an idealistic chimera" ("Appearance," 172). To be sure, we might question the Cashier's success from the first scene, given his profoundly misguided—and the playwright's own deeply cynical—notion that money, honestly come by or not, is the key to personal and social fulfillment. At the cycling competition in the velodrome, the Cashier believes that he can sponsor prizes so large that he will move the mass audience to new heights of rapture; later, he attempts to lure beautiful women to his side in a cabaret by setting his table with "pinnacles" (158)—the ultimate in luxurious food and drink. But at the velodrome, several competitors, as it will be revealed in the final episode, are injured in their attempt to win the prize money, and a lowborn spectator is killed when he tumbles from his viewing stand high up in the cheap seats. At the restaurant, all of the alluring masked women are in fact ugly and sordid, and in his demoralized exit, the Cashier inadvertently sticks the sickly headwaiter, with a wife and children to support, with the bill.

More misguidedly—and cynically—yet, the Cashier is not motivated on his quest by any kind of authentic love feelings for the Italian Lady. He is simply aroused by the touch of her "naked hand in [his]" (149), and as she is marked as a prostitute from her first appearance by the other "gentlemen" at the bank, the Cashier can have few expectations with this woman beyond a bought-and-paid-for sexual tryst. Like the Italian Lady, almost all of the female characters, save the Cashier's immediate family, present as figures of staged sexuality of a notably degraded form—even when, as in the case of the Italian Lady, this turns out not to be the case. Though Kaiser may be using his play to protest the yoking of modern women to the whore's role, he certainly deepens the association in his own way by assigning almost all of his female characters (the masked women at the cabaret, the female penitents in the Salvation Army hall) to this predicament. Though not sexually profligate, his wife, mother, and daughters are instead more victims of the Cashier's unapologetic, Supermanian search for self-interested self-realization. They lose him as their breadwinner when he abandons the family, and his mother dies from the shock. Moses calls Kaiser "the arch-Expressionist" and quotes a remark he made to the theater historian Barrett H. Clark: "Not until we forget our old notions of forgiveness and pity will it be possible to found a new order" ("Expressionism," 135). In response, Clark observed that if it was Kaiser's aim to "discard human beings in his scheme, it was only in order that he might more effectively show us humanity" (qtd. in Moses, "Expressionism," 135). In Moses's summation, "You feel Kaiser groping in the substance for the shadow, and the shadow is spiritual truth" ("Expressionism," 135).

Although many late-nineteenth- and early-twentieth-century dramas were transferred to the screen, German Expressionism is one of the earliest artistic movements born alongside and thus profoundly shaping of the continental film medium. As a manifestation of German Romanticism, German Expressionism was realized on the stage by the likes of Kaiser and his fellow dramatists Gerhart Hauptmann and Ernst Toller just as it was coming to light (more correctly, to chiaroscuro) in the films of F. W. Murnau, Fritz Lang, Robert Wiene (of *Dr. Caligari* fame), and theater director Karlheinz Martin, who filmed Kaiser's play as a silent masterpiece in 1920. The author of the blog *A Cinema History* suggests that this film was so much more radical in its pessimism and cynicism than *The Cabinet of Dr. Caligari* that it never received an ordinary release in Germany in its own day. Luckily, the only surviving copy was found in Japan "where it was favorably received, maybe because of a certain similarity with Noh Theater" (*A Cinema History*) in 1963.

Trifles (1916)

Susan Glaspell (1876–1948)

Shortly after her graduation from Drake University in June 1900, 24-year-old Susan Glaspell achieved a rare distinction as a female reporter for a major newspaper—the *Des Moines Daily News*. Rarer yet, her main assignment was not feature reporting or society news, but the complex doings of the Iowa State House, and then even more remarkably the sensational murder trial of Margaret Hossack, accused of bludgeoning her husband to death with an ax handle in December 1900. Notably, Glaspell's and Hossack's lives would be intertwined thenceforward: shortly after Hossack was sentenced to life with hard labor in April 1901, Glaspell left reporting for a life of letters, left the Midwest for New York's bohemian-feminist Greenwich Village, and wrote a play based on the trial that would ignite the interest of the actors and audience of her Provincetown Players and secure her artistic legacy to the present day.

Glaspell covered for the *Daily News* the entire trial from December 1900 to April 1901, demonstrating her flair for the dramatic in reports that emphasized sensational turns of events and secrets to be revealed at a later date. In an early article among the two-dozen-plus filed, Glaspell is impressed with Margaret Hossack's physical appearance—"tall and powerful and looks like she would be dangerous if aroused to the point of hatred" ("She Prepares to Fight")—but is careful to show later how the strain of the trial has reduced her piteously: "worn and emaciated … she has begun to show signs of weakness and … red and swollen eyelids indicating she has been weeping" ("Now Before Grand Jury"). Margaret's hearty physical bearing led to a rather damning reputation before the murder as especially adept at ax handling; her legal status as the main landowner in the marriage, intriguing to the proto-feminist Glaspell, perhaps offended the male prosecutors and jurors responsible for the case. Yet Glaspell emphasized sympathetic if not exculpatory evidence regarding the Hossacks' volatile marriage: they quarreled frequently over how to treat their children, and according to a neighbor, Mrs. Haines, Margaret Hossack "had asked her and her husband to come down to her farm, … as she was afraid her husband would kill the family before morning" ("Hossack Begged Wife").

The role played by the Haineses in the trial is remarkable: until his regrettable bout of insanity mid-proceedings, Mr. Haines had been the prosecution's chief witness, as he claimed that Margaret had wished out loud more than once that her husband could be gotten rid of. When Mrs. Haines testified to the abuse suffered by Margaret, it was a smoking gun of a motive for the jury, yet for Glaspell, the incipient cause for acquittal, whose modern name is battered wife syndrome. Hossack's defense team sought to pin the murder on the now-insane Haines himself, but they'd have done so at the expense of impugning Mrs. Haines's testimony regarding the abusive marriage, and clearly Glaspell's investment included no such discrediting of this narrative. As Glaspell's biographer, Linda Ben-Zvi, observes, the Iowa State Supreme Court, on hearing the appeal of this case, "acknowledged John Hossack's repeated beatings of his wife—with his hands and with a stove lid" ("Murder," 152); this court ordered a new trial that resulted in a hung jury, subsequent dropping of charges, and Margaret Hossack's release in April 1903.

Although the husband's first name, John, is retained by Glaspell in her dramatic rendition, she transforms the powerfully built Margaret Hossack into the birdlike Minnie Wright, who ironically commits a murder requiring much more main strength than ax murdering—stringing her husband up for hanging in his sleep—as comeuppance for his having wrung the neck of her pet songbird and for her own lifetime of suffocating oppression. The Haineses are reproduced as Mr. and Mrs. Hale; although Mrs. Haines is famous for "singing" in court regarding the abuse suffered by Mrs. Hossack, in Glaspell's play Mrs. Hale blames herself for her silence about her neighbor Minnie's loneliness and repression. She shoulders some of the jailed woman's guilt by asking, "Who's going to punish that?" (23). As Ben-Zvi notes, Glaspell herself played Mrs. Hale in the original production, and Mrs. Hale's role as Minnie's chief advocate "seems to indicate Glaspell's awareness in 1916 of her omission and commissions in 1901, of her failure to recognize and respond to Mrs. Hossack's disenfranchisement at the trial" (*Susan Glaspell*, 175).

Glaspell's play is famously set in the kitchen, where Minnie's female associates, Mrs. Hales and Mrs. Peters, the sheriff's wife, locate comfort items to bring her in jail and happen upon the evidence so avidly searched out by the men upstairs, in the parlor, in the barn, and everywhere but the place where women's lives actually unfold. For the wives, Minnie's unwiped kitchen table and disorderly quilting stitches are sure signs of her emotional distress in the hours preceding the murder; when they find the dead bird hidden in a box in Minnie's sewing basket, they locate the motivation sought by the sheriff and join their jailed counterpart in criminal behavior when one hides the evidence in her coat pocket just as the men return. In fact, the men burst into the women's sanctuary several times in the course of the story; each time it feels like a violation, an invasion of the women's own and the jailed Minnie's privacy and person. When the prosecutor complains of "dirty roller towels" (11) at the sink, the women point out that men usually fail to wash their hands sufficiently before drying them off. When he kicks open the doors of Minnie's kitchen cabinets, the subtext is of a specifically sexual violation; the association is completed in the women's discovery of Minnie's broken jars of cherry preserves, shattered due to her husband's niggardly use of heating fuel throughout the home.

The sexual subtext of the men's several kitchen invasions underscores the fact that the real-life Margaret Hossack was very much tried and convicted "in the bedroom," where women have faced judgment for centuries. Much was made, for instance, regarding the blood-spatter patterns on the bedroom walls and the sheets, and at one point the Hossacks' blood-drenched bed was brought into court to challenge Mrs. Hossack's contention that she slept through the crime, because of the bed's small size. The Hossacks' bedroom activities were also implied throughout the trial in the presence of the nine devoted children—Glaspell draws Minnie Wright as, like herself, childless—who insisted on their mother's innocence at all times and created a melodramatic portrait of sobbing supporters gathered around her during the trial. And yet the youngest son, John Jr., became an implicating factor in his mother's prosecution when it was learned that the couple fought over Margaret's tendency to spoil him; as an 11th-hour bolt from the blue, their eldest son Alex is revealed to have been born just as—or just before—the couple were married in fall 1868 ("Allege Haines"). As Ben-Zvi remarks, "The jury may not have been convinced that she was guilty of murder, but she certainly was guilty of questionable female behavior. She had left her husband, discussed her marital troubles with neighbors, and—most damaging—had been pregnant before marriage" ("Murder," 152).

Notably, disgust with this trial may have motivated Glaspell to give up both court reporting and the Midwest altogether, such that this case has proven a motivating impulse for modern drama in the American context. Ben-Zvi observes several features of Glaspell's play that were as innovative as what O'Neill attempted in the same period: the dashes that characterize the uncertainty and dawning awareness of Mrs. Peters, for instance "indicate the hesitancy of the women to face the implications of what they are discovering." Another modern technique was the "mutual monologue"; "rather than have the two women respond to each other ... [each speaks] her thoughts not to an addressee but to herself, marking the fact that real drama resides in the separate minds of each woman" (*Susan Glaspell*, 176). Although Glaspell was a well-published novelist and short fiction writer by the time she wrote *Trifles*, this was the first drama she had attempted, and as an afterpiece to their production of O'Neill's electrifying *Bound East for Cardiff*, was instrumental in establishing the viability of the Little Theater movement—and of the theme of women's equality—in early twentieth-century American drama.

The Adding Machine (1923)

Elmer Rice (1892–1967)

Although he lasted in the profession only two years, Elmer Rice trained as a lawyer in 1910s New York, caring so little for the contents of his coursework that he read plays during some of the duller lectures. Yet he went on to make his mark in American drama by drawing frequently on this rejected legal background; among many other titles, his two most famous and lucrative stage works were *On Trial* (1914), cowritten with Frank Harris and being the first American drama to relay its events in reverse-chronological or flashback format, and the once frequently revived *Counsellor-at-Law* (1931). Both were made at least once into successful feature films. In the markedly expressionistic *The Adding Machine* (1923), Mr. Zero moves through seven episodes (or stations) in his life, hinged around the crime of murdering his boss, and the absurd futility of the subsequent trial, sentencing, and execution. Following an astonishingly long monologue, wherein he details his difficult life and the adversities facing him now, the jury declare his fate with one word—*"Guilty"* (60)—and disperse. Aside from these specific legal references, life in general is "a trial" for Zero and his various beleaguered counterparts, especially his once admired and now soured coworker Daisy Diana Dorothea Devore. Both live lives of endless drudgery, disappointment, and self-betrayal, and like the characters penned by Kafka, who are obvious kin, they scramble for proper answers to momentous questions and know these answers do not exist.

Because their waking realities are so painful, both Zero and Daisy fantasize constantly about personal and (for Zero) professional fulfillment—"picturing" themselves as stars in their favorite movies or even as victims in high-profile crime proceedings covered voraciously by the yellow press. Zero half-fears and half-hopes to find fame as the tragic hero of a scandalous affair: "Girl Slays Betrayer" (11). In the typical female-masochistic fashion, Daisy imagines herself gaining headline recognition as "Girl [Who] Takes Mercury after All-Night Party" or "Woman in Ten-Story Death Leap" (15). In a remarkable scene from early in the play, the two engage in the "mutual monologue" technique on display in Glaspell's *Trifles*. Interspersed with numbers called out and added up, and childish sniping over tones of voice and personal appearance, each drifts off into memories or dreams of a better life, often in each other's company. Each time they come close to admitting their regard for each other, they seek refuge from the risk in defensive criticism, and the scene is suffused with longing and deeply regretted lost chances. Late in the story, in a scene set in Elysian Fields, Zero has a poignant reunion with Daisy, who finally acted on her suicide fantasy when she learned of Zero's execution for murdering his boss. But he leaves her in a moralistic huff (learned from his judgmental wife in life) over how many "bums" they allow into Paradise.

Zero is married to a frumpy harridan with her own obsession with popular film and lurid press coverage; her speeches are nothing but grating, vacuous jabber. Frank Durham remarks that "it is the talk of all the drab, embittered wives to all the inadequate husbands; it is the talk all husbands hear every night, every year" (41). Despite his hatred for his wife, Zero once allowed her to instigate removal of an attractive, half-dressed tenant whom Zero enjoyed spying on—another disappointment and self-betrayal. On the day the story opens, Zero has been pointlessly adding numbers in his dreary corporate cell for 25 years. When his boss arrives at closing time—not to give him the raise and promotion he is expecting, but to replace him with an actual adding machine—Zero commits murder in dramatically expressionist style with loud music and garish red lighting; "they are entirely motionless, save for the boss's jaws, which open and close incessantly" (29–30). Later, his wife notices "red ink" on his collar, and he must hurriedly don a clean one before a horde of their equally mean-spirited, misguided, vacuous friends arrive for a night's gathering.

Following Zero's trial and execution, Rice's drama shifts into absurd-comic mode in a manner unique among the expressionist tragedies by Kaiser, O'Neill, and Treadwell and verging closely to the sharp satire of Sinclair Lewis's *Babbitt* (1922) and *Dodsworth* (1929). As Robert Hogan remarks, "A main reason, certainly, for the play's continued popularity is that it is comic.… We indict the Zero mentality and presumably by some mental osmosis become less like Zero" (*Independence*, 31). Macabre humor abounds in the graveyard scene, where Judy, the dishabille young tenant once jailed at the Zeros' behest, wants to have sex on Zero's grave but is only talked out of it by her skittish lover. Mosquitoes bother the resurrected corpses of Zero and his mysterious guide to the underworld, Shrdlu (played originally by Edward G. Robinson), whose odd name is never actually pronounced by the other characters and is a lino-type-setter's notation for "strike this line." As Russell E. Brown observes, "this nonsense, mistake, to-be-removed word is the verbal equivalent to Zero in the numerical system" (269). Rounding out the nonsense in this scene is a third body (or at least head) who pops up from his plot and in a comic rewrite of *Hamlet*'s graveyard scene, flings a skull at Zero and Shrdlu for waking him up. In the play's final scene Rice anticipates Wilder's cosmic farce *The Skin of Our Teeth*, when Zero finds himself adding numbers in a clearing house for souls migrating to their next lives. There he learns that, although he has evolved from ape to galley slave to serf—"You wore an iron collar then; white ones hadn't been invented yet" (133), he is actually "get[ting] a little worse" (130), not better, with each inching move up the drone worker's chain of being.

For the 1922 Samuel French edition, Philip Moeller, who ingeniously directed the Theater Guild production of 1923, wrote in his introduction, "Pitilessly and pityingly, with a curious conglomeration of tenderness and scorn, [Rice] has … exposed the starved and bitter littleness but at the same time the huge universality of the Zero type … that from eternity to eternity expresses the futility and the tragedy of the mediocre spirit" (ix, x). In the phrasing of Rice's biographer Frank Durham, Zero's world is "of soul-destroying drudgery and routine, of grubby passions unsatisfied, of grubbier dreams unrealized, and of the eternal babble of long-dead clichés" (40–41). Crediting the skills of the Guild staff, especially director Moeller and set designer Lee Simonson, Brooks Atkinson called *The Adding Machine* "the harshest, most provocative and illuminating play about American society that any American had written…. When an American submitted an explosive manuscript, the Guild had the good sense to accept it and the artistic experience needed to produce it" (*Broadway*, 217–18).

Machinal (1928)

Sophie Treadwell (1885–1970)

This remarkable example of feminist expressionism resembles its forebears in form and content, with nine episodic stages in the journey undertaken by the story's protagonist, the Young Woman, whose victimization at the hands of social, professional, and ultimately legal bureaucracies run by uncaring males is unique, in Treadwell's estimation, to the female sex. Performing mindless secretarial work with other drudges in a large corporation, the Young Woman (whose given name, Helen, is mentioned late in the play, almost as an afterthought) is harassed by the overweight, middle-aged vice president into a marriage that is loathsome to her. Freed from her underpaid employment to a life of relative ease, she is better able to support her nagging mother but traumatized by the need to submit sexually to her repulsive husband and speechless with despair at the birth of her baby girl, who she knows will face the same life of sexual subjugation. In her own life, Treadwell supported her mother, who had been abandoned by her husband when Treadwell was a child. The playwright suffered debilitating bouts of nervousness and eating disorder that had her in and out of sanatoriums throughout her adult life (see Rodríguez, 78–79).

After a fleeting but electrifying night of intimacy with a rakish stranger, the Young Woman makes the break with her oppressive past that all expressionist heroes must: she bludgeons her husband to death but is immediately caught and tried for the crime, then sent to the electric chair. Her only consolation is a short reconciliation with her mother, in which she asks to have her baby daughter looked after. As Judith E. Barlow noted in a 1993 reprint, "The cacophony of urban sounds that underlies each scene" (e.g., typewriters, jackhammers, jazz bands, arguing tenement-dwellers) that set the play's dispiriting tone and account in part for its title (Fr. "mechanical") "is remarkably similar [to our own], while *Machinal*'s repetitive dialogue, woven of clichés, foreshadows the work of Samuel Beckett, Harold Pinter, and … David Mamet" (ix). In his review of a 1990 revival Frank Rich coined "Mamet-ese" for the characters' empty speech stylings and referred to "the repetitive, staccato short-hand of Babbitt-era salesmanship" (C13). Treadwell scholar Jerry Dickey observes that another experimental feature, the Young Woman's several introspective monologues, "subvert audience expectation … by moving [her] into the subject position" ("Real Lives," 177), following early exposition that positions her as the object of office gossip, criticism, and envy.

Like her fellow feminist/experimental dramatist Susan Glaspell, Treadwell was a journalist who drew from her own reporting assignments to inform her literary work (novels as well as plays). She was renowned on both coasts as a reporter for newspapers in San Francisco and New York and as an intrepid war correspondent and an expert on US-Mexico relations. Her exclusive access to the revolutionary-in-hiding Pancho Villa figured in her novel *Gringo* (1922) and in the backstory of Helen's lover, the First Man, who himself committed murder to escape capture by Mexican bandits. It is as incorrect to read the scene between them, however significant it is to the protagonist's future actions, as an instance of "true love" as it was in the case of Kaiser's Cashier and Italian Lady. Marked by his own indifferent character assignment, the First Man is simply a handsome figure with "dark wavy hair," literally the first man to come along, who warns Helen throughout their brief time together that he will be on his way before morning. Their meeting is little more than a pickup in a speakeasy and more an experience of quick, however moving, sexual gratification than lasting emotional connection. Although played in the original Broadway run by a very young (and even then unforgettable) Clark Gable, it seems key to Treadwell's dark vision that the Young Woman murders her husband and loses her own life not for any kind of love conventionally construed, but more correctly for the love she could never have or even for nothing and no one at all (see also Rodríguez, 76–77).

Treadwell was known in San Francisco for two multipart exposés—one on the mistreatment of homeless prostitutes, in which she presented herself in the guise of same to various local charities to test their willingness to help, and one more fictionalized account regarding modern marriage. She was able to use her acting abilities (which she had originally envisioned leading to her own stage career) and literary skills in these assignments, and again, each theme resurfaces in *Machinal*, where marriage is plainly equated with sexual selling out by any woman attractive enough to do so, and where Treadwell archly reconsiders the title of her marriage exposé, "How I Got My Husband and How I Lost Him," through murder as the chosen method. Treadwell's own marriage, to sports journalist William O. McGeehan, seemed much more companionable than passionate. They admired each other's talents but were very different kinds of people; lived for a time in separate houses; and survived at least one affair, by Treadwell with the artist Maynard Dixon (see Gainor and Dickey, 45).

Like Glaspell, Treadwell also found herself bearing witness to sensational crime stories that inspired her work. Miriam López Rodríguez reports that Treadwell had covered for the *San Francisco Evening Bulletin* the trial of Leah Alexander, who shot to death the philandering, already-married ad executive who talked her into quitting her job in view of their impending marriage, then left her for another stenographer (73). Two years later, for the *New York American*, Treadwell covered the trial of Elizabeth Mohr, who paid three men (including her chauffeur) to shoot her husband while he was riding around with his mistress. In covering both trials, Treadwell stressed the egregious gender bias on display; regarding the Alexander case, Treadwell "highlighted the sexism of the police officers and the district attorney who questioned the defendant's morality for being the mistress of a married man but did not question this same man for his adultery" (Rodríguez, 73). But *Machinal* is most famously based on the notorious trial of Ruth Snyder from Queens, New York, who, with her milquetoast lover, Judd Gray, did in her husband with a blunt object in 1925. They were both caught immediately, confessed to their crime, and tried in a case attended by celebrities and followed avidly internationally. Snyder's execution in the Sing Sing electric chair in 1928 was made famous by her being a rare woman dispatched in this manner, and by an iconic photo taken surreptitiously by *New York Daily News* photographer Tom Howard just as the currents reached her body. Though the image may shimmer due to movement of Howard's leg as he extended the camera strapped to his ankle, there is a ghost-like aura about the image that weirdly suggests the electrocution itself. Though Treadwell, like Glaspell, took pains to present her murderess as a beleaguered and thus partially justified housewife, the real-life Ruth Snyder (very much like the real-life Margaret Hossack) was no shrinking violet, but a large, imposing woman with a strong personality. She took over the killing when her boyfriend's weak-wristed attempt barely grazed their victim. However, her similarity to Treadwell's heroine therefore ends early on, as Helen is importantly depicted as acting alone—not only at the moment of the murder, but in each stage of depressing, disconnected life.

Machinal was Treadwell's best-received play, running only three months originally but receiving strong reviews in *The New Yorker*, *The World* (see Kabatchnik, 217), and *The New York Times*, in both its theater review and editorial sections. Brooks Atkinson considered the play "a triumph of individual distinction, gleaming with intangible beauty" (qtd. in Barlow, viii), and

Burns Mantle included it in his annual *Best Plays* edition for 1928–1929. It was renamed *The Life Machine* for its first British production in 1931 and has been revived on and off Broadway and even as a mid-1950s teleplay since that time. *Machinal* has received attention from feminist- and expressionist-theater researchers throughout recent decades, although Kornelia Tancheva makes the notable claim, based on thorough study of original reviews, that critics' admiration of and intensive focus on the play's expressionist features tended to obscure its feminist complaint. This slant, says Tancheva, toward mainstream (masculine?) expressionist theater enabled the play's success. But J. Ellen Gainor and Jerry Dickey, who compare Susan Glaspell's career in the Little Theater movement to Treadwell's consistent attempt to gain the Broadway stage, argue that "Treadwell always envisioned herself as not only succeeding on a large, national platform like Broadway but also using her success to reform this platform" (51).

Drama in Dialogue: *The Adding Machine* and *Machinal*

One of the more obvious points of contrast between these two early twentieth-century expressionist American dramas is the gender assignment of both the authors and the main characters. As Ginger Strand points out, "[W]riting a type of play meant to highlight the universality of a subject's experience [hence generic character names and understated acting], Treadwell begins by suggesting her subject's specificity—a woman, and a woman based on one individual woman" (163), Ruth Snyder of Snyder-Gray murder case infamy. As Miriam López Rodríguez has determined, Treadwell might have based her character on an amalgamation of Snyder and other famous murderesses of the era (73; see also Dickey, "Expressionist Moment," 72), "universalizing" her character to at least some extent. But in the estimation of Jerry Dickey, "Ruth Snyder may have been one particular woman, but Treadwell's *Machinal* suggests that the forces which drove her to violence could do the same for 'any woman' similarly disempowered by modern society" ("Expressionist Moment," 73). Treadwell thus shares with Susan Glaspell an interest to intensify the feminist impact of her work—as well as "worry the abstract mode of Expressionism itself" (Strand, 163)—by rooting her character in an actual, controversial figure of her time. To that extent, Treadwell may stand guilty of succumbing to the very craze for sensationalist press coverage that she (as a former courtroom journalist) helped foment and that her fellow dramatist Elmer Rice could treat with sheer irony and harsh critique.

Even without the connection to Snyder and her sister murderesses of the mid-1920s, Treadwell's Young Woman is indeed rooted in, trapped by, her female sex in ways that Rice's male protagonist never is. She is even eventually revealed to have a given name, Helen, though her surname, Jones, immediately subtracts from whatever individuality this bestows, in that it first and foremost belongs to her husband, not to mention many other dozens of Joneses at any urban street corner on any given day. Although Rice's Mr. Zero moves through the stations of his expressionist drama more or less shedding women as he goes, even abandoning the devoted Daisy when he decides to leave the Elysian Fields, Helen is unable to escape the barrier established by her future (then actual) husband from the first scene and escapes the results of her crime against him only in execution by the state. In her own "Elysian Fields" scene, with the "First Man" who gives her an inkling of sexual attraction and fulfillment, she is abandoned just as Daisy is, and on even flimsier pretenses. Just as Daisy commits suicide in Rice's play when she learns that her one true love (Zero) has met his fate in the prison gas chamber, so Helen enters the path of assured self-destruction when her own best shot at romance and togetherness leaves her behind. (Notably, Treadwell breaks from the historical record of the Snyder case with this action, as Ruth Snyder's lover co-murdered her husband and went, laying blame on her every step of the way, to his own execution for the crime.) Treadwell seems to suggest that "the average young woman" makes such impossibly fraught decisions every day—marry a loathsome man or starve; live a life of quiet desperation or "commit suicide" (i.e., open yourself to prosecution and execution) in your radical break from matrimonial bonds.

Taking their place in the tradition established by Kaiser, Rice's and Treadwell's plays both present early scenes at the stultifying workplace, where repetitive, useless, compulsive motions and conversations characterize the emptiness of white-collar existence. Where both Kaiser's Cashier and Rice's Zero find (or at least think they find) romantic fulfillment with female customers or coworkers, Treadwell presents a fine rendition of sexual harassment that has clearly been a hazard for women office workers—and women workers of all kinds—throughout history. In my reading of *from Morn to Midnight*, I noted Kaiser's tendency to suggest, as he simultaneously critiques, a persistent equation between women and degraded sexuality; positioning her audience in the woman's shoes, Treadwell shows in *Machinal* how women are insistently sexualized despite their own steady attempts to act like professionals (or just make a living). As the many male workers stand around in gangs sneering at the sexual propriety of the Italian Lady in Kaiser's play (and again, while Kaiser half-critiques and half-"banks" on such sneering assumptions to complete his female characters in almost every scene), so Helen is ganged up on by both male and female coworkers who may envy Helen's chance to quit work by marrying the boss but who also implicitly accept their panderer's role: to countenance the affair, encourage and applaud it, and to keep their complaints about the favors shown to Helen to themselves.

As noted above, Rice's Mr. Zero is free to move through his seven stations in unimpeded, masculine fashion; even death does not disable him: he pops up from his grave in the second half of the play and enters and exits the remaining several scenes, acting as a free agent. Even in the last scene, when he is *sent* by Lt. Charlie to rejoin the living in reincarnated form, he is yet back to the land of the living to have another go at succeeding or failing by his own lights. Treadwell's Helen, by contrast, moves inexorably through the first four scenes into marriage and then motherhood, both radically disavowed. She is pushed toward her husband by both her taunting female coworkers and her needy mother; later, when her lover leaves her, she has no choice but to rebound to her husband. Against him, she commits her most independent action in the play—his murder—but this action propels her inexorably, we might almost say mechanically, into the clutches of priest, jailer, and executioner. Strand observes that Treadwell meant to engage with Rice's text by echoing his title, *The Adding Machine*, with her own, *Machinal* (73). Notably, the last scene in Treadwell's play is also called "the machine" and refers implicitly to a whirring "aeroplane" that passes over her prison cell (the droning, needling sounds of modern industry being everywhere in the play) and explicitly to the modern mode of government-sponsored death dealing, the electric chair. One reporter worries to another, "Suppose the machine shouldn't work!" and is assured by his compatriot, "It'll work! It always works!" (82). We are to assume that this miracle of then-modern technology functioned perfectly on this occasion, especially as the play takes its final turn back to historical precedent—or at least famously sensationalized treatment of same—by invoking the widely published image of Snyder frying in the electric chair. The reporters in this last scene belong to that historical moment as well, and the final machine implied is the camera attached to the leg of Tom Howard, photojournalist at the scene of the Snyder execution, whose technological initiative was immediately curtailed at all future execution scenes, so disturbing were its results. Eschewing the comic elements of Rice's *Adding Machine*, as well as the superlative humor of the remarkable "caught in the gears" scene from Charles Chaplin's *Modern Times* (1936), Treadwell's Helen is ground in the gears of a machine that has been in motion throughout her adult life and that subjects its female victims to a unique fate.

The Children's Hour (1934)

Lillian Hellman (1905–1984)

The Children's Hour was the first play written by Lillian Hellman; it was very notably passed over for a Pulitzer Prize in 1934 and very famously responsible, in part, for the inauguration of the Drama Critics Circle Award (about which more below). Hellman was cued to the source material of an 1810s Edinburgh girls school, shuttered after accusations by one of the students of sexual activity between the two headmistresses, when she read Scottish author William Roughead's *Bad Companions* (1930). Both the 1810 scandal surrounding Marianne Woods and Jane Pirie of an elite girls' school in Drumsheugh Gardens and the accusations leveled against Karen Wright and Martha Dobie in Hellman's play resulted in "acquittals" that resolved matters not at all: Woods and Pirie ended in poverty—using most of the damages awarded them to pay their legal fees—and banished forever from their chosen careers; in *The Children's Hour* Karen and Martha lose a court case, but the charges against them are finally revealed to be false. Cleared in this manner, the engagement between Karen and Dr. Joe is still ruined (mainly by Karen's own insistence), while Martha, realizing that she does in fact "love" Karen in a sexual way, commits suicide. Hellman thus writes a play about the impossibility of clearing one's name following sensational allegations. Such scandal attaches throughout the life of the person accused, whether she is actually "guilty," whether she is ever convicted, or not.

Notably, Woods and Pirie were exonerated from their charges largely by the utter incredulity of "one of the Judges in the case, Lord Meadowbank, who … declar[ed] that sex between women was 'equally imaginary with witchcraft, sorcery, or carnal copulation with the devil'" ("Drumsheugh"). Such views regarding the "absence" or "lack" of female sexual organs, drives, and so on, have oppressed women (gay and straight) throughout human history (see also Shedd). The sheer unimaginability of lesbian sex in the early nineteenth century may have spared Woods and Pirie from jail, but it never released them from the cloud of suspicion that was its own life sentence; closely attuned to the ironies and tragedies that befell these women, *The Children's Hour* is much less about forbidden activities than permanent indeterminacy, as minor characters wrestle with the question of "Did they or didn't they?" just as intensely as the major characters wrestle with "Are we or aren't we?" in their own minds.

As the British novelist Jeanette Winterson remarked in a recent blog about the play, "Hellman had an unerring sense of what makes drama. Joe [Karen's fiancé] is not there to provide a love interest; he is there to provide ambiguity." Winterson adds, "Karen is more or less indifferent to him, not because she may or may not be gay, but because she puts everything into the school she and Martha have been working to build for eight years." Thus the career-mindedness of Martha and Karen is as big an affront to the small community where the play is set as is the prospect of their sexual relationship. In her own life, Hellman would face charges she refused to admit to—most notably membership in the Communist Party as alleged by the House Un-American Activities Committee in 1952. As a skilled writer for the stage and screen throughout this period, Hellman herself was as thoroughly, unnaturally career oriented as were Karen and Martha. *The Children's Hour* thus speaks against our tendencies to suspect and condemn independent women of all kinds, those who choose to make their living or find romantic and sexual fulfillment without involving men. Winterson points out that as Hellman was refusing to name names for HUAC in 1952, the *Children's Hour* was enjoying a Broadway revival and Arthur Miller (who would later appear before Congress and refuse to speak himself) was writing *The Crucible*, which debuted in New York in 1953. As Thomas P. Adler notes, the revival of Hellman's play "assumed a political meaning and resonance it did not originally have…. The House Committee on Un-American Activities … found homosexuality almost as great a threat to the nation's security as 'the Red Menace'" ("Lillian Hellman," 125). The connection between Hellman's and Miller's plays is strengthened by the recollection of Lord Medowbank's declaration that lesbian sexuality was as preposterous an accusation as witchcraft. But in fact, the hero of *The Crucible*, John Proctor, suffers social opprobrium and eventual death for clinging to an unpopular truth, whereas Hellman's play is very much in search of actuality at many levels in each scene. Even when "the truth"—that Mary has lied—is revealed late in the story, it is a highly contested, highly qualified truth and has come so late in the proceedings as to be useless if not meaningless.

Because there was a fair amount of bed sharing between teachers and students at the Drumsheugh school (ordinary for boarding schools of that period), the evidence against Woods and Pirie was detailed and persuasive, whereas in Hellman's play the protagonists' innocence holds sway while student Mary Tilford has lied about Karen and Martha for no other reason than utter, inexplicable evil. Hellman's biographer, Jacob Adler, called the child "psychotic" (30), and as Hellman told reporter Harry Gilroy on the eve of the 1952 revival, "When I read the story, I thought of the child as neurotic, sly, but not the utterly malignant creature which playgoers see in her…. It's the results of her lie that make her so dreadful—this is really not a play about lesbianism but about a lie" (25). Although almost all modern commentators on this play feel differently, "the lie" is indeed a theme close to Hellman's heart in many of her plays. As a Jew who early in life left her studies in Hitler's Germany when Fascism was on the rise, and as a committed leftist suffering greatly on behalf of the beleaguered peoples of Europe in this period, Hellman was intensely concerned about the damage done to careers and lives when false witness overpowers right thinking. As Alice Griffin and Geraldine Thorsten argue, Hellman felt that "harm is done by so-called 'good people,' who do not challenge evil" (28), specifically in *The Children's Hour* by Mary's grandmother, Amelia, who fails to question the young accuser closely enough, and Martha's Aunt Lily, who runs off to Europe when she should have stayed and testified at Martha and Karen's failed libel suit (see also Lederer, 35). Such weak-willed bystanders play a role in Hellman's other important work from this period, *The Little Foxes* (1939) and *The Searching Wind* (1944). In the view of Thomas P. Adler, "[T]he 1952 revival of her first hit, *The Children's Hour* (1934) assumed an added dimension under Hellman's own direction ... in the context of the excesses of anticommunist fervor during the Cold War" (*American Drama*, 52).

The 1936 trailer for *The Children's Hour*'s first film adaptation, *These Three* (dir. William Wyler), splashes the word "slander" across the screen, and Bosley Crowther's *New York Times* review of the 1962 film adaptation relies on it again and again. *These Three*, written by Hellman herself, made such hash of the original plot that it eschewed all references to lesbian sexuality and pitted Martha and Karen in a contest for Joe's affections. The 1962 remake, titled *The Children's Hour* (again directed by Wyler), returned the orientations and motivations of the three main characters. But all three texts, despite their shared interest to explore the crises surrounding rumor, vendetta, and unfounded allegation, are equally certain with respect to certain "facts of the case": that Karen at least is in the clear with respect to her sexual orientation and marital intentions, and that Mary Tilford tells vicious lies because no "unnatural" activity between the women ever occurred, although she ultimately does not "lie" at all, as Martha is indeed a lesbian. All three versions of this text regard the "crime" in question to be false or irresponsible accusation and hysterical reaction to same, not the crime of homophobia that a modern viewer might assume. This same modern viewer might ultimately decide that the crime of this play is that the truth Mary told—having read out the sexual identity of Martha Dobie, despite her own vigorous self-denials—was not met with acceptance and understanding by the students and parents of the girls' school, Karen's fiancé, Karen, and ultimately Martha herself. As Jenny S. Spencer remarks, "This is not a play that a feminist director would eagerly seek out" (44). But the modern reading, however unrelated to the original text and the author's original intentions, surely adds to our understanding and appreciation of *The Children's Hour* each time it is revised.[2]

Though the location (and even existence) of the truth is thus open to debate in this play, it is, according to Winterson, "its power and truthfulness" that caused it to be passed over for the Pulitzer Prize in Drama in 1934 because of its controversial subject matter. New York's drama critics, who hailed the play and defended it against all such critiques, had grown disgusted with the excessively mainstream views of the Pulitzer committee, who had been passing over many now-canonical dramatists in this period—including Hellman but also Clifford Odets and Robert Sherwood—to give the prize to traditional fare (e.g., Zoë Akins's *The Old Maid* in 1934). They thus inaugurated their Critics Circle Award the following year, being sure to bestow one on Hellman for *Watch on the Rhine* in 1941 and *Toys in the Attic* in 1959; the Circle Award has sometimes coincided with, but often served as a check on, the more mainstream choices of the Pulitzer committee throughout subsequent decades.

Waiting for Lefty (1935)

Clifford Odets (1906–1963)

Like the vigorously leftist expressionist texts by Rice and Treadwell in the 1920s, Odets's agitprop classic, *Waiting for Lefty*, from the even redder decade of the 1930s, recalls Rice's *On Trial* through its use of the flashback technique, and expressionist format with its own simple "station" structure of several flashback episodes interspersed by present-time action at an ever more tumultuous union meeting. As Gerald Weales discovered several decades ago, Odets borrowed much inspiration and some situation from Joseph North's

---

[2] Other readers, early and modern, have indeed taken issue with the confusion between truth and falsehood in this play. As early as his review for the 1934 production, James Craven complained about the complete reversal of audience attitude demanded by the final moments of the play (see Tufts, 64). In a review of the 1952 revival, Eric Bentley believed that the play was seriously flawed in its attempt to tell two stories: "The first is a story of heterosexual teachers accused of lesbianism; the enemy is a society which punishes the innocent. The second is a story of lesbian teachers accused of lesbianism; the enemy is a society which punishes lesbians" (qtd. in Tufts, 64). As Carol Strongin Tufts observes, Hellman had spent the play generating indignation against the lies told by Mary and believed by townsfolk; when, moments before they are finally declared to be lies by Mary's grandmother, they are in fact revealed to be true, "What is [the audience] to feel now?" (64).

1934 article for *New Masses*, "Taxi Strike" (*Odets*). Although the characters on display in North's article and in the present time of Odets's play are indeed the blue-collar "hackies" belonging to the class readiest to use its fists—in communist salutes or left hooks—to gain rights, *Waiting for Lefty* moves up the class scale as it goes, including the demoralized pencil pushers of interest to Kaiser, Rice, and Treadwell and even well-paid chemists and medical doctors abused for political or ethnic (anti-Semitic) reasons. All are thus enjoined to "Strike! Strike! Strike!" at the end of the play. Finally, even humble Joe and Edna—in despair over Joe's low wages, the furniture repossessed as a result, and with Edna threatening to leave—recall Ibsen's middle-class Torvald and Nora and the monetary crisis that ended their marriage. They suggest the universality of such dilemmas across the class scale in the modern, realist age (see also Brandt, 205). As Harold Cantor observes, "[I]t is more than a propaganda piece [aimed at the proletariat], because of the vitality of the language and its vivid, colloquial invocation of middle-class myths and attitudes" (18). In agreement, Gabriel Miller describes *Lefty* as "transcend[ing] the boundaries of the didactic, revolutionary play. It remains today the only such play that is read and anthologized" (165).

The flashback and station techniques are only a few of the features that *Lefty* shares with the other dramas of this era. A pathetic scene between cabbie Sid and his girl Florrie, too poor to marry, ends when they "dance to a 'cheap, sad dance tune played on a small portable phonograph'" (Seward and Barbour, 45). It recalls the equally dispiriting affairs between Zero and Daisy in Rice's *The Adding Machine* and especially the fleeting, doomed encounter between Helen and the First Man in Treadwell's *Machinal*. With *The Children's Hour*, it shares the reputation of tremendous controversy, being "the most widely suppressed play in the history of the American Theater" (Seward and Barbour, 41; see also G. Miller, 166). Perhaps most striking (pun intended) of all are the many ways that *Waiting for Lefty* anticipates Wilder's *Our Town*, radically breaking the fourth wall between stage and audience with its planting of cast members in the orchestra seats and with its direct address to the audience. A character "lolling against the proscenium down left" (Odets, 5) for much of the play prefigures Wilder's Stage Manager, who spends much of his time in this position of somewhat ominous power and necessary critical distance; instead of a godlike overseer as in Wilder's play, the man at the proscenium in Odets's is a hired gunman. In the final, explosive scene, he exacerbates the conflict between the union heroes (especially Agate who, originally played by Odets, rushes up from the audience and calls for a strike) and heels (especially Fatt, a union man in name only, employed by the company to fend off a strike). When another character runs onstage to announce that Lefty, whose chair has been empty at the back of the room the entire time, has been murdered, the classically overdetermined contradiction occurs, and strike and riot become indistinguishable.[3]

From the article by North for *New Masses*, Weales notes the "hackie's fable" that serves as an epigraph to the article, wherein the wife of a cabdriver threatens to leave if he does not strike for higher wages. In the first flashback of *Lefty*, Edna delivers the same ultimatum to her husband (and echoes the harangue of Mrs. Zero in the first episode of *The Adding Machine*, except that Edna is much more of a goad to action than was Zero's dispiriting wife). Agate is identified with Pondsie, a cabbie who speechifies heroically at the end of North's piece (11) and has a mean left hook; Fatt clearly represents the "company union" targeted relentlessly in North's article. Weales (*Odets*, 44) and others have called attention to the cartoonlike qualities of this opposition and the characters themselves; Harold Cantor refers to the characters as "caricatures" (18), and Richard J. Dozier regards certain "portions of the play ... [as] little more than cartoon drawings turned into speech" (597). These statements are mainly admiring, however, with respect to the effectiveness of Odets's stark political message.

Theater historians Lori Seward and David Barbour relate the ways in which *Waiting for Lefty*, beyond several artistic choices, dismantled the fourth wall between play and public. Foregoing his royalties for many of the early productions, Odets allowed amateur, school, and workers' groups to produce his play—and spread its message—in theaters across the country (40–41), and the Group Theater's Longacre Theater production cost an astonishing $8 to mount: "An itemized account, vouched for under oath by the Group business staff, revealed that $4.25 of this sum was spent on taxi fares, $3 for surgeon's white jacket, ... and 75 cents for repainting a table" (qtd. in Seward and Barbour, 42–43). The Group also managed exceedingly low ticket prices— $1.65 for the orchestra and $.40 for the upper tier, recalling the low-priced peanut galleries from earlier centuries, such that rich and poor could share the same theatrical experience. For Odets's play, "[T]he cheap seats went quickly, and night after night the balcony was filled" (Seward and Barbour, 42). As is the case for several other classics in American drama (see the discussion of *Long Day's Journey* below and *Death of a Salesman* in the next section), the deeply affected audience is part of the theater annals: as Ruth Nelson, who played Edna in the original cast, remembered, "When [the audience] couldn't

---

[3] Seward and Barbour relay an incident of breakdown between artifice and real life, when a staged fistfight between Carnovsky in the role of Fayette the Industrialist and Tony Kraber, who played Miller the lab assistant, resulted in a broken nose for Carnovsky (45).

applaud anymore, they stomped their feet.... all I could think was, My God, they're going to bring the balcony down. It was terrible, it was so beautiful." Cast member Morris Carnovsky, who played Fatt and two other powerbrokers, added that after the performance on the sidewalk outside, "There they were, the audience, arguing, talking, agreeing, clapping hands.... there was almost a sense of pure madness about it" (qtd. in Seward and Barbour, 40). Director and Group Theater cofounder Harold Clurman remarked on the "exultancy of communication" between actors and audience: "It was the birth cry for the '30s" (qtd. in Cantor, 18; see also G. Miller, 165).

Our Town (1938)

Thornton Wilder (1897–1975)

This Pulitzer Prize-winning drama narrates the joys and tribulations of ordinary Americans in small-town America; these include love, marriage, and childbirth but also depression, alcoholism, suicide, and untimely death. All of these profound experiences, Wilder suggests, constitute the daily lives of an individual and a community; the playwright speaks through his heroine, Emily Webb-Gibbs, when, after death, she laments her failure during life to savor every moment. In the story, George Gibbs and Emily Webb court, marry, and separate by death; an equally important character is the Stage Manager, who literally ushers in the play's scenic and dramaturgic breakthroughs, setting a few spare furnishings on the darkened stage, speaking directly to the audience, "constantly call[ing its] attention to the fact that it is witnessing a play" (Murphy, "Plays," 336), and assuming the role of facilitator (druggist at the soda counter, wedding minister) in many scenes. His speech is a perfect blend of folksy innocuousness and ominous omniscience. Early on he comments, "Hitching posts and horse blocks in front of [the stores]. First automobile's going to come along in about five years" (6). In Wilder's fully automated late 1930s audience, this statement surely caused a pang of nostalgia for the innocence lost with the passing of the horse-drawn age. They would have also felt the stab of mortality in contemplating how long ago that seemed, and such feelings only intensify the further modern audiences come from Grover's Corners (the New Hampshire "every-town" where the play is set) circa 1901. Notably, George's father, Doc Gibbs, and Emily's father, Editor Webb, are stage managers in their own rights, overseeing the life cycles of individuals and communities, respectively, and doing so with the gentle detachment required of them.

Further into the Stage Manager's first monologue, we learn of the death of the horse-drawn carriage and also of several characters we are more or less warned we will come to know and love in the course of the play (see also Klaver, 114). Mrs. Gibbs "died first," in the loving, life-affirming act of visiting her daughter in another town, by a fluke encounter with pneumonia. Even her husband, Doc Gibbs, a figure hoped to be immune to ordinary human frailty, has passed, and the town has feebly if not ironically "named the new hospital after him" (8) to make up for his loss. The Stage Manager spoke indeed from a more fragile age, when demise from many illnesses treatable today was an "ordinary" occurrence, and even the heartbreak of the young bride Emily's death in childbirth would have been common enough in the early decades of the twentieth century to be tragically statistically meaningless. Although the play ends with George Gibbs deeply mourning the death of his beloved wife, we have learned from this play that he is a young man with his life before him and is bound to relentlessly move on. More disturbing, young Emily herself, in the play's last moment, has already forgotten her happy life on earth, having no way and no interest to join her husband in his grief.

The story regards as much forfeited chance as it does uncontrollable fate. Rolling beneath the otherwise-excellent marriage of Dr. and Mrs. Gibbs is the current of discontent emerging from the latter's thwarted dreams to visit Europe, now that a piece of old furniture has been offered a princely sum by an antique dealer. Mrs. Gibbs has ordinary, admirable longings to see other places, but Dr. Gibbs jokes back that "it might make him discontented with Grover's Corners to go traipsing about Europe" (20). The Gibbs's dilemma with respect to going or staying is renewed when George and Emily reach a fateful intersection, their own private "corners," shortly into their courtship. Emily is speaking honestly—or manipulatively—regarding a change in George she's noticed: his having gotten quite stuck up lately. George, being the thoroughly unstuck-up young man he is, immediately apologizes and promises to make amends. The conversation turns to George's impending departure for agricultural college, at which point Emily confesses her concern, echoing her future father-in-law, that "being away three years you'd get out of touch with things. Maybe letters from Grover's Corners wouldn't be so interesting after a while" (66). Still perhaps inordinately focused on his desire to mend his conceited ways, George soon talks himself out of going. All Emily must do, passive aggressively, is utter cries of surprise tinged with admiration—"Why George … My!" (67)—and George has given up his chance to learn, grow, and change. He commits to life in Grover's Corners with Emily, and nine short, blissful years later, his wife has died in childbirth, leaving him with a young son to raise. Would George have spared himself the pain of loving and marrying Emily had he gone off to school? Would he have made the better choice had he done so? *Our Town* is silent on the answers to such unanswerable questions and leaves its survivors (including its audience) with only the bittersweetness of life's fleeting joys to fill the void. *Our Town* is regarded as a masterpiece of American drama, second only to O'Neill's finest work.

Long Day's Journey into Night (1941–1942)

Eugene O'Neill (1888–1953)

Although O'Neill had placed a 20-year posthumous moratorium on the staging of *Long Day's Journey*, his widow released the play in 1956, entrusting its American debut to José Quintero. Quintero had recently completed a rejuvenating production of O'Neill's *The Iceman Cometh*, and now cast Jason Robards (who had memorably portrayed Hickey in Quintero's *Iceman*) as Jamie the elder son. In four intense acts, *Long Day's Journey* rakes through numerous painful details from O'Neill's own life, including the death in infancy of one brother (when another brother, infected with measles, failed to avoid the baby's room); the resulting alcoholic self- and other destructiveness of this surviving brother, Jamie; and the morphine addiction of his beautiful but doomed, manipulative, and self-deluded mother, Mary, upon the occasion of the birth of the youngest son (Eugene in real life, Edmund in the play). In the play Mary is victimized by a drug-pushing quack employed by her tightfisted husband, a crumbling matinee idol with stark similarities to O'Neill's own father James (famously associated with *The Count of Monte Cristo*) and with barely sufficient courage to face his thick culpability in the family's several tragedies and the misguided decisions of his professional life. Brenda Murphy adds that the play takes place in 1912, "the year of [O'Neill's] attempted suicide and his tuberculosis" ("Plays," 303) as well as of his days bumming around flophouses and barrooms before he found his artistic calling. *Long Day's Journey* thus draws heavily from O'Neill's own life, as does *A Moon for the Misbegotten* (1943), regarding the end of his elder brother's life from alcoholism, again realized in the character of Jamie.

In scenes constituted more often by whispering pairs or threesomes (i.e., the male family members) than soul-baring foursomes, the characters bicker, misrepresent past misdeeds and present concerns, and construe schemes regarding absent family members (how to get Mary to give up the needle, whether to tell Edmund about the seriousness of his illness). Whenever the conversation threatens to close in on painful truths, refuge is sought in drinking or taking drugs; in constantly hashed-over past incidents, discrepancies, and deceptions come to light; and in passive-aggressive shifts to belligerence, then defensiveness, denial, and moments of acceptance and love, depending upon who enters or exits and how late in the day it has become. As Murphy observes, each of the four acts concludes with a "sustained self-revelatory modified monologue" from each main character "that provokes understanding and sympathy from the audience" ("Plays," 305). Despite the play's title, which suggests some meaningful progress from gladness to perdition (or conversely from delusion to understanding), in fact the Tyrones live and relive an endless cycle of betrayals, never forgiven or forgotten, and chemical addictions endlessly reinstated. They disguise the men's alcoholism as hearty Irish fellow-feeling, and Mary's much more shameful morphine addiction is banished to closed rooms upstairs and confronted or denied over the course of multiple vituperative arguments among the family. As Murphy observes, "O'Neill's implication is that their life will continue in an endless cycle of pain and escape, approach and avoidance. Although the audience comes away with new insight into the human condition and new charity for human failure, the characters do not escape being trapped" ("Plays," 305).

As is often noted, the Edmund and Jamie types are everywhere in O'Neill's oeuvre: sensitive, dreamy, frail misfits—Christopher Bigsby terms them "poets who inhabit prose" (*A Critical Introduction* 47)—conned and forgotten by a faster-paced, hyper-materialistic, profit-driven world; and attractive, cynical raconteurs whose slick exteriors disguise tortured, self-hating souls. Not surprisingly, brothers or brother figures (often fitted into these profiles) are everywhere as well: Robert and Andy Mayo in *Beyond the Horizon*, Eben and his brothers in *Desire Under the Elms*, Dion Anthony and Billy Brown in *The Great God Brown*, Parritt and Larry in *The Iceman Cometh*, the gulled hotel clerk Charlie and his fast-talking visitor Erie in *Hughie* (1941), and of course the Tyrone brothers in the final plays. The dreamer outsiders long for escape, forgetfulness, and peace (see Lewis, 16–17) while their seemingly caring, worldlier mentors only exploit their vulnerabilities. As David Krasner points out, the dynamic is identical between O'Neill and his older brother: "O'Neill was often impressed by those, like his brother, who 'put on the act': the blarney, the mountebank, the snake-oil salesman ready with a tall tale and a glad hand" ("Eugene O'Neill," 151). With respect to the autobiographical element of O'Neill's work, Bigsby asserts, "It was, of course, precisely when he chose to confront [his] personal ghosts that O'Neill created his greatest drama" (*A Critical Introduction*, 111); he told his publishers that *Long Day's Journey* had been "written in tears and blood" (qtd. in Murphy, "Plays," 305), but world audiences have cherished O'Neill for a century for the exquisite personal honesty, squaring almost always with universal human truths, that he brought to all of his works.

The 1956 production transported its audience to new heights: actor Robards and O'Neill biographer Arthur Gelb tell the story of opening night, when the audience sat (or slumped) in silence—stunned and drained—as the curtain fell. Then, as the cast returned to take its bows, the audience not only leapt to their feet but rushed the foot of the stage in frenzies of appreciation, so desperate they seemed to somehow permanently, physically attach themselves to the unforgettable theatrical event they had just witnessed (interview with Rose). The mayhem recalled, in exponentially intensified fashion, the excitement generated by the opening night of *Bound East for Cardiff* on that foggy wharf in Provincetown forty years earlier, and the thrills O'Neill has been generating in audiences ever since.

Part V

American Drama's Golden Age (1945–1959)

A canon of serious American drama, inaugurated by O'Neill, Wilder, Hellman, and others in the early twentieth century, was significantly strengthened by the contributions of two giants of the post-WWII stage, Tennessee Williams and Arthur Miller. Williams, the gay Southerner invested in the sweeping romance of grand dreams, betrayed hope, and failed escape; and Miller, the Jewish New Yorker combining realism and experimentation to challenge complacent mid-century audiences, both approached their vocation from divergent standpoints but shared the ability to enthrall audiences with their dramatic output throughout the golden age of American drama in the late 1940s and 1950s.

As a young man in the 1930s, Williams wrote social-protest plays for radical groups in St. Louis, where he grew up and where his first important play would be set. Indeed, his career as a major American dramatist began with the production of *The Glass Menagerie* (1944), a minutely autobiographical play—down to the protagonist sharing his own name and dispiriting job history—that dissects the destructive relationship between a displaced, impoverished southern belle and her two grown children. Amanda Wingfield is the indomitable mother; Tom, her son, is the reluctant provider; and Laura, her daughter, is the shy and game-legged dreamer for whom we fear the most: the titular menagerie of glass figurines belongs to Laura, and the breakage of her prized unicorn's delicate horn signals both a painful but necessary coming of age and the death of her own hopes for happiness and escape. It likewise reflects the real death-in-life suffered by Williams's sister, Rose, subjected to incarceration and lobotomy while Williams was in college, and guilt over which he suffered from all his life. The play won the Drama Critics Circle Award for the 1944–1945 season and established the postwar drama milieu as the most exciting in US history.

When Williams's *A Streetcar Named Desire* (1947) proved just as electrifying as his opening gambit, his reputation as a master dramatist was assured. Once again, complex female characters are in the foreground, especially Blanche Du Bois, who is trapped by the tragic missteps of her past. She is caught in a lie by her brutish brother-in-law, Stanley, while clinging desperately to the semblance of respectability he offers her as his guest in his cramped French Quarter apartment. Once her sexually incontinent past is exposed to her potential romantic rescuer, Mitch, Blanche is cut off from her last avenue and driven mad by Stanley raping her on the night his wife gives birth to their son. As Brenda A. Murphy observes, "The conflict between Blanche and Stanley is an early formation of a fundamental dualism that Williams was to express in his plays throughout the period of his greatest work" ("Tennessee Williams," 181)— between the realist and the dreamer, the sensualist and the spirit, the domineering body and the fragile soul. Again the Drama Critics (and the Pulitzer committee) hailed this play, which was made into a successful film, provided Marlon Brando (as Stanley) his most celebrated role, and is staged almost constantly by professional and community theaters in the United States to this day.

Williams's *Summer and Smoke* (1948) and *The Rose Tattoo* (1950) were moderate successes that continued to explore body–soul dualism (in the latter play to comic effect), but his early, absurdist *Camino Real* (1953), peopled with literary figures including Lord Byron and Esmeralda from *The Hunchback of Notre Dame*, trapped in a dystopian version of *Casablanca*, did not fare well. Then "Williams [was] embittered and … so depressed that he … even considered abandoning his career" (Bigsby, *Modern American Drama*, 53). His spirits and career revived with *Cat on a Hot Tin Roof* (1955), the story of the catlike survivor, Maggie, who restores herself to the semblance of successful marriage and accession to great wealth on the death of her father-in-law, Big Daddy. It was not the first time the fateful theme of homosexuality would complicate Williams's plot—in *Streetcar*, Blanche's rejection of her queer husband leads to his suicide and her eternal guilt—and in this play it is Maggie's husband, Brick, who is suspected of homosexual feelings for the surely gay Skipper, who has just committed suicide out of shame. Audiences embraced Williams's ultimately triumphant story for its original run of almost 700 performances; it won the Pulitzer in 1955 and has enjoyed several successful Broadway revivals. It likewise lives on as a famous film starring Elizabeth Taylor as Maggie and Paul Newman as Brick.

Orpheus Descending (1957) had only minimal success (68 performances) in its original Broadway run but was made into a film renamed *The Fugitive Kind* (1959), directed by Sydney Lumet and yet again starring Marlon Brando. Val Xavier, another earthy and powerful life force, sexually rejuvenates the demoralized Lady, victimized by her thuggish husband, a member of the gang that killed her father for serving Negroes in his establishment. When Lady becomes pregnant with Val's child, her husband murders her in retaliation and sees to the tortured death of Val. Where sexual celebrants like Stanley, Maggie, or Alvaro (from *The Rose Tattoo*) had triumphed in Williams's earlier works, even this universal energy flags before the menace of bigotry and violence here, as Williams moved toward the end of his own renown, professional affirmation, and psychological well-being in the early 1960s. *Suddenly, Last Summer* (1958), an even darker and more psychologically offbeat "memory play," (as Williams described *The Glass Menagerie*) was written while Williams himself sought psychological counseling (Murphy, "Tennessee Williams," 185) and performed only off-Broadway in its original run. In the story, Sebastian Venable is a sensitive and mysterious poet, attracted to young boys; he is dead as the story begins—at the very hands of the beach urchins who had once been Sebastian's sexual prey. He exploits his cousin Catharine (also played by Elizabeth Taylor in the film) to lure the young men; she again represents the lost Rose—as she is at one point unjustly threatened with consignment to a mental institution (Bigsby, *Modern American Drama*, 61).

The Night of the Iguana (1961), regarded as Williams's last great play, involves the defrocked minister T. Lawrence Shannon, who leads a group of Baptist tourists to a bohemian Mexican outpost in an effort to forget his past. Suffering an emotional breakdown, he must be tied to a hammock as if confined to a straightjacket; he and the other desperate characters are likened to the iguana tied by the foot below the porch where the main action occurs. As Shannon is soothed in his panic by the understanding Hannah Jelkes, so he frees both the beleaguered iguana and Hannah's nonagenarian father, a poet who has come to this forgotten place to die peacefully and is at last able to do so. Murphy observes that the 1960s marked a permanent downturn in the quality of Williams's works and a falling-out with the critics, from which he never recovered. He severed his hugely consequential partnership with director Elia Kazan in 1960; his life partner, Frank Merlo, died of cancer in 1963, and the radicalism and experimentalism of the 1960s seemed to leave Williams behind ("Tennessee Williams"). As Christopher Bigsby notes, "[A]t a time when the mood of the American theater tended to be confident and celebratory, when sexuality was deployed as an image of freedom and liberation, Williams's bleak dramas of defeat, of sexual depletion and spiritual collapse seemed largely irrelevant" (*Modern American Drama*, 64). He wrote nearly 20 more plays between the early 1960s and his death by freak accident (choking on the cap of an asthma inhaler) in 1983, but he is remembered almost entirely—and entirely deservedly—for his resounding triumphs of the immediate postwar period.

Arthur Miller's current assessment is similar; he is another undisputed giant of the mid-century American stage whose career past the 1960s is regarded unevenly. In his later years, Miller debuted many of his works in London, where he remained a major figure throughout his final decades. There, according to Bigsby, "[F]or cultural, class, and educational reasons, language remained central and physicality [the frank sexuality and violence that characterize the contemporary American stage] was distrusted. Miller's theater, resolutely committed to the word, was readily embraced" (*Modern American Drama*, 115). Though he wrote almost until his death in 2005, Miller is thus remembered in the American dramatic canon for his major early works, *All My Sons* (1946), *Death of a Salesman* (1949), *The Crucible* (1953), and *A View from the Bridge* (1955); all of his work engages deeply with its immediate social context and includes themes of betrayal, integrity, and principle within families and/or communities. Miller's relationship to his own father was fraught with such betrayal and mutual disappointment; he looked on his father, whose business dissolved in the Depression, as a professional failure, and the largely illiterate Miller Sr. denigrated the career in wordsmithing sought after by his son. Thus in Miller's plays fathers, sons, uncles, and male cousins act in selfish, misguided ways, perhaps to solve an immediate problem but also in ways that impinge on a male relative's chance for happiness for years to come. Based on historical events (Schlueter, 296), Miller's first Broadway production, *All My Sons*, tells the story of Joe Keller, who sells faulty aviation parts to the government during the war to save his business, but at the cost of many young pilots' lives. When his own son, a pilot in the military, learns of his father's grievous subterfuge, he commits suicide, and Joe, learning the news, kills himself with a gunshot to the head. This is one of Miller's "Greek plays," in that it observes the Aristotelian unities of time and place and features a tragic hero whose past mistakes haunt him throughout his ill-fated present. *All My Sons* won the Circle Award for the 1946–47 season, beating out O'Neill's *The Iceman Cometh*.

Death of a Salesman, widely regarded as Miller's best work, may be the single play most responsible for announcing the arrival of American drama—specifically tragedy—on the world stage. It tells the story of yet another profoundly failed father, Willy Loman, whose days as a successful salesman are long behind him, if they ever existed at all. The problem, as the story indicates, is that Willy had the "wrong dreams," having bought into the ethos of glad-handing one's way up the ladder of success with little concern for the integrity of one's product or the time and energy necessary to develop technical skills. Although the Lomans' neighbor Bernard studies and succeeds, eventually arguing a case before the Supreme Court, Willy encourages his sons,

Happy and Biff, toward prowess on the football field and an easygoing way; yet the two flounder as young men back under their parents' roof. Willy has thus both embraced and profoundly misinterpreted the American dream he feels he has little chance to revise on his own terms. When he realizes the hollowness of the values passed to his sons, their resulting hollowness as men, he takes his life for the insurance money that will at last pay off his mortgage and give his sons the only chance he can give them. In a famous essay regarding Willy Loman as a tragic hero, Miller wrote, "I believe the common man is as apt a subject for tragedy in its highest sense as kings were.… [T]he tragic feeling is invoked in us when we are in the presence of a character who is ready to lay down his life, if need be, to secure one thing—his sense of personal dignity" (1). Critics agreed that Willy Loman, speaking as he did for a generation of aging, flawed but forgotten common men, had indeed achieved tragedy in its highest sense; they bestowed on this work a Pulitzer, a Circle Award, and a Tony for Best Play, the first drama ever recognized with this coveted "triple crown."

Miller's *The Crucible* spoke in pointed allegorical terms to an immediate political context with which he was intimately involved. Famously called (and refusing) to provide the names of 1930s Communist associates to the House Un-American Activities Committee in 1956, Miller three years earlier reeled from the HUAC testimony of close friend and artistic collaborator Elia Kazan, who jeopardized many careers in an effort to save his own. In *The Crucible*, set during the Salem witch trials of 1692, the hero, John Proctor, adheres to his strong sense of personal integrity, confessing to an affair in court, in order to save his wife, who has been jailed for witchcraft, and revealing the treachery of Abigail Williams, the spurned mistress and source of false accusation. Although recorded as Miller's most often staged play, it received a luke-warm reception in its original run (only 197 performances), due perhaps to a national mood that was focused on self-gratification and material acquisition and that, if anything, favored those who spilled their guts for putatively patriotic reasons. *A View from the Bridge* resumed the theme of familial betrayal and the hero's death as a form of atonement; its controversial subtheme of an uncle's incestuous love for his niece suggests more Greek-tragic undertones as well as Miller's own conflicted feelings about his extra-marital affair with and eventual marriage to Marilyn Monroe, 11 years his junior and famously in search of her own affirming father figures.

After the Fall even more notoriously references Monroe, whom he divorced in 1961 and who died of a drug overdose in 1962, two years before the play premiered. Audiences felt that the confused, tragic character of Maggie was in bad taste and turned away from Miller's seeming attempt to traffic in prurient interest in his marital secrets so as to sell tickets to his play. Miller redeemed himself with his tragicomic *The Price* (1968) in which two brothers—a cop who had sacrificed his future to provide for his failed father and a surgeon who did not let parental need stand in the way of his own success—meet in the attic of their family home upon the father's death, to sort through the goods with an elderly comic Jewish furniture dealer and settle the score between themselves. *The Price* enjoyed a respectable run of 429 performances and three major revivals since then. Per Bigsby, in this story "the debate seems to be one between idealism and self-sacrifice, on the one hand, and cynicism and self-concern on the other. That it is never quite that simple is what gives the play part of its fascination and integrity" (*Modern American Drama*, 105). Although Clive Barnes declined in his original review to declare *The Price* "serious theater," he did find it to be "good theater" that "will give a great deal of pleasure to many people and deserves a long and profitable run" (37). Miller's later plays include *Incident at Vichy* (1964), *The Archbishop's Ceiling* (1977), *American Clock* (1980), and the fairly well received *Ride Down Mt. Morgan* (1991) and *Shattered Glass* (1994). His autobiography, *Timebends* (1987), is a widely referenced text discussing Miller's personal life and theory of stagecraft.

In the 1950s also rose and fell the career of William Inge, whose string of hits included *Come Back, Little Sheba* (1950), the Pulitzer Prize–winning *Picnic* (1953), *Bus Stop* (1955), and *The Dark at the Top of the Stairs* (1957). All of these dramas received respectable Broadway runs and star-studded, Oscar-garnering film treatment and have been frequently revived onstage since then; Inge also wrote the Oscar-winning screenplay for *Splendor in the Grass* (1961), and each of these dramatic works presented the daring themes of sexual hypocrisy, repression, failure, and fulfillment—frequently outside the bonds of matrimony—that surprised and engaged their original audiences. Thomas P. Adler considers Inge's themes "paradigmatic" for the decade, although he observes that "What marks and finally delimits the women in Inge's play[s] is their nearly total subjugation to what might be called the curse of the romantic imagination" ("Fissures," 163). Like his fellow St. Louis native Tennessee Williams, from whom he received early vital encouragement, Inge was a conflicted gay man and admitted alcoholic from the late 1940s; he committed suicide in 1974, though he stayed active in theater, television, and as a novelist until that time. Tracing the focus on "domestic realism" from Miller and Williams to Inge, June Schlueter observes, "If there was a playwright who shared the respect of Miller and Williams in the fifties, not for innovation of form but for the sensitivity with which he dramatized the American family, it was William Inge" (307; see also Aronson, 110–11). Per Bigsby, "While celebrating a particular kind of Americana, he managed to convey a sense of the terrible loneliness and frustrations of ordinary life" (*Modern American Drama*, 155).

Yet another celebrated domestic realist from this decade is Lorraine Hansberry, whose landmark *A Raisin in the Sun* (1959) deservedly enjoyed a 530-performance run in its original production, numerous Tony awards (including Best Play), and the Drama Critics Circle Award for 1959, the only play by an African American female (at the young age of 29) ever to receive this award. The story of the misguided but noble Walter Lee Younger (played on stage and screen by Sidney Poitier to massive acclaim) and his oppressed but aspiring Southside Chicago family (his wife, son, mother, and sister), Hansberry's play presents the vital themes of neighborhood integration and white resistance to same, the injustices of the inner city, and the embrace of African heritage. Hansberry followed up with less well-received plays in the early 1960s and died tragically of duodenal cancer at only 34.

In another key, the rapidly transforming tradition in American musical theater, begun with the staging of Edna Ferber's *Showboat* by Jerome Kern and Oscar Hammerstein in 1927, reached a peak in the middle decades of the twentieth century through the efforts of George and Ira Gershwin (with the operatic *Porgy and Bess* [1935]); Irving Berlin (*Annie Get Your Gun* [1946]); Cole Porter (*Anything Goes* [1934] and *Kiss Me, Kate* [1949], which won the first Tony for Best Musical); Richard Rodgers and Lorenz Hart (*I'd Rather Be Right* [1937] and *Pal Joey* [1940]); Frank Loesser (*Guys and Dolls* [1950]); Leonard Bernstein (*West Side Story* [1957]); and Alan Jay Lerner and Frederick Loewe (*Brigadoon* [1947], *My Fair Lady* [1956; considered by many—e.g., Mordden, 194; Naden, 25—to be the most outstanding American musical of all time], and *Camelot* [1960]). In general, these musicals are hailed for integrating the dramatic or comic plot with the song and dance; as is often said, the musical numbers established character or advanced the plot instead of being contrived "time-outs" in a farcical storyline as was traditional for late nineteenth- and early twentieth-century musicals such as *Beauty in Dreamland* (discussed in Section III). These later musicals likewise included serious themes, complex anti-heroes, sexual candor (as opposed to girlie-show titillation), and an all-around improved quality to the song lyrics and compositions themselves. At last the American musical could measure up to yet another pacesetter from across the Atlantic, the enduring canon of Gilbert and Sullivan, whose complicated but delightful operetta tradition had been the musical's gold standard throughout the West since the 1870s.

It was especially Rodgers in collaboration with Oscar Hammerstein II, beginning in 1943 with their phenomenally successful *Oklahoma!* (a staggering 2212 performances during its original run, no major stars in any lead roles, and more than a dozen hit songs), who are credited with establishing the golden age of American musical theater, due to the sheer number of smash hits, revived almost constantly on Broadway and across America to this day. *Oklahoma!* told the story of feuding farmers and ranchers in a Western territory on the threshold of claiming statehood, and famously included a moody dream ballet, a favorite stylistic trend in this era, that added tragedy and pathos to the main story. Rodgers and Hammerstein followed up with the equally well-remembered *Carousel* (1945), *South Pacific* (1949), *The King and I* (1951), *Flower Drum Song* (1958), and *The Sound of Music* (1959). Musical theater historian Ethan Mordden observes that Rodgers and Hammerstein reliably wrote "family shows" with little violence or lewd action, although many deaths or serious situations (e.g., the death of the villain Jud Fry in *Oklahoma!* and of the raffish hero Billy Bigelow in *Carousel*, as well as the Nazi threat in *The Sound of Music*), such that they belong less to the tradition of musical comedy than musical drama. Per Mordden, "Clearly, R&H all but reinvented the musical. *Oklahoma!* and *Carousel* weren't more integrated than musicals had been: they were more influential" (170).

At the height of his career, Hammerstein also mentored the leading lyricist-composer of the contemporary American stage, Stephen Sondheim. Having written the lyrics for both *West Side Story* and *Gypsy* (1959), Sondheim composed both lyrics and music—in his signature tonally complex, verbally witty, sophisticated style—for long-running, critically acclaimed hits from then on: *A Funny Thing Happened on the Way to the Forum* (1962), *Company* (1970), *Follies* (1971), *A Little Night Music* (1973), *Pacific Overtures* (1976), *Sweeney Todd* (1979), *Sunday in the Park with George* (1984), and *Into the Woods* (1987). Sondheim's work has earned numerous recognitions, including the Pulitzer Prize for *Sunday in the Park with George*, eight Grammies, five Tony Awards for Best Musical, and a Lifetime Achievement Tony Award in 2008.

This section includes a key play from the major dramatists of this period. Chekhov's work leads the discussion, 40 years after inception, for being a key influence on Miller, Williams, and numerous dramatists throughout the contemporary period.

A Transatlantic Touchstone: *The Cherry Orchard* (1904)

Anton Chekhov (1860–1904)

Although this canonical dramatist belongs to an earlier era, his influence on major mid-century (and contemporary) American playwrights is well documented, and his iconic story of an era's passing is therefore discussed here.

In *The Cherry Orchard*, Madame Ravenska returns from five years in Paris to her beloved estate—but only to sell it to the highest bidder, as she can no longer afford the taxes on the property. When it is purchased by Lopakhin, the self-made son of peasant stock, Madame Ravenska and her aristocratic family must face the reality that their society has changed in traumatizing but potentially liberating ways: in the estimation of Montrose J. Moses, "the sad theme of a dying regime, the exultant theme that it is over and that life is free to face a better life to come" ("Anton Chekhov," 4). If Ibsen focused on the internal and interpersonal/marital crises born by a rapidly modernizing industrial age, Chekhov used a wider lens, tracing the shift (or fall) of generations and ages in the face of sweeping historic and economic transformation involving conflicting social classes and sometimes including societal revolution.

Thomas P. Adler has traced the influence of Chekhov on several mid-century dramatists, noting with regard to Lillian Hellman, for instance, that her autobiographical *Little Foxes* and *Another Part of the Forest* are "swan songs for a cultured, genteel way of life, now dying out, only to be replaced by a more pragmatic and utilitarian business model" (*American Drama*, 47). Later, Adler describes Hellman as a "daughter of Chekhov … along with [being] the disciple of Ibsen she had always been" (*Modern American Drama*, 50). Adler regards Hellman's widely acclaimed *Autumn Garden* (1951) as "the most Chekhovian of all American plays in its reduction of outward plot, its wistful, elegiac tone of loss, and its handling of an ensemble cast" (*American Drama*, 54). With respect to *The Autumn Garden*, William Wright avers that although "[Hellman's] judgmental approach to her characters is still present" and the play lacks "Chekhov's quirky humor and his lyricism" (236), his influence on this play is yet "unmistakable" (236). With regard to the plays of Tennessee Williams, Adler sees there a prevailing Chekhovian theme of tension between "an agrarian South [looking] back nostalgically to a partly mythical past of gentility and refinement and an industrial North that rewarded business acumen and practicality" (*American Drama*, 131). Adler discusses the contest between Stanley and Blanche as "the strength of the industrial North against the decadence of the agrarian South" (*American Drama*, 140); per the findings of Jacob H. Adler, "Blanche has something in her of culture and beauty; … as with the aristocrats in *The Cherry Orchard*, we must regret its passing, even as we recognize the decadence and futility and even degradation that makes its passing both necessary and inevitable" (qtd. in Cardullo, "Birth," 169). Williams famously replied, when asked to name his three favorite playwrights, "Chekhov, Chekhov, and Chekhov."

Later in the decade, Brooks Atkinson notably considered Hansberry's *A Raisin in the Sun* to be readable as a "Negro *Cherry Orchard* … [as] the knowledge of how character is controlled by environment is much the same, and the alternation of humor and pathos is similar" ("The Theater," 24). The theme of a genteel, agrarian way of life giving way to cold corporate pragmatism is also significant in Arthur Miller's *Death of a Salesman*, and in a conversation with Henry Brandon in 1960, Miller might have been talking about his own masterwork in his rumination on *The Cherry Orchard*: "[W]hen the real estate developer destroys with his axe the lovely but unproductive basis of the characters' lives, Chekhov was not merely describing a picturesque piquancy, but the crude thrust of materialism taking command of an age." In this and other plays, Miller discerned that Chekhov "was seeking some reconciliation for these much-loved people and the forces displacing them" (Brandon, 59). Miller's reconciliation with respect to Willy's long-denied dream to grow a garden or work with a batch of cement lies in his elder son Biff's intention to return to the West following Willy's death at the end of the play. He will never make significant money, or perhaps even rise above poverty, as a ranchhand in Texas, but he will live the satisfied, self-aware life that his father died refusing himself.

Many, when considering Chekhov's plays, refer to his large ensemble casts, and though never as large as in Chekhov, Miller's and Williams's plays and also Hansberry's *A Raisin in the Sun* include "ensemble" casts with several generations of adults under the same roof. As opposed to the marital conflict taking center stage in *A Doll's House*, for instance (a conflict in part fomented by the *absence* of an older generation in the form of Nora's father), the crises in *The Glass Menagerie*, *Death of a Salesman*, and *A Raisin in the Sun* involve parents contesting with their adult children over whose values shall predominate in a new age. Although the adult sons, daughters, and (in the case of *Raisin* and *Streetcar*) siblings may wish that the dominating couple or elder generation might simply die away, clearing the stage (and home) for the advent of the new arrivals, this retiring generation reads the return or persistence of adult children to the parental home as both a sign of its own failure and an unnatural stoppage of the flow—a decline in prosperity, fertility, or general forward momentum—essential to a vibrant society.

Elsewhere in his discussion with Henry Brandon, Miller noted that Chekhov's plays "are great, for one thing, not because they do not give answers but because they strive so mightily to discover them, and in the process draw into view a world that is historical" (59). Many have observed this tendency to leave questions unanswered or matters unresolved in Chekhov's plays, such that Richard Gilman makes reference to Chekhov's "drama of the undramatic" (qtd. in P. Lewis), and Pericles Lewis argues that "[l]ike life itself, Chekhov's plots generally lack resolution." Although it is Chekhov whose famous maxim dictates that "if you say in the first chapter there is a rifle hanging on the wall, in the second or third chapter it absolutely must go off," in fact plenty of guns do not go off in Chekhov's dramatic works. As Lewis notes, Uncle Vanya shoots at his hated brother-in-law twice but misses, and no prosecution or any other reaction ensues. In *The Cherry Orchard*, "a minor character boasts in the second act, 'I always carry a loaded pistol.' ... Yet as Chekhov announced proudly, 'There's not a single pistol shot in the whole play'" (P. Lewis). Although flesh-and-blood wrongdoers bring crisis to the lives of the protagonists in each Chekhov play, what these heroes would be shooting at is the tide of progress itself, and any such shot is bound to miss. As Lewis observes in a similar vein, the titular characters in *Three Sisters* simply endure, never getting to Moscow despite their ardent intentions to do so. In this way, they clearly resemble, and thus Chekhov clearly anticipates, Vladimir and Estragon of Beckett's *Waiting for Godot* (1952) (Gilman qtd. in P. Lewis), and his anticipation of Beckett is also recognized in Chekhov's strong bent for the comedic. Although Miller and Williams take inspiration from Chekhov to enlarge their respective tragic visions, and although "the lugubrious naturalist stagings" of Chekhov's plays at the Moscow Art Theater made him famous (P. Lewis), Chekhov insisted that *The Cherry Orchard* was a comedy, though an unconventional one. Denying its audience the expected marriage between Lopakhin and Varya, instead the image of the elderly servant Firs, lying down onstage, waiting for someone (or death) to reclaim him, is best played for farce and not tragedy, again paving the way for Beckett 50 years later. Per Beckett's clownish characters and his widely known admiration for the comic genius of Chaplin, Chekhov himself was famously described by Gorky: "By appearance he was a tramp, but inwardly this is a rather elegant man" (qtd. in Moses, "Anton Chekhov," 5).

If even the best of the human players in *The Cherry Orchard* suffer persistent short-sightedness and self-interest, that likely leaves the orchard itself as our most reliable principle of unchanging goodness, even if not of heroic action. Per the details of his own biography, Chekhov's fluctuating family fortunes, and later his faltering health following the onset of tuberculosis, required numerous moves, many of which entailed leaving behind a beloved estate or region that he would later learn suffered development or deforestation. When he moved, or even simply traveled, he appreciated the beauty of the natural environments he found himself in, and likely suffered guilt that his family's diverse failures to maintain their properties led to encroachments from profit-minded strangers with no emotional investment in the forests, orchards, or other natural beauty that came with the purchase of the land. There was a Lopakhin-type "savior" who rescued his family from destitution when Chekhov was a teenager, but at the cost of the family home, and as his parents and grandparents had struggled to buy the family out of serfdom in an earlier generation, so Chekhov shored up his parents' finances (and maintained his sister as well as his wife) through his successful career as a journalist, fiction writer, and playwright throughout the short years of his life. His medical degree, taken in 1884, never earned him much income, as he saw many patients for free; nor did it save him from his impending fate from tuberculosis, which he succumbed to in July 1904, six months after the triumphant debut of *The Cherry Orchard*, his last play. Though Beckett employed absurdism to sharpen the edge of his already significant pessimism with respect to the prospects of human survival, Moses argues that this statement from *The Cherry Orchard*'s Trophímof captures "Chekhov's attitude toward life": "There is happiness, there it comes; nearer and nearer; I hear its steps. And should we not see it, should we not know it, what matter? Others will!" (qtd. in Moses, "Anton Chekhov," 4).

A Streetcar Named Desire (1947)

Tennessee Williams (1911–1983)

Like almost all southern writers, from Poe to Faulkner to Styron, Williams presents much of his work through the lens of romanticism. Though he may critique (and all but destroy) his leading women who insist upon "magic! magic!" (*Streetcar*, 545) even when the tax collectors, police, or men in white coats are beating at the door, Williams himself was clearly in love with the romantic idiom and plied it with remarkable effectiveness in a realist age. In her defense, director Harold Clurman referred to Blanche as "the potential artist in all of us…. Her wretched romanticism is a futile reaching toward the fullness of life" (qtd. in Adler, *American Drama*, 141). *A Streetcar Named Desire* is easily readable as an encounter (shifting into violent conflict) between a realist/naturalist everyman and a once-beautiful, once-refined woman whose obsession with pretense, fable, and fabrication assumes gothic proportions by the end of her story (see also Holditch). Williams surely loved both the romance and the realism he found on the streets of the French Quarter in New Orleans, where he lived for the first time in the 1940s and where the story is set. The gritty, interracial, frankly sexualized street scenes that likely drew Williams in the first place provide the setting and inform much of the characterization in his play. Blanche's brother-in-law, Stanley Kowalski (named for and based on a sexually magnetic coworker from Williams's own shoe factory days) exudes the animal lure that Blanche's sister Stella openly lusts after and that draws Blanche as well, despite her recognizing him as a mortal enemy as soon as they meet. In Gerald Weales's early but still trenchant observation, "Blanche became the symbol of the Old South, that romantic invention of Southern ladies and Northern historians, whose cultural and human virtues were doomed to destruction in the face of the vitality and vulgarity of the New South—Stanley" (*American Drama*, 24). The Kowalskis live a noisy, sometimes crude, but utterly satisfied life, and Blanche's repeatedly reminding Stella who she once was—despite her hysterical attempt to flee from her own shameful, tragic past—creates tension throughout the play.

The past Blanche longs to forget is the realist element in her own character—traumatizing death for her older family members, losing the southern mansion to foreclosure, and a series of scandalous sexual affairs, including some with her own high school students, that has Blanche not just visiting but banished from the town of Laurel, Mississippi, where her once-proud family has fallen from grace. In an early scene, Stanley suspects that all of Blanche's "feathers and furs" (485) come from an inheritance she has yet to share with her sister and, under the dictates of the Napoleonic Code, himself. Their "cards on the table" scene is literally Blanche's only moment of truth. With the papers documenting the loss of Belle Reve riffling expertly through her hands, Blanche makes an impassioned speech, proving an intelligence far superior to Stanley's and an ability to look—literally throughout the reading glasses surreptitiously donned for the occasion—at hard facts in all of their ugly intransigence: "There are thousands of papers going back hundred years, affecting Belle Reve as piece by piece, our improvident grandfathers and fathers and uncles and brothers exchanged the land for their epic fornications…. I think it's wonderfully fitting that Belle Reve should finally be this bunch of old papers in your big, capable hands!" (490–91). Stanley is silenced, and thwarted in his attempt to vanquish Blanche, but only temporarily. For the remainder of the story, Blanche's attempt to whitewash her past and win the affections of Stanley's poker buddy Mitch is no match for the realist and realistic Stanley, who has networks of information, and the bitter truth, on his side.

Blanche is a neurotic narcissist with all manner of related psychological hang-ups and an overall infantile personality. Stella, though younger, acts the protective mother figure around Blanche, tolerating her "white lies" and bids for compliments; her demanding, critical attitudes about Stella's life choices; and her generally boorish behavior in their small apartment. Blanche presents as a sexually demure, teetotaling Southern lady (when in fact she is neither), impressing Mitch (whom she does not love, but needs desperately) with her refined ways and withholding sexual favors long enough to elicit from him a marriage proposal. Blanche fears most discovery of how old she is and looks; she hints to Mitch that she is younger than Stella and insists upon low lighting in any room she is in, regarding a naked light bulb as offensive as "a rude remark or a vulgar action" (499). Blanche has no tolerance for the adequate lighting that would enable the men in her world to "have a real good look at [her]" (544), and although her story gets darker, stranger, and more unsayable as the play progresses, the awful truths of Blanche's past and present come inevitably to light. Regarding the play's remarkable use of light and shadow, John Gronbeck-Tedesco observes that early in the play, "Blanche separat[es] from Stella by stepping out of the light into the shadow, so that Stanley sees only his wife. Sight soon becomes one of the epistemological issues in the play. Who sees whom? When? Who wants to be seen and who does not? Whose sight is trustworthy whose is not? Whose presence is lit and whose is darkened and … in what dramatic situations?" (104).

The lie that started Blanche on her lifelong path of desperation and deception regards the sexual orientation of the deeply beloved husband of her youth. Williams paints the entire long-ago episode—her marriage to "the boy," his discovery with an older man, her bitter rejection and public humiliation of him, and his resultant suicide—as unspeakable horror, that is, as a ghost story that has been driving Blanche mad with feelings of hurt, betrayal, and guilt ever since. As Keith Dorwick observes, Blanche's dead husband belongs to an important group in Williams's canon: "One thinks [also] of Skipper in *Cat on a Hot Tin Roof* and … Sebastian Venable in the film version of *Suddenly Last Summer*…. All of these queer characters are dead before the actions of the plays that that mention them, but all remain central, often in devastating ways, to the conflicts between the major onstage characters" (80). Scenes 7 through 10 of Williams's 11-scene play occur during one fateful night—when Mitch, who has learned the truth about Blanche from Stanley's traveling sales associates, stands her up on her birthday, Stella is taken to the hospital to deliver the Kowalskis' baby boy, and Stanley confronts Blanche in a scene that ends in rape. Per the conventions of the gothic horror story, the French Quarter apartment is shrouded in shadow, Blanche wanders alone and drunk through its several rooms, and an eerie Mexican woman sells her wares on the corner, calling out mournfully, "Flores, flores para los muertos…." (546). When a young man comes to the door, looking to collect for the Kowalskis' newspaper subscription, Blanche attempts to seduce him, taking on the role in this haunted house of the rapist revenant, with the hapless newsboy as the fleeing damsel in distress. Yet surely Blanche herself assumes this traditional role, draped per convention in a white evening gown from days of yore, at the hands of the monstrous, marauding Stanley later that night. His attack permanently curtails Blanche's romance with lies and magic by permanently curtailing her ties to reality. Rather than believe her story about the rape, Stella has Blanche committed to an insane asylum, and she tragically, ironically pays dearly and permanently for confronting her sister with the truth of her victimization, Stanley's character, and her marriage. As Philip C. Kolin observes, "*Streetcar* innovatively presented a theater of interiority, converting Blanche's fluctuating mental states into stage action. *Streetcar* staged the disintegration of Blanche's mind and its impact on those around her, including the audience" (*Williams*, 4).

In its original Broadway run, *Streetcar* enjoyed 855 performances and massive critical acclaim. It won the 1948 Pulitzer Prize in Drama and the Drama Critics Circle Award; Williams himself regarded it as his best work, and in the estimation of Thomas P. Adler, it "may arguably be the finest work ever written for the American stage, possessing as it does, along with technical brilliance, what relatively few other American dramas attain: the psychological and thematic complexity most often attributed to the novel" (*American Drama*, 140).

Death of a Salesman (1949)

Arthur Miller (1915–2005)

Arthur Miller is regarded by many as America's premier playwright; only O'Neill and Williams rival him for this title, yet Miller's *Death of a Salesman* is widely considered the most theatrically profound, thematically significant American drama yet written. Notably, *Salesman* has been singled out for its universal (not simply American) themes; it has been translated into numerous languages and enjoyed a notable production in Beijing in the early 1980s, overseen by Miller himself. Although the occupation of its tragic hero, Willy Loman, in the Chinese version was reconceived by the lead actor as an old-fashioned caravan wrangler (sales in China being a disreputable profession), it is Willy's role as a salesman that has so captivated Western audiences and that took audiences by storm at its mid-century moment of origin: as one of the lowest rungs on the ladder of white collar success, many in Willy's generation transitioned from long family histories of manual labor into the indoor world of corporate, managerial, education-based work across the hardscrabble proving ground of road sales. Readable to many as an important step up, in fact the "drummer's" life was a questionable improvement over the older ways, with long, lonely hours endured on the road and salary paid mainly or entirely on commission. Though he represented a sophisticated corporate concern, a traveling salesman might find himself trudging through the very hinterlands he had worked so hard to escape, suffering the indignities of his precarious professional perch and the physical travails—witness Willy's heavy sample cases—of demonstrating, marketing, and pushing his product. Many in Willy's (and Miller's) generation, for whom college and the skills it availed were not an option, would never move beyond this bottom rung, and Miller's play addresses key questions (that remain important to this day) regarding the choice between vocational and professional work and whether any move, no matter how bedeviled, up the ladder is to be seen as success. In the phrasing of Thomas E. Porter, Miller's "play is an anti-myth, the rags-to-riches formula in reverse so that it becomes the story of a failure in terms of success, or better, the story of the failure of the success myth. The events in the play are a mirror-image of the hero's progress. Willy Loman's history begins at the end of the line" (27).

Although Americans were overall jubilant with postwar power and prosperity in 1949, everyone also remembered the desperation of the Depression era, and in the boom years after war Americans found themselves awash in newly fabricated consumer goods and the high-pressured cynicism of the advertising age. If the promotion of dubiously necessary products was itself a hollow art, what about those many of us lacking coveted skills, with nothing to market with "a smile and a shoeshine" (*Salesman*, 111) but our ingratiating selves? Willy's plight as the salesman whose goods no one was ever interested in, with a home, a wife, and two grown sons to support nevertheless, struck original audiences as terrifying and profound—as eliciting those cathartic emotions of pity and fear essential to classic tragedy. It threatened the foundation of that most devoutly followed of national faiths known as the American Dream. Per Miller's own recollection of opening night, "[T]here was no applause at the final curtain…. Some people stood to put on their coats and then sat down again, some, especially men, were bent forward covering their faces and others were openly weeping. People crossed the theater to talk quietly with one another. It seemed forever before someone remembered to applaud, and then there was no end to it" (*Timebends*, 191). It was a historic opening night in American theater and a historic American drama that had been written, defining an age against its more optimistic judgment and introducing a uniquely American version of modern tragedy.

In his well-regarded essay "Tragedy and the Common Man" (1949), Miller spelled out his rationale for ascribing to an ordinary, deeply flawed protagonist the heroic stature befitting tragedy. For Miller, such a man's most noble gesture is his readiness to "lay down his own life, if need be, to secure one thing—his sense of personal dignity" (1). Thus the tragic-heroic mindset is that of "indignation," accompanied by the bold actions of "total examination of the 'unchangeable' environment" (1) and the "sketching and tearing apart of the cosmos," whereby the character "gains 'size,'" the tragic stature that heretofore had only been accorded to the royal and high-born in classical custom. Miller enjoins his audience to receive tragedy with a sense of optimism, narrating as tragedy does "the indestructible will of man to achieve his humanity" (3) despite the self-destruction he may undergo in the attempt. Less than a decade later, Miller published "The Family in Modern Drama" in the *Atlantic Monthly*, and surely described his own politically committed works—*Salesman* high on this list—when he advocated a blend of the poetic and the prosaic, the political and the psychological, the social and the familial in modern drama: "It is within the rightful sphere of drama—it is, so to speak, its truly just employment and its ultimate design—to embrace the many-sidedness of man" (84).

Miller was born in 1915 into an upper-middle-class Jewish family on 110th Street overlooking Central Park. His father's garment factory failed during the Depression, and Miller developed his leftist commitment to economic equality and political justice during this time. He matriculated at the University of Michigan in the mid-1930s and was there a two-time winner of the school's highest literary prize, the Avery Hopwood Award. He had his first Broadway production in 1940, *The Man Who Had All the Luck*. Although it closed after only four nights, Miller scored a hit in 1947 with *All My Sons*, about a corrupt war-munitions manufacturer, whose pilot son kills himself in shame. The play ran more than 300 nights and won that year's Drama Critics Circle Award and two Tonys. It was championed by Brooks Atkinson, the reigning theater critic of the *New York Times* in that era, who later referred to *Death of a Salesman* as "a superb American drama. From every point of view … it is rich and memorable" ("At the Theater," 27). Willy was based on a blustering, boastful, pathetically insecure uncle who fascinated Miller and who had two sons whom he placed into perpetual competition with Miller and his brother. The name Loman echoed that of a key character from Fritz Lang's *The Testament of Dr. Mabus* (1933; see also Lahr, "Walking"). Miller wrote numerous other dramas until his death in 2005 but is best remembered for his masterworks in the 1940s and 1950s; as Christopher Bigsby remarks early in his two-part biography, it was "in the first half of his life, that … he was being shaped, [that] he began his conversations with America, [and that], no matter his later doubts, he did, indeed, change the world" (*Arthur Miller*, x).

Death of a Salesman is noted for its experimental form, with an original working title of "The Inside of his Head" and an original set design conceived of as a cranial space wherein the actions would be portrayed as the memories, delusions, and other mental workings of the main character (see Lahr,

"Walking"). In his autobiography, Miller described his desire to achieve a cubist or chordal effect by having lines overlap, scenes from different moments taking place in the same space, and fluid movement between present and past to convey the dynamics of Willy's active, often frantic mind. Willy, his wife, and two sons play younger versions of themselves in scenes from the past, and Willy's successful but ruthless older brother, Ben, appears as both a living character in early scenes and a haunting memory during Willy's lonely reveries. As Enoch Brater remarks regarding the scene design, "On a multi-level constructivist set, time past and time present could be in dialogue with each other as a rhythmic pattern of negotiation and renewal emerged. All that was needed to signal transition was stage lighting, accompanied by the haunting sound of a flute playing somewhere in the distance" (*Arthur Miller*, 42).

Miller's take on stream-of-consciousness drama is both an emulation of the ordinary mind at work—and indeed a fair replication of the meandering style of Miller's aptly named autobiography, *Timebends*—and the dramatization of a fragile mentality spinning tragically out of control. Willy experiences less the typical aging process (he is in fact only 63) than a form of madness finely calibrated to the atmosphere of his lived experience: being fired by his young, uncaring boss on the day he was planning to gain from him a raise and promotion, then learning of his elder son's professional failure, stemmed directly from the trauma he suffered as a youth witnessing his father's affair with a secretary. Willy bounds toward total dementia yet makes a last calculated act in the car crash that takes his life, so that the insurance money can pay off the mortgage and enable his sons to a fresh start. At his graveside, Biff, the elder son, declares that Willy had "all the wrong dreams" and that he will learn from his father's mistakes by finding happiness in ranch land out west. Meanwhile, Willy's misguided, less favored younger son, Happy, vows to win his father's lost battle on the business front, and Linda expresses her confusion, despair, and desolation. *Death of a Salesman* won the 1949 Pulitzer Prize for Drama, and Tony Award for Best Play. It has enjoyed four Broadway revivals and hundreds of stagings in regional theaters nationwide and in professional theaters around the world.

Come Back, Little Sheba (1950)

William Inge (1913–1973)

Gerald Weales remarked of Clifford Odets that "he is so identified with the 1930s that a mention of his name elicits stock responses, the recollection of a time when literature was a weapon and leftist optimism almost mandatory"

(*Odets*, 15). In a very different decade, the 1950s, William Inge is just as evocative and meaningful a watchword; he scored hits with *Come Back, Little Sheba* (1950), *Picnic* (1953), *Bus Stop* (1955), and *The Dark at the Top of the Stairs* (1957), and won an Oscar for his screenplay for *Splendor in the Grass* (1961). All tell stories of sexual longing realized or repressed in small Midwestern towns like Independence, Kansas, where he grew up. Yet Inge's own life until 1950 had not been easy; the son of a philandering father and a repressed mother, Inge was bullied as a mama's boy in his youth and spent life thenceforward firmly ensconced in the closet of homophobic repression. He was a "full-blown alcoholic" (Teachout, 72) by the time his string of 1950s hits began, and success onstage cured neither the heavy drinking nor the repression of his gay orientation. Per biographer Ralph F. Voss, "*Sheba* had changed his status but not himself" (117), and when the 1960s arrived, Inge found it impossible to maintain his artistic stride. Somehow trapped in the decade preceding, which he had so effectively defined and diagnosed, he never had another success onstage and committed suicide, "a deeply troubled ... man who slept as much as he could to obliterate his pain, perhaps to recover in his dreams some fragment of the more hopeful years of his life" (Shuman, "Preface"), in 1973. As both Voss and Inge archivist Diana Bertolini observe, Inge may have never recovered from a blistering review for *Harper's* by Robert Brustein, who pronounced at length on "the mediocrity of [Inge's] work" (52). "Inge's friends and colleagues agreed that the article was a turning point from which he never recovered. He struck out with [his final three plays for Broadway, and] after the initial success of *Splendor in the Grass* Hollywood wasn't much better" (Bertolini). In Terry Teachout's admiring retrospective, "Those who criticize him because he was incapable of writing for America in the '60s with similar skill ... are missing the point of his achievement. Within his limits he was close to perfect, and it was only when he felt obliged to move beyond them that he faltered" (74).

Teachout places Inge in the pantheon of leading postwar dramatists—Williams and Miller—each of whom is remembered today for three or four excellent and/or widely successful plays from that period. Williams's *Glass Menagerie* was deeply inspiring to Inge, who saw the out-of-town Chicago premiere with Williams in 1944 and who then realized "that common people in ordinary settings are the stuff of which moving drama can be made" (Shuman, 8). They had an intense, short romance in the late 1940s and remained in each other's orbit throughout their lives. Williams was jealous of Inge's hits from the 1950s, all of which were striking while Williams was in the midst of his own commercial downturn (Shuman, 7), and claimed that Inge's dialogue was better (Shuman, 13). Quoting David Savran, Albert Wertheim locates another important connection between the two writers: "'Williams's homosexuality is endlessly *refracted* in his work: translated, reflected, and transposed.' Much the same can be said of William Inge" ("Dorothy's Friend," 197). Elsewhere, comparing Inge to Arthur Miller, specifically his probing political allegory, *The Crucible* (1953), Wertheim considers both writers to have looked honestly at the sexual and social neuroses that led to a sick society: "'Why does America's sickness exist and how can health or rehabilitation occur?' are questions [these] playwrights posed and attempted to answer" ("American Theater," 15). Wertheim includes Williams's *Cat on a Hot Tin Roof* and Hellman's *Autumn Garden* as two other plays from the 1950s that "explore the maladies that can affect sexual relationships" ("American Theater," 18).

In *Sheba*, Inge presents his signature theme of sexual frustration, exacerbated this time by professional disappointment and barely maintained sobriety for Doc Delaney, a washed-up chiropractor married to dumpy, brassy Lola in the depressed Midwestern town where the story takes place. When a sexy boarder, Marie, moves in, Doc is tempted physically, demoralized by thoughts of wasted opportunity, and reacquainted with the bottle; though he returns to his wife by story's end, modern critics have cautioned against reading Doc and Lola's reunion as happy. Lola will never recover from the loss of her miscarried child, and Doc's failure to succeed with Marie can be likened to Marie's choice of safe, boring Bruce over the sexually exciting but unreliable Turk. As Steven R. Centola argues, all three of *Come Back*'s main characters "live in bad faith. Having relinquished their freedom and abdicating the responsibility for emotional collapse, ... [they] sentence themselves to a torpid life of disillusionment and isolation, a life of compromise and repression" (113). With only slightly more optimism, Thomas P. Adler compares Doc and Lola at the end of the play to Vladimir and Estragon, the eternal waiters of Beckett's *Waiting for Godot*, who ultimately "can only be certain of one another's presence" (*American Drama*, 89). *Sheba* is notable for its references to Alcoholics Anonymous, which Doc belongs to and whose members rescue Doc from his fateful attempt to take Lola's life at the end of the play. Inge himself had copious if only minimal successful personal experience with AA, founded in 1935, and brought this background to the story.

No end of Freudian trouble may be (and has been) read into the pet names that Doc and Lola use to refer to each other. Though Doc as "Daddy" and Lola as "Baby" suggest an air of earthy role-playing sexuality, in fact the bizarre shift from husband-wife to parental-child roles is the more reliable indicator. Doc and Lola are, notably, tragically childless, having married due to an unplanned pregnancy, which Lola miscarried and was never able to replicate as Doc's wife. Scholars have suggested that their current marriage configuration, pet names included, is a means by which to allow Lola cope with "the child she lost and then was unable to conceive in marriage" (Centola, 110). True to her pet name, Lola seems not to recognize how the years have worn on her; like the coquettish young woman she used to be, she flirts absurdly with local service providers and identifies vicariously with Marie, whom she encourages in her pursuit of both wealthy Bruce and sexy Turk. "Sheba" of the title refers to Lola's missing puppy; he has disappeared long before the start of the story and represents the lost youth, lost sexual vitality, lost children, and lost opportunity for both Doc and Lola. Also true to his pet name, Doc is very much the "father" figure, strongly repressed in his sexual feelings for the young, flirtatious Marie, almost as if these were forbidden by the incest taboo. As a doting father would, he clings to the notion that Marie is chaste and prudent in her behaviors; it is his learning of her affair with Turk that sends him back to drinking and to the violent attack on Lola that forms the play's climax.

Sheba was a hit with critics and an even bigger hit with audiences, whose views led to decisions to turn each of Inge's Broadway hits into successful Hollywood films. Inge's partnership with Joshua Logan, who directed Broadway and Hollywood versions of *Picnic* and the film version of *Bus Stop* and who aimed to make Inge's work as "marketable" (Shuman, 12) as it could be, is emblematic of the serious-popular intersection where Inge worked throughout his career. Despite the success of each play from the 1950s, Inge evidently enjoyed little of it, being described by biographer R. Baird Shuman as "nervous," "worried," and "fretting" (10–12) much of the time. In his own words, "The experience of my first production on Broadway was frantic and bewildering.... [Following its] modest success ... I was in a funk" (v). Inge added that whenever one of his four plays succeeded, he felt no elation or triumph, only "deep gratefulness, like a man barely escaping a fatal accident, that he has survived" (vi). Notably, Voss subtitles his authoritative biography of Inge *The Strains of Triumph*; Inge's talent ensured that *Sheba* and his other plays of the 1950s would succeed, but failure was hardly more terrifying than the adulation and publicity that were their own sources of anxiety and discomfort for this reserved, shy, private, and "secret" (Voss, xiv) man.

A Raisin in the Sun (1959)

Lorraine Hansberry (1930–1965)

Lorraine Hansberry lived a tragically short life, dying in New York of duodenal cancer at the age of 34; a night later, her second Broadway play, *The Sign in Sidney Brustein's Window* (1964) closed. In fact, the play had been struggling for months and was kept onstage mainly through the generosity of its actors and backers; although each had its own merits, none of Hansberry's other plays has ever enjoyed the well-deserved success of her masterwork, *A Raisin in the Sun*. The play had a critically acclaimed initial run of 530 performances and won the 1959 Drama Critics Circle Award for Best American Play. Hansberry was the first African American woman to have a play produced on Broadway, as well as being the first African American, the first woman, and the youngest American at that time to win the Circle Award. The play featured one of the era's most engaging screen and stage stars, Sidney Poitier, who also played the lead role in the 1961 film version. Hansberry's drama was adapted as a musical, *Raisin* (1973), by Hansberry's ex-husband and executor Robert Nemiroff, and has enjoyed two stage revivals (in its original, nonmusical form) in 2004 and 2014.

The play tells the story of the Younger family on Chicago's segregated Southside, just as various members of the black community were attempting to better their lives by a move to more commodious (though at that time all-white) suburbs. Hansberry's own father was a real estate developer who understood the problems caused by racially discriminatory, legally sanctioned, "restrictive covenants," which prevented black families in supposedly integrated northern regions from moving into white neighborhoods throughout the early decades of the twentieth century. He took his own struggle for freedom in housing to the Supreme Court where *Hansberry v. Lee* (1940) was decided in his favor on a technicality and led to little change in the actual housing market in Chicago or elsewhere. Notably, Hansberry's father died in Mexico during an attempt to move his family there for a better life, and Hansberry tells the story of her mother patrolling their hard-won suburban home at night with a loaded gun (*To Be Young*, 51). In the play, "Big Walter" dies before the story opens—also seemingly due to the pressures of making a better life for his family in a racist society. His death has brought an insurance settlement of $10,000, however, that enables the family's move to the suburbs but creates several dilemmas for Walter and his wife, their son Travis, and Walter's sister and mother. They all share cramped quarters in the same inner-city tenement and create "role confusion" for the beleaguered Walter, who longs to act the man in his family but for financial reasons is forced to maintain his wife and son under his mother's roof. Although many have remarked on the ensemble quality of the story, with each character facing her or his own crises and resolutions, in fact it is Walter who grows the most, entering the action intent to grease palms and get ahead in the capitalist system that oppresses him and finding selfhood in radical political resolve at story's end: after losing much of the insurance money through his association with sketchy friends, Walter stands up to a white emissary from their new home's "neighborhood improvement association." Turning down Mr. Lindner's offer to buy the house away from them, Walter leads his family into a more hopeful, however politically fraught, future.

Throughout its life, critics have debated the political import of Hansberry's play, specifically its location on the integrationist–separatist spectrum that confronted black artists throughout the postwar period (see also Matthews, 588). In 1967, the radical black activist Harold Cruse famously denounced Hansberry's play as a "glorified soap opera" (69) and critiqued "the quasi-white orientation through which [Hansberry] visualized the Negro world" (283). To be sure, in the play's opening scene, Walter reads not from Chicago's working-class daily paper, the *Sun-Times*, but the staunchly middle-class, rightward-leaning *Tribune*, and many have raised eyebrows at the expensive pursuits (e.g., horseback riding, photography) of Walter's sister Beneatha. Reviewing the original production for *Commentary*, Gerald Weales anticipated Cruse's complaint but set it in aesthetic terms: "Although Miss Hansberry, the daughter of a wealthy real estate man, may have enjoyed poking fun at a youthful version of herself, the result of putting the child of a rich man into a working-class home is incongruous" ("On the Horizon," 529). More recently, James C. McKelly faulted *Raisin* for its "picture of the African-American family that white culture generally found to be charming, heroic, and hospitable in every respect. Part of the reason for the unparalleled enthusiasm of the play's reception is that it posed no real threat to this dominant culture" (87).

Hansberry herself insisted that *Raisin* was first and foremost a racially inflected drama (see Matthews, 572, n.2; and also Carter, 26). And Amiri Baraka, Cruse's fellow black nationalist (and author of the play *Dutchman*, discussed in Section VI), was once as critical as Cruse but revised his opinion in 1987, on the occasion of a tribute edition of *Raisin in the Sun*: "The Younger family is part of the black majority, and the concerns I once dismissed as 'middle class'—buying a house and moving into 'white folks' neighborhoods' —are actually reflective of the essence of black people's striving and the will to defeat segregation, discrimination, and national oppression" (qtd. in Carter, 25). Kristin Matthews also argues for the radicalism of Hansberry's vision, located in the coalescing of the Younger family members' diverse intentions into a shared determination to move and live as they please: "There is a multiplicity of voices in Walter's words [to Mr. Lindner at the end of the play] …[Their] source and matter emerge from the idealistic community of individuals living in his home, and the result is a small victory of 'social justice'" (567–68).

Lorraine Hansberry was born into a cultured middle-class household on the south side of Chicago in 1935 and developed her race consciousness amidst racial tensions as a high school student. She discovered art—specifically theater—while a student at the University of Wisconsin and was especially influenced by the affirming working-class visions of Sean O'Casey. Arriving in New York after college, she was an activist for civil rights and peace causes, and married the songwriter and social activist Robert Nemiroff in 1953. Steven R. Carter reports that she spent the night before her wedding protesting the Rosenberg executions (11). Following the success of *Raisin*, she completed its screenplay in 1960 and wrote other plays (including *Sidney Brustein, What Use Are Flowers?* [1961–62] and *Les Blancs* [1964, 1970]); the unproduced teleplay *The Drinking Gourd* (1960); and numerous essays, articles, and letters. She and Nemiroff moved to Croton-on-Hudson in 1961, divorced in 1964, but remained close friends and artistic collaborators until her death. In the midst of cancer diagnosis and treatment in 1963, she left the hospital to join an important meeting of African American activists, with Attorney General Robert F. Kennedy, regarding the nation's vital race questions. She died on January 12, 1965 (see Carter, vii–x).

Drama in Dialogue: *Death of a Salesman* and *A Raisin in the Sun*

The conversation between these two classic mid-century works is dynamic and wide ranging. Despite their similar experimental features (i.e., time-bending forays into the past), both are clearly in the realist vein established by Ibsen, Chekhov, and their turn-of-the-twentieth-century brethren in this canon. Criticizing *Raisin*'s somewhat outdated, "naturalist" set—"as murky and crowded and gadgety as the slum apartment it represents" ("On the Horizon," 528)—Gerald Weales even likened it to director David Belasco's wallpaper-and-all reconstruction of the rundown boarding house in Eugene Walter's *The Easiest Way*. Both Hansberry's and Miller's plays echo Chekhov's *Cherry Orchard* theme (with or without the comic undertones) of the beleaguered extended family facing the prospect of group demise at the hands of a society no longer willing to include them and their worldview.

If the traditional melodramatic storyline concluded with the felicitous approach to the altar of a virtuous young woman and a wealthy suitor, whose marriage financially rescues all penurious family members attached to the lucky bride, we can credit Ibsen as one of the innovators who *opened* his story with that fairytale wedding, then followed the happy couple over the threshold to mark how long the festivities would last. In this tradition, both Miller and Hansberry tell the story of families fallen from connubial grace— the marriages are quarrelsome; the children grown, underemployed, and thus trapped in their parents' household; the elders unwanted or at odds with the younger generation. Perhaps the most modern aspect of both these works is the profound ironizing of a classic melodramatic element—the boon windfall that arrives in the form of a recovered deed, a well-timed inheritance, or, as above, a marriageable millionaire. In both Miller's and Hansberry's plays, the money arrives, but at what cost? How is it to be spent, and is it ever enough? We recall that in *A Doll's House*, the marriage of Nora and Torvald foundered on the shoals of financial insolvency, and a key theme engaging modern dramatists since then has regarded the damage done to all the hallmark romantic virtues—love, honor, fidelity, and so on—when the bank account runs dry. *Salesman* and *Raisin* provide their protagonists with the windfall that might have rescued Nora in an earlier era but that now bleakly equals an entire life of undercompensated sacrifice and causes its beneficiaries no end of interpersonal conflict and ethical uncertainty.

Many commentators on *A Raisin in the Sun*—including Hansberry herself— have noted the resemblance between Hansberry's Civil Rights–era play and Miller's postwar forerunner; she echoed Miller's "Tragedy and the Common Man," when she asserted that "the most ordinary human being … has within him elements of profundity, of profound anguish. You don't have to go to the kings and queens of the earth—I think the Greeks and Elizabethans did this because it was a logical concept—but every human being is in enormous conflict about something" (qtd. in Carter, 26). Christopher Bigsby referred to Hansberry's protagonist Walter Lee Younger as a "black Willy Loman, self-deceiving and self-destructive" (qtd. in McKelly, 87), and Steven R. Carter regards Hansberry's play has having "the same visionary force as Miller's *Death of a Salesman*" (26). Thomas P. Adler compared the sun-starved potted plant carried to their new home by Mama in *Raisin* with Willy's garden, which will never see the light of day, in *Salesman* (*American Drama*, 187). Finally, Weales remarked in his review, "Walter Lee's difficulty … is that he has accepted the American myth of success at its face value, that he is trapped, as Willy Loman was trapped, by a false dream" (529). Hansberry later cited this piece as the only original write-up to establish this important connection ("Willy Loman," 7).

In a remarkable essay written for the *Village Voice* in August 1959, "Willy Loman, Walter Younger, and He Who Must Live," Hansberry indicates "a simple line of descent between Walter Lee Younger and the last great hero in American drama to also *accept* the values of his culture, Willy Loman" (7). She is less than surprised, however, that few reviewers have hit on the resemblance, due to the white-minded tendency to categorize Walter Lee as "an exotic" for his audacious dreams regarding liquor store ownership and his refusal to be at home with the poverty and degradation that defines the "catfish row" stereotype. If Willy is entirely recognizable, says Hansberry, "Walter Lee Younger jumped out at us from a play about a largely unknown world" (8). By contrast, Hansberry insists that the important difference is less their belonging to different worlds—as there is nothing so exotic about Walter's ambitions after all—than the salient fact that Willy must die at the end of his story, whereas Walter chooses life: unlike Willy, Walter "draw[s] on the strength of an incredible people who, historically, have simply refused to give up" (8). Despite the many achievements of postwar America, Willy's failure and suicide, Hansberry attests, belong to the current "vogue of despair" (8) perpetuated by Miller, absurdist playwrights, and existentialist intellectuals. She critiqued such attitudes in her landmark address to a group of young black writers in 1959, "The Negro Writer and His Roots" and a later article, "On Arthur Miller, Marilyn Monroe, and 'Guilt'" (1964). Considering the dramatic tendencies toward absurdism, violence, and despair characterizing many white-authored dramas in the wake of Beckett's arrival, Hansberry suggests that by contrast, the black community represented in Hansberry's play cannot afford such fashionable intellectual luxuries, that "*the weight and power of their current social temperament intrudes upon and affects* [Walter Lee], *and it is, at that moment, at least, gloriously and rigidly affirmative*" ("Willy Loman," 8).

As valid as Hansberry's distinction is, in fact *Raisin* includes tragic aspects that connect it to Miller's play. Specifically, two children—Mama Lena's infant son, who died of treatable illness in the distant past, and the pregnancy that Walter's wife, Ruth, considers aborting early in the story—are positioned as victims of an uncaring society and the stark poverty resulting from it. Even more significant is the death of Mama's husband, Big Walter, in the story's prehistory; just as Miller's audience pondered whether Willy Loman took his own life or whether he was done in by desperation and despair, so Steven R. Carter describes Big Walter's death by natural causes in distinctly Lomanesque terms: "an unconsciously calculated form of protracted suicide … And if suicide is not intended, even unconsciously, it nevertheless becomes the inevitable result of pushing oneself too hard too long in the attempt to provide for one's family, while ensuring that they will get more after one's death. (Big Walter's death is also, in another sense, systematic murder.)" (23).

Though critics have understandably compared Willy Loman and Walter Lee as two characters misguidedly subscribing to the capitalist value system that oppresses them, the parallels between Willy and Big Walter are equally significant—including the generational parallel and the death that elicits the insurance payment. In both plays, the money creates more problems than it solves: in Miller's, Willy's wife, Linda, pays off the mortgage but goes home to an empty house; his younger son, Happy, has just the inspiration (and modicum of financial incentive) he needs to continue pursuing his father's benighted dreams. In Hansberry's play, Mama makes a down payment on a house in an all-white neighborhood, causing consternation among her children and a scramble for the remainder of the proceeds between Walter, who wants to open a liquor store, and his sister Beneatha, who wants to go to medical school. As we map the Loman family dynamic onto the Younger household, Walter Lee, in the beginning of the play, is readable as the counterpart of the ironically nicknamed Happy, the grown son whose father's legacy has, if anything, encouraged his journey down the wrong path. Walter Lee then grows into the self-aware status of Biff, and both men demonstrate their maturation by leaving the family home. (Similarly, younger Beneatha is another Biff counterpart, with her own foibles and self-interest but who is better-focused and more committed to honest identity formation throughout the story.) In this light, Hansberry seems interested—as was Ibsen, following the bride and groom into the bower—to ask of Miller's play, what then? How does blind faith in postwar prosperity settle on the shoulders of the younger, seemingly more enlightened generation once the fathers have learned from, and died for, their shortcomings?

If by the end of the play Walter succeeds—where both Willy and likely Happy fail—in shaking off the ideological traces that have kept him in thrall to the hollow goal of quick riches through petty graft and business schemes, it is hardly the case that his heroically achieved race- and class-consciousness spell the end of the Younger family's troubles. Though the play ends with the Youngers proudly packing their belongings for the move, the original version notably ended with the family in their new suburban home, armed against bullets and brickbats hurled through the windows by hostile neighbors. Even in the much more upbeat final version, the Youngers have surely traded one set of worries for another even more deadly one. Yet harking back to Miller's prescription for the common man's attainment of "tragic [or heroic] stature" through his "total questioning of what has previously been unquestioned," we see that Hansberry's Walter Lee Younger is the "younger" ideal of Miller's common man and that—although Hansberry bars her audience from bearing witness—tragedy may yet be his outcome. Regardless of whether Walter

Lee and his family physically survive their transition to Cylbourne Park, Hansberry's play presents not the happy ending characterizing the melodramatic fairytale, but the affirming, however more dangerous choice made— an ennobling bid for dignity and a family's willingness to risk their lives in achievement of same. Miller said that such tragic action should not depress its audience but be a source of "optimism," eliciting as it does "the onlooker's brightest opinions of the human animal" ("Tragedy," 3). Hansberry's play is equally effective in guiding an audience to such realization.

Part VI

Albee, Others, and the American Absurdist Tradition (1959–1980)

Though he famously denied the association, the influence of the Irish-born master dramatist Samuel Beckett on the career of the first major playwright of the American contemporary era, Edward Albee, is plain. Often linked with his European contemporaries Eugene Ionesco and Jean Genet, it is Beckett who has most effectively provided the American theater scene its transformative encounter with the theater of the absurd, and his deservedly renowned *Endgame* (1957) is the Transatlantic Touchstone for this section therefore. Absurdist theater comprised the uniquely postwar (indeed post-nuclear) dramatic response to a humanity that many left-wing intellectuals were sure had come unhinged, had sacrificed its last semblance of commitment to self and other in the catastrophic instances of the Holocaust, Hiroshima, and Nagasaki; the Vietnam War; and the many assassinations, riots, and revolts of the late 1960s. Beckett's absurdism confronted its audience with a bleak, ruined setting; equally deteriorated and deranged (though often darkly comic and clownish) characters; and stringent mockery of any pretense to hope, survival, or fellow-feeling. In *Waiting for Godot* (1953), the Chaplinesque tramps, Vladimir and Estragon, famously await "Godot"—widely interpreted as a god figure—who never arrives, then endlessly insist to each other that they both "go," though neither ever does. Beckett's influence on Albee's off-Broadway contemporary Jack Gelber is clear in *The Connection* (1959), in which a group of heroin addicts wait endlessly for their dealer to arrive, panhandle the audience during intermission, and otherwise threaten the conventions of dramatic realism. Perhaps no transatlantic influence is more illustratively Americanized than in the shift from Beckett's "God" to Gelber's heroin dealer; as throughout the history reviewed here, the American dramatist puts his distinctively earthy, plebian, and shocking spin on the philosophical, cosmological themes of his European predecessors.

Much of Albee's work continues in this dark-comic register and often stages the violence so ominously referenced in the works of Beckett; his remarkable one-act drama *The Zoo Story* (1959) concludes with a knife suicide, and dead, dismembered, or nonexistent children are frequent themes, observed by critics as related to Albee's own adoptive status and unhappy childhood (see Price, and also Bigsby, *Modern American Drama*, 149). At the end of his more recent *The Goat; or, Who Is Sylvia?* (2002), Stevie decapitates and drags out the body of the title character in a dramatic late moment, in revenge against her husband, who has confessed to having had sex with and even fallen in love with Sylvia, the goat. Albee enjoyed great success early in his career (*The Zoo Story, Who's Afraid of Virginia Woolf?*[1962], and his Pulitzer Prize–winning *A Delicate Balance* [1966]); he weathered many critically and commercially failed productions in the 1970s and 1980s, and revived his reputation more recently with *Three Tall Women* (1991; based on his adoptive mother), *The Play About the Baby* (1998), and *The Goat*. Although Bigsby calls *The Zoo Story* "the most impressive debut ever made by an American dramatist" (*Modern American Drama*, 129), he observes also that "[f]rom the perspective of the 1990s [before his later successful works appeared], Albee's career has been a disappointing one…. His tone became petulant, his language pedantic, his characters pure constructs drained of function and conviction" (*Modern American Drama*, 126). Steven Price, however, describes "the extraordinary creative renaissance" that began with the three later plays, the last of "which bears comparison with his best work" (252; see also Roudané, "Plays," 336).

In *The Zoo Story*, Jerry is an offbeat loner with a room in a seedy boarding house on New York's Upper West Side. One Sunday afternoon, he approaches the conventionally middle-class Peter on a bench in Central Park, dragging him into their fateful encounter with his insistent announcement that "I've been to the zoo. I said, I've been to the zoo. MISTER, I'VE BEEN TO THE ZOO!" Peter, seeking every Sunday a few hours' respite from his stultifying home life, resents Jerry's intrusion into his private time and even onto "his" park bench, and is ultimately horrified by Jerry's unstable rants, the loneliness and degradation he confesses, and the knife that Jerry forces him to hold while Jerry runs himself through in the play's final moments. As Price remarks, "Jerry brings the shock of the new, breaking without warning into Peter's too-settled existence, anticipating all those figures in Albee's plays—babies, adoptees, fictional creatures, or foundlings—whose arrival in the present, like Albee's on the New York stage, seems unencumbered by the past" (248). In the hugely successful follow-up, *Who's Afraid of Virginia Woolf?*, George is a bitter, aging professor, married to the daughter of the president of the backwater college where he has squandered his career; the couple drink heavily and bicker incessantly, even in the presence of two after-hours guests, a junior faculty member and his timid wife. After a grueling night of insults, betrayals, and ruinously revealed secrets, shocking violence is again in store, this time in the symbolic "murder" of George and Martha's son at the hands of George, who reveals to the younger couple that in fact there never was any boy, that the elder couple's marriage has been held together by the lie they tell each other regarding his birth and life. Widely regarded as deserving the Pulitzer that year, it was considered by an especially puritanical member of the selection board to be "a filthy play" (qtd. in Price, 251) and passed over. Albee's later *A Delicate Balance* received the recognition instead as a "belated apology for the fiasco over" *Virginia Woolf* (Price, 251). Albee's *Three Tall Women* again challenges realist conventions by transforming three separate characters (A, age 90; B, 52; and C, 26) in Act I into early, middle, and late versions of the same character thereafter. In the later scenes, the two older versions of this woman "join forces in opposition to C" (Roudané, "Plays," 337), who is yet to experience the disappointment, betrayal, and infirmity that constitute life. Described by Albee as "an exorcism" (qtd. in Roudané, "Plays," 337) of emotions related to his vigorous though unfeeling adoptive mother, it was hailed by critics and audiences for its honesty and intensity, and won Albee another Pulitzer in 1994.

In general, the 1960s was a graphic decade in American drama, with copious violence and political conflict, nudity and sexual themes, and darkly acerbic comedy. It was also the decade during which Broadway lost its status as the only or ultimate venue for many dramatic works regarded as important if not canonical today. As explained by Christopher Innes et al., "Broadway [has become] a showcase theater. It is a place where musicals, classic revivals or guaranteed contemporary sensations animate the stage" (ix). As these authors observe, plays by major American dramatists may receive a Broadway debut if a major entertainment star, such as Madonna in David Mamet's *Speed-the-Plow* (1988) or Mos Def in Suzan-Lori Parkes's *Topdog/Underdog* (2002) play a leading role. Or a play with proven success in a regional theater may convince nervous investors to roll the dice with an ever more expensive Broadway mounting. As Mel Gussow observes, the off-Broadway movement that began in the mid-1950s, and has flourished (along with its even less commercialized offshoot, off-off-Broadway) since that time, has functioned as another proving ground for Broadway-worthy productions. Just as vitally, it has hosted the work of important, if less commercially successful, dramatists who never made a break for the Great White Way (see Gussow, "Off and Off-Off-Broadway," 196; also Aronson, 109,138–40; and Maslon, 191–92). The first "Obie" Awards, bestowed by the *Village Voice* for excellence in off-Broadway theater work, were given in 1956.

Serious if noncommercial plays from this period include Arthur Kopit's *Oh Dad, Poor Dad, Mamma's Hung You in the Closet and I'm Feeling So Sad* (1961), which ran for only 47 performances at the Morosco in 1963 but has attained cult status since then. Amiri Baraka's Obie Award–winning *Dutchman* (1964) narrates the seduction, betrayal, and murder of Clay, an intellectual young black man, at the hands of a flirtatious white woman named Lula, who then orchestrates a group of racist subway riders to dispose of the body. Adrienne Kennedy's *Funnyhouse of a Negro* (1964) includes themes of suicide and child abuse, dark comedy, and formal experimentation, with the main character Sarah taking on several identities, including the Duchess of Hapsburg and Patrice Lumumba (see Schlueter, 321–22; and Olsen, 232–33). That same year, Megan Terry's *Ex-Miss Copper Queen on a Set of Pills* (1964) "present[ed] a … confused young woman, caught, without resources, between her sense of herself as a former Midwest beauty queen and that of her current drug-addicted life as a prostitute on the streets of New York" (Schlueter, 322); Terry is also credited with the first rock musical, *Viet Rock* (1966). Kenneth H. Brown's violent military drama *The Brig* (1963) was staged successfully by Judith Malina and Julian Beck's Greenwich Village Living Theater collective (as was Gelber's *The Connection* two years before).

Also active on the 1960s alternative theater scene was Lanford Wilson, who wrote numerous short plays for Caffè Cino early in the decade, then his first full-length play, *Balm in Gilead* (1965), the story of failed love among junkies and prostitutes at a rundown urban diner, for Ellen Stewart's La MaMa Experimental Theater. Wilson helped found the Circle Repertory Company and scored several hits in succeeding decades, including *The Hot l Baltimore* (1973; later a TV series of the same name), *The Fifth of July* (1978), *Talley's Folly* (1979), and *Burn This* (1987). William Hanley's *Slow Dance on the Killing Ground* (1964) concerns three demographically diverse, desperate characters who find themselves in a convenience store in a rough part of town, "engag[ing] in a 'slow dance' filled with tension, bitterness, and regret, immersed in a quagmire without any means of escape" (Olsen, 232). Howard Sackler's *The Great White Hope* (1967) tells a racially charged story about the African American heavyweight champion Jack Johnson and his long, bitter struggle for international recognition. David Rabe wrote four important Vietnam plays in this period, based on his own experience as a draftee working at an Army hospital in Long Binh in 1966: *The Basic Training of Pavlo Hummel* (1971); the dark-comic and violent, Tony Award–winning *Sticks and Bones* (1971); *The Orphan* (1973); and the widely anthologized, also violent *Streamers* (1976). Joseph Papp, director of the New York Shakespeare Festival and the Public Theater, and another hugely influential figure in the off-Broadway scene from the mid-1960s until his death in 1991, sponsored many of Rabe's early works. Rabe is known also for his gritty tale of a go-go dancer, *In the Boom Boom Room* (1973), and later *Hurly Burly* (1985), a dark comedy about four low-level Hollywood hangers-on who engage in profuse self- and other-destructive behaviors, including cocaine binging and violence toward women, until the main character, Eddie, reaches an epiphany, thanks to the arrival of the waif, Donna.

The hugely influential, multi-Obie Award–winning Cuban American playwright Maria Irene Fornés has been an active presence in New York's alternative theater scene since the early 1960s. She founded and directed the Hispanic Writers-in-Residence Workshop for INTAR (International Arts Relations) from 1981 to 1995, and as a dramatist "her greatest critical success" (Sofer, 444) was *Fefu and Her Friends* (1977). In this uniquely structured work, hailed by feminists since its inception, eight female friends gather at a country house in 1935 to plan a charity event. Their host Stephany ("Fefu" of the title) presides over the proceedings in Parts 1 and 3; Part 2, in the original production at New York's Theater Strategy, broke out into four separate scenes taking place in the home's kitchen, a bedroom, study, and lawn, staged four times in succession as parts of the audience viewed each scene on location throughout the theater. Scott T. Cummings observes of this text, "Its unorthodox, provocative, and joyous celebration of women being together as women made it a landmark in feminist drama and one of the most important plays of the twentieth century" ("Maria Irene Fornés," 26; see also *Maria Irene Fornés*, 70–73). In 1967, the musical *Hair* debuted off-Broadway at Papp's Public Theater, moving to Broadway a year later, with its notorious nude scene and generally shocking countercultural response to the wholesome qualities of most Broadway musical fare. Mart Crowley's *The Boys in the Band* (1968) introduced straight theatergoers to dramatic and tragic gay themes, and Charles Ludlam's Ridiculous Theater Company surprised and engaged downtown audiences with its campy parodies. Lighter comic hits from that decade include Herb Gardner's *A Thousand Clowns* (1962), Joseph Stein's *Enter Laughing* (1963), the socially relevant plays of Murray Schisgal (*The Typists* [1963]; *The Tiger* [1963]; and most famously, *Luv* [1964]), and the zany escapades of Woody Allen (*Don't Drink the Water* [1966] and *Play it Again, Sam* [1969]).

One monumental counterpoint to the experimentalism and alternative theater making of the 1960s is the career of Neil Simon, whose half-century dominance of the Broadway comedy scene began at that time with *Come Blow Your Horn* (1961), *Barefoot in the Park* (1963), *The Odd Couple* (1965), *Plaza Suite* (1968), and *The Last of the Red Hot Lovers* (1969). Schlueter regards

Simon as "a master of the running gag, the circular joke, and the witty one-liner....[A]t one point in the sixties, four of his plays were in simultaneous runs on Broadway" (325). Bigsby adds, "Though now [even] his plays tend to open elsewhere in the country, he is the quintessential Broadway writer, highly skillful and creating plays which probe anxieties in such a way as to cauterize the wounds which he momentarily opens.... This is Woody Allen without the angst" (*Modern American Drama*, 160).

John Guare's intelligent, serious-minded farce satires target the American obsession with celebrity, wealth, and inordinate faith in the common man's ability to strike it big—in Hollywood, on Broadway, or through infamous violent crimes (see Plunka, "John Guare"; and Urban). His style blends naturalism with surrealism; Bigsby remarks that "he has been called the Jackson Pollock of playwrights" (*Contemporary American Playwrights*, 1) and in Guare's own words, his goal is to "get the play out of the kitchen sink and hurl it into the Niagara Falls of life" (qtd. in Bigsby, *Contemporary American Playwrights*, 46). His major works include *The House of Blue Leaves* (1971), *Rich and Famous* (1976), *Landscape of the Body* (1977), *Bosoms and Neglect*, (1979), and *Six Degrees of Separation* (1990), a career-defining text for many of Guare's admirers. His quintessential protagonist from the early work manifests in both Artie Shaughnessy of *Blue Leaves* and Bing Ringling of *Rich and Famous*—both deluded as to the nature of their artistic talent, egged on by ultimately self-serving well-wishers, and awakened to realty by the devastating betrayal of a childhood friend who has achieved enviable success. In *Six Degrees*, Ouisa and Flan Kittredge have great wealth as Upper East Side art dealers but are lured by a prospective brush with celebrity—Sidney Poitier, whose aura includes both Hollywood glamour and political pioneering—when a con man posing as Poitier's son promises them a role in his father's film version of *Cats* and otherwise inserts himself into their elegant home and guilty consciences. The play won the Drama Critics Circle Award for 1991.

Sam Shepard is a major figure in this era, equal in stature to and mentored in his youth by the canonical Albee. He began, as have many others, in lower Manhattan's alternative theater scene and has enjoyed much success in New York, on the West Coast, and in the United Kingdom since his first plays in the mid-1960s. Shepard has a widely recognized set of signature themes: familial discord of Oedipal intensity with neglectful or abusive fathers, ineffectual mothers, siblings or spouses at each other's throats, and the sordid psychological and sexual detritus of dysfunctional lives lived under too-small roofs (or in disorienting evacuated spaces), unable to escape each other's company. Too, Shepard dwells on the myth of the American West, the death of the cowboy and the rugged individualism he represented—with history, politics, and Hollywood all to blame for his demise—and the direction America now takes in a blind, drunken, desperate search for its next habitable mythos. As with Albee, much of his work springs from the autobiographical: raised on a series of military bases by a drunk, abusive father, Shepard eventually settled with his family on a ranch in Duarte, California, and it is in this region that Shepard himself settled after stints in New York and the UK and where he has premiered many of his plays, specifically at the Magic Theater in San Francisco. Shepard has enjoyed simultaneous careers as a rock musician and an Oscar-nominated actor (cast often as the cowboy type idolized in his dramatic texts) and has shifted from a libertarian-style statement in earlier plays (see Wade, 295) to an antiwar, anti-jingoism stance in more recent plays (e.g., *States of Shock* [1991] and *The God of Hell* [2004]) that aligns more with the Left.

His key works of the 1970s and 1980s are a trilogy of family-themed dramas beginning with *The Curse of the Starving Class* (1977), the Pulitzer Prize–winning *Buried Child* (1978), and *True West* (1980). Each of these is marked by realistically detailed sets, dark humor, bizarre or mysterious occurrences in the midst of quotidian family proceedings, and threatened or explicit violence (see also Roudané, "Plays," 347–53). *Curse* regards two culpable parents and their largely victimized adolescent children; the elders each plan to sell off the family farm, and Weston (the father) drinks, verbally abuses his children, and ultimately flees the premises when his criminal associates threaten physical harm. The curse is figured in this impoverished family's inability to prosper or even sustain each other, as well as daughter Emma's menstrual onset, for which she blames her mother. *Buried Child*'s dysfunctional crew is headed by Dodge and Halie, parents to three sons: one killed during a military stint; one missing a leg due to a chainsaw accident; and the third, Tilden, psychologically fragile and guilty of an incestuous union with his mother, leading to the birth and murder of the title character. Tilden is also father to Vince, who arrives mid-story with his girlfriend, Shelly, a breath of vitality from the outside who successfully escapes the family's corrupting influence by play's end; Vince, however, is not so lucky—settling into the couch where his now-dead grandfather has been ensconced throughout, and into his family's heinous morass.

True West is celebrated for its comic characters and situations and centers on the destructive relationship between two brothers: Austin, a successful Hollywood screenwriter, and Lee, an aimless drifter and petty criminal ten years his senior. As the brothers circle each other in the home of their absent mother, their conflict is interrupted by the arrival of Saul Kimmer, a Hollywood producer whom Lee persuades to pursue his own version of a movie Western instead of the accomplished Austin's. As the brothers collaborate on a successful script, they soon begin to switch roles, then return to verbal abuse and at last engage in physical violence. Their mother's last-act return to the homestead results in more comic upheaval as well as her ominous, ultra-Shepardian utterance, "I don't recognize it [her home? Her life?] at all" (see Roudané, "Plays," 353). Also well regarded in this period are *The Tooth of Crime* (1972), staging the Oedipal conflict between an aging and an up-and-coming rock musician; *Fool for Love* (1983), about the incestuous affair between half-siblings who both adore and abuse each other; and *A Lie of the Mind* (1985), an involved and violent tale of Faulknerian scale, about an abusive husband and his traumatized wife, their extended families, and the vengeance wreaked by one clan on the other. In addition to his Pulitzer for *Buried Child*, eleven of Shepard's plays have won Obie Awards, and he has received numerous other recognitions.

This section discusses key works from the post-WWII period, many revealing the influence of Beckett and a more generalized interest in frank sexuality and violence, per the broader cultural trends of the period.

A Transatlantic Touchstone: *Endgame* (1957)

Samuel Beckett (1906–1989)

In 1960, the director and critic Martin Esslin famously coined the term "theater of the absurd" to delineate the genre newly developed by diversely European-born and -schooled but ultimately French-identified playwrights of the period, including the Irish Samuel Beckett along with Eugène Ionesco and Arthur Adamov. The theater was European first and foremost, as it responded so thoroughly (like its brother movement, existentialism) to the traumas and losses of World War II, including the massive bombings in London, Dresden, and across Europe during the conflict; the nightmare of the Holocaust; and the great waves of displacement, disorder, and starvation that engulfed European survivors in immediate aftermath. Beckett received the *Croix de Guerre* and the *Médaille de la Résistance* for his work in the French Resistance, but he was silent or dismissive about his wartime heroics in later life (Knowlson, 303–5) and seems to have approached his postwar work for the theater with the mindset that "resistance" to life's grim inevitabilities was a waste of energy. Per Esslin, absurdist theater conveys not only "the futility and pointlessness of human effort" but "the … impossibility of human communication" and the "fundamentally tragic view of human experience" (5).

Absurdist theater pieces, with their puzzling action (if "plot" is too strong a word) and clownish, though also often direly injured or depleted, mechanically moving characters, clearly responded to the crises of their age: "the decline of religious faith, the destruction of the belief in automatic social or biological progress, the discovery of vast areas of irrational and unconscious forces within the human psyche, the loss of a sense of control over rational human development in an age of totalitarianism and weapons of mass destruction" (Esslin, 6). It is remarkable that in the period (1950–1961) during which the American William Inge took Broadway and then Hollywood by storm with his plays and screenplays diagnosing post-WWII sexual neuroses, Beckett took a very different pulse, in a markedly different, much more adversely war-affected social context, with *Waiting for Godot* (1952), *Endgame* (1957), *Krapp's Last Tape* (1958), and *Happy Days* (1961). The first two of these were originally written in French, then later translated by Beckett into English; the last two were written originally in English. Though English audiences did not know what to make of the earliest plays, and many American theatergoers have never known how to receive Beckett's work with anything other than confusion and fear,[1] he has been celebrated on the English-speaking stage since early on, and his influence on major American dramatists is broadly in evidence to this day. Drama critics (e.g., Wertheim, *Dramatic Art*, xii) regularly use the term "son of Sam" when tracing the line between Beckett and Edward Albee, Sam Shepard, David Mamet, the British Harold Pinter, the South African Athol Fugard, and many others. Surely various contemporary female playwrights such as Maria Irene Fornés and Suzan-Lori Parks, both of whom claim Beckett as an influence; Sarah Ruhl; and the British Caryl Churchill deserve the designation "daughters of Sam" in their own right.

Esslin traces the influence of earlier movements on absurdism, singling out Brecht's "theater of alienation" and "Artaud's "theater of cruelty," but also comic forms as diverse as Rabelais, Chaplin, and the Marx Brothers and experimental texts such as Joyce's *Finnegans Wake*. The expressionist dramatists of

---

[1] Biographer James Knowlson relates the disaster that was the US premiere of *Waiting for Godot* in, of all places, the Coconut Grove Playhouse in Miami in January 1956, where it had been billed, absurdly, as "the laugh hit of two continents": "It was a fiasco… the audience left in droves at the intermission" (378). Producer Michael Myerberg blamed director Alan Schneider for his mishandling of comedian Bert Lahr in the role of Estragon but later himself admitted, "In casting Bert Lahr and Tom Ewell I created the wrong impression about the play. Both actors were too well known in certain types of performance. The audience thought they were going to see Lahr and Ewell cut loose in a lot of capers. They expected a farcical comedy, which *Waiting for Godot*, of course, is not" (qtd. in Knowlson, 378).

the early twentieth century and the proto-absurdism of Luigi Pirandello are also clear forerunners. Regarding its debt to Brecht, Esslin argues that absurdism realized ideas that Brecht himself never did. To enable its audience to critical perspective and radical self-reflection, Brecht's "epic theater" sought to block all emotional identification with characters. As Esslin said of the absurdist theater experience, "It is impossible to identify oneself with characters one does not understand or whose motives remain a closed book.... Emotional identification with the characters is replaced by a puzzled, critical attention ... [and] eventually spectators are brought face to face with the irrational side of their existence" (5). As Brecht always proponed the didactic function of theater, leading the audience to new insight enabling social change, absurdist theater likewise confronts complacent audiences with disturbing truths, although Beckett would likely reject Brecht's view that such understanding can change anything.

Endgame is very plainly post-apocalyptic and likely specifically post-nuclear, in setting, action, character, and tone. Hamm and his servant, Clov, along with Hamm's "accursed progenitors" (9), Nagg and Nell, seem prevented from venturing past the door of their bare, tanklike enclosure, so "corpsed" (30) is the outside environment, as would be the case following nuclear war. The food source is close to depleted, and Hamm is desperately injured: his eyes bleed on a nightly basis, and he cannot get up from the chair that Clov occasionally wheels to the windows so that he "can feel the [nonexistent] light on [his] face" (62). He waits in anguish for a painkiller that, when at last it is time to take one, he learns has been used up. Despite these dire circumstances, the play opens with Clov comically meaning, always forgetting, then finally remembering to drag a stepladder from one window to the next in a futile search for signs of life. He has a "brief laugh" (1) at what he sees outside each window and then again when he removes the sheeting from two ashcans where Hamm stashes his elderly, legless parents and has a look inside. *Endgame* is a perfect, and perfectly unnerving, mix of slapstick and apocalyptic; because the characters cannot move, leave, love, alleviate each other's suffering or even evidently find the nerve to do themselves in, all there is left are absurd bits of business and repartee.

The last sheet Clov removes reveals Hamm himself, whose first line, "Me— (he yawns)—to play" (2)—comments on the play's English-translation title, "endgame," a chess term describing the game's final action, with very few pieces left on the board; very few moves that each is allowed to make; and the king, protected in earlier phases, now able to take center-board and move into attack mode. Hamm is clearly the king figure in this beleaguered vestige of a kingdom; Clov, the pawn, with traditionally the most mobility in a chess game, is the only character with any mobility, however awkward and painful that may be. Hamm makes Clov push his chair toward the walls and windows but always insists that his chair be perfectly centered when it is time to go back:

HAMM:	Am I right in the center?
CLOV:	I'll measure it.
HAMM:	More or less! More or less! … I'm more or less in the center?
CLOV:	I'd say so.
HAMM:	You'd say so! Put me right in the center!
CLOV:	I'll go and get the tape.
HAMM:	Roughly! Roughly! (26–27)

Ruby Cohn observes that Hamm in his kingly role is the play's main conduit to the tragic (and certainly the Shakespearian). When Hamm asks, "Can there be misery—(he yawns)—loftier than mine?" (2), "the yawn undercuts the tragic tone, but the tragic tone is there to be undercut. In traditional tragedy lofty misery distinguishes the hero, and his eloquent suffering commands center stage" (Cohn, *Just Play*, 60–61). Like a Lear whose entire world has turned into blasted heath, or a Prospero with his Caliban at the end of long, futile attempt to get off their shipwreck island, Hamm, says Cohn, must "be recognized as the remains of a tragic hero, and Clov a comic servant" (*Just Play*, 61). Though utterly dependent on Clov, Hamm is abrasive and controlling of Clov's physical movements and emotional state of mind; Clov threatens to leave more than once, and in yet another echo of Ibsen renounces his servant's role (even if never actually going) in the final scene. By then Hamm's mother Nell has been rescued from her misery by death, with her grieving spouse Nagg seemingly soon to follow; Hamm is center-stage with only his bloody handkerchief—his reliable "old stancher!" (84)—to dry is tears and/or sop the blood.

One more thing these characters have left, as they exhaust their food and medicine and wait for death, are thoughts of the past. As the elder generation, Nagg and Nell reminisce fondly, even when the memory is grim. Their having "lost [their] shanks" in a bicycling accident in the Ardennes recalls not only personal tragedy but the dreadful large-scale losses incurred by all parties involved in the Battle of Ardennes at the opening of World War I; as they relive the incident "they laugh heartily" (16). They are loathed by Hamm, evidently for having brought him into the world; he never changes the sand they live and shed their waste in and orders Clov to "bottle them" (24) when he tires of their stories and pleas. Hamm, however, is just as avid a reminiscer and raconteur;

if "ah, yesterday!" is the mantra of the older couple, Hamm and Clov wring maximum accusation, hope, and regret out of "once" (e.g., 6). Nagg and Nell share a poignant affection and concern for each other that is powerless to lessen their suffering and is snuffed out for good at the death of Nell.

Beckett once told an interviewer that he chose Nell as a character name because her death is itself the "death knell" of the pathetic remnants of humanity lingering on in the story. Others have also observed the hammer/nail references in the names: Hamm being the root of "hammer" and Clov being close to the French *clou* ("nail"). "Nagg" is close to German *nagel* (also "nail"), and Nell is a cognate in English. As Lee A. Jacobus observes, "The characters thus seem equipped to rebuild their society, but they refuse to do so. By using English, French, and German versions of *nail* Beckett involves the principal combatants of modern European wars" (1048). Certainly such political allegory might contribute to the playwright's own sense that *Endgame* was "dark as ink" (Brater, *Essential Samuel Beckett*, 78); of all his plays, it was also "the one [he] disliked the least" (Brater, *Essential Samuel Beckett*, 85). Throughout *Endgame*, the sense of time passing, the story and its players "getting on" (9) and ending both their revels and miseries as they inch toward night and death, is equaled by the pervasive sense that all are simply trapped forever in an unbearable now. In the words of interviewer Lawrence Shainberg, "It was always here, 'in the clash,' as [Beckett] put it to me once, 'between can't and must' that [Beckett] took his stand." As Enoch Brater adds, "There is, for audience, as well as player, simply no exit" (*Essential Samuel Beckett*, 81).

The Zoo Story (1959)

Edward Albee (1928–)

The Zoo Story was Edward Albee's first play; it was originally denied a Broadway production so premiered instead in 1959 at the Schiller Theater in West Berlin on a double bill with Beckett's *Krapp's Last Tape*, both having been written the year before. Back in the United States, this same program premiered off-Broadway at the Provincetown Playhouse; it ran for 582 performances, and Albee's play won four Obie Awards that year. It is fitting that Beckett's third play was booked to play directly in front of Albee's in this original production history, as Beckett clearly opened the way for younger playwrights who challenged audiences with volatile, even violent subject matter. Albee's remarks in this period about Harold Pinter aptly describe his own relationship to the Theater of the Absurd: "[He] could not have written *The*

Caretaker had Samuel Beckett not existed, but Pinter is, nonetheless, moving in his own direction" ("Which Theater," 66). In *The Zoo Story*, Peter endures the life of empty, static waiting that befalls the figures from Beckett's *Waiting for Godot, Endgame*, and many other works, while Jerry exhibits the clownish, anarchic, but ultimately violent aspect of these same waiting figures' situations. As Hamm, the kingly character, sits while Clov the servant moves about at his behest in *Endgame*, so the same power differential settles on the seated Peter and the rambling Jerry for much of the play. Although advantage is periodically gained and exploited by the mobile figure, at the end of *Endgame*, Clov is ultimately powerless to leave, whereas in *The Zoo Story* Jerry retains power in his own permanent immobilization, his Christlike self-sacrifice at the feet of Peter, which "moves" Peter profoundly and forever.

For a revival/premiere at the Hartford Stage in 2004, Albee wrote a first act to *The Zoo Story* called "Homelife," with the new two-act version titled *Peter and Jerry* but known in current publication and production as *Edward Albee's at Home at the Zoo*. Even before the Hartford commission, Albee had often remarked that he considered *The Zoo Story* uneven in its fleshing out of the Upper West Side drifter Jerry but much less detailed regarding the reserved East Sider Peter. Peter indeed has many fewer lines than Jerry in *The Zoo Story* and is often literally and metaphorically little more than Jerry's straight man. "Homelife" stages the afternoon leading up to Peter's journey to his favorite bench in Central Park; he and his wife, Ann, at her urging, discuss their married life as lacking as far as Ann is concerned, especially in their failure to share troubles with each other and in the bedroom, where Ann wants sex of a more "animal" nature. Though she herself is so habituated to playing it safe that she is considering a preemptive double mastectomy, she ends the scene by slapping Peter across the face before kissing him—a precursor to the physical challenge Peter will face at the end of *The Zoo Story*. Since inception of this "prequel" act, Albee has forbidden any professional theater company to stage *The Zoo Story* in its original one-act form, but in fact "Homelife" has not met with audience or critical favor in any measure comparable to the original text. In her review for the *New York Times*, Jane Gordon notes, "We learn that [Peter and Ann] are formal with one another, careful with hurt feelings, steady but stifled. And we learn that they made a pact early on that marriage would be a safety net, not an exploration. But this is often laborious learning" (CT5). Gordon adds that "the weaker 'Homelife' falters before the power of 'Zoo Story'" and represents an "attempt to needlessly fix a flaw.... Besides, small flaws to a playwright are typically all but invisible to an audience willing to forgive idiosyncrasies for tight dialogue, a challenging premise and an unsettling ending. 'Homelife' has none of those" (CT5).

The focus here will be on the role *The Zoo Story* has played as Albee's entrée to the late-1950s/early 1960s stage context and as a harbinger of much provocative, quite literally visceral drama in this period. Of course life itself got more sexual, violent, unpredictable, and inexplicable as the 1960s wore on, and *The Zoo Story* stands at the threshold of a decade that it forecasts (and instigates) with remarkable accuracy. Its appearance marked the last moment in US history when a man of such obviously meager means as Jerry could approach a man such as Peter on his home turf (New York's still entirely exclusive and forbidding Upper East Side) and not risk being arrested or even shot; though today, the well-to-do have commandeered all but the most notorious precincts of poverty in the five boroughs in the late 1950s, the rich and the poor roughly divided the city down its center and were therefore much more evenly matched when they met: Central Park was the DMZ (too sprawling and meandering to be very tightly policed) separating the ritzy, conservative Upper East Side from the bohemian, eclectic but downtrodden and dingy Upper West Side. A modern New Yorker would hardly recognize Jerry's description of his squalid Upper West Side environs, now as exclusive as most other Manhattan neighborhoods:

> [O]ne of my walls is made of beaverboard; this beaverboard separates my [laughably small] room from another laughably small room, so I assume the two rooms were once one room, a small room, but not necessarily laughable. The room beyond my beaverboard wall is occupied by a coloured queen [who] has rotten teeth, which is rare; he also has a Japanese kimono, which is also pretty rare. (22)

Setting the play in a specifically post-nuclear context, Thomas P. Adler notes the bare stage (which recalls the all-but-emptied setting of *Endgame*) and reads the park as "a fallen world of discord rather than harmony" (*American Drama*, 207). As New York slid into the recession-era demoralization and disrepair that characterized much of the late 1960s and 1970s, Albee's New York—even iconic, bucolic Central Park—is already a post-realist, minimalist, and violent dystopia.

Like the characters in Beckett's *Endgame*, Jerry is a raconteur who fixes Peter to his spot on the Central Park bench with his lurid tales of sordid living from the other side of the city. Jerry eventually shares most of what is important and importantly missing from his life in the course of his several monologues; he is not only poor but lonely for a loved one, and the "two picture frames, both empty" (23) where his mom and dad's (or his parents' and a sweetheart's) photos should be signal both orphanhood and alienation, themes that echo throughout Albee's canon. Jerry's lengthy, darkly comic story about his randy but hideous landlady and her vicious dog echoes Hamm's climactic narrative about the man who begged him for bread to feed the son who was likely already dead; both monologues reveal as much about the craven disillusionment of the tale-tellers as they do about the meaningless lives of those they encounter. Throughout, Jerry promises to relate what happened that day when he went to the zoo; as time is mocked and manipulated in *Endgame*, (through the pointlessly set alarm clock, the hour for medicine taking that finally arrives but without the medicine itself) so the remarkable thing that has happened at the zoo that morning—"Wait until you see the expression on his face" (19) when the incident is reported on the news that evening—is actually the mortal encounter between Peter and Jerry, whose face it is that Peter sees as he lies bleeding to death.

Certainly, *The Zoo Story* represents a clash of psychosexual personalities, a superego and an id, with fatal results. Peter and Jerry also represent warring ages (not much older, Peter is yet a dying breed and Jerry the grim face of an under-resourced American future) as well as opponent social classes. Comparing it to Rice's *Adding Machine* and Odets's *Waiting for Lefty* among others, Matthew C. Roudané considers *Zoo Story* "bold social protest drama" (*Understanding*, 29). Within the decade, we will recognize Peter and Jerry's contest as that unfolding between the establishment and the counter-culture; in the play's climactic action, Jerry crowds Peter on his park bench until he has no space for himself, just the way that white conservatives of the 1960s felt hemmed in all sides by off-putting or downright fearsome Abbie Hoffmans, Huey Newtons, and Charles Mansons. They felt challenged to stand and "defend their benches," but the audience cannot but laugh when Jerry throws down this gauntlet to Peter, because it surely never was his bench in the first place. Finally, if Jerry is the sacrificial GI—a modern Christ figure (e.g., Bigsby, 14–15; Cohn, 9–10)—and Peter the "suit" who sends him to Vietnam, it is certainly not the case that Peter "walks away" from his encounter despite the fact that he ends *The Zoo Story* alive and Jerry dead. Jerry forces a knife into Peter's hand and impales himself against it; his death implicates and engulfs Peter in ways he will never recover from.

With his dying breath, Jerry reassures Peter that "you're not really a vegetable; it's all right, you're an animal" (49), but if Peter has reclaimed his impugned masculinity by assuming the animal's role, all Jerry has really suggested is that in our zoo society, each is a brute pacing a cage, nervously marking turf when threatened, and regarding any attempt to connect as a gesture of aggression that must be met with mortal force. As Christopher Bigsby remarks in his early study of Albee's work, "[T]he zoo has suddenly become a horrifyingly accurate image of a society where furious activity serves only to mask an essential inertia and whose sociability conceals a fundamental isolation" (*Albee*, 9). Placing this work in a broader context, Roudané sees all of Albee's most unforgettable themes coming to life: "the necessity of ritualized confrontation, the primacy of communication, the paradoxical mixture of love and hate, the cleverly abrasive dialogue, the religious and political textures, the tragic force of abandonment and death … all coalesce in Albee's first and in many respects most successful composition" (*Understanding*, 27–28).

Dutchman (1964)

Amiri Baraka (1934–2014)

Baraka's Obie Award-winning one-act narrates a deadly encounter between Clay, an intellectual black man, and Lula, an unhinged white temptress, on a New York subway. Strikingly beautiful, Lula is also forward in her actions, sitting next to Clay despite there being seats all over the train car, offering him an apple in classic Eve fashion, laying her hand on his thigh, and fantasizing with him about a party Clay will take her to, followed by a trip back to her place for seduction and lovemaking. Though Clay is irresistibly drawn—in some ways, the entire play is about the journey he takes from wariness to enthrallment, from seduced to attacker, and from safe distance to dangerously within Lula's reach. While she draws Clay in with lines like "Walked down the aisle … searching you out" (ellipsis in original) and "What are you prepared for?" (204), Lula's every other line is an insult: "God, you're dull" and "What do you think you're doing?" In other words, Lula is a classic pricktease, but her racial difference charges the encounter with particular tensions and indeterminacies. Even some of her tough talk may be part of her come-on, but Lula's language gets more virulently, unmistakably racist as the tension mounts. Her presumptuous attempt to "get real" with Clay turns quickly into sheer ugliness, and finally Clay is fully hooked—no longer drawn by lust (or lust alone) but by the irresistible urge to dress Lula down, if not do her in. At the moment he takes the bait, delivering an impassioned speech that constitutes the play's climax, Lula "retaliates" with two sharp stabs to his heart. The play concludes with her bizarre collusion with fellow straphangers to dispose of the body as the next unsuspecting victim enters the car.

Dutchman is of its moment in numerous ways, staged as a realistic rendition of a modern (but always iconic) New York subway occupied by people in modern (even, for Lula, mod) dress, engaging in what was then a modern prospect for race relations—something bold, consensual, and shorn of the outdated conventions governing men and women, whites and blacks of previous generations. To be sure, Lula's greatest crime in this realist reading is that she is a women's libber—a zealous beneficiary of the sexual revolution whose measure of personal independence has gone disastrously to her head. Baraka may hold up for special contempt such liberated women, because they represented exactly the kind of sexual threat—a threat of sexual encounter historically fatal to the black men caught up in them—militated against by supervening white males. At the start of his climactic tirade against her, Clay mocks her as "you great liberated whore!" (218). Despite her temptress presentation, she is very much the phallic aggressor; early in the story she poses the classic macho challenge of one street tough to another—claiming to have slept with Clay's sister, despite his own attempt when he was 10 years old (205). Matthew Rebhorn argues that Lula "mimic[s] the same black masculinity Baraka was after in Clay's final monologue" (797). Her aggressive sexuality—when she tries to make Clay get up and dance with her and "rub bellies," just before he lashes back—is another claim to the masculine mantle, and of course her use of deadly knife violence against Clay is phallic in the knife's shape and in its being a form of weaponry rarely taken up by women.

Despite the trenchant topicality of its plot and characterization, *Dutchman* is a remarkably multilayered text with numerous historical, cultural, and Biblical references that interpreters of this play have gained from working through since its first day. Starting with the name of the play itself, several have suggested a parallel between the subway car and the Dutch-owned ships of the Middle Passage, which brought African slaves to the North American continent for the first time in the 1690s; at least one staging modeled the subway to resemble a ship's hold (Cardullo, "Names," 51). Likewise the title invokes the doomed ghost-ship of nautical mythology and Wagner's opera of 1843, roving forever the seven seas, due to a pact made by the captain with the devil. Robert Cardullo adds that "Dutchman" might even be a reference to 1920s-era mobster Dutch Schultz, one of the first white men to enter Harlem and take over the numbers rackets originally run by residents themselves; "thus, the title of the play may suggest that there is little difference between the economic enslavement enforced by Schultz and the economic as well as physical enslavement enforced by the American government for almost 250 years" ("Names," 52). Once Lula produces the apple in the first scene, her Eve figure plays off "Clay" as an Adam figure, who was fashioned out of clay in the Book of Genesis and who is read by several as malleable and vulnerable to Lula's attack. He is likewise, as far as Lula is concerned, common as dirt, a debased character dressed up in white man's clothing (a suit and tie), who is literally indistinguishable from the next black male victim to enter the subway car. Regarding Clay's aspirations to appear and speak in "white" fashion, Cardullo points out that "Clay" and "Adam" reference that era's congressman from New York, Adam Clayton Powell, one of the first African American powerbrokers in Washington, known also for his light skin and Caucasian features (Cardullo, "Names," 53).

Lula has been read as several temptress figures from the Bible and popular culture (see Baker, 111), including Lola from Josef von Sternberg's *The Blue Angel* (Cardullo, "Names," 54), Lilith (another feminist icon) who tried to be equal with Adam, and the Strange Woman from the Book of Proverbs (Baker). She certainly is a principle of strangeness, weirdness, and madness in the play; once more per his name and conservative dress, Clay appears as the ordinary Man on the Street (or underground, in this case) to whom Lula "happens" as if he had suddenly entered into a nightmare scenario. In his conservative suit against her short dress and summer sandals, he is, despite designation by the playwright as 10 years younger than Lula, very much a staid father figure—even the classically urbane Sidney Poitier is a likely invocation. He is thrown for a loop by this daffy, perhaps just plain daft, child of the streets, with whom he is expected to have endless patience. In this way Clay figures an ancient African culture whose progenitor role in the United States manifests everywhere from the slave labor that built American wealth and American infrastructure to the various indigenous African American cultural forms (e.g., jazz, the blues) that white Americans have been expropriating throughout the centuries. In the play's opening moments, Lula gazes at Clay eerily from the platform outside his window, seemingly left behind as the train leaves the station; moments later she materializes in the aisle beside him. As George Piggford observes, *Dutchman* is readable for its gothic setting and title and especially the nightmarish Lula; he regards Clay as in a "dream-like" (147) state, moving inexorably toward his fate. The two proceed to have their date (with destiny), and the *Twilight Zone* quality of the narrative recurs in Lula's uncanny ability to know the particulars of Clay's background—where he is going, who his friends are—that is simultaneously just another garden variety of her overweening racism: "I told you I don't know anything about *you* … you're a well-known type" (206) The tone of simmering oddity boils into full-on surrealism in the play's final seconds, when Lula orders the others on the train to "get this man off me!" (220), toss his body off the train, and then all exit together at the next stop.

Elijah Muhammad famously depicted America as a seductive white woman whose beautiful body the Nation of Islam (figured as the proud black man) had to recognize his infatuation with and resolutely keep his distance from.

In this same vein, Lula is very much an allegory for America itself, a seductive terrain of leisure, prosperity, and popular culture that any man might be drawn to. But also like white America, Lula is a bag of contradictory emotions regarding race, who repeatedly pulls her black counterpart close to her, then pushes him away, each time with increasing anger and intensity. She constantly tells Clay that she is "a liar," signaling the history of betrayal and subterfuge that characterizes America's bargain struck with its African American inhabitants since the late 1690s. Though she accuses Clay of his own fakery, his long speech at the end of the play lays various claims to his insiderism to black culture, regardless of his chosen manner of dress, and his blind hatred of Lula is the most heartfelt emotion expressed in the play. As Kimberly W. Benston observes, "Language itself, as in [his] poetry, is a major protagonist throughout Baraka's drama. A struggle for control of the available syntax lies at the very heart of the early plays" (15).

Drama in Dialogue: *The Zoo Story* and *Dutchman*

In his assessment of the shift in dramatic styles, Thomas P. Adler compares important short plays from the early twentieth century, such as Glaspell's *Trifles* and O'Neill's *Bound East for Cardiff*, with a string of exciting one acts presented in short succession by the likes of Edward Albee, Jack Gelber, and Arthur Kopit in the 1960s. One should certainly add Baraka's *Dutchman* to the mix that heralded the contemporary period; both *Zoo Story* and *Dutchman* are manifestos declaring the arrival of new breed on the American stage: "Both groups of artists, separated by half a century, wrote against the Broadway establishment of the times for audiences desiring something more than commercial pap" (Adler, *American Drama*, 201). Albee is cited by many as an inheritor of the Beckett/absurdist tradition, and Matthew Rebhorn has included Baraka in this company with his astute placement of Baraka's work within Artaud's Theater of Cruelty tradition: "Theater in Artaud's view should challenge us, jolt us into action, and offer a new arena of sensibility. Baraka seems to have followed this directive in his own dramaturgy" (799; see also Piggford, 145). Not only is *Dutchman* one of a group of challenging texts to come out of this revolutionary period in US history, but it is also a trenchant citation of and response to *The Zoo Story* in addition to the many other intertexts that echo through Baraka's drama (see discussion of this play above).

The structural similarities between the two texts are many and obvious; each is a one-act play featuring mainly or solely two actors, set on a rather bare stage yet meant to invoke an iconic New York setting (Central Park and the subway). Throughout *The Zoo Story*, the only set is a park bench, while in the first scene of *Dutchman* only Clay's seat and the one next to it is visible; and even in the second scene, just a few more seats come to light. Both Central Park and the subway are fluid, dynamic, integrated spaces—they are neither of them neighborhoods given over to any particular racial or ethnic enclave; the rich and the poor rub elbows in both, and the potential for such interpersonal understanding is utterly blasted in the violent knife assault that concludes each play. A conservatively dressed straight man opens each play, simply minding his own business with some innocuous reading matter, when he is approached by an oddball from the counterculture with whom he initially wants no contact. As David Krasner remarks, "Peter and Clay have buried their undeveloped talents and sacrificed their inner selves in routine and appearances. They have swallowed pride in order to secure a place in the food chain" (*American Drama*, 71). Each, however, is lured by the exotic qualities of this passerby and especially with his or her ability to weave a spellbinding yarn. Both Jerry and Lula describe their rundown living arrangements, Jerry in a boarding house on the Upper West Side and Lula in a tenement that may or may not be her real home. As Lula herself warns Clay on several occasions, she is likely lying about her residence as she lies about everything else in the story, and although Jerry's circumstances are probably as downtrodden as he narrates them to be, there is a lurid, comic-book quality to his descriptions of his neighbors, his landlady, and especially her vicious dog, such that much of it seems staged for Peter's enjoyment and enthrallment.

Both Jerry and Lula present a sexual subtext to their friendly conversational gestures; Lula's come-on is pronounced throughout *Dutchman*, while Jerry's is very much a coming-out story to Peter, including his one brief period of having been loved by another man in an earlier day and his approach to Peter at the end of the play, which includes tickling, crowding him on his bench, and engaging with him passionately with respect to anger and action. Lula also provokes Clay to stand and defend his bench, so to speak; as Jerry is often read as sacrificing his own life to provide Peter his transformative moment, so Lula's breed of racism is depicted as that which brings out in Clay his revolutionary manhood. Throughout their respective plays, both Jerry and Lula tell stories that are an uncanny blend of events that may or may not have already happened and predictions of future action that are full of mystery and intrigue: Jerry promises Peter, "Wait til you see the expression on his face" (19) regarding an incident that occurred at the zoo, while Lola simply promises sexual activity following her and Clay's trip to a party. At the end of *The Zoo Story*, Jerry asks, "[C]ould I have planned all this…. No … no, I couldn't have. But I think I did" (48, ellipses in original), and it is clear from the beginning of *Dutchman* that Clay is not Lula's first victim, that even while still on the platform she "begins very premeditadedly to smile" (202). Nita N. Kumar's comments about Lula, that she appears to be a random passerby but that she takes on a "sinister, premeditated aspect" (277) as the story proceeds, apply to Jerry as well.

Though Jerry and Lula move in characterological lockstep for much of their respective plays, the final assignments are reversed in *Dutchman* to great political effect. If the white man Jerry, Baraka seems to suggest, gets to stay in charge of the action, despite his down-and-out-status, and makes the radical choice to end his own life, in New York's interracial context, even the equalizing one of the 1960s, it is still the black man, no matter how conservative and middle-class, who goes down. Jerry is allowed to play the Christ figure, bestowing benediction as he dies for others' sins, whereas Clay is simply stunned by his own murder, completely caught off guard and, as the entrance of Lula's next victim makes clear, dying for no purpose whatsoever. One need only compare the permanently traumatized state of Peter as he exits the stage in *The Zoo Story* with Lula's blasé, "businesslike" (220), assembly-line handling of Clay's murder at the end of *Dutchman*. Baraka has been discussed by critics with respect to Clay's revolutionary statement at the end of *Dutchman*, followed by his failure to act—violently against Lula and the other whites in the train car—on these ideas (see Kumar, 274). But in fact *Dutchman* is readable as ironically citing a long line of characters of color in American drama—including Stone's Metamora, Aiken's Uncle Tom, and Boucicault's Zoe (all discussed in Section II)—who must fall before the curtain does. At the end of the play, Lula taunts Clay with and Clay even refers to himself as an Uncle Tom; "I sit here, in this buttoned-up suit, to keep myself from cutting all your throats" (218). Baraka suggests that though we have entered by the 1960s a new age of racial equality and black liberation, with statements as radical as Clay's last stand, the rules—of who survives and who does not at the end of the day and in the American play—have little changed.

House of Blue Leaves (1971)

John Guare (1938–)

Jane Kathleen Curry observes that John Guare "has expressed his gratitude to Edward Albee, who not only inspired a new generation with *The Zoo Story*, but also invested much of his earnings from *Who's Afraid of Virginia Woolf?* into the staging of American plays" (7). The Albee-Barr-Wilder Playwrights Unit produced an early play of Guare's in 1965, and Guare is indeed readable as one of Albee's zanier offspring. Per Curry, "His works feature the juxtaposition of characters' dreams, imagination, and utopian hopes, with the harsher realities of life, which often include violence and death. Guare uses an eccentric mix of tone and style, for instance employing an outrageously farcical plotline to treat a painfully serious topic" (5). As Guare himself suggests, quoting a prescient line from William Dean Howells, his plays tell "the Black heart's truth" ("Preface", vii). In his sharp satire *The House of Blue Leaves*, hapless, no-talent songwriter Artie Shaughnessy; his schizophrenic wife, Bananas; and his self-serving mistress, Bunny Flingus, await the arrival of Pope Paul on an international visit to their humble borough of Queens. Equally exciting is the arrival of Artie's childhood friend and now successful Hollywood director Billy Einhorn, who may hold the key to Artie's success but actually only absconds with Artie's mistress when his own girlfriend is killed in a freak elevator-bombing instigated by Artie's AWOL son, Ronnie. Curry notes that Guare struggled to develop the second act of *Blue Leaves* (9), which introduces the character of grieving but wheeling-dealing Billy Einhorn, who with his mythical last name (one horn = unicorn) might have easily remained the mirage he seems to be in Act I. The entire story has the slightly askew quality of alternate history or alternate reality; we will see the same offhanded blend of the real and the surreal in the work of Fornés and Shepard, discussed below.

In addition to his considerable comic gifts, Guare is a talented composer and parodist of popular musical forms. Early in his career, he collaborated with Jerome Robbins, Leonard Bernstein, and Stephen Sondheim on a project that never came to light (Curry, 9) and wrote the lyrics for a Tony Award–winning adaptation of *Two Gentleman of Verona*. Instead of writing musical comedy as typically construed, however, Guare writes "back-stagers" or more accurately "off-stagers" populated by characters with big dreams and few prospects. *Blue Leaves*'s Artie writes songs such as "Where's the Devil in Evelyn?" and "Back Together Again," schlocky rip-offs of Tin Pan Alley standards with inane lyrics. Many of Guare's characters, if not songwriters, are simply ready to burst into song or break into showbiz in any way they can; his plays with titles such as *Muzeeka* (1968), *Rich and Famous* (1974), and *Marco Polo Sings a Solo* (1977), as well as his Tony- and Oscar-winning *Six Degrees of Separation* (1990), treat ordinary Americans' obsession with celebrities, including the Pope and the Kennedys, and their own envisioned fame as entertainers. *Blue Leaves* is set in Queens, Guare's home borough, which he has spoken of in comically denigrating terms as never the place "people clapped for on quiz shows if you said you came from there" (*Blue Leaves*, 3). Guare mocks Queens for its pretentious place names such as Kew Gardens and Astoria "(after the

Astors, of all people)" (*Blue Leaves*, 3), Linsley Hall and Alhambra apartments; for Guare Queens is the quintessential American way station that only the lucky get to leave. As Christopher Bigsby observes, *Blue Leaves* is "centrally concerned with limits, in the depiction of people limited by a lack of talent, limited economically, emotionally, and geographically…. Artie and the others [are] rooted in a Queens they wish to escape, desperate to break out of fixed roles and determined circumstances, are frustrated and deformed by a world less expansive than their dreams" (*Contemporary American Playwrights*, 13).

Bananas may be the only character certified insane, but each major character in the play, as well as several of the minor ones, are cuckoo for the prospect of being discovered—even just singled out in the crowd by the Pope—and destined for greatness thenceforward: Bunny reads movie magazines and is up at dawn to get her place along the Pope's motorcade route, Artie longs for a big break writing music for the movies once his friend Billy comes back to town, and even three nuns who invade the Shaughnessy apartment at the end of Act I fall over themselves with excitement to see the Pope on Artie's TV. In the monologue that begins Act II, Artie's son, Ronnie, relives a rollicking incident from his childhood—cribbed from an autobiographical story involving Guare and his uncle, an MGM casting director—in which Ronnie auditions for visiting Billy Einhorn for the role of Huckleberry Finn in preposterously overplayed fashion. Ronnie is mistaken for being mentally retarded, and his intention to blow up the Pope with grenades pilfered from his basic training camp is both a revenge for his earlier rejection and a renewed bid to attain the celebrity that eluded him in childhood. Per Guare scholar Gene Plunka, the play's comment is that "[t]his infatuation with celebrities allows us to dream of fame and fortune while we tend to ignore the reality around us, including what may be meaningful relationships with family and friends, as well as valuable spiritual connections" (*Black Comedy*, 75).

Plunka also suggests that Bananas is actually the conduit to the truth that Artie refuses to acknowledge; she reminds him that most of his songs are variations on the tune of *White Christmas*, and zings him with "No man takes a job feeding animals in the Central Park Zoo [Artie's day job, in yet another nod to Albee] unless he's afraid to deal with people" (qtd. in Plunka, *Black Comedy*, 78). By contrast, the ostensibly sane Bunny "keeps the future alive for the aspiring songwriter" (Plunka, *Black Comedy*, 77) by insisting that his mediocre music is wonderful. The play's title refers to the insane asylum where Bananas is scheduled for dispatch, where on a visit Artie had seen a tree full of beautiful blue leaves that turned out to be an almost as miraculous flock of blue birds that vacate their perches in one majestic swoop. But Guare clearly suggests that the Shaughnessy apartment itself is its own ward full of loonies, all suffering from delusions of grandeur encouraged by the popular media surrounding and suffocating them.

The television is explicitly likened to a modern shrine (Guare, *Blue Leaves*, 85) or holy relic; several of the nuns kiss it, as does Bananas, as if it were the Pope's ring, and both she and Artie kneel before it when the Pope passes by, praying to it for rescue from Bananas's mental crisis. The play's crowning irony is given to the producer to declare, when he informs Artie that he can never take Artie with him to Hollywood, as he and his wife are "my touch with reality" (84). He can only make successful films so long as he knows that Artie and Bananas are back in Queens enjoying them. Artie's dreams implode at this moment, when Bunny leaves on Billy's arm, his hopes of Hollywood stardom are dashed, and he is left alone with his permanently incapacitated wife. Bananas calls attention to the couple's solitude for the first time in the story—"like it's taken us eighteen years to get from the church to the hotel room" (86)—and the quiet that descends on the once densely crowded, manically paced apartment is suffused with the eerie menace we are familiar with from the final moments of Beckett, Albee, and Baraka: Artie kisses Bananas good-bye and strangles her to death in another shocking turn of violence between two lover-combatants locked in mortal embrace. Though Artie's act is readable as a gesture of loving mercy, Plunka suggests that "once the superficial and self-deceptive dreams are exposed and we are left with a real world that does not measure up to our fantasies, we are reduced to violent behavior in trying to cope" (*Black Comedy*, 75). Later, "Artie kills Bananas because she is a witness to his failure and would serve to reinforce his humiliations for the rest of his life" (*Black Comedy*, 79).

The House of Blue Leaves premiered off-Broadway in 1971, where it ran for 337 performances and made Guare a major name in American drama, winning an Obie for Best Play that year and a Drama Critics Circle Award. It has received distinguished revivals at Lincoln Center in 1986, winning a Tony for Best Revival and several other recognitions, and at the Walter Kerr in 2002.

Fefu and her Friends (1977)

Maria Irene Fornés (1930–)

In this classic experimental work from the end of the second-wave feminist movement, Fefu and seven well-heeled female friends gather at her country home to plan a fundraiser. Over the course of the play's three parts, each of the main characters explores her damaged, oppressed psyche and/or celebrates triumphant self-reclamation in an extended monologue. Fefu is controlling, fond of guns, and in conflict with her husband, who is only ever addressed offstage; the main onstage conflict is between Fefu and Julia, hysterically confined to a wheelchair after being in the vicinity of a hunter shooting a deer. In a climactic moment of eerie surrealism, Fefu dreams of—or actually sees— Julia getting up from the wheelchair and walking languidly across the floor; later Julia vigorously denies her ability to walk, though Fefu angrily insists that she did: "Fight with me!—Fight!—I need you to fight" (140). Scott T. Cummings refers to Julia as the catalyst to the play's "principle of narrative indeterminacy that erupts into full-blown mystery when [she] arrives" (*Maria Irene Fornés*, 67); she is also "a complex and resonant metaphor for the way women internalize the stifling forces of patriarchy and misogyny" (*Maria Irene Fornés*, 68). As W.B. Worthen argues, "[T]he authority of the absent male is everywhere evident in *Fefu*, and particularly in Julia's imagined paralysis" (70), and Helene Keyssar remarks that Julia "is no more or less mad, no more or less paralyzed than Hamlet ... Like Hamlet, Julia is paralyzed from too much knowledge, and she worries that Fefu is approaching that same state" (188). Because of Julia's association with the hunted dear, Elinor Fuchs reads this character as a Christ figure whose wounds resemble saintly stigmata, "appearing by some process of intense and mysterious identification" (105). Fornés has extolled the influence of Beckett on her work, regarding her viewing of the original production of *Waiting for Godot* as a life-changing event, despite not having "understood a word" (Savran, 54) of its original French. Julia is thus readable as an incisive feminist manifestation of the figure of Hamm, confined to a wheelchair for reasons that are ultimately beyond words, beyond language itself.

The play's experimentalism is characterized by its lack of interest in a pronounced plotline; for much of their time at Fefu's estate, the women simply visit, engage in girlish hijinks (e.g., a water fight), and enjoy each other's company. As conversations flow from one subject to the other, so afternoon flows into evening, and in the famous middle part of the play, the audience is literally asked to leave their seats and flow from theatrical space to space, established as Fefu's kitchen, study, bedroom, and front lawn. In each of these diverse settings, the conversation continues between two or more actors; as Cummings points out, the breakout-scene structure "requires precise timing: Fefu appears in three of the four scenes, leaving Emma on the lawn to go get some lemonade, poking her head in the study to see if Cindy and Christina want to play croquet, and then entering and exiting the kitchen after taking the pitcher from the fridge" (*Maria Irene Fornés*, 70). "Flow" may certainly be said to characterize women's lives, especially in the context of this second-wave, somewhat essentialist moment: their menstrual flow is a sign of their fertility and life-giving abilities; they must move from home to parental, to spousal (and sometimes to professional) duties each day without missing a beat; and fluidity, flexibility, and even circuitousness have been read as classically feminine principles—both embraced and critiqued—throughout the history of feminism.

If a linear plot trajectory is a masculine principle, this only interrupts the flow on rare occasions in *Fefu*—in part 3, the rather prosaic planning session at last takes place, and the conflict between Fefu and Julia reaches its climax. Fornés even rewrites the Chekhovian edict regarding the gun in the first scene that must go off by the end of the play. In fact, Fefu's gun goes off almost immediately, except that she is firing blanks, such that it does not quite go off at all. In the final scene, she kills a rabbit offstage that results in yet more ambiguity: the non-realist death of Julia onstage from a bloody head wound. *Fefu*'s final moment is yet another scene of unexpected, quickly inflicted violence that has become de rigueur in this period. As Cummings notes, "This abrupt and violent ending triggers an immediate desire to know exactly what happened, but the play frustrates such an urge, ending on a note of profound ambiguity" (*Maria Irene Fornés*, 67). Though Beverly Byers Pevitts reads the death of the tortured and hysterical Julia as necessary "in order to enable the emergence of a new self-determined female identity" (Farfan, 446), Penny Farfan's view is that the shooting impugns the role of Fefu, "that her male-identification is ultimately as self-destructive and ineffectual a strategy of resistance … as Julia's hysteria" (446).

Cummings notes that *Fefu and her Friends* signaled a more explicit focus in Fornés's writing on female characters seeking to break free of dependent or oppressive relations with male characters, a shift that lasted for more than a decade and led to Fornés's characterization as a "'woman playwright' and a feminist" (*Maria Irene Fornés*, 64). Meanwhile, "in [the men's] absence, the restlessness of the women manifests itself in a variety of ways, some playful and relaxed, some agitated and ill at ease, and some that suggest that 'the mind and the spirit' of women carries with it the force of its own oppression or liberation" (*Maria Irene Fornés*, 68). Piper Murray voices a more pessimistic reading: "It is the male (or his absence) … that holds the women—and each woman—together" (399). Murray explores *Fefu*'s themes of abjection—its repeated attention to plumbing, both of the home and of women's bodies—and the continued dependence on men: "Indeed by the play's violent ending, we might wonder whether constructing feminist homosociality is possible at all …" (407). Concurring, David Savran remarks, "All of Fornés's plays are about the dark underneath" (*In Their Own Words*, 53). In a more hopeful vein,

Worthen draws attention to the device of the audience moving from space to space in Part 2, calling attention to their role as audience: "*Fefu and her Friends* decenters the absent 'spectator' [Fefu's husband Philip and the other men referred to in the play] as the site of authentic interpretation, replacing 'him' with a self-evidently theatricalized body, an 'audience,' a community sharing irreconcilable yet inter-dependent experiences" (74).

Buried Child (1978)

Sam Shepard (1943–)

This widely hailed drama of the contemporary stage is hardly the Sam Shepard play most representative of his major themes. Nowhere does it mourn the loss of the cowboy or the cowboy state of mind; it is not recognizably set in the American West (but in rural Illinois, where Shepard was born); it does not make major use of the tropes of rock music or Hollywood and seems more directly descended from O'Neill's *Desire under the Elms* (see also Porter) than the post-WWII masters most often named as his influences: Beckett, Pinter, Albee. Yet *Buried Child* surely explores (though "ransacks" or "autopsies" might be the more accurate term) "the American family," which Matthew C. Roudané regards as Shepard's most recurring concern ("Introduction," 5). As a postmodern "American Gothic," aging patriarch Dodge and his faithless wife, Halie, preside over the decline of this legacy—one son is dead, another maimed physically, and a third suffering some kind of PTSD. Tilden, this third son, may figure a universalized Vietnam War veteran, but the trauma that has most likely left him emotionally paralyzed is the shameful affair with his mother, whose issue of the title is inevitably unearthed.

Buried Child employs a recursive, fugue structure that is identifiable in the work of later playwrights such as Sara Ruhl; Richard Gilman draws the analogy to collage and mixed media (xiv) and cites Shepard's "rejection of linear construction" (xv); Christopher Bigsby's terms are "poetry of the theater" and "unrevised jazz scats" ("Born Injured," 16). As an example, Tilden enters in an early scene bearing an armload of corn; later it is carrots, and finally the buried child; in Act III, Halie enters with an armful of yellow roses. In a sort of Fisher King fertility ritual (see also Orbison), Tilden showers Dodge with corn husks in Act I, and Halie tosses a single rose on his blanket, which lands between his knees, in Act III. The Greek-tragic dimension is heightened by the various incest themes, as well as Halie in the role of both faithless Clytemnestra and child-murdering Medea. Thomas P. Adler observes numerous burying rituals, including all of the times that Dodge is covered with a blanket and Shelly's coat, and reads his blood-letting haircut from his son Bradley as a "removal of potency" ("Repetition," 118). As Tucker Orbison notes, "The vision of *Buried Child* is characterized by a bitter irony. While the natural world is renewed, the human world is not" (509). Halie's son Ansel has died before the play begins, as has her illegitimate child with Tilden, who is, with his own air of being "profoundly burned out and displaced" (Shepard, 69), a figure of walking death. Halie spends most of Act I upstairs, calling down semi-incestuous reminiscences of her three sons, especially the dead Ansel, endlessly replaying their lives and deaths. Her sexual unsavoriness is reprised in her memories of a horse breeder who used to court her and later in her flirtations with Fr. Dewis; she is read by Orbison as the Terrible Mother who "dismembers, devours, and destroys" (512) and as a witch dressed all in black (513).

Tilden "had some trouble in New Mexico" (70) and has now resurfaced at the homestead; his arrival is echoed by Bradley at the end of Act I, then by Vince at the start of Act II, who is on his way with Shelly to New Mexico to see his father, Tilden, not realizing that he is here instead. Bradley's stumble through the porch screen door in Act I anticipates Vince's crash through the same door in Act III. When Dodge awakes at the beginning of Act II, he mistakes Vince for Tilden, then does not recognize him at all. Shelly's rabbit coat, with its connotations of fur equaling murder, invokes the play's innocent dead sons. Whereas Halie is a figure of corrupted sexuality, desired by offstage or minor characters in unnatural ways, Shelly is a breath of freshness and fertility, sought after by each of the onstage men, but who makes a last-minute escape from the house of decrepitude and derangement. Vince is not so lucky. In a gesture of self-castration, he allows Shelly to drive away and seeks the mortifying comforts of his grandfather's couch. At the climax, Halie cries out, "Ansel … was a man. A whole man! What happened to all the men in this family?" (124), pronouncing on each of the play's surviving but broken men as she does.

The psychiatric condition of the fugue state goes a long way to explaining the "nonrealism" or "modified realism" (Roudané, "Introduction," 5) in the play as well. Defined as a temporary but sometimes prolonged of reversible amnesia for personal identity and memories, such a diagnosis can be applied to Dodge's persistent refusal to recognize his grandson Vince, as well as the truth regarding the buried child. The fugue state also includes somnambulistic wandering, and although Dodge is couch-bound for much of the story, the symptom certainly manifests in the peripatetic habits of the sons, especially Tilden who makes frequent trips to the back field, his younger brother

Bradley who slows down only once his wooden leg is stolen, and grandson Vince just in from his road trip with Shelly. Bigsby describes "that sense of removal—from other people, from a rooted surrounding, from a self—[as] a central concern of a writer [Shepard] whose plays explore the American psyche at a time of failed dreams and lost visions" ("Born Injured," 7).

This play's citations, intentional or not, to *Endgame* are numerous; Shepard's title itself evokes the "brat" from Hamm's long narrative at the close of the play, and both plays hinge around a recurring sense of menace and pathos regarding the obscured identity of fathers and sons. In both plays, three generations of men are main characters; in *Endgame*, Clov may or may not be Hamm's son, and may or may not be the "brat" dying in the hinterlands; as above, Vince is denied by his own grandfather, and all vigorously attempt to ignore the child buried in the field and dragged back aboveground by Tilden in the last scene. Whereas Beckett's Nell, per the traditional woman's station at mid-century, is pathetic and disabled, the first to die, Halie is vigorous and malicious, causing misery to all the men in her family and intensifying the vertiginous nightmarishness of Shepard's universe thereby. The ruined field behind Dodge's house suggests some dreadful environmental alteration, recalling the post-nuclear wasteland outside Hamm's shelter. As Clov opens *Endgame* up on a ladder, looking for signs of life outside the shelter's windows, Halie reports" blue sheets" of rain coming down "up here" (64); she reports from the upstairs bedroom, and in this out-of-kilter universe, it may in fact only be raining at that higher latitude. Clov's word for the scene outside is "corpsed"; Dodge's is "catastrophic" (64). Halie tries to get Dodge to "take a pill. Be done with it once and for all" (65), and Hamm begs Clov for a painkiller—and later for assisted suicide—and gets neither. Like the paraplegic Hamm, ensconced front and center on his wheelchair throughout the play, Dodge is another stricken king, seemingly rooted to his sofa, giving the space to the usurper Vince only in death. As Hamm bleeds from his eyes overnight and feels "a little vein" dripping in his head throughout the play, Dodge is ruthlessly subjected to a haircut by Bradley at the end of Act I and spends the rest of the play with a bloody, cut-up scalp. Like an overgrown baby, Dodge whines constantly to Tilden about having "my blanket" and "my bottle," just as Nagg nagged endlessly for his sugarplum to his son Hamm.

Buried Child won the Pulitzer Prize in Drama in 1979, though notably did not make the typical transition to Broadway following the award until almost 20 years later, in 1996. As Ben Brantley explained the situation in his 1996 review, *Buried Child*, "which once seemed to represent the very essence of Off- Broadway cool [now] comfortably fills a big Broadway stage.... [It] operates successfully on so many levels that you get dizzy watching it" ("A Sam Shepard Revival," C15). Recently off-Broadway's the New Group completed an all-star remounting, starring Ed Harris and Amy Madigan, that was also commended by Brantley in the *Times* ("In Shepard's *Buried Child*").

Drama in Dialogue: *House of Blue Leaves* and *Buried Child*

John Guare and Sam Shepard, two contemporaries graduated from the off-off-Broadway proving grounds of the mid-1960s to Broadway success (if also the occasional miss) since then, are masters of dark comedy whose stories of radically dysfunctional families tell equally essential, however divergent, stories of the American experience. If the viewer who enters Guare's broadly comic *House of Blue Leaves* is surprised by its slide into mayhem and even violence, there is no such surprise once inside the dismal living room of *Buried Child*: "a sadness pervades ... most of Shepard's [plays] ..., a sadness that dissolves into a sense of menace, then uncertainty.... In Sam Shepard's entropic world, the primary family unit—whose members seem to be on some grand cosmic disconnect—is trapped within its own lies of the mind" (Roudané, "Introduction," 2). Though the ratios of light to dark may be opposite in these two playwrights, they both challenge middle-class shibboleths regarding the sanctity of the home and the American dream, and they raise equally disturbing questions about the violence at the heart of our most intimate relationships.

   In both plays, a TV is a prominent feature of the largely (but not entirely) realist set; in the sunny (however frigid) daytime context of Guare's play, it is a locus of farce, with various characters kneeling before it, kissing the images that appear there, and draping arms around it to scream, "Get [a photo of] me with Jackie Kennedy!!! ... Get me with ... Mayor Lindsay!" (59–60). In the brooding silence of Shepard's low-lit wee hours, the television's blue light casts an eerie glow on the sleeping Dodge and the sizzle of its overnight static (this play originated in the analog days), suggesting the white noise of permanent oblivion. The images on the TV in *House of Blue Leaves* are specifically described and integral to the plot; all the static on Dodge's TV suggests is a world cut off from communication with the outside world, a world beyond the reach of even the meager solace offered by insipid daily programming. Equally impugned is the living room sofa and all its enervating effects. Both Artie of *Blue Leaves* and Dodge of *Buried Child* open the play asleep on their living room couches and spend long scenes seemingly trapped there. Their removal from the bedroom connotes the estrangement of their respective wives, and the older, more decrepit Dodge—his and the other men's diverse injuries recalling the alarming physical breakdown of *Endgame*'s quartet— dies on his couch at the end of the play; in another echo of *Endgame*, no one seems to take much notice.

As the wounded Fisher King is a pronounced allegorical subtext in Shepard's play, in fact both he and Artie are emasculated by the women in their lives. Dodge's wife, Halie, is the treacherous wife of Clytemnestra's epic tradition, and even lovely Shelly cannot or will not sacrifice her safety for his. Artie's mistress, Bunny, sells him out as soon as the chance presents itself, and although Bananas seems disabled and thus harmless in her mental confusion, she exploits her husband's weak spots as deftly as any wife can, as when she mocks his inability to come up with original song material; her demise at his hands is readable as payback for this humiliation, yet audiences must decide whether Shepard's husband-vanquishing harpy or Guare's wife-murdering schlemiel presents the darker vision. Finally, the impotence of both men is dark-comically displayed in the violent revolt of their respective sons. Instead of avenging the wrongs their fathers endure, the sons in each play add insult to injury by being feckless, damaged, and damage-causing embarrassments to the family name. The ability of any one of them to bear forth the next generation is either called into question or abruptly curtailed in the various deaths and emasculations they themselves undergo.

The settings account for important distinctions between the plays; though a theme of both is the shattering (and shattering effects) of illusion, Guare's play is rooted in logistical particularities—the Pope's 1965 visit to New York, passing through Queens; studio-era Hollywood in its last gasps; the Vietnam War—that are nowhere to be found in the disorienting shifts and reboots of *Buried Child*. The setting of Shepard's play is generically rural and bleak, almost accidentally central Illinois, and as above, it makes its references to ancient mythologies—the Fisher King and related fertility legends—instead of current events. Despite its rampant pop-Catholicism, the prevailing tone of *House of Blue Leaves* is New York-style shtick, schlock, and kitsch; in *Buried Child* it is postmodern gothic, a mix of updated Beckett and prototypical David Lynch. The atmosphere of *Blue Leaves* is noisy and manic; in *Buried Child* (per the reception on Dodge's TV), it is static, disconnected, and desolate, with menace suffusing even the moments of comic bickering and sight gags regarding Bradley's missing leg, Tilden's armloads of corn and carrots, the haircut scene, and others. Though Artie is devastated by the loss, the audience looks upon the late-hour departure of sexually profligate, aptly named Bunny Flingus as good riddance, whereas it simply breathes a sigh of relief at the flight of Shelly, in suitably gothic white—this time the "bunny" reference is her rabbit jacket—from the haunted house of Halie and Dodge. Gene Plunka remarks that in *House of Blue Leaves*, New York is "drab reality" (*Black Comedy*, 75) and Hollywood the land of fantasy; such oppositions collapse into each other in the wide swath of dying heartland that is the province of *Buried Child*.

Part VII

Diversity and Social Change (1980–present)

The contemporary scene in American drama includes major contributions from a diverse array of gay authors (who now write openly on gay themes; see also Roudané, "Plays," 404), playwrights of various ethnic and racial backgrounds, and an improving representation of women from all groups. Not surprisingly, the goal of many underrepresented writers is to bring their story to the American stage, developing dramatic work from the unique perspective of their personal/contemporary and collective/historical experience. Many continue tapping into the absurdist tradition established by Beckett and others, and many mix dark humor with implicit or explicit violence per the genre-blending tendencies of the wider contemporary stage. As have the dramas, so the stages themselves have continued to diversify beyond the bounds of Broadway; important regional theaters such as the Magic in San Francisco, the Mark Taper in Los Angeles, the Guthrie in Minneapolis, the Goodman and Steppenwolf in Chicago, Yale Repertory Theater New Haven, and the McCarter Center in Princeton have sponsored plays by many of the artists represented in this section; the Public Theater's Joseph Papp (in New York), Yale Rep's Lloyd Richards, and McCarter's Emily Mann are cited as key mentors to these writers in their early and mid-careers, as are important playwriting teachers such as Marie Irene Fornés and Paula Vogel, who directs the playwriting program at Brown. Theatre Communications Group is an active publisher of contemporary American plays and a sponsor of theater-related research; its *American Theater* and *BOMB* are two online magazines with frequent updates regarding theater news and interviews with contemporary playwrights.

David Mamet is a Chicago-born dramatist whose most notable works call acerbically into question the hollow promises of the American Dream. He writes frequently about the world of work, spanning the class spectrum from junk shop owner to college professor, to Hollywood producer. He repeatedly confronts his audience with the difficult equation between capitalist business practice and socially sanctioned theft, mixing criminal persons and activities among legitimate workplace doings and presenting characters whose main business it is to con their customers. David Savran refers to "Mamet's realization that in a capitalist economy all relations are, to some degree, commercial relations" (*In Their Own Words*, 133). Mamet also draws from his personal life, including his regrettable childhood under the roof of a violent stepfather, his Jewish background, and his dealings with Hollywood. A large number of his plays have been made into films, and Mamet has written several scripts directly for film and television. He has penned controversial plays regarding American race relations, including *Edmond* (1992), *The Old Neighborhood* (1997), and *Race* (2009), and is equally interested in the mutual exploitation by men and women in works such as *Sexual Perversity in Chicago* (1974), *Speed-the-Plow* (1988), and *Oleanna* (1992). Mamet's dialogue is marked by pauses and staccato one-word exchanges—reminiscent of the broken language (and resulting broken social contract) in Beckett's universe—or conversely by characters who speak in rapid, lengthy monologues as a sign of desperation and social subservience (e.g., Ruth in *The Woods* [1977]) or of confidence and social dominance (e.g., Teach in *American Buffalo* [1975] and Ricky Roma in *Glengarry Glen Ross* [1983]). As with his contemporaries Albee and Shepard, onstage violence is frequently the cause or outcome of verbal conflict and social isolation.

Mamet has not had a truly successful original Broadway run since 1992 (with *Oleanna*), but his most renowned work, including *American Buffalo, Glengarry Glen Ross, Speed-the-Plow*, and *Oleanna* have enjoyed successful film adaptations and/or revivals on and off Broadway until the present day. In *American Buffalo*, Don is the owner of a Chicago junk shop; Bobby, his trusting assistant; and Teach, a cynical denizen of the neighborhood. They all plot to rob a customer they suspect of being a wealthy collector. In their minds, the very fact that this customer may have "buffaloed" Don in the purchase of a buffalo nickel is an offense they feel entitled to repay with burglary of his home. When Teach suspects that Bobby has already done the job without cutting the older men in on the deal, he attacks Bobby; Don leaps to his defense while Teach retreats in defeat. *Glengarry Glen Ross* takes place in a real estate office, where agents battle each other to score the hottest leads and ascend to top place on the office "board," where awaits a Cadillac, or to avoid at all costs the lowest ranking, where awaits summary dismissal. Once again, intricate cons and cat-and-mouse games play out, leading to the exposure of Moss in his attempt to sell leads to a competing firm, subsequent job loss, and likely criminal charges. This play won the Pulitzer Prize and Drama Critics Circle Award in 1994 and a Tony and Drama Desk Award for Best Revival in 2005.

In *Speed-the-Plow*, Karen is turned against by her mogul boss, Bobby Gould, and his sycophantic associate, Charlie Fox, when she is exposed in her scheme to trade sexual favors for favor shown to an artsy novel she desires to lead into film production; in *Oleanna*, the college professor, John, faces job loss and jail time when his befuddled student, Carol, parleys John's poorly executed show of sympathy into a charge of sexual harassment and then of attempted rape. This late work found somewhat less favor than Mamet's earlier plays: Roudané says of *Oleanna*, "Despite the popularity of this play, Mamet's control of language disappoints. Brittle, awkward, unnatural, the repartee never gains theatrical momentum" ("Plays," 371). Roger Ebert panned the film version, and the 2009 revival closed after only 65 performances. Nevertheless, Mamet is credited with "a powerful social vision, ... brilliant linguistic sensitivity, ... and plays of genuine originality" (Bigsby, *Modern American Drama*, 201) and with pointed relevance for the new century: "Mamet's dramas speak ever more profoundly to a terrorist-hunting and haunted America as the characters fight for a piece of a disintegrated Dream, struggling hopelessly to conquer by performing popularized American roles" (Haedicke, 409).

August Wilson is a Tony- and Pulitzer-winning dramatist who came into his own in the early 1980s, when *Ma Rainey's Black Bottom* was selected by Lloyd Richards (renowned for having directed Hansberry's *A Raisin in the Sun* in 1959 as Broadway's first black director) for a staged reading at Yale Repertory Theater. Richards shepherded this play to Broadway, where it found wide acclaim, and Wilson completed a ten-play cycle, each featuring the African American experience from a different decade in the twentieth century, before his tragically early death, at the age of 60, months after completion of *Radio Golf* (2005), set in the 1990s. As Harry J. Elam Jr. points out, the central conflict in Wilson's plays often involves the theft of black cultural expression (music, athletic talent, years lived) by white perpetrators (*Companion*, 323); even if these figures (e.g., Sutter's ghost, Joe Turner) are long dead, their damaging legacy remains, causing conflict between the surviving African American characters. They wrestle with traumatic memories, wrong turns taken, and debts unpaid in their attempt not to flee the inescapable past, but to integrate it into an affirming, forgiving communal present. Michael Downing adds that "Wilson's dramatic technique follows a certain pattern. He consistently takes pejorative, racist stereotypes [e.g., watermelons] and turns them into holy archetypes—sacred symbols which are imbued with new meaning and power ... " (augustwilson.net). Finally, Joan Fishman explores the relationship between Wilson and his fellow Pittsburgh native, the artist Romare Bearden, whom Wilson greatly admired. Bearden's own work entitled *The Piano Lesson* (1984) inspired Wilson's 1990 multi-award-winning play of the same name, and Bearden's earlier *Millhands Lunch Basket* (1978) inspired Wilson's *Joe Turner's Come and Gone* (1988): " ... these two artists ... present a rainbow of the life cycle incorporating the past and the present, the dead and the yet-to-be-born, offering images and inspirations intended to heal the community" (Fishman, 133).

Ma Rainey's Black Bottom (1984) is set in the 1920s and is Wilson's most historically inflected drama, narrativizing a scene from the life of Gertrude "Ma Rainey" Pridgett, a blues pioneer from the 1920s, known as the Mother of the Blues. In the story, the conflict between Ma's two band members, the flashy, high-spirited Levee and the politically self-aware Toledo, leads to the stabbing death of Toledo by Levee and the resulting senseless ruination of both men's lives. In *The Piano Lesson*, set in the 1930s, brother Boy Willie and sister Berniece debate whether to sell the piano that was intricately carved with African totem figures by their great-grandfather, stolen by the white planter who enslaved their family, and retrieved by the siblings' father, who died for his efforts. Per Roudané's observation, "The brother-sister conflict is deliberately left unresolved, thus inviting the audience to participate in the larger moral dilemmas with which the characters themselves struggle" ("Plays," 391). *Fences* (1987) is set in the 1950s and tells the story of larger than life Troy Maxson, a retired player from the Negro Baseball Leagues who rues his luck of having been born too early to test his mettle—and earn national recognition—in an integrated sport. He takes his hard feelings out on his long-suffering wife, Rose, and his athletically gifted son, Cory; Troy betrays his wife by sleeping with another woman and belittles his son's desire to play college football, insisting that his son will face the discrimination that integrated sports have, by then, alleviated to some degree. His death in the midst of matters unresolved imbues the story with its tragic element. *Fences* won the Pulitzer Prize in Drama and the Tony Award for Best New Play and has been widely anthologized.

Influential gay dramatists at the turn of the twenty-first century include Tony Kushner, whose *Angels in America* (1993) won the Pulitzer Prize and is notable for its broad thematic canvas—including the Cold War past and the AIDS-affected present and the stories of straight and gay, black and white, Jewish and Mormon, male and female, living and dying characters. Terence McNally's plays have focused affirmatively, however controversially, on gay identity and frank sexual themes since the 1960s; he has received major acclaim for his mature plays—including *The Lisbon Traviata* (1989), *Lips Together, Teeth Apart* (1991), *Love! Valor! Compassion!* (1994), and *Master Class* (1995); the first three deal with gay and AIDS-related themes; the fourth shines a probing but admiring light on the opera diva and gay icon Maria Callas.

David Henry Hwang is known for his comedic, music-infused portraits of the Chinese American experience; *FOB* (1980) tells the story of a Chinese American woman's choice of a Chinese immigrant ("FOB," or "fresh off the boat") at home in his ethnic identity over a more Americanized rival. It won the 1981 Obie for Best New Play. Hwang's most acclaimed drama is *M. Butterfly* (1988), a deconstruction of Puccini's opera, *Madame Butterfly* (1904) and based on a historical incident involving a 1960s French diplomat mistaking a male Chinese opera star for a woman, with whom he fell in love and betrayed professional secrets. This play won the Tony for Best Play for 1989—the first time the award was bestowed on an Asian American playwright. Nilo Cruz, arriving to the US from Cuba in 1970, has written more than a dozen plays produced off-Broadway and across the country. His best-known work is the Pulitzer Prize-winning, historically-based *Anna in the Tropics* (2002), in which the lector (hired to read novels and newspapers to workers) at a 1920s Tampa cigar factory disrupts the workers when their lives take on the romantic and tragic dimensions of his selected text, *Anna Karenina*.

Donald Margulies explores Jewish themes in his work, often through domestic dark comedies such as *The Model Apartment* (1988) and *The Loman Family Picnic* (1989). He won the 2000 Pulitzer Prize for *Dinner with Friends*, which chronicles the marital breakup of two upper-middle-class East Coast couples. Jon Robin Baitz is well regarded for *The Substance of Fire* (1991), about a Holocaust survivor who becomes a New York publisher and desires to bring out a six-volume history of Nazi medical experiments, leading to conflict with and eventual estrangement from his commercially oriented adult offspring. Before her tragically early death in 2005, the widely regarded Wendy Wasserstein worked frequently in a similar well-to-do, well-educated, East Coast Jewish milieu; her episodically structured, warmly comic, widely acclaimed plays include *Uncommon Women and Others* (1977), *The Heidi Chronicles* (1988), and *The Sisters Rosensweig* (1992). Matthew Roudané observes that despite the clear feminist intent behind much of her work, "Such [privileged] characters have left Wasserstein open to charges of writing elitist drama.... Unquestionably, Wasserstein's work lacks a streetwise grittiness" and may "provoke mistrust on the part of certain theatergoers and critics" ("Plays," 380).

Other important women playwrights of the contemporary period include Marsha Norman, who is celebrated for two early works—*Getting Out* (1977) and *'night Mother* (1982), both telling stories of working-class Southern women, with tragedy in their pasts, who triumphantly take control of their futures: Arlene, the ex-con heroine of *Getting Out*, by choosing life; and Jessie, the impaired and demoralized heroine of *'night Mother*, by choosing death (see Roudané, "Plays," 377). Norman's fellow Southerner, Beth Henley, has numerous works to her credit, although "to date, her reputation rests chiefly on her comedy *Crimes of the Heart*" (1980; Roudané, "Plays," 382). In the story, Lenny, Meg, and Babe McGrath are three sisters facing life's difficulties, even tragedies, with a regenerating measure of dry Southern wit. Tina Howe is an experimental playwright with a pronounced absurdist streak in many of her earlier works. She has received the most critical acclaim for her more realist works, however, including *Painting Churches* (1983), *Coastal Disturbances* (1986), and *Pride's Crossing* (1997). These largely autobiographical works feature resilient, artistic heroines often in conflict with well-to-do, once-illustrious, but now-declining, parents or other family members. As Bigsby observes, "the 'chaos,' 'lunatic climaxes,' and 'flying language' of [earlier works] gives way to a measured concern with those anxious to discover or impose some shape on the flux of experience…. [Howe] edges her characters towards an epiphany, a moment of reconciliation, with death no less than with life" (*Contemporary American Playwrights*, 84–85). Paula Vogel's two most well-regarded works are *The Baltimore Waltz* (1992) and the Pulitzer Prize-winning *How I Learned to Drive* (1997). The former is a dark comic satire on AIDS hysteria in the 1980s, and in the later play, narrated in flashbacks by the heroine, Uncle Peck begins molesting his niece-by-marriage, Li'l Bit, at age 11 while teaching her important lessons in surviving a harsh world. Per Johanna Mansbridge's assessment, "[I]n the play's most poignant irony, he teaches her how to protect herself from the very harm he imposes on her" (382).

Christopher Durang is a rollicking dark satirist whose most acclaimed works include *Sister Mary Ignatius Explains it all For You* (1979), *Beyond Therapy* (1981), *The Marriage of Bette and Boo* (1985), *Betty's Summer Vacation* (1999), and most recently *Vanya and Sonia and Masha and Spike*, which won the 2013 Tony for Best Play. His plays have created controversy for their marked anti-Catholicism; his "more general questioning of authoritarian personalities, social structures, and belief systems" (Savran, *In their Own Words*, 19); and his dark-comic takes on serious themes such as incest, alcoholism, and child abuse. As David Savran has observed, in Durang's plays, "Comedy arises in large part from the use that characters make of various deceptive or obscure orthodoxies to rationalize their brutality" (*In their Own Words*, 19). Durang's remarkable website (chrstopherdurang.com) includes not only useful summaries and production histories of his many works but revised passages offered for substitution in various scripts whose comic reference points are so rooted in their original 1980s context that they may be lost on certain modern audiences. Although Durang ultimately recommends simply setting each work in the time period of its original production, the variant texts for several of Durang's works (e.g. *Beyond Therapy, Baby with the Bathwater* [1983]) are only known via this website. Notably, even references in his recommended revisions [e.g., Elián González replacing Marv Albert] have become dated and difficult to recall.

Neil LaBute is a clear successor to both Shepard and Mamet, to whom he has dedicated one play each (Innes, "Neil LaBute," 132), and with whom he shares the regrettable history of childhood under an abusive father. Reminiscent of the work of both, his plays are peopled by few but desperate characters playing insidious mind games against each other, indulging in tour-de-force verbal assaults, and resorting to physical violence, even murder, when the occasion presents itself. Where Shepard and Mamet frequently bring fathers and sons, brothers, and coworkers into intense conflict, LaBute ups the ante by submitting female characters to men's psychological and physical predations, or by setting up pitched battles between the sexes in which any attempt at warmth and compassion is ultimately mockingly undermined. Scenes of humiliation, physical abuse, even infanticide, occur; not surprisingly, LaBute has been tagged more than once with the names "misogynist" and "misanthrope." He was "disfellowshipped" from the Mormon Church (which he joined in college) for *bash: latterday plays* (1999), in which Mormons are depicted as homophobes and child-murderers, and one playgoer famously cried out "Kill the playwright!" during an especially offensive scene from *Filthy Talk for Troubled Times* (1992, 2010).

LaBute's work focuses frequently on destructive sexual relationships, as in his two early award-winning and broadly representative films, *In the Company of Men* (1992) and *Your Friends and Neighbors* (1998), and in his plays *The Shape of Things* (2001), *Fat Pig* (2004), and *Reasons to be Pretty* (2008). In *The Shape of Things*, an attractive art student, Evelyn, wins the affections of clumsy, unattractive museum guard, Adam, causing him to change his physical appearance (including cosmetic surgery) and abandon his group of friends. When she announces, during her thesis defense, that Adam himself was her project, resculpted into a better version of himself but through sheer artificial manipulation, with no love or desire for him whatsoever, he is publicly devastated. In *Fat Pig*, the more typical theme of men's cruelty toward women is to the fore, as the overweight Helen is insulted by friends of her love interest, Tom, then betrayed by Tom himself when he refuses to acknowledge her in front of his superficial group. In many of the relationship narratives, LaBute depicts physically attractive characters in the cruelty roles; per his remarks to Pat Jordan in the *New York Times*, " [P]retty guys have this glow. No matter how bad they are, people keep going back to them. I always keep an eye on the pretty guy who can hurt me" (30). As Christopher Innes remarks, "[T]he provocation of LaBute's plays is primarily aimed at making us question the way American society substitutes surfaces for substance, personal appearances for principle" ("Neil LaBute," 144).

Suzan-Lori Parks is a MacArthur "Genius" grant recipient whose widely regarded *Topdog/Underdog* (2001) received the Pulitzer Prize. In the story, two African American brothers abandoned by their parents as teenagers eke out existence in a rundown tenement through odd jobs. Ironically, Lincoln is an Abraham Lincoln impersonator at a waterside arcade; his younger brother, Booth, gets by on petty crimes but longs to con tourists with the three-card Monte so expertly plied by Link. At the end of the story, Link hustles Booth out of his share of his parents' inheritance, whereupon Booth reenacts history by gunning Lincoln down. Obviously, there is a good bit of postmodern "play" in this, as in all Parks's work, although play with a deadly earnest, historically informed bent, as she questions the validity of Lincoln's legacy and the tendency of Americans to both pride themselves on and endlessly reinjure themselves with constant recourse to traumatic historical narratives.

As Parks here reviews and rewrites the Lincoln legacy, so *Topdog/Underdog* is a purposeful "restaging" of an earlier work, *The America Play* (1994), which, although different in situation and outcome, also includes an African American Lincoln impersonator referred to as the Lesser Known. Earlier in her career, Parks earned public acclaim with her double-billed retake on Nathanial Hawthorne's *The Scarlet Letter: In the Blood* (1999) and *Fucking A* (2000), known together as *The Red Letter Plays*. In them, Parks creates an African American heroine whose first name is Hester and who suffers the same opprobrium as her nineteenth-century namesake. Once again, Parks remixes history, literature, race, and society with a technique she has famously described as "Rep & Rev"—repetition and revision—to provide her audience with multilayered, deeply ironic, movingly tragicomic (re)takes on the national past and her characters' various personal histories. That many of her characters are impersonators, costumed performers, or con artists returns viewers to Parks's abiding interest in the vital importance, but often, finally, the impossibility, of distinguishing "what is" from "what ain't." As Ilka Saal observes, "Parks's protagonists tend to be possessed by a past that has forsaken them. Through digging (literally and figuratively) they attempt to locate a form of inheritance, which—even as it does not turn out to be exactly a treasure—can nonetheless provide them with a sense of historical continuity and recognition" (256).

Other contemporary writers include A. R. Gurney, who began writing drama full-time only in his fifties, when his well-regarded *The Dining Room*

(1982) scored a major success. The play contains 18 scenes set in the same dining room, through which travel different families (although all well-heeled New Englanders) with different travails, chronicling elegiacally the wane of America's WASP culture. Gurney's excellent website (argurney.com) usefully reviews his dozens of works. Actor and playwright Wallace Shawn is known for his controversial *Aunt Dan and Lemon* (1985), in which the charismatic Aunt Dan makes a persuasive case for the role of government as the brutalizing force that ensures civilized life for those sheltered from international conflict; her gullible protégé, Lemon, concludes that Nazism therefore served a necessary historical function. Many in Shawn's audience hated the play for failing to include a liberal rebuttal, and many incorrectly assumed that it presented a pro-fascist position (see Savran, "Plays," 214–18). John Patrick Shanley's most noted work is *Doubt* (2004), in which a young, forward-thinking priest is accused by a conservative nun of molesting a young African American boy in his charge. Per the work's title, there is never proof as to whether the allegations are true, and the boy's mother argues with Sister Aloysius that Father Flynn's interest in her son is beneficial, no matter its unseemly aspects. The play won numerous awards in 2005, including the Pulitzer Prize in Drama, the Tony for Best Play, the New York Drama Critics Circle Award, and the Drama Desk Award.

Richard Greenberg has written numerous plays and adaptations since his career began in the mid-1980s. His work is characterized by gay themes, verbal wit and erudition in the mode of the British dramatist Tom Stoppard, and an interest in US history, especially the early twentieth century (see Achilles and Bergmann, 53–54). His plays demonstrate the ironies of false hopes, failed expectations, and the painful acuities of hindsight; he is best known for the multi-award-winning *Take Me Out* (2003), about a major-league baseball player who comes out at the height of his career and is devastated by the negative reaction. Oklahoma native Tracy Letts is a Tony Award–winning actor as well as dramatist; most critically acclaimed is *August, Osage County* (2007), which won the 2008 Pulitzer Prize and Tony Award for Best Play. Autobiographical in both setting and situation, it narrates the travails of three sisters in the wake of their long-suffering father's suicide and their damaged, sadistic mother's descent into pill addiction, in the final stages of mouth cancer.

Richard Nelson writes plays especially illustrative of the "drama in dialogue" phenomenon that is a key thematic in this text. Himself an editor of early American plays (see Bigsby, *Contemporary American Playwrights*, 206), Nelson wrote two plays in the 1990s, *Two Shakespearean Actors* (1990) and *The General from America* (1996), that hark back, respectively, to the

Forrest-Macready dispute that fomented the 1849 Astor Place Riots and the historical circumstances that led William Dunlap to write *André* (1798). In *Two Shakespearean Actors*, the classically framed "contrast" between Forrest and Macready—with respect to acting styles, audiences, and so on—is deconstructed through exploration of the rivals' shared love of dramatic language, particularly Shakespeare's, and their shared tendency to shelter themselves from personal and social upheaval by retreating into the artificiality and adulation of performance. In *The General from America*, Washington's aura is diminished when he condemns the somewhat minor war profiteering of Benedict Arnold in a baldly political (i.e., theatrical) gesture, triggering Arnold's impulse to betray his country. Ironically (though not at all surprisingly at this point), the Royal Shakespeare Company originally staged both plays, and Nelson's career exemplifies the ongoing dialogue between American drama today and yesterday, as well as its remarkable continuing engagement with its parent cultures across the Atlantic.

Sarah Ruhl's impressive career to date includes her own "Genius" grant and a dozen well-regarded original plays and adaptations, including *Eurydice* (2003), *The Clean House* (2004), *Dead Man's Cell Phone* (2007), and *In the Next Room (or the Vibrator Play)* (2009). Typically, her sets are spare (though giving way frequently to gorgeous theatricality and comical unrealism), and characters act in the present, with little if any motivating backstory, as Ruhl regards psychological explanations for all present action as overly "rational" and "explained" (Lahr, "Surreal Life" 82). Mixing realism with surrealism, Ruhl observed to John Lahr in the *New Yorker*, "I like to see people speaking ordinary words in strange places or people speaking extraordinary words in ordinary places" (Lahr, 78). In agreement, Charles Isherwood observes that Ruhl's work "blends the mundane and the metaphysical, the blunt and the obscure, the patently bizarre and bizarrely moving" (6).

Like Ruhl, Christopher Shinn is a young playwright with a dozen well-received works to his credit thus far. He is known for chronicling "what it *felt* like to live in the United States at the beginning of the twenty-first century" (Bottoms, 336), whether the issue be 9/11 (*Where Do We Live* [2002]), the Iraq War (*Dying City* [2006]), liberal tolerance for Islamic extremism (*Now or Later* [2008]), or gay baiting on college campuses (*Teddy Ferrara* [2013]). Shinn said of this last play that it attempts to deconstruct the dichotomy between villain and victim in national tragedies such as the Tyler Clementi case, wherein a gay Rutgers student committed suicide after being outed by an intrusive roommate (christophershinn.com). Writing in the *LA Times*, Rob Weinert-Kendt adds, "If playwright Christopher Shinn has a signature character, it is the manipulative victim—the half-sympathetic, half-deplorable sort of person whose suffering is real but who uses it as a rationale for bad behavior."

Although this text has not focused on American musicals to any extent thus far, it is impossible to complete discussion here without in-depth reference to the modern-day phenomenon that is Lin-Manuel Miranda's *Hamilton* (2015). Although academic research on this play is yet in the offing, *Hamilton* is extolled by serious theatergoers and music experts throughout the popular press and raucously hailed by New Yorkers and Broadway attendees from all walks of life, who have taken Miranda's "young, scrappy, and hungry" bastard orphan immigrant turned founding father to their innermost hearts. *Hamilton* has broken so many records with respect to attendance, box office, and accolade that it is difficult to keep track of them all, but the final Note below will do its best to provide a semblance of the factors constituting *Hamilton*-mania in American drama today.

This section includes representative plays from diverse contemporary playwrights; the transatlanticism of its Touchstone text, Athol Fugard's *Blood Knot*, is duly complicated by the fact that South African–born Fugard has moved between South Africa and the United States for the last several decades. His desire to use his drama to effect social change coincides with the goals of many US playwrights in this section, whose works instruct, revise, and enlighten both home communities and diverse audiences with respect to cherished national narratives and stories not yet heard.

A Transatlantic Touchstone: *Blood Knot* (1961)

Athol Fugard (1932–)

Fugard's important early text from the Apartheid era tells the story of two colored (mixed-race) half-brothers, one dark-skinned and one light enough to "try for white," in South African parlance, but who has returned home exhausted and shamed by his passing experience. Morris, the lighter brother, now shares the meager shack of the darker Zachariah in Korsten, a dilapidated section of Port Elizabeth abutting a stinking industrial lake. Throughout, Morrie is preoccupied with the dreadful smell, and his nose is extra-sensitive to his brother's body and clothes, in a manner that plays on and challenges black stereotypes of the period. Morrie waits on Zach like a housewife (there is a homoerotic undercurrent to their relationship), setting a clock to make sure his brother's footbath is ready when he comes home from his exhausting day as a guard at a gate. As the two fuss over the trivialities of home-keeping (e.g., which foot salts are superior) in the first of the play's seven scenes, they develop this context of a bickering husband and wife while also replicating the style of sniping enmeshment engaged in by Hamm and Clov throughout Beckett's *Endgame*. Beckett's desolate, absurdist works are clearly invoked here, and his pessimism regarding the human condition takes on special meaning in the absurd and atrocious context of Apartheid-era South Africa.

The bare inner sanctum and ruined outer wasteland of Beckett's post-apocalyptic world is concertized in the impoverished shack of the typical South African black homeland and the polluted, unbreathable air and undrinkable water outside (see also Wertheim, *Dramatic Art*, 20). Albert Wertheim regards the final moments of *Blood Knot* as Zach and Morrie's "endgame"; "like Hamm and Clov, Morrie and Zach have a pastime to pass time, a relationship to occupy them while they live out their lives without a future. They are destined to continue on hopelessly, like so many other blacks and coloreds, their lives devoid of meaning because they can look to no future" (32). Calling attention to the theatricality of the Beckett-style silent comedy (even after Zach's entrance) of the play's early moments, Robert L. King observes that "'When [Zach] sees Morrie smile,' he directs our attention to acting as a technique of social control: 'He frowns, pretends to think, and makes a great business of testing the water with his foot'; ... we are led to laugh at Zachariah's 'great business' at the same time that his role playing takes over the scene from Morris, the one who has elaborately prepared it" (40).

Fugard himself has always cited as an influence the existentialism of Camus and Sartre over the absurdism of Beckett, especially the guilt and responsibility of bearing witness to the suffering of a "brother" and being powerless to alleviate same. The white Fugard's own white brother presented him with just such an existential dilemma when he once came home from travels after a long time, his face lined with the suffering of his difficult life. Dennis Walder locates two more racially inflected instances of witness-bearing in Fugard's life: he was a reporter in the mid-1950s for the Port Elizabeth *Evening Post*, doing a story on beleaguered blacks in a literacy class, who studied so that they could read the white man's signs and stay out of trouble (409). Later he was employed "as clerk in a 'Native Commissioner's Court,' where pass-law offenders were jailed every few minutes" (414). Too, Fugard was thoroughly engaged with the black theater community in 1960s South Africa and thus translated his personal epiphany with his brother into a play for an interracial cast, which had its own dramatic impact: although the play was allowed to tour South Africa for six months in 1962, laws against white and black actors appearing on stage—the original cast was Fugard as Morrie and Zakes Mokae as Zach—were passed shortly thereafter. But in the longer, more important run, plays such as *Blood Knot* instilled in white South Africans an awareness that eventually led to the dismantling of Apartheid. Although *Blood Knot* identifies the brothers as mixed-race, white and black actors have traditionally played the parts, such that they demonstrate less a biological than an allegorical brotherhood and such that their symbolizing of racial difference "under one roof" is clear: the brothers portray the national family that is South Africa and the love–hate bonds that permanently attach and mortally threaten the white brother as well as the black. Fugard said in a 2008 interview with Jessica Werner Zack that he saw "both brothers as equally oppressed" (10).

Blood Knot spends its early scenes establishing an opposition between the brothers that goes beyond the ability of one to pass, although this certainly has a profound impact on their relationship: Morris is torn apart by the dilemma of whether or not to reach for a better life; Zach, as abject as he is in his permanently stigmatized state, at least suffers no such identity crises. He is quite simply who he is and can rest assured in the lifelong consistency between self and appearance. His life, of course, is anything but restful, as he is clearly the more set-upon brother in the Apartheid context; Morrie has managed to earn for himself literacy and freedom of movement, but Zach's utter powerlessness in his workplace and his primitive, even animal-like qualities are emphasized as evidence of Apartheid's brutalizing effects: not only the bad smells of Zach's body and clothing but his unfamiliarity with the use of toilet paper, his past history of having raped a local woman (whom he regards as a former girlfriend), and his repeated bellowing, like a Neanderthal in a cave, for "Woman!" In Derek Cohen's estimation, "Morrie has tried to civilize his brother, make him aware of the finer things ... has tried to make him conscious of the future, and willing to hope" (76–77). Yet Morrie's dream of saving money so that the brothers can eventually own a two-man farm in more neutral territory is no more admirable (because so much less realistic) than Zach's fantasies about instant sexual gratification, drinking, and listening to music with his friend Minnie. In his impulsive demands for quick, furtive enjoyments in the here and now, Zach grasps the realities of his political condition while his misty-eyed brother with his light skin and unwinnable (white) goals does not.

Many have drawn attention to the female characters in this play who never appear onstage—the tragic Connie of Zach's younger days; the brown-skinned mother whose preference for the lighter or darker child is a permanent sorrowful mystery to both men; and Ethel Lange from the distant locale of Oudtshoorn, the pen-pal who answers Morrie's response (writing as Zach) to her ad in the personals section of the local paper. Ethel sends her "snap," and it is revealed, to the brother's amazement, amusement, and then—when she writes again to announce an impending visit in the company of her brother the policeman—terror that she is white. Ethel's brother appears accidentally in the photo; his boot sticking into the foreground is a harbinger of the thrashing the men will receive if they are ever caught in their act. The brothers contrive a scheme to extend their ruse and fend off the threat represented by Ethel: O'Henry-style, they sacrifice the funds they have stashed for the farm to buy Morrie a white man's suit of clothes, which it is soon determined they will not even need when Ethel's last letter announces her engagement to another man. When she is still on her way, Morrie contemplates the sartorial splendors his brother brings home, and hesitates:

MORRIS: Give me time.
ZACHARIAH: For what?
MORRIS: For God's sake, Zach! This is deep water. I'm not going to
             just jump right in. Men drown that way. You must paddle
             around first....
ZACHARIAH: (*Offering him the hat.*) Try it on.
MORRIS: The idea, man. I got to try it out. There's more to wearing a
             white skin than just putting on a hat. You've seen white men
             before without hats, but they're still white men. (80)

Zach comically insists that although a white man might be white without his hat, he's never seen a white man "without sock and shoes. Never a barefoot white man" (81).

As the brothers search out a prospective white identity for Morris, he tells a long story, reminiscent of Hamm's narrative late in *Endgame* of the begging father who crawls to him in search of bread for his dying son. In his own memory-dream, Morrie walks a long distance, following a man in front of him, with whom he seeks comfort and communion as night falls. The other man, however, recognizes his mixed-race status and raises a stick against him. Haunted by the incident, Morris uses the admiration and envy (not to mention anger and humiliation) he felt at that time "to walk properly ... and to sound right" (83) in preparation for his meeting with Ethel. Finally both Morrie and Zach (who provokes him until he explodes) find this white identity in the racist epithet—"Hey, swartgat!" (86; "black-ass," an extremely derogatory South African term for a person of color)—Morris hurls at Zach as he role-plays a peanut vendor in the park. At the end of the scene, Zach even fails to recognize his brother; Morris "tear[s] off the jacket and hat in a frenzy":

MORRIS: Now do you see?
ZACHARIAH: It's you.

MORRIS:	Yes!
ZACHARIAH:	That's funny, I thought—
MORIRS:	I know, I saw it again…. The pain, man, the pity of it, and all the pain … in your eyes. (86)

Deeply shamed by his outburst, Morris resolves to move away the next day, then decides to stay when the letter announcing Ethel's engagement arrives. Yet the brothers, sadomasochistically, tragically, absurdly, seem unwilling or unable to give up their "game." Morrie dons the fancy clothes again, resumes the action with another taunt of "swartgat!," and concludes by viciously beating Zach with an umbrella. In the course of things, Zach has called Morrie a bastard, and the brothers have treated themselves to the fantasy of stoning their poor, half-naked mother to death. Per King, "through [Morris], Fugard virtually equates role-playing with identity, and once into the role, Morris must pursue its full implications" (45). As he administers the beating, Morris curses Zach for "crawling around like that. Spoiling the view. Spoiling my chances!" (101). Deeply shaken and saddened, yet also perversely "relieved" by his violence against Zach, Morrie concludes the play by stating that the brothers will have their game to play over and over, now that there is no "future" (having traded the farm money for the suit). Zach might wish to end the cycle or separate from his brother, but Morrie insists that both are "home" and that they are "tied together" (104) in the blood knot.

As Fugard himself has remarked, "Anything that will get people to think and feel for themselves, that will stop them delegating these functions to the politicians, is important to our survival. Theatre has a role to play in this" (qtd. in Cohen, 74). With regard to Fugard's township play *The Coat* (1966), actor Mulligan Mbikwane remarked during its first run, "We want to use the theatre. For what? … Some of us say to understand the world we live in, but we also boast a few idealists who think that theatre might have something to do with changing it" (qtd. in Walder, 420). In *Blood Knot*, black and white players enact an ordinary relationship (of mixed-race brothers) under the most socially challenging terms: black and white actors pretending both to belong to another racial caste and to be related, with the broader social "act"—game, sham, scheme—of racial difference and separation thoroughly undermined in the process. The story calls much meta-theatrical attention to Zach and Morrie as role-players; they recall games of make-believe from childhood and spend much of their time trying out habiliments, voices, and gestures not naturally their own. As Wertheim observes, "The on-stage presentation of *acting* two racial roles provides insight not merely to Morrie but to the audience, which is made aware, through the deconstruction of racial roles, that those roles are very much a form of acting, that apartheid is a form of theatre" (29). The "mixed race" men in the story enact the even more controversial gesture of courting a white woman; that there is no such actual character (let alone actual person) as Ethel hardly mitigates—and thus challenges as completely paranoid—the scandal of interracial romance presented in the story. Morrie and Zach stage an attempt, complete with scripting (the letters to Ethel) and costuming (the suit), to cross closely guarded racial lines, and Morrie, as a mixed-race man who can pass for white, may represent a bigger bogey in the racist imaginary than the easily demarcated Zach. When the audience is forced to recall, meanwhile, that an actual white man portrays Morrie and the actual white woman literally never materializes, the complications, confusions, absurdities, and futilities of maintaining racial distinctions come fully to light.

Fugard's play is an important touchstone for this review of contemporary American drama because, like many plays in this section, it tells a story of racial oppression experienced by diversely situated humans in a complex national landscape, managing despite its bleak context expressions of humor, truth, hope, and the triumph of insight if nothing else. Fugard has been cited by August Wilson as a chief influence (Savran, *In Their Own Words*, 292), and it is not possible to know the story of the destitute and motherless, role-playing, advantage-trading brothers in Suzan-Lori Parks's *Topdog/Underdog* without noting the uncanny resemblance to Fugard's Zach and Morrie. Many playwrights in this section (e.g., Hwang, Vogel, Yellow Robe) explore the exploitations perpetrated by relatives or compatriots against each other, those who by virtue of shared class, ethnicity, or "blood" poignantly, if not tragically, commit oppressions more effectively than does the disembodied social authority they insidiously bring home. Like Fugard, many contemporary playwrights (e.g., Parks, Ruhl, Cruz, Miranda) productively allegorize the stage as a microcosm of the modern world. Their characters, as actors who self-consciously don costumes and enact roles, use such role-playing to gain advantage over other characters and to call an audience's attention to their own roles as scripted social actors. Finally, Fugard and his fellow postmodern playwrights employ the concepts of play, uncertainty, and indeterminacy to undermine the conventions that equate theater with escapism in less motivated contexts.

Blood Knot was the first Fugard play to receive staging abroad (Cohen, 75), and Fugard himself is a "dual citizen" of both his home context of South Africa and the dramatic stages of the United States, especially on Broadway (where he revived his role as Morrie with Mokae reprising Zach in *Blood Knot* in 1985); at Yale Repertory Theater; and on the West Coast, where he makes his American home for part of each year. Significantly, Fugard commented in an interview with longtime collaborator Lloyd Richards, artistic director at Yale Rep, that his several roles as playwright, actor, and director in the original staging of *Blood Knot* were of "economic necessity.... I only started enjoying the luxuries so taken for granted in American theater when I came to Yale. I never had designers in my life. I never had dramaturges. I'm still trying to figure out what to do with that animal; what *do* you do with a dramaturge?" His work is produced regularly in South Africa, the United States, and worldwide, and his habitual transatlanticism in life and work bespeaks the dissolution of borders of national belonging and exclusion, as well as the notion of a homogenized national drama itself. The writers in this section clearly demonstrate that there are as many American dramas as there are Americans to stage the story, and that each will radically revise, enlarge, and improve the national narrative in the process.

FOB (1980)

David Henry Hwang (1957–)

FOB is David Henry Hwang's first play, and although it did not storm Broadway and international stages in the way that his multi-award-winning *M. Butterfly* (1988) has done, the playwright observes that it "may be my favorite play, because it was written so much out of instinct, before I acquired any so-called tools" (Savran, *In Their Own Words*, 123). To be sure, this play was presented first in Hwang's college dorm at Stanford in 1978, and when it received a well-acclaimed off-Broadway staging at the Public Theater in 1980, Hwang was a mere 23 years old. One of the ways to read *FOB*, in fact, is as the story of a young writer paying homage to "two figures from American literature," as Hwang states in the Playwright's Note: Maxine Hong Kingston, whose mythic heroine from *The Woman Warrior*, Fa Mu Lan, returns as an alter-ego for *FOB*'s heroine Grace, and Frank Chin, whose god from Chinese folk tradition, Gwan Gung, is the main identity claimed by the "FOB," the fresh-off-the-boat Chinese immigrant, whom Grace tags with the Americanized "Steve." Per Esther Kim Lee, "Kingston and Chin influenced Hwang equally, and he thought about how he would position himself as a Chinese American working alongside such important voices" (*Theater*, 13).

Notably, Steve himself never identifies with the name; instead he is a mysteriously regal if not immortal (or perhaps just obnoxiously arrogant) figure who happens into Grace's restaurant early in the story, demanding to be served *chong you bing*, a savory Chinese pancake, and whose identity and history shift throughout. In addition to his Gwan Gung persona, "god of warriors, writers, and prostitutes" (Hwang, 11), Steve presents as the son of a rich merchant who has come over in an airplane (instead of in steerage on some arduous ocean journey, as early Chinese immigrants have done) and as a desperate immigrant from the turn of the twentieth century, begging unseen officials to grant him entrance to the United States, then later begging an unseen wealthy white women to trade his laundry services for food. He also shifts languages and accents throughout the play, from Chinese to ordinary English when alone with Grace, to broken "Chinese" English when interacting with Dale, the third character in the story. Likewise, Grace, a seemingly ordinary UCLA student helping out in the back room of her parents' restaurant in Torrance, California, where the entire story takes place, monologues as Kingston's mythic queen, then shifts into blasé "southern Californian" dialect (E. Lee, *Theater*, 18) when interacting with the two men; in all three Hwang mixes "the mythic and the mundane" (E. Lee, *Theater*, 18) as he does in many of his works.

Comedy follows from Steve's Gwan Gung–style posturing and Grace's deadpan refusal to be impressed; she informs her visitor that no modern-day Chinese Americans have ever heard of Gwan Gung, that her own information comes only from a Chinese American history course at UCLA attended by dental technicians and bored housewives. When Steve later questions the patrons of the restaurant, he is dismayed to learn that the indifference is indeed universal, because as Grace remarks, "No one gives a wipe about you around here. You're dead" (14). (Later, Dale will attempt to humiliate Steve by making him wipe up the table they've been eating on.) Dale is readable as a comically self-deprecating rendition of Hwang himself; he is an "ABC" (American-born Chinese) who is "dressed in preppie clothes" (7), has no accent, and drives an expensive sports car, typical of wealthy Los Angelinos. Josephine Lee remarks that Dale "rejects the notion of ethnic identification and collectivity and overtly celebrates the individualism of the 'free self.' At the same time, [his] preoccupation with material goods is satirized" as excessive and in its failure to achieve for him "personal satisfaction" (175). Yet his wisecracking attitude about the greenhorn mannerisms of the newcomer Steve is balanced by the doubts and anxieties regarding the racism he himself faces throughout life—"I've had to work hard, real hard, to be myself. To not be a Chinese, a slant, a yellow, a gook. To be just a human being" (33)—that he voices in a soul-searching monologue. As Josephine Lee observes, "Dale is [also] haunted by his father's betrayal of his grandfather's trust" (177), in his refusal to return home following his American education. Dale sees his grandfather's "hopes reduced to a few chattering teeth and a pack of pornographic playing cards" (qtd. in J. Lee, 177) and attempts elsewhere in the play to transfer his shameful family history onto Steve.

During the time the play was written, Chin had famously criticized Kingston for Americanizing the Chinese mythology on display in *The Woman Warrior* to suit western expectations (see E. Lee, *Theater*, 13). Throughout *FOB*, Grace (the Kingston avatar) and Steve (the Chin avatar) snipe at each other sharply and even break into a sword fight at the end of the play. As Esther Kim Lee observes, "By the time Hwang wrote *FOB* he was aware of the public exchange between Kingston and Chin…. Instead of taking sides, he let the mythic characters created by [them] clash onstage" (13). But the arrival of Dale mid-play causes Grace to feel pulled between the two men and the cultural narrative each represents. Esther Kim Lee argues that in Grace "Hwang complicates the dramatic conflict and opens the possibility of moving beyond a simple binary (FOB vs. ABC) and towards a more ambitious articulation of assimilation" (12). Grace spends time as the men's mediator and as the object of their mutual interests, increasing the tension between them, but at last Fa Mu Lan is reconciled with her adversary, Gwan Gung, and Grace leaves on the arm of the FOB, Steve, leaving Dale to ponder his rejection. Grace herself, despite her highly assimilated values, goals, and speech patterns, is first-generation, having arrived in the United States at the age of 10 and suffering continued humiliation at the memory of the ABC girls in her grade school who "just stay with themselves and compare how much clothes they all had, and make fun of the way we [immigrants] talked" (31). Despite her tendencies to emulate the American-born Dale, she at last claims what seems to be romantic attachment and political solidarity with the FOB, Steve. His Gwan Gung persona indicates that despite his greenhorn exterior, within beats the heart of a noble son and worthy heir of Chinese culture transferred to American shores. Per Josephine Lee, "Unlike Dale, Grace and Steve ultimately find their relation through the use of legends. Notably, these are specifically Asian American rather than Asian versions of the traditional myths" (180). The play's Coda is a repetition of the speech Dale made in the Prologue, where he comically criticized the newly arrived immigrant as "loud, stupid, four-eyed…. Big feet. Horny…. Before an ABC girl will be seen on a Friday night with a boy FOB in Westwood, she would rather burn off her face" (7). But as Esther Kim Lee notes, "[E]verything [Dale] says about the FOB the second time around is more questioning than mocking" (*Theater*, 15). She adds that "Dale is confused, but is he also angry? How has his attitude toward FOBs changed? … By withholding the details of Dale's feelings, Hwang creates ambiguity and openness for those [actors and audience members] interpreting the play's meaning" (19).

Hwang has remarked on the influence of his fellow Californian Sam Shepard, and Maria Irene Fornés, "one of the best playwriting teachers on earth" (Savran, *In Their Own Words*, 119), both of whom mentored him during a residency at the Padua Hills Playwrights' Festival in 1978. Both of these earlier dramatists experiment with linear plot structure and realist characterization (above, I described the "fugue" elements in Shepard's *Buried Child*) and in similar fashion, says Hwang, "*FOB* goes from one thing to another without any explicit reason" (Savran, *In Their Own Words*, 120). To be sure, loosely attached motifs such as the gift Grace is wrapping at the start of the play, arguments about which young man's car to take on the outing that ultimately never occurs, ordering and eating *bing*, and the several persona shifts of Grace and Steve surface and resurface; the effect is diffuse and cumulative instead of pointed and universally agreed on. *FOB* suggests that Chinese immigrant identity is a shifting, relative, guilt-inducing, and pride-instilling space of habitation that each Chinese American must create for him or herself and stabilize to whatever degree possible or desirable.

The play's setting itself is meaningfully liminal, if not chimerical, a space between the Westernized main dining room where Grace's parents serve American customers as well as their fellow Chinese immigrants, and the kitchen occupied by Grace's parents, where the hot, difficult work of running the restaurant is closed off from the eyes of patrons. Per Esther Kim Lee, "The Chinese restaurant functions as a microcosm of Chinese America, as both an imagined and real space where assimilation is played out in multiple ways" (*Theater*, 14). And "[Hwang's] choice to set the play in the back of the restaurant" accords with his interest in many of his plays "in revealing what takes place behind the scenes—both literally and metaphorically—and in complicating the view the average individual perceives of Chinese America" (14). That the kitchen and its parental occupants are never seen implies the shame or discomfort that the younger generation feels for the unassimilated elders (with this lack of respect itself a sign of Americanization). It likewise suggests the shame the elder generation may itself feel for living their lives as backroom cooks (instead of in the professions they may have trained for in their homeland) and watering down their recipes so as not to offend the timid American palate. Firmly associated with this transitional backroom space, Grace herself is torn between identifying with her parents' first-generation experience of oppression and exclusion, and joining the assimilating demographic of the dining room, whose members are free to come and go or not to patronize her family's establishment at all. Early in the play, she insists that the three young people get out of the restaurant "before 5," when it opens for the dinner service, suggesting that she would rather eat at a mainstream American restaurant and that she desires to avoid the menial waitress role she plays when at the family shop. When Grace later decides, both as regards where to eat dinner and where to spend their after-dinner time together, that the three should stay where they are, she indicates her growing awareness of the value of her home culture. The reconciliation of her mythic persona with Steve's is part of her personal epiphany. Having suffered in her ancestral past from the battle raids of Gwan Gung, present-day Fa Mu Lan vanquishes present-day Gwan Gung in the operatic sword fight, at which point "he becomes a 'Chinaman' begging for food" (E. Lee, 18). She redeems him with the gift of *bing* (the contents of the box that she wrapped in the first scene), although Steve has proven his manhood by his ability to consume great qualities of spicy food in the dinner scene. With a final chant in praise of Steve (or Gwan Gung) the man, Grace celebrates "your mouth … your teeth … your tongue … your throat" as "beautiful" (Hwang, 30), and celebrates her own power to nurture others and self.

FOB won the 1981 Obie Award for Best New American Play and a Performance recognition for John Lone in the role of Steve. It has been revived numerous times in regional US theaters and internationally.

The Independence of Eddie Rose (1986)

William S. Yellow Robe Jr. (1950–)

William S. Yellow Robe Jr. is a member of the Assiniboine nation of northern Montana and the author of dozens of well-regarded plays produced in regional theaters nationwide. He claims several contemporary Native American writers and contemporary American dramatists as influences; within the former group are James Welch, Joy Harjo, and Lewis Owens, and the latter group includes David Henry Hwang, August Wilson, and Suzan-Lori Parks. Himself three-eighths African American, Yellow Robe claims special affinity with the work of Wilson, his stories of family in struggle and his effort to "move people along" (qtd. in Beete). His recent play, *Grandchildren of the Buffalo Soldiers* (2009) works through the internal and external conflicts experienced by Native people whose African American blood comes from cavalry soldiers fighting alongside white regiments to exterminate Natives from the Western states in the late 1800s; this play received a production with Lou Bellamy's African American theater company Penumbra in St. Paul, as "There aren't many Native American writers who have dealt with the history of the Buffalo soldiers…. He has personalized a very large issue and brought it down to one family" (qtd. in Rooks). Yellow Robe has claimed Eugene O'Neill as another major influence (Rathbun, 343), and to be sure *The Independence of Eddie Rose* presents centrally the ruinous theme of alcoholism in a family, reminiscent of O'Neill's *Long Day's Journey into Night*. Though the two children in O'Neill's play were adult men, trapped permanently in their family's cycle of deception and denial obscured by the stupors of alcohol and morphine abuse, *Eddie Rose* belongs to the "long Native tradition of 'leaving home' plays, in which young boys enact an Oedipal narrative by fighting for their independence from an oppressive father/loving mother, eventually breaking free and starting a new life" (Mojica and Knowles, 3–4).

Themes such as these take us as well to the central conflict in Wilson's *Fences* (see below). It is as if *Eddie Rose* were written from the standpoint of Troy's son Cory, who joins the military at the end of Wilson's play to escape his own Oedipal struggle with his overbearing father. Reminiscent of Wilson's salvific Raynell, there is even a charming younger sister in this play, a 10-year-old named Theia. Unfortunately, the loving mother of Native tradition and Wilson's play has been all but destroyed by her own enthrallment to alcohol in *Eddie Rose*, but there is a loving, sober, proudly Native aunt in the ensemble, who rescues Theia from her abusive home when Eddie departs for school. As Alexander Pettit observes, with Eddie's release from his own home-based travails, "[T]he play thus transcends the anxiety about solutions that characterize much realistic drama" (277). Meanwhile, Eddie is readable as descending if not from the doomed Tyrone brothers of O'Neill's play, then from another departing son from the height of the realist era, Biff Loman in *Death of a Salesman*, who sees through the shams of his father's, mother's, and brother's lives and resolves to go West. Finally, comparing Eddie Rose to another famously disaffected youth from the twentieth century, Holden Caufield, David Krasner argues that Yellow Robe's drama is a "Native American Bildungsdrama," or coming-of-age story: "Eddie's 'independence' is, ironically, not equated with having the freedom to travel the world with his friend Mike; rather, it is circumscribed by his sister's *dependence* on him. His commitment to Theia … breaks the cycle of self-destruction in his family, imbuing him with the characteristics of adulthood" ("Coming," 175).

Yellow Robe has remarked that what one critic terms the "kitchen-sink naturalism" (qtd. in Däwes, 453) of his plays tends to bother white audiences who expect mysticism and magical realism in Native American texts. More interested to confront his Native and white audiences with the poverty, substance abuse, and lack of options actually faced by Native peoples on a daily basis, Yellow Robe has remarked to interviewers, "I don't do Sundance 101 in my plays. I leave that for others" (Uno, 101). In another interview, Yellow Robe considered the conflict between sensationalism and stereotypes (e.g., regarding Native American alcoholism) and the "hard slice of life" he wished to portray in his drama. "We have people who are so concerned about being politically correct that they don't really understand why that stereotype existed, how it came to be" (Rathbun, 349). Later, "on the one hand you can't talk about alcoholism because it's a stereotype; at the same time, if you don't deal with it, people will die" (Rathbun, 350).

The story's grim themes are established at the outset, when the set includes "metal folding chairs and a table" with no mention of any other furniture (although later a couch is employed). Theia sits on one of the chairs, clutching "an old gray Snoopy doll" (7), and she and Eddie's mother, Katherine, are in the midst of tossing her deadbeat boyfriend, Lenny, out of the house for having stolen the money Eddie was planning to use to get himself to school. Theia is in tears, and yet Eddie prepares for leave-taking, his suitcase being a "paper sack." The story's moral crisis is established at this moment as well; Katherine is as violent and difficult as her loathsome boyfriend (whom she will take back in Act II); by the end of the first scene, she will make a sexual pass at her own son. Theia is helpless, and Aunt Thelma, to appear in the next scene, is the saving angel. She cleans up the beer cans and cigarettes from Katherine's carousing, makes the kids' dinner, and tries to respect the rights of their mother by doing all she can to keep them in the home. Meanwhile, Eddie is caught in a bind: he packs up (he is squirreling away cans of food in the cemetery where is grandmother is buried) in the midst of family crisis, when it is clear that his sister needs his protection so long as she is trapped in Katherine's house. Even where to go presents a dilemma: should he head to boarding school with the hopes of an education and meaningful work, or should he help his friend Mike, with his own neglectful, alcoholic mother, get away from sadistically sodomizing guards at the jail where he's been booked for drug possession? Notably, Mike also has a loving aunt in Seattle, where the boys plan to run, and is also traumatized by a sexual encounter with his own mother: in the woods with friends one night, he was propositioned by a local prostitute who then realized she had approached her own son in a moment of humiliation for Mike. With these sexually threatening mothers on the scene, Yellow Robe completes the Oedipal complex in a gritty, modern mode: in this markedly dysfunctional environment, the fathers are downright murderous, and the mothers only intensify the conflict and trauma. Finally Mike makes his own getaway; Eddie is bound for school; and Aunt Thelma, following a violent showdown with Katherine and Lenny and Lenny's dreadful rape of Theia in a night of drunken anger, has brought the law to bear. Katherine is made to sign papers against Lenny (for the rape) and releasing both her children to Thelma's custody; deep irony attaches to Eddie's statement at the end of the play, "Thank you Mom. You gave me life again" (72); she has done so by making herself, in Aunt Thelma's words, dead to the rest of the family forever. Seeing Eddie's leave-taking as a necessary "separating ... from his biological roots," Rachel Däwes observes that in *Eddie Rose*, "Cultural identity becomes a dynamic process: instead of being fixed by categories of blood quantum or genetic heritage, it depends upon an individual's affiliations, mobility and choice" (453).

Although Yellow Robe eschews the dream-catcher mysticism (and optimism) expected from Native authors, in fact Aunt Thelma is a capable conveyer to the youngsters of a proud Native tradition. While gently brushing Theia's hair in an early scene (after Katherine has abusively yanked at it in a fit of jealous rage), she burns the leavings from the hairbrush in an ashtray, per Native custom. As Thelma explains, "If you let the hair go without taking care of it [disposing of it], it can bring you bad things. Even ghosts" (32). Thelma reminisces about how good Theia's grandmother was: "Your grandma ... never drank. She used to say it was never part of the Indin' people" (32). As the grandmother was well loved and deeply mourned when she passed, and as is also according to Native custom, "[Y]our mom and I, we cut our hair. We women do that when someone dies. When it is someone close to you and you love them" (32). Later in the play, Thelma cuts her braids with the pained declaration to Katherine that "[y]ou are dead for me" (44), and her remarks here to Theia indicate that this is a gesture of love and mourning for the sister with whom she was once so close. When, at the end of the play, Eddie begins to perform the customary burning of his aunt's braids, Katherine takes the first step toward reclaiming her proud heritage when she tells her son, "My boy, women do this. Just go" (73).

Notably, Lenny, Mike, and Sam (the vicious guard at the jail) are described as mixed-race in origin, and aside from Eddie they are the only male characters in the play. Yellow Robe depicts, therefore, a reservation environment largely abandoned by full-blooded men who can carry on Native custom for a young man coming of age such as Eddie. Their absence echoes their decimation at the hands of white invaders in prior centuries, as well as modern Native men's own tendency to simply leave home or to pass away early due to alcohol abuse or other oppression-related health issues. It is therefore once again up to Aunt Thelma to school Eddie in the particulars of even traditionally male rituals. In the cemetery next to his grandmother's plot one night, Aunt Thelma finds Eddie and prepares him as adult men might have steeled a young warrior for battle in earlier times: setting a match to some sage leaves in a bowl, Thelma says a prayer and tells her nephew, "Now wash yourself in the smoke," demonstrating with gestures of taking a bath. Her nephew "dips his hands in the bowl and begins to bathe himself." Thelma tells Eddie, "Now you are ready my ... my son.... I want you to go into that house of death and bring Theia to me if you can" (47; first ellipsis in original). Clearly this purification rite has had its transformative effect on Thelma as well: for the first time in the play she dares to usurp her sister's role, calling Eddie her son and agreeing to shelter his sister from future conflict. Eventually, Eddie succeeds in his quest to save Theia and prepares for his departure to school. Although he is yet another proud Native man leaving women and reservation behind, it is on this occasion under the best, most hopeful circumstances.

Theater scholars and professionals regard *The Independence of Eddie Rose* as Yellow Robe's "signature piece" (qtd. in Däwes, 451) and "most popular play" (Haugo, 56). It was first staged at the University of Montana under the direction of Rolland Meinholtz in 1986 and given its first professional production by the Seattle Group Theater in 1987. It has received several staged readings and regional productions since then and is frequently anthologized in collections of Native American dramas. Yellow Robe is the recipient of numerous awards and honors, including a TCG National Theater Artist Residency fellowship, an NEA fellowship, and a First Nations Book Award for Drama, for *Eddie Rose* and his other work. Oskar Eustis, current Artistic Director of the Public Theater, is a significant admirer and supporter of Yellow Robe's work. He regards *Eddie Rose* as "powerful and revelatory—and upsetting as well.... It is hard to write a play that is so honest about such brutal things but, nonetheless, hopeful at the end" (qtd. in Rooks).

Fences (1987)

August Wilson (1945–2005)

In this Pulitzer- and Tony-winning drama from Wilson's ten-play cycle regarding African American life in the twentieth century, ex-Negro League baseball player Troy Maxson is declared by his best friend, Bono, early in the play to have "come along too early" (16) to achieve greatness in the integrated leagues of the late 1950s, when the play is set. In *Fences*, Wilson presents his audience with a crisis unique to the African American dreamer in US culture: by the simple fate of a life beginning, unfolding, or even ending before integration milestones open necessary doors, African Americans like 53-year-old Troy may spend their lives bitterly lamenting misfortune—and ironically, stubbornly maintaining a mindset suited to earlier times. Attempting to persuade Troy to allow his son Cory accept a football scholarship to college, Rose informs her husband, "Times have changed from when you was young, Troy.... The world is changing around you, and you don't even know it" (40). Although the stellar athletic and political accomplishments of Jackie Robinson, and later Roy Campanella, Henry Aaron, and Satchel Paige, were cause for universal celebration within the African American community of the late 1940s and 1950s, Troy speaks disparagingly of these national heroes, insisting to his wife and best friend, "I done seen a hundred niggers play baseball better than Jackie Robinson" (16) and to his son that "Hank Aaron ain't nobody" (36). Susan Koprince points out that the powerfully built, heavy-hitting Troy is likely modeled on the great slugger Josh Gibson of the Negro League's Pittsburgh Crawfords (351); per James Robert Saunders, with *Fences*, "[W]e are allowed to imagine how it might have been if Gibson, who died [of a stroke] at age 35 had lived to be age 53" (50). Gibson is referenced in the play as being twice as talented as many white players, but whose daughter walks around Pittsburgh in falling-apart shoes. Koprince also points out that like Troy, many Negro League players regarded Jackie Robinson as more of a gentleman than an athlete, someone who was selected as the first black player in the major leagues for his ability to tolerate great amounts of abuse (351; see also Saunders). But in his angry dismissal of otherwise highly regarded baseball greats, as well as his insistence that instead of attending college his son get a job fixing cars and his grievous betrayal of his stalwart wife (from the first scene it is indicated that he is having an affair), Troy is at odds with his late-1950s, progressively-minded African American community. In his stage notes, Wilson specifies a front porch, added recently by the skilled woodworker Troy. Like its builder, it is large, protective, and "sturdy," but it "lacks congruence" (n.p.) with itself and the rest of the house.

Kim Pereira remarks that historical events of the period, such as the career of Jackie Robinson, *Brown v. Board of Education*, and the Little Rock integration story "are not Wilson's primary territory," interested as he is instead to "register… the mythology of the period" (66). Yet when Rose remarks that the world is changing around Troy, she herself seems mindful of the inroads made by talented black athletes and aspiring college graduates and desires to give her son the chance she sees others gaining for themselves. Importantly, Troy has, through his courage and integrity, achieved an important promotion on the job—from garbage lifter to truck driver, breaking the color line in that local industry. Yet Troy resolutely turns his face from such milestones of the present, insisting—and he is certainly largely correct with respect to his own middle-aged, blue-collar, under-unionized context—that there is no chance in America for a black man with a dream. Troy spends much of the play complaining about the bosses, storekeepers, and furniture-dealers who have limited his workplace advancement, denied him credit, or overcharged him for goods; most of his conversations with his family regard money, and he has no encounters with either Cory or Cory's half-brother Lyons that are not occasions for cynical reproach. Thus *Fences* is very much the dissection of a psyche profoundly misshaped by not only the lost opportunities of a professional calling but also daily degradation as a black sanitation worker in 1950s Pittsburgh.

Troy's brother Gabriel is a veteran of World War II, dealing with resulting permanent head injury; he was compensated by the military only $3000, which Troy has used to purchase the home that he and his family (and until recently, Gabe also) live in. Although Gabe presents as a beloved, addle-brained foil to his brother, Troy deals with almost-as-serious psychological limitations; his wife complains that she "cannot get no sense out of [him]" (40), and it is difficult not to regard Troy's every decision as perversely disastrous for all involved. Harry J. Elam Jr. regards Gabriel as one of Wilson's visionary fools whose "racial madness" (a term he adopts from Fanon, DuBois, and writers such as Ellison and Baraka) "largely results from confrontations with white power structures" (64). To be sure, Gabriel's intellect has been badly damaged in service to the white-run military during the war. But Koprince also borrows Elam's term to also describe "Troy's efforts to prevent his son from playing football." She agrees that in *Fences* Gabriel is the most vivid indicator of the phenomenon of racial madness, but "it is also revealed in Troy himself, who is so overwhelmed by bitterness that he destroys his son's dream of a college education" (354). Up until he signs the papers that get Gabriel recommitted to the mental hospital, Troy argues with his wife over Gabe's need to be "free"; in truth, Gabe is readable as much freer in his total incapacity than is Troy, who is driven to a form of madness by feelings of regret regarding his lost baseball career, envy and bitterness with respect to his sons, and guilt and betrayal with respect to his wife and brother. As Elam points out, Gabe is "'outside of history'… beyond the threat of earthly events" (*Past as Present*, 64). Notably, Troy also "came along too early" to suffer the losses endured by Gabe during the war; being seven years older, and likely already with a wife and son to keep him from the draft, Troy suffers guilt for having used his brother's compensation to buy his own home. He declares in another moment of righteous anger, tinged with a rare admission of guilt and shame, "If my brother didn't have that metal plate in his head… I wouldn't have a pot to piss in, nor a window to throw it out of" (31).

Wilson imbues Troy with a mythic aspect through his several occasions of having met Death and the devil and beaten them both. As John Lahr observed in a *New Yorker* profile in 2001, "Under [Wilson's] focused gaze, characters take on uncanny, sometimes awesome, life" ("Been Here," 32). In an early scene Troy recalls how he struggled through a bout of severe pneumonia, wrestling with Death for "three days and three nights" (18), winning reprieve through superior strength. At that point, Troy also boasts of having spoken to the devil; although this comically devolves into an unmasking of the local furniture financer as the devil in disguise, Troy later tells the story of having seen "the devil himself" (31) in his own father, who threw his 14-year-old son off his 13-year-old girlfriend so that he could have her for himself. Troy emerges from the contest physically battered but morally victorious by leaving home, walking 200 miles to Mobile to begin life on his own. Operating in its own mythic vein, Gabriel's madness takes the form of his delusion that he is the angel Gabriel. While guilty Troy repeatedly outwits the approach of Death, righteous Gabriel gladly visits St. Peter at the heavenly gates, boasting of his ability to use his trumpet to fend off the hounds of hell (40). At the drama's climax, Cory challenges Troy three times, then "strikes out" when Troy sees "the devil in [his son]" (80) and vanquishes him once more. As Troy wrestles his son to the ground and threatens him with his baseball bat, Cory disappears from his father's life to join the Marines. Yet Troy's victory is qualified at best; Cory accuses his father of having "never done anything but hold me back. Afraid I was gonna be better than you" (79). He rightly challenges Troy for having cheated on his mother and taken his uncle Gabe's military severance to buy his own house. Troy fends off the accusations, but the audience is inclined to share his son's determination that, in taking Cory for the devil, Troy has in fact gone "crazy" (80). Troy indeed seems to have met his match; at his son's exit, he once again sees Death coming for him, and the next scene, seven years later in 1965, is the morning of Troy's funeral.

Wilson defended this epic father-son battle to David Savran, when he stated that "Troy would have been tremendously disappointed if Cory had not challenged him…. [But] the only world Troy knows is the one that he made. Cory's going to go on and find another one, he's going to arrive at the same place as Troy" (*In Their Own Words*, 300). But as Matthew Roudané remarks, "it is difficult to agree fully with the playwright" ("Safe," 140) in his defense of Troy. Roudané points to the father's "pent-up rage" and "inability to understand his son's point of view" and concludes that "the same audience [who detects Troy's love for Cory] may also detect much resentment, misunderstanding, and ignorance within that love" (140).

Per the play's remarkable focus on the fates handed its male characters by virtue of their dates of birth, Cory comes home as a corporal in the Marines in the year that began the American occupation in Vietnam. Lyons advises Cory to "stick with Uncle Sam and retire early" (85), downplaying the prospects that the early retirement facing a low-ranking African American Marine in Vietnam could easily be dismemberment, debilitating brain injury, or death (see also Savran, *In Their Own Words*, 301). The audience hopes that Cory will follow his own thinking on the matter, "I got six [years] already. I think that's enough" (85). Wilson has staggered the ages of Troy's several relatives, such that the generation between Lyons and Cory can be said to account for the younger man's more informed understanding of the weight behind his military options. Rose is ten years younger than Troy, and while he was alive, the disparity in their ages may have accounted for Rose's ability to inhabit the modern sensibilities that her husband could not. Meanwhile, upon Troy's death, she very much adopts the voice of the senior generation; though she herself never forgave Troy for his sexual betrayal, resulting in the birth of a daughter now being raised by herself, she insists that Cory forgive and honor his father despite his several misdeeds against him. Cory eventually does agree to attend his father's funeral, although his mind (and heart) may be changed less by Rose's speechmaking than by the clean break with the past represented by his darling half-sister, seven-year-old Raynell. Notably Raynell has planted a garden in what had been a dirt yard in all earlier scenes, and per Elam, "for Wilson children are a fertile soil in which the lessons of history can be planted" (*Past as Present*, 58).

Depicting Troy and Cory as more or less doomed to relive the crisis that Troy underwent with his own father, Wilson remarked, "I suspect with Cory it will repeat with some differences and maybe, after five or six generations, they'll find a different way to do it" (Savran, *In Their Own Words* 301). But *Fences*'s youngest characters seem primed to move beyond the old cycle with more rapidity than Wilson suggests; Cory and Raynell share a warming memory of their father by singing about a dog named Old Blue; Cory finds it in his heart to bury his father with his dignity intact; and Gabriel breaks into a "slow, strange dance, eerie and life-giving" (91) to commemorate past and future as the curtain falls. As Roudané observes, "[B]y the play's end, an earlier [Amiri] Barakian rage has yielded to a Hansberryan sense of renewal and hope" ("Safe," 143). Wilson famously lamented that by the end of the play, everyone "is institutionalized. Rose is in the church. Lyons is in a penitentiary [doing three years for stealing welfare checks]. Gabriel is in a mental hospital, and Cory is in the marines." Yet Wilson considers that "the black church [associated with Rose throughout the play] has been our saving grace" (Savran, *In Their Own Words*, 301); he therefore effectively establishes the affirmative context of the play's final scene through focus on Rose and her children, especially the bond forming between Cory and Raynell. Wilson singled out this youngest character as "free" from the institutions defining the rest of her family and as "the hope for the future" (Savran, *In Their Own Words*, 301). Although *Fences*, like all of Wilson's plays, pays homage to a long-suffering but consummately dignified ancestry attempting and often managing to bestow its invaluable legacy, Wilson also pointed out to Savran that "I try to position my characters so that they're pointed toward the future" (*In Their Own Words*, 298), and that is assuredly the direction prevailing as *Fences* comes to a close.

Drama in Dialogue: *Death of a Salesman* and *Fences*

Although *Fences* author August Wilson rejected the association throughout his life, the conversation cross-staged between Arthur Miller's iconic family drama from the late 1950s and Wilson's just as iconic revision from the 1980s (set, let us note, in the same moment as the Loman family tragedy) is too important to disregard. This conversation is even more remarkable given the fact that Wilson was himself a rare playgoer and claimed no knowledge of Miller's work when interviewed the year after *Fences* debuted on Broadway (Savran, *In Their Own Words*, 292). Several scholars in fact regard Wilson's denial of familiarity with *Death of a Salesman* as "figural rather than literal" (Wattley, 1). Mark Rocha sees Wilson as "repeat[ing] and revis[ing] the work of literary antecedents which in Wilson's case means 'getting in the face of' the American triumvirate of O'Neill, Miller, and Williams" (qtd. in Wattley, 2), and Michael Awkward considers the citation "self-conscious" (qtd. in Wattley, 1). Miller and Wilson, in their respective eras, make the case that the story they tell, of family, betrayal, and the "tragedy of the common man," is classically American yet thoroughly subject to revision per the dictates of the succeeding generations and unique communities contributing their version of the story.

Both plays are significantly autobiographical, as both Miller's hero, Willy Loman, and Wilson's, Troy Maxson, are based on family members: Miller's is closely tied to an uncle with deep regrets, defenses, and eccentricities never worked through. Following the collage technique of his artistic inspiration Romare Bearden, Wilson developed Troy from his experience with numerous father figures (as his own father, a hot-headed German immigrant who stayed away for much of the time, did not deserve the commendation): a mentor from across the street who was a garbage collector; his stepfather in later years, who, like Troy, spent a long stretch in prison for killing a man in the course of a robbery; and a local drug-dealer turned poet who protected Wilson from embroilments on the street (see Lahr, "Been Here," and see S. Freedman, ix). Even Wilson's overbearing mother figures forth in Troy to some extent; theirs was a fractious relationship after his stepfather had passed away, and like Cory, Wilson joined the military to get away from home (Lahr, "Been Here," 38). Although Miller's own avatar in *Death of Salesman* is the hard-working, unassuming, eventually tremendously successful Bernard, Wilson may be best represented in *Fences* in yet again Troy himself; as Matthew Roudané notes, Wilson "experienced the full force of white racism" ("Safe," 135) as a high school student and as a young man in this same late 1950s/early 1960s in which Troy's story is set. Troy's deep suspicion regarding white well-meaning may be said to represent Wilson's own. As Samuel Freedman remarks, it was Wilson who quit the high school football team, a move that "incensed" his stepfather (x), and Wilson thus seems to use Troy to make the case against college-level sports that he himself made when he was Cory's age.

A key difference between the two plays regards final assessment of the hero himself: despite Miller's reading of Willy in "Tragedy and the Common Man" as a tragic hero, *Salesman*'s controlling perspective at the end of the play is Biff's, who declares that Willy had "the wrong dreams" and that by contrast, "I know who I am" (111), and who will find happiness in a more honest life. At the end of *Fences*, meanwhile, this countervailing view has been silenced, and Troy is largely redeemed in the eyes of his community. Per Roudané, Willy heavily invested, to a damaging degree, in the prospects of his son attending college on a football scholarship, whereas Troy "wants [his son] to mend fences and secure a vocational job rather than attend ... college.... If Biff Loman saw his father as a fake, Cory sees Troy as a paternal oppressor" ("Safe," 139). On a related note, Ama Wattley remarks, "Willy and Troy's contrasting beliefs about their ability to attain the American dream, beliefs which reside in their racial identities, play a large role in how they relate to their sons" (3).

Almost all of the characters in Miller's play are repeated and revised in Wilson's: Willy and Troy are the two patriarchs who regrettably missed their calling in life; Willy, a mediocre route salesman, was in fact "a happy man with a batch of cement" (110), and Troy, who hauls garbage instead of playing in the major leagues, likewise works well with his hands as a talented carpenter. Each man has a loyal friend who provides emotional support (to the point of enabling troubling delusions) but eventually draws on his own clear-eyed sense of things to spell out hard truths. Each man has two sons—one more attached to his father's way of doing things, one more in rebellion—and each enjoys the undying devotion of a hard-working, under-respected wife. Both men cheat with a mistress of inferior caliber; both are exposed in the act by the favorite son; and both put up a frantic but flimsy wall of defense. Both men die following a final showdown with this beloved son, and the last act of each play is the funeral scene wherein the community, led by the loving wife, reassembles to celebrate what was best in the departed man. Miller's impassioned defense of Willy as tragic hero—as he who is "willing to lay down his life if need be, to secure one thing: his sense of personal dignity" ("Tragedy," 1)—applies with equal force to Wilson's Troy; Kim Pereira's description of Troy, as a man "whose idea of victory lies in moving from the back of the [garbage] truck into the driver's seat and who becomes an expression of a wider fight for dignity and purpose" (66) echoes Miller's definition of the modern hero of tragic stature. Although Troy seems to die of natural causes several years following his showdown with Cory, Wilson sequences the scenes to move immediately from Cory's departure to Troy's funeral. It is as if in both plays the father has done all that he can for (or to) his favored son and understands that it is time to accept Death's coming for him.

Both of the plays are known for their experimental features, and in both plays the mythic element emanates mainly from the mind of the main character; Troy is presented in *Fences* primarily as a visionary, but in *Salesman* Willy's vivid mental journeys into the past mark his decline into dementia. Ironically, both men engage with what is most real and most true in their lives through their fanciful excursions to a mythic world: Willy speaks from the heart to his (illusory) brother Ben about missing the father who left both boys at a young age and about his fears with respect to how he has raised his sons. In several scenes, his sons regard him as going senile, but Willy is only outside planting seeds for the garden that used to grow in less urbanized times, and the action represents the best, most essential part of who he is. Troy's stories of Death and the devil are disregarded by his more realistic wife, Rose, but Wilson clearly attaches to Troy's narratives a visionary significance that the others around him, more rooted in day-to-day particulars, fail to share. Although Willy can never know the oppression and limitation that his late-1950s African American counterpart endures on a daily basis, both men find themselves trapped by their age in an earlier era and suffer the sense of obsolescence at work and at home as time speeds into a more modern age. That said, we recall that in the late 1950s, Hansberry mellowed Miller's tragic conclusion—and Willy's wasted garden—by leading her Younger family triumphantly toward a better life, symbolized in the meager potted plant that Mama has coaxed into survival. In Wilson's own affirming view, Willy's failed crop growing is redeemed in the garden planted by Raynell, which comes vigorously to life in the midst of her father's funeral rites and family's mourning.

Oleanna (1992)

David Mamet (1947–)

This controversial drama examining the polarized implications of sexual harassment and political correctness pits an arrogant college professor, John, against his befuddled student, Carol, whom John condescends to in his office and attempts to comfort with an improper hug. In the second act, Carol, spurred on by militant feminist students in her cohort, turns her confusion into anger and accuses John of sexual harassment, jeopardizing his job, home purchase, and marriage. Like many Mamet plays, *Oleanna* (the title refers to a failed nineteenth-century utopia, as Mamet feels academe has become) concerns itself with a work environment where special languages—often suffused with obscure jargon—cause a power struggle between those who can and cannot use the terms effectively. In the first act, the conventional hierarchy asserts itself—John plies his erudition adroitly (that is, mystifyingly) and thus holds sway over Carol; in the final two acts, however, John's propensity toward mystification does him in: because none of his words and actions in Act I are finally clearable from the charges of impropriety and harassment, he can offer no proof of his innocence any more persuasive than Carol's proof of his guilt. In an interview, Mamet specifically likened John to Oedipus, as "he undergoes absolute reversal of situation, absolute recognition at the last moment of the play" (qtd. in Murphy, "*Oleanna*," 134); since John himself is "perhaps … the cause of plague in Thebes" (qtd. in Murphy, "*Oleanna*," 134), he is both the victim and the perpetrator of the tragedy engulfing him.

As many have noted, this play premiered during the days of the Clarence Thomas-Anita Hill hearings before Thomas was appointed to the Supreme Court; the early 1990s were also a peak moment for high theory in the humanities, when the language of scholarship and even teaching was especially intimidating to beginning users, as well as the moment when political correctness got its own strong start throughout the academic setting. Though Mamet has eschewed any such current-events contextualizing of these characters and their elemental struggle, it is difficult to view this play from the vantage point of twenty-first-century academe and not regard John's words and actions as egregious from the very first. Likely it is cultural phenomena just like *Oleanna* that have led universities to the protective—and, to be sure, improved—position that a student's perimeters, emotional, physical, and otherwise, must be respected by the professor in every instance. Office doors are never to be closed; the only contact allowed is a handshake; and the subject of discussion should never be other than the content of the class in question—certainly never "you" or "I" and the "feelings" of same, as is the case with easily 90 percent of the statements made in *Oleanna*. One is struck by how very much of Carol's valuable time John *wastes* in this play—his tenure situation should go into adjudication on those grounds alone—in addition to all of the valuable time of his own taken up encouraging an inarticulate student to sputter on and on, and when that line has run its course, divulging a series of his own personal truths. As Naomi Morgenstern notes, regarding the importance of tenure in the play, "Tenure, traditionally speaking, opened up a protected space for the risk of learning, the risk of thought.... And David Mamet's 1992 play seems peculiarly attuned to the role tenure plays in what we might call the academic border crisis" (2).

As the curtain rises, John is on the phone, rattling on to his wife about the house they are about to purchase. Although the constant interruptions to answer the ringing phone are construed as a power play—John more than once rubs Carol's face in the fact that he has a spouse and a son and a new home while she does not—this is the play's first example of John exposing himself, his personal information and his agitated state of mind, to a student in a manner grossly inappropriate under any circumstances. It is a performance of busyness and importance easily read as an attempt to impress, intimidate, and trap that has no place in the forthright, all-business setting of a professor's office. The refrain of every phone call is "I can't *talk* now," but in fact John interrupts his discussion with Carol constantly to talk yet more into the phone, although it is the case that John speech's is as truncated and inarticulate over the phone as it is over his desk to Carol; both he and Carol approach an aphasic state in their marked inability to "talk," and this is surely the play's prevailing question: When there is disagreement or miscommunication, why cannot the parties involved just say what they mean? This apparently erudite scholar, with plenty to say in his books, is stuck in Mamet-speak for much of the play, when not issuing "lame catch-phrases" (Murphy, "*Oleanna*," 127) regarding his research:

JOHN: ... how ...
CAROL: ... I have to pass it ...
JOHN: Carol, I:
CAROL: I *have* to pass this course, I ...
JOHN: Well.
CAROL: ... don't you ...
JOHN: Either the ... (8–9)

Mamet indicates with long senseless exchanges like this that John's role as an almost-tenured professor provides him no superior position from which to speak, be understood, or help a confused student focus her thoughts. Though the entire play thematizes the difference between his and Carol's way of using words, for much of the time their styles are indistinguishable. Christopher Bigsby cites Mamet's "belief in the critical importance of absence [or silence] and his desire to define the use of language" as establishing his connection to Beckett and Pinter, but I am more in agreement with Richard Badenhausen, who comments, "*Oleanna* ultimately explores the perils of inferior teaching … and functions as a dire warning both to and about those doing the educating" (2).

The tutorial setting is frequently regarded as a scene of seduction (or therapeutic transference; Morgenstern, 3), wherein an otherwise well-spoken sexually flustered professor might trip over words in just the fashion written here. He also might attempt certain verbal gambits—promising to "break rules" and (the Holy Grail of off-limits subject matter) bestow an "A" before the term is even half over, sharing stories from his past and encouraging the student to do the same, and repeating how much "I like you," though the student has done nothing to prove herself likeable in the least—to get her to linger on. The persistent ringing of the phone, with almost always the wife on the other end, sets up the scene between John and Carol as something illicit, transpiring after hours, that is, on his wife's own time and in a manner that causes her to constantly call to monitor John's actions and progress towards home. One is only too glad for Acts II and III, when at last the obfuscation dam begins to break:

CAROL: I don't *care* what you feel. Do you see? DO YOU SEE? You
              can't *do* that anymore. You. Do. Not. Have. The. Power. (50)

And later,

CAROL: …To lay a hand on someone's shoulder.
JOHN: It was devoid of sexual content.
CAROL: I say it was not. I SAY IT WAS NOT. Don't you begin to see
              … ? Don't you begin to understand? IT'S NOT FOR YOU
              TO SAY. (70)

As many have observed, in the final two acts, Carol has learned from John the language of power; in fact she has an attachment to the verifiable that John, in his arrogant preference for abstraction, does not. "Thus her note taking, which John took as a sign of submission, of 'obesiance,' in Act I, is transformed into a sign of power" (Murphy, "*Oleanna*," 130).

Pushed past his limit with her accusations of attempted rape, John concludes the play by throwing Carol to the floor, calling her a cunt, and making as if to smash a chair over her head. With such overtly criminal activity, clearly tenure is lost, and even jail time is imminent; Carol picks herself up and utters the cryptic statement "Yes. That's right" to John and once again to herself as the curtain falls. Murphy reads the moment as "an image of defeat, not of triumph" ("*Oleanna*," 135), in that Carol succumbs to agreeing with John's insulting assessment. Many an audience reaction corroborates Murphy's view: there are often gasps when Carol levels the charge of attempted rape in Act III, and "audience members [have] cheered John's violence to Carol in the play's closing sequence" (Garner, 39). Stanton B. Garner Jr. argues that "the play … harness[es] outrage to a gender politics it does little to question. That the audience is led to frame the play's earlier interactions in terms of Carol's manifestly outrageous behavior in Acts 2 and 3 leaves her character and the positions she represents targeted in unfair and ultimately reactionary ways" (39). As Badenhausen points out, just as many feminists as misogynists saw the play as an attack on women's rights (1, 7), simply hating instead of loving the play therefore. Marc Silverstein asks of this play, "What can *Oleanna* tell us about misogyny, about the frightening 'need' for misogyny, at the particular cultural moment at which we find ourselves?" (104).

Angels in America: A Gay Fantasia on National Themes (1993)

Tony Kushner (1956–)

Tony Kushner's widely acclaimed two-part play cycle *Millennium Approaches* (1991) and *Perestroika* (1992) were key dramatic texts of their late 1980s/ early 1990s American moment. The Clinton administration had yet to prove itself as a force for good or ill; the first post-AZT antiviral HIV therapies had just begun to move from clinical trials to general availability; and progressive America felt it had barely survived—scattered, weakened, and unsure of its next steps—a decade-long firestorm of far-right rhetorical vituperation and punitive legislation against the environment, the most disenfranchised of urban America, and HIV-positive gay men. As Lee Siegel remarks in an ultimately negative review of *Angels in America*, "The San Francisco theatergoers who applauded the play's first full production in 1991 were also applauding their own still-beating hearts" (28); gay men were indeed most immediately and detrimentally impacted by the presidency of Ronald Reagan and the popularity of conservative public figures such as columnist William F. Buckley and TV minister Jerry Falwell, because lives depended on national action and were lost in droves when this failed to materialize. Kushner's play cycle thus presents an icy undercurrent of bruising, inescapable trauma but is also suffused with the optimism (verging on sentimentalism [Bigsby, *Contemporary*, 120]) of not just a new decade and a new US president but also the fall of the Berlin Wall, the warming of relations between the US and USSR, and whatever hope, heaven, or apocalypse the impending turn of the century would bring. As Charles McNulty remarks, "Communal consciousness, provoked by loss [of the kind staged in *Angels*], has translated [since that time] into militancy and activism" (90), and indeed radical, terrifically theatrical groups such as ACT-UP, Queer Nation, and the Names Project have in subsequent years caused changing attitudes. These have in part enabled political and legal victories with respect to gay military service, marriage, and adoption, and thankfully much more effective treatments for HIV. The numerous recognitions accorded *Angels in America* bespeak the power it had to move and encourage in its original moment: the 1993 Pulitzer Prize in Drama, Tony Awards for Best Play in 1993 and 1994, and raves in major newspapers nationally and in the UK.

Millennium Approaches introduces the main characters, including WASPy, effeminate, HIV-positive Prior Walter, who in an early scene reveals the Kaposi's sarcoma tumors on his arms that mark him as moving from HIV-positivity into the symptomatic phase referred to in that era as "full-blown AIDS." His lover is Louis Ironson, an intellectual Jewish liberal who lacks the courage to stay by Prior's side during the final stages of his illness. They are joined by a Mormon lawyer, Joe Pitt, and his Valium-addicted wife, Harper, trailed later by Harper's repressed mother, Hannah, who winds up as a good friend and caretaker to Prior. The third figure in Prior and Louis's purview is Prior's ex-lover, the African American ex–drag queen and registered nurse, Belize, who also cares at home for Prior and in the hospital for the last major character, the historical Roy Cohn. Cohn gained fame during the McCarthy era for prosecuting Ethel and Julius Rosenberg into the electric chair and remained a Washington powerbroker—despite his Jewish ethnicity, his closeted homosexuality, and his own imminent AIDS diagnosis—as late as the Reagan era. All of these characters, save Roy, abandon their primary associations early in the story to form alliances they would have once found unimaginable: the indignantly liberal Louis engages in a passionate affair with the ultra-conservative Joe; Joe embraces (after mortally wrestling with) a gay identity; and his wife, Harper, through her first-fantastic and then-literal association with Prior, can be said to do the same. Hannah Pitt becomes a lesbian, and Belize reaches an understanding with both Louis and Roy Cohn, whose only transition is from this world to the next. In *Perestroika*, the Angel (who crashed through Prior's ceiling in the last moments of *Millennium*) and her cohort play a bigger role; Roy is visited on his deathbed by the ghost of Ethel Rosenberg; and Prior, who rejects an offer to join the heavenly train asks the Angel to "bless me anyway. I want more life" (133). He is alive and accessing his first course of AZT at the end of the play, surrounded by Louis (with whom he has reunited in friendship only; see below), Belize, and Hannah, at the feet of the Bethesda Angel in Central Park. His final words to the audience have received much critical attention (also see below) and are a benediction to all survivors in a time of plague: "We won't die secret deaths anymore. The world only spins forward.… You are fabulous creatures, each and every one. And I bless you. More life [a traditional Jewish blessing]. The Great Work Begins" (146).

Essential to an understanding of *Angels in America* is Kushner's deployment of the angel figure. Beyond its role in 1990s popular gay iconography, the angel has for Kushner "a prototypical[ly] American" (Savran, "Tony Kushner," 310) manifestation in the Mormon angel Moroni and especially a profound historical significance as a figure inspiring to Kushner's political, intellectual, and philosophical hero, Walter Benjamin. Kushner's main character, Prior Walter, converses at the end of Part One with the ghosts of Priors prior to himself, both of whom died of plague (85–89). But the most important "prior Walter" in the story is Benjamin himself (see also Savran, "Tony Kushner," 305). Benjamin owned, and practically adored, a painting by the Swiss-German modernist Paul Klee, *Angelus Novus* (1920), until his suicide following a failed attempt to flee Nazi-occupied France in 1940; he famously described Klee's painting, renaming its figure "The Angel of History" in his ninth thesis from "Theses on the Philosophy of History" (1940), a description reproduced frequently in scholarship on *Angels in America*:

> His eyes are staring, his mouth is open, his wings are spread.… His face is turned toward the past. Where we perceive a chain of events, he sees one single catastrophe which keeps piling wreckage upon wreckage and hurls it in front of his feet.… [A] storm is blowing at his feet … [that] irresistibly propels him into the future to which is back is turned, while the pile of debris before him grows skyward. The storm is what we call progress. (qtd. in J. Freedman, 100)

This description, though bearing little on the actual contents of Klee's painting, has been influential to thinkers since Benjamin presented it; it has signified tremendously for Kushner in these two plays. That and another comment from Benjamin—"*even the dead* will not be safe from the enemy if he wins" (qtd. in McNulty, 90)—clarify the scope and stakes in view for Kushner as he wrote. In an interview with David Savran, he provided this apt summation: "As Walter Benjamin wrote, you have to be constantly looking back at the rubble of history. The most dangerous thing is to become set upon some notion of the future that isn't rooted in the bleakest, most terrifying idea of what's piled up behind you" ("Tony Kushner," 300).

In *Angels of America*, this bleak and terrifying past is concretized throughout Part One with the eulogizing of Louis's grandmother, an Old World figure whose suffering through life refers to early twentieth-century pogroms in Russia and Eastern Europe, as well as the nightmare of the Holocaust, and with reference to American narratives of religious persecution, including Puritanism and Mormonism, the McCarthy-era witch trials that caught the Rosenbergs and many other Jews and leftists in its snare, and the phobic hysterias and hypocritical self-absorptions of the Reagan era. As McNulty observes, "Kushner understands that the future needs to have its roots in the tragedies and calamities of the past in order for history to not repeat itself" (91). Elsewhere, "Kushner believes this sad fact [of AIDS] may very well force Americans to confront the consequences of their blind individualism. The trauma of AIDS holds for him the greatest potential for social change" (90).

Meanwhile, the plays have been criticized for their "reconciliationist politics" (Kornhaber, 728), and for the fact that Kushner, "torn between the reality of protracted calamity and the blind hope of a kinder, gentler millennium, ... opts for the latter, hands down" (McNulty, 91). Despite his overall admiration, McNulty questions the final moments of *Perestroika*: "Such uncritical faith in progress would have been anathema to Benjamin.... The playwright has quite emphatically turned his attention away from the past and present turmoil to a future that seems garishly optimistic in contrast" (92; see also Savran, "Ambivalence, Utopia," 214). Jonathan Freedman critiques the excising of Roy Cohn from the final scenes, as well as the anti-Semitic features of Cohn's character throughout: "At the end of the play, there is room for angels and angelic queers in utopian America, but there is no place for monsters" (97). Freedman questions "the turn to Christian thematics by the privileging of the Prior plot" (98). Finally, from more mainstream quarters, Lee Siegel, in *The New Republic*, takes issue with every aspect of Kushner's original drama and its 2003 HBO adaptation: "*Angels in America* hits the screen with so much glamour and noise that [director Mike] Nichols and company almost succeed in burying the play's essential mediocrity in the production's illusion of significance.... [It] is a second-rate play by a second-rate playwright who happens to be gay, and because he has written a play about being gay, and about AIDS, no one—and I mean no one—is going to call *Angels in America* the over-wrought, coarse, posturing, formulaic mess that it is" (27).

Siegel completes his review with an equally negative assessment of Kushner's follow-up to *Angels*, the autobiographical *Caroline, or Change*, which was then having its off-Broadway premiere at the Public. He regards the story as "condescending" (29) to the black servant characters taking care of the Jewish family in the story, especially its spoiled young son. Regarding the character of Belize in *Angels*, Christopher Bigsby reports that Kushner was "to some degree uncomfortable about creating a black character and …worried later about making Belize a nurse, afraid of racial stereotyping" (*Contemporary*, 114). To be sure, the black-servant figure *is* a problematic portrayal by white authors, regardless of the broader political or artistic context; in their wide-ranging abilities to make the lives of their white clients more livable, they belong to the "magical Negro" tradition criticized by Spike Lee in 2001 ("Magical Negro"), and described with respect to Belize in Kushner's play as "the stock-wisdom figure of the drag queen in countless gay plays" (Siegel, 28).

Audience members from the disability rights community would also take issue with *Angels*'s regrettably typical handling of the sick or disabled characters—Prior, Harper Pitt, and Roy Cohn. As in much gay- (and straight-) authored fiction and drama from this period and throughout history, the symptomatic, dying character is relegated to the caring hands of some minority figure—the African American servant type, the drag queen, or the woman (e.g., Hannah for Prior, and Ethel Rosenberg for Roy)—leaving the healthy, able-bodied central characters to pursue their ambitions and romances unencumbered by the chronically ill ball and chain. Kushner told an interviewer in the *New York Times*, "The supernatural moments in the play are always ambiguously related to AIDS" ("Secrets," 44), and the immortality bestowed on Prior by his association with the ghosts of his ancestors and the Angel who offers him a swinging door on heaven's gate is another form of this relegation. Another trope in abelist works (e.g., Clint Eastwood's *Million Dollar Baby* [2004]) is the sick or disabled character who firmly rejects the offer of the able-bodied loved one to stay around and provide care (see Longmore); in the final scenes of *Perestroika*, Harper wants only Joe's credit card (139), and Prior tells Louis, "But you can't come back. Not ever" (140). In this manner, the able-bodied character is freed from the tedium (and potentially catastrophic expense) of having to tend to the long-term sick or disabled person while also conveniently freed from the moral aspersion of having abandoned this character of his own accord. Unfortunately, *Angels* presents many such ableist treatments despite its conscientious attempt to portray a diverse cast and include many of these in its final vision.

How I Learned to Drive (1997)

Paula Vogel (1951–)

This Pulitzer Prize–winning tragicomedy regarding the harrowing subject matter of childhood sexual abuse relies upon reverse chronology to attract (or seduce) the audience to the sides of both Li'l Bit, sexually molested throughout her girlhood, *and* her molesting uncle-by-marriage, Peck, who loves and understands his intelligent niece when no one else in the family does. The story is told in a series of flashbacks by the grown woman who survived the ordeal; the first remembered scene is with Li'l Bit at age 17 and the audience unaware of the relationship between the young woman and the older man engaging in sexual foreplay in the front seat of a car. By the end of the scene, however, Li'l Bit refers to the man as "Uncle Peck," and the connection between the two of them intensifies as it moves into the past: slightly younger, Li'l Bit is taken out to celebrate high school graduation, and gets drunk on martinis; Uncle Peck is credited for never taking advantage of his niece in an inebriated state. Later scenes at younger ages include Li'l Bit posing for risqué photos at age 13 and finally a putative driving lesson at age 11, during which Uncle Peck cajoles Li'l Bit to sit on his lap so she can steer the car, then rubs himself to climax against her backside.

In the midst of her freshman year at college, Li'l Bit at last has the courage and wherewithal to say good-bye to Peck forever, and Peck has the decency to honor her request and then drink himself to death seven years later. Though not all abuse victims are nearly so lucky, Li'l Bit is enabled by his passing to look back with both anger and appreciation for the role Peck played in her life. At a key moment in the driving instruction that actually takes place, Peck warns Li'l Bit against ruinous influences such as himself: "You're going to learn to think what the other guy is going to do before he does it…. you're the one who's going to steer through [a multicar accident], put your foot on the gas if you have to, and be the one to walk away" (50). As Christopher Bigsby observes, Peck "warns her against himself, thus surrendering the one thing that holds him back from despair, an action that has led Vogel to call him 'heroic'" (*Contemporary*, 321); as Vogel remarked in an interview with Mary-Louise Parker, "*How I Learned to Drive* was 'about the gifts from people who've hurt us.'" Critics appreciate the final scene, wherein Li'l Bit races off in her high-powered automobile and, adjusting her rearview mirror, "a faint light strikes the spirit of Uncle Peck, who is sitting in the back seat of the car" (92). In the estimation of Graley Herren, "Li'l Bit has relegated Uncle Peck to the back seat, and she is in the driver's seat now. No longer frozen in the backward glance and reverse gear of trauma, she ends the play facing forward into the future, and floors it" (112). Also, Vogel refuses to "define her victim completely in terms of her victimization" (Herren, 112), and Li'l Bit "overcomes her personal demons" (Kimbrough, 48), "break[ing] the stereotype of the helpless victim by taking active, creative control over the staging of her memories" (Herren, 112). For David Savran, Peck's "unexpectedly comforting" ("Haunted," 121) reflection in the rearview mirror enables Li'l Bit to "put … the past to rest in what counts as something of a triumph" ("Haunted," 122). But Peck's advice is, to a notable extent, too little too late. He himself has prevented Li'l Bit from "steering past" many years of psychosexual wreckage and only leaves her alone when she finally develops the maturity and independence to shove him away, some two-and-a-half years following his self-negating statements during the driving lesson.

The play is built upon the erroneous assumption that "victims are not always blameless and perpetrators are not just villains" (qtd. in Kimbrough, 48) and that Uncle Peck's love for Li'l Bit redeems him despite his heinous actions against her. Although critics and scholars have praised this play, its controversial subject matter has turned others away, who feel that the subject is ill-suited to the weak comic drollery framing it throughout Vogel's text. Even Herren, in her sympathetic reading, remarks, "Imagine what a drastically different play this would be had the events been recounted in chronological order, beginning with the initial violation when she was a prepubescent. Sympathy for Uncle Peck would have been impossible from the start—for the few spectators that might have stayed to see that version of the play through to the end" (109).

Topdog/Underdog (2001)

Suzan-Lori Parks (1964–)

Topdog/Underdog is Parks's most critically acclaimed and commercially successful play, having enjoyed an off-Broadway premiere at the Public Theater in late 2001, followed by a move to Broadway's Ambassador in 2002. The star actors playing brothers Lincoln and Booth—Geoffrey Wright as Lincoln at both venues (and later at the Royal Court), Don Cheadle as Booth at the Public and rap artist Mos Def as Booth on Broadway—enabled two memorable productions and many accolades, including the 2002 Pulitzer Prize for Drama (Parks being the first African American woman playwright so honored), several Obie and Outer Critics Circle Awards, and two Tony nominations. Jochen Achilles notes also that "[o]n account of its psychologically rounded characters and quasi-realistic plotline, *Topdog/Underdog* is more accessible than some of Parks's earlier plays" (104; see also Foster, 24–25). Named by a father with a sense of humor and doomed thereby to repeat national history in the cramped privacy of their shared room in a rundown boarding house, Lincoln and Booth were abandoned by their parents as teen-agers—mother driven off the premises by her "side man" and leaving the younger Booth $500 in the toe of a nylon stocking as she went. Their father, two years later, bestowed the same handkerchief-wrapped legacy on the elder Lincoln. Despite his tendency toward the responsible, job-holding, caretaking role, Lincoln has evidently spent his inheritance years ago, whereas loose-cannon Booth has never broached the intimacy of the sexual item containing his money, and in the play's final moments, the actuality of the stocking's contents comes into question: has Booth's mother "played" him like the mark he turns out to be in his elder brother's three-card Monte scheme? The prospect is so dreadful that, repeating history, Booth sneaks up behind Lincoln and shoots him dead.

Ironically, Lincoln works as a Lincoln impersonator at an arcade in an Atlantic City–style entertainment venue, dressed in stovepipe hat, frock coat, beard, and even whiteface, and waiting for tourists to pay an entrance fee and have a turn at assassinating the president with a cap gun. His job is to sit quietly, as in the box at Ford's Theater, then keel over again and again as the tourists, "housewives with they [*sic*] mouths closed tight" (55) and various other marks, come through. Booth spends his days shoplifting suits of clothing and fancy tableware to impress his girlfriend, Grace and practicing at home for his own intended role as a con artist with three-card Monte, with which he has no facility whatsoever. Notably, John Wilkes Booth is remembered as the lesser stage talent compared to his elder brother, Edwin Booth, hailed internationally as a gifted Shakespearian and easily the leading American actor of the late nineteenth century. *Topdog*'s elder brother, Lincoln, is also the better actor—paid to impersonate the 16th president until he is laid off, and a spellbinder when dealing cards. As Parks has remarked to Rick DesRochers, "People like their history in different ways, and when you come into the theater … you see these characters named Lincoln and Booth, and you see a handgun introduced early in the play.… Some people like [their history] by the book, as it was; some like it as it *could* be" (107–8). Despite Parks's own openness to diverse audience viewpoints, Lincoln spells out the play's tragic inevitabilities when he informs his brother, "People are funny about they Lincoln shit. Its [*sic*] historical. People like they historical shit in a certain way. They like it to unfold the way they folded it up" (57).

Parks's "rep and rev"—repetition and revision—technique is well displayed in this play; her character of a black Lincoln impersonator is even repeated and revised from her earlier *The America Play* (1994), and she trenchantly allegorizes important national questions by bringing Lincoln back to life—ironically, he is replaced at the arcade late in the play by a wax dummy—as she has: Do *all* Americans get to recognize themselves in founding fathers such as Lincoln, to adopt his manner of dress, historical significance, and value system as part of their national heritage? Or is Lincoln's impersonation of Abraham Lincoln as mirthless a joke as his father's bestowal of the names on his sons or the whiteface he must don to ply his trade at the arcade? Do the tourists taking potshots at his Lincoln engage in harmless historical hijinks, or is Lincoln getting paid to let white tourists exercise their anti-democratic, racist attitudes by seeking personal revenge on a black man dressed as the Great Emancipator? Given President Lincoln's own ambivalence with respect to hating slavery but sharing many of the white-supremacist and separatist values rampant in his day, how "black" was the historic Lincoln, and how right, therefore, was Martin Luther King Jr. to stage his March on Washington and give his famed "I Have a Dream Speech" at the Lincoln Memorial in 1963? Does Lincoln belong to King as much as he does to white Americans? More so? (See Goto, 120.) Parks's play suggests that because US society struggles to this day with the questions meant to be resolved by the Civil War—and for some, by the assassination of Lincoln—we are all, like the two brothers, doomed to reenact these same violent disagreements. Quoting Sara Warner, who reads Parks's work as "drama of disinterment," Philip C. Kolin adds that it is also a "theater of resurrections ... [E]ven as [Parks] deconstructs the fantasies of white power, she converts the black body into a theater of trauma" ("Puck's Magic," 10).

As the play travels its mythic, allegorical path, it also tells an entirely realist story of black oppression that connects it with numerous dramatic predecessors of the contemporary period. As noted above, *Topdog/Underdog* engages in scintillating dialogue with Fugard's *Blood Knot*, and the themes of economic hardship and racism—Lincoln as the typical black worker ("last hired/first fired") is cut from his job and was paid less than his white predecessor while employed—tie this play back to Albee's *The Zoo Story* and Baraka's *Dutchman*. It is as if we have transferred this play to the depressing Upper West Side rooming house endured by the also-orphaned Jerry in Albee's play; as Jerry used violence in the last moments of *The Zoo Story* to lash out at a society that refused to recognize his desperate needs, so Booth's late-hour murder of Grace (who, like the women in Fugard's play, never appears onstage) and Lincoln is readable as social and economic desperation pushed to its limits.

Kolin and Harvey Young compare Lincoln and Booth to the feuding brothers in Sam Shepard's *True West* (15; see also Malley, 188), and with respect
to Parks's experimental language and the centrality of the con, John Dietrick
sees in this play a connection to the work of David Mamet (48). Dietrick also
sees in these two brothers Biff and Happy from Arthur Miller's *Death of a
Salesman*; as the younger Happy Loman is the more avid defender of fanciful
talk and bogus dreams in Miller's play, so Booth spends almost the entirety of
Topdog spouting lies and indulging in magical thinking (see also Dietrick 50,
63; and Malley, 88). In another echo of Fugard, Achilles observes that "both
brothers seem to have settled into a husband-and-wife arrangement, with
Booth in the feminine role" (107; see also Wolfe's comment to DesRochers,
108) and likely partially motivated to murder by this emasculation at the
hands of his higher-earning brother. Verna Foster (25–27) sees elements of
not only realism but naturalism (that is, economic determinism) in the play;
though the brothers might be tragic figures on a collision course with destiny,
they are also doomed by numerous socioeconomic factors to a Beckett-style
existence of repeated, meaningless actions (see also Tucker-Abramson, 95; and
Dietrick, 48). Myka Tucker-Abramson comments, "[I]f masculinity is based
on economic worth and economics become unhinged from their Real value
[in a postmodern context], then the notion of masculinity itself becomes
increasingly difficult to maintain…. Parks forces us to confront the vast issues
of racial and economic inequalities in America through their impact on the
psyches of two characters" (77–78).

Both brothers imagine careers as performers—either Lincoln impersonators,
shoplifters, or card sharps; as Kolin remarks, "The métier of acting—pretending, assuming a role, adopting multiple identities, donning costumes, engaging
with an audience—is at the heart of Parks's canon" ("Puck's Magic," 7). Later:
"Her plays are filled with commentary by characters who announce, exaggerate,
or undercut the trappings of their performativity" (13). Jennifer Larson reads
the many stolen, abandoned, and changed articles of clothing in the play, "even
the 'suits' of cards in the brothers' three-card Monte game [that] symbolize elements of the brothers' identity." She asserts that "clothes highlight the fluidity,
exteriority, and superficiality of identity, especially in its relation to history and
memory" (183). And yet, per the economic-determinist readings above, the
entire play, taking place as it does in the cramped quarters of their single room,
is a place of Lorraine Hansberry–style thwarted dreams—endlessly repetitious
practice instead of performance per se. As Michael LeMahieu observes, "Unlike
A Raisin in the Sun, however, *Topdog* denies its audience a conciliatory conclusion" (34); in other words, while the Youngers triumphantly exit their cramped
apartment at the end of the play, the setting in *Topdog* seems very much a

permanent entrapment. In this room, in addition to constant rehearsing of his Monte patter, Booth uses masturbation as a substitute for an actual relationship and marriage, and Lincoln practices dying more dramatically when shot by his tourists and also regaining his skills with cards. Even as he manages to cheat Booth out of some "real" money in the game they play at home, Lincoln admits, "We're missing the essential elements. The crowd, the street, thuh traffic sounds, all that" (101). Tragically, therefore, these two energetic performers seem doomed to a second- or third-string existence of constant practice and postponement. Although Lincoln comes home late in the play with the wad of conned cash, demonstrating his return to the card-sharping stage, he is tragically gunned down by the brother who has no talent for such displays or for winning a woman's affections—but only schemes; brag; frustrated intentions; and, following the murder of his brother at his own hands, a lifetime of guilt and solitude. Though he will likely exchange life in his cramped city apartment for a prison cell, Parks indicates that the history Booth was doomed to repeat has already imposed its life sentence.

Drama in Dialogue: *Angels in America* and *Topdog/Underdog*

In an interview given in 2007, Suzan-Lori Parks described her days as the child of a US Army sergeant stationed in Germany and of her family's trip to the passion play staged every ten years at Oberammegau. Influenced by her viewing of this spectacle, Parks remarked, "My plays are very much like that— the community gets together and creates this pageant … [T]he idea of pageant is intrinsic to [my canon]" (Kolin, "Puck's Magic," 11). In another interview, in the company of her director George C. Wolfe, Wolfe remarked that despite the two-character, one-room setup of *Topdog/Underdog*, "the *whole world* is inside this room. The relationship between the brothers is astoundingly real and astoundingly mythic at the same time" (DesRochers, 107). Remarks such as these point to the meaningful connection between Kushner's "Gay Fantasia on National Themes" from the early 1990s and the expansive, spectacular features of Parks's work at the turn of the twenty-first century. Both dramatists are duly recognized as bards of the American narrative who use their broad visions to rewrite and enlarge the meaning of American identity, to centralize those not regarded as "typical" citizens due to their race, class, or sexual orientation. If Kushner hews to the "inclusive vision of Walt Whitman" (Bigsby, *Contemporary*, 110), with *Angels*'s cast of diversely religious, ethnic, racial, gendered, and sexual characters (not to mention the hermaphroditic angels and various ghosts), Parks might be said to take inspiration from Langston Hughes, whose famous poem "I, Too" presented the speaker as Whitman's "darker brother" who yet also "sings America." Whitman celebrated the diversity recognized in the rivers of humanity flowing all around him in nineteenth-century New York, but later writers such as Hughes and Parks may both appreciate Whitman's sweeping vision but also perform a "rep and rev" on some of its inevitable blind spots. *Angels in America* is sprawling, outlandish, and fantastical—Kushner calls it his "theater of the fabulous" (Savran, "Tony Kushner," 292); *Topdog/Underdog*, confined to its one room and two characters, is in certain ways bigger than Kushner's play, specifically in its more informed understanding of the race- and class-based realities (and mythologies) of life in the United States.

Both Kushner and Parks are clearly committed to exploring how the national past suffuses and shapes the national present, and their respective experimental techniques often involve the attempt to resurrect and reconsider stories and figures from the past. In *Angels* the ghosts of Prior Walter's fourteenth- and seventeenth-century ancestors relate to him their own experience of death from plague (bubonic) while the ghost of Ethel Rosenberg (and of the 1950s anti-communist, anti-Semitic hysteria she symbolizes) gloats over Roy Cohn on his deathbed with the news that he has been disbarred. Joe and Harper's Mormonism invokes the spirit of Joseph Smith and the story of his indigenous American religion; the ghost of Eisenhower is summoned (and shamed) by Reagan Republicanism; and the ghosts of past partners, actions, and uncertainties surface on the skin of Prior Walter in the form of AIDS-related Kaposi's sarcoma.

Parks's play is also crowded with "the community" that has come together to create its spectacular effects: the "ghosts" of each brother's former partner, Lincoln's ex-wife, Cookie, and Booth's former girlfriend, Grace, are spectral presences of disappointment and condemnation that motivate the men's moods and actions; though Cookie departs the scene unscathed, Grace is literally ghosted by the offstage violence of Booth, who confesses to his brother her murder at his hand. The ghosts of the brothers' parents haunt the play just as significantly, especially in the transparent material of his mother's nylon stocking, in which her $500 legacy to Booth may be just as ghostly a presence. The parents are also resurrected in both the brothers' frequent recollections of childhood and in their comically inhabiting of the roles "Pa" (Lincoln, who brings home a weekly salary) and "Ma" (Booth, who stays home and cares for the apartment) at the beginning of the play.

Parks's busiest emanations from the past are the ghosts of Abraham Lincoln and John Wilkes Booth, who bring forward a long train of historical

occurrence, from the Middle Passage to the assassination of Lincoln following the Civil War. As Kushner democratizes his American story by making the
straight white characters a minority (and the wealthy WASP figure a minority of one), so Parks opens portrayal of the historic Lincoln and Booth to her
modern-day African American brothers; so doing, she "travesties the exclusiv-
ity and legitimacy of an icon of white history" (Kolin, "Puck's Magic," 14).
Elder brother, Lincoln, earns an honest paycheck (though criminally smaller
than the one given his white predecessor) impersonating Honest Abe at a
seaside arcade; he explains his choice to Booth with the simple defense, "It's
a living" (39), but the expression is tragically reversed when his impersonation is realized in death at the hands of his assassinating brother. As the
brothers fatefully reenact history thus, Parks calls into question the national
obsession with mythologizing historical figures and events through endless
reenactments, commemorations, and enshrinements. Parks might feel comfortable borrowing Kushner's ethos regarding the need to know the past so as
to avoid repeating its mistakes, yet both playwrights would likely acknowledge
the extremely difficulty—the frequent occasions of violence and tragedy—
involved in achieving social change.

Both plays call playful attention to the theatricality of their presentations;
Kushner specifies "no blackouts!" (5) between scenes and requests that the
actors act as stagehands for the minimalist sets. Regarding special effects, such
as the angel crashing through Prior's bedroom ceiling, "it's OK if the wires
show, and maybe it's good that they do, but the magic should at the same time
be thoroughly amazing" (5). He designates the same actor to play numerous parts; for instance, the Angel also plays a nurse, a real estate broker, and
a homeless woman; and Hannah also plays a male rabbi, a male doctor, and
Ethel Rosenberg. Finally Kushner stages several double scenes, in which two
actors stage left reach some crisis or resolution while two actors stage right
engage over related themes. Parks's *Topdog* is equally multilayered; reading
the layers literally, Jennifer Larson remarks, "Both Lincoln and Booth believe
that switching identities involves merely taking off old and putting on new
clothes, as an actor puts on a costume to get into character.... As a whole in
this play, clothes highlight the fluidity, exteriority, and superficiality of identity, especially in relationship to history and memory" (183). Myka Tucker-
Abramson calls our attention to the play's "collapse [of] differences between
historical slavery and [the] modern wage slavery" (88) that causes the brothers' economically depressed condition in the present day. In a more symbolic
register, their given names invoke prior (to borrow a Kushnerian term) man-
ifestations. As Kevin J. Wetmore Jr. remarks, "[Parks's] plays are concerned
with ritual, memory, history, language, gender, ethnicity, acts of viewing and

performing and the interaction of all of the above elements" (xvii), a statement equally applicable to *Angels in America*.

Anna in the Tropics (2002)

Nilo Cruz (1960–)

Anna in the Tropics won the 2003 Pulitzer Prize for Drama, having been selected over the work of better-known playwrights, including Edward Albee for *The Goat, or Who is Sylvia?* and Richard Greenberg for *Take Me Out*. It was the first Pulitzer for Drama ever awarded on the basis of the script alone, as the play had only had a first production in Coral Gables, Florida, and none of the jurors had seen it. It had already been invited for staging at the prestigious McCarter Theater Center on the Princeton campus when its award was announced, however; and under the direction of playwright Emily Mann, it then moved to Broadway for a three-month run at the Royale Theater. It was nominated for two Tonys in 2004.

Anna tells the story of a family of Cuban émigrés, cigar factory owners in Tampa, Florida, whose lives are changed when a "lector" (professional reader) hired to entertain their workers chooses as his text *Anna Karenina*, and their own situations begin to resemble those in Tolstoy's epic novel: the patriarch Santiago admires Tolstoy's hard-working Levin; his passionate love for Kitty revives the flagging romance between himself and his wife, Ofelia, and through this rekindled love, Santiago gets his gambling and drinking under control. Their elder daughter Conchita warms to the passionate affair between Anna and Vronsky; she embarks on an affair with the lector, Juan Julian, yet the interlude ends up strengthening her own marriage to Palomo. Younger daughter Marela has a girls' crush on Juan Julian, but just as this ripens into the prospects of true romance, he is shot to death by Cheché, Santiago's half-brother, described by Henry Pérez as the drama's "agent of change": as the one member of the family who has lived in the North, married a non-Cuban woman, and insisted upon taking steps to modernize the factory in the near future, Cheché is the outsider and the spoiler. Even the jilted Palomo comes to appreciate the role played by Juan Julian and his reading of Tolstoy before the play is over, but Cheché, whose wife ran away with another lector years ago, loathes and fears Juan Julian at every moment. As Pérez remarks, "It is ironic that the agent of change in the cigar factory has not grown like the rest of the characters in the play; perhaps the author is differentiating between real personal growth and overblown advances in technology." Cheché remembers his own loss every day that the lector reads, and he regards this old-world custom of giving culture to the workers as standing in the way of his intended machine renovations: once the factory is fully mechanized, the lector's voice would be completely drowned out. The increased efficiency due to machines, combined with much lower wages for the machine operators (who actually pay the lector's salary), would require the immediate dismissal of lectors like Juan Julian and the tradition he represents. The family's attachment to Juan Julian is one of many reasons that they repeatedly veto Cheché's bid to modernize; when the lector finally wins the attentions of Marela, the half-niece that Cheché has lasciviously eyed for himself, it is the last straw, and Juan Julian, the last best representative of a way of life ebbing away, is destroyed.

Although the story's many romances and marriages occupy the characters for much of the play, what critics have admired frequently are its broader historical contexts. Like Tolstoy's novel, *Anna* has its own epic sweep, set as it is in 1929 in the moments before the stock market crash of that October would plunge this family's adopted nation into a decade-long depression and wreak its own great changes to the local economy, regardless of the incursion of the machine age. Not helping matters is the waning of the cigar industry itself; as Juan Julian remarks at a crisis moment, "Moving pictures now feature their stars smoking cigarettes: Valentino, Douglas Fairbanks" (53), suggesting the way that movies and cigarettes are usurping the roles once played by more thoughtful, leisurely habits such as reading and smoking cigars: "The truth is," adds the lector, "that machines, cars are keeping us from taking walks and sitting on park benches, smoking a cigar slowly and calmly" (53). But Cheché's insistence on modernizing the factory will have its inevitable effects as well, as Cruz's audience knows full well that the beautiful dreamers and skilled artisans populating his play belong to an era gone with the wind. Interviewing the playwright in 2004, director Emily Mann remarked, "[Y]our writing reminds me of Chekhov. With *The Cherry Orchard*, for instance, you're seeing the end of an age, a certain way of life coming to a close. And there's something of that in your play, a society that was so deeply rooted in the cigar factories, the social clubs....They don't know that they're on the verge of a huge change."

Closer to home, Cruz has cited the influence of playwrights Maria Irene Fornés, Paula Vogel, and Emily Mann; he has additionally remarked upon the strong influence of female mentors and supporters throughout his life, including his mother, who gave him his first typewriter, and his many other female family members. It was the poetry of Emily Dickinson that, as a student in America (he emigrated with his family from Cuba in 1970), inspired him to study literature and be a writer, and Cruz has remarked upon all of these female sources of inspiration when explaining the preponderance of female characters and women's perspectives in his work. As Mann remarked, "You have always understood women on an exquisite level." In *Anna*, Juan Julian enables Conchita to her own sexual agency by performing as a partner (sometimes even a submissive partner) during their lovemaking, instead of as the macho, dominant male of traditional Latin cultures. Through his example, both Santiago and Palomo learn to be more loving, sharing spouses to their wives. To be sure, Juan Julian is such a cipher, with equally strong masculine and feminine sensibilities, and an old-world charm, grace, and elegance so impeccable and enthralling as to verge on the other-worldly, that he is readable as a magical-realist element in this play (see Paran)—a figure beamed into the midst of these lives gone astray to renew in them the devotion to their spouses and children that will help them through their impending age of uncertainty.

Cruz has also identified August Wilson as a primary influence, as Cruz shares Wilson's interest in dramatizing the history of his ethnic community; Cruz remarked with a laugh that matching Wilson's ten-play achievement would be "a big responsibility" (Gussow, "Nilo Cruz," B5), and indeed per his own communal roots, Cruz's plays are set in Cuba or Spain as often as they are in the United States. They also tend to aim much of their political ire at the betrayals of the Castro regime, as the American Cuban experience—especially for wealthy, more culturally conservative dissidents to Castro's communism—has been much less fraught with oppression and exclusion tragically common to the African American, Puerto Rican American, and Mexican American experiences. Thus in *Anna* the mood is wistful, elegiac, and lyrical instead of bitter, cynical, and tragic as in, for instance, Wilson's *Fences*. Likewise, the focus on the characters' love lives takes such precedence that, in fact, members of the laboring class are not named; given lines of dialogue (except the for the cockfight operator, Eliades, who speaks only in Spanish and only in the opening scene); or even, it seems, portrayed in many productions of this play. One rather curious scene involves the prospect of mechanizing the plant, which is widely understood to affect the non-owner workers on the floor much more adversely than it would the family itself. Cheché has come in with a prototype of the machine that would roll cigars automatically, and Cruz designates "a crowd" of workers gathered around to look upon the mechanism of their imminent doom. At various points in the scene, their agitated presence is indicated in stage directions, such as "*The Crowd is getting anxious*," "*He is interrupted*," and "*Assertive comments from the crowd*." Again, however, the play's production notes and available photographic archive indicate that many if not all productions of this play have been staged without any characters aside from the main family, Juan Julian, and Eliades in the opening moment. Cruz has commented that the family would have had socialist leanings and therefore be automatically interested in the Russian novel being read to them, but, as noted above, much of the family's preoccupation is of a middle-class, romance (even a bodice-ripping, telenovela-type of romance) variety. They manage to strengthen their various marriage partnerships and, compared to Chekhov's aristocrats facing loss of home and identity to an erstwhile serf, may fare even better in the onslaught of mechanized industrial capitalism that they and their illiterate workers will contend with on their respective terms.

Fat Pig (2004)

Neil LaBute (1963–)

Representing Neil LaBute's recurring interest in attractive men and the women they victimize, *Fat Pig* begins as a love story between an office worker named Tom and a plus-sized librarian he meets and falls for, Helen. At work, Tom is badgered for information about his new girlfriend by the superficial Carter and Tom's erstwhile love interest, Jeannie. At a beach party, Tom is forced to choose between his looks-oriented friends and including Helen in their activities, and chooses to abandon Helen. As Christopher Bigsby remarks, *Fat Pig* explores "the thin line between civility and betrayal, genuine feeling and calculation, concern for others and concern for the self. For LaBute, it is the step from one to the other that compels attention, and not because of the distance between his characters and those who see or read his plays but because of their moral proximity" (*Neil LaBute*, 8). Although LaBute remains most famous for his theater (and cinema) of cruelty from the 1990s—especially *In the Company of Men, Your Friends and Neighbors*, and *The Shape of Things*—*Fat Pig* won the 2005 Outer Critics Circle Award for Outstanding Off-Broadway Play and has enjoyed productions throughout the United States and internationally.

LaBute has remarked that he has gotten more reaction to this play than all of his others, touching as it does upon a national obsession with physical perfection and including characters who are more morally ambiguous than the heartless predators and duped victims of the standard LaBute text. LaBute's plays of the turn of the new century also strike critics as taking on mellower tones than those from his first decade. As David Amsden remarks, "It was *Mercy Seat* [2002, about 9/11] that marked a truly subtle shift in tone for LaBute, the cursory introduction of something new: genuine emotion in the form of human weakness" (116). Amsden quotes the playwright himself: "In [*Fat Pig*], people hurt each other, yes, but I think sometimes they do so out of kindness and honesty" (116). Writing for the *New York Times* in 2004, Liesl Schillinger titled her interview with the playwright "Is Neil LaBute Getting … Nice?," and per Bigsby, "[*Fat Pig*] is a play in which [LaBute] forsakes irony, even as his characters deploy it as a weapon or protection. He remains as interested as ever in human cruelty but explores it in the context of a play which does indeed seem to have an unequivocally good character at its heart" (*Neil LaBute*, 166).

LaBute's Preface to *Fat Pig* includes a comment regarding his own attempt to lose weight, as well as his indifference to others' views of his failure to do so. He describes having lost 60 pounds in eight months, then "feeling happy, healthy, and in good spirits" (ix), but also like a "preening fool" (x), newly obsessed with his image in the mirror and with shopping for smaller sizes. Like his fictional creation Adam in *The Shape of Things*, who starts frantically eating when he's rejected by the woman he thought was his devoted girlfriend, LaBute admits that "I'm a stress eater." Following "a few personal and professional mishaps" ("Preface," x), he went right back to his own comforting, inspiring habits. Watching LaBute direct *Nurse Betty*, a mainstream film from the late 1990s, theater critic John Lahr noticed LaBute munching compulsively on raisins (with even a package "tucked in the cuff" of his slicker ["A Touch," 44]), Cheetos, and Doritos as if eating were a way to dispel or absorb the nervous energy that comes with the director's role. Similar to Helen, who describes the comfort of a big bowl of popcorn while watching movies with her family when boys did not call to ask for dates in high school, LaBute remarks, "My mother taught me this self-medicating trick [of reaching for a bag of chips or a bucket of popcorn] years ago, and I've stood by it for a long time now" ("Preface," x). He adds that since having regained 40 of the lost 60 pounds, he is "wearing those same [fat] pants again, thank you for asking. Oh, yeah, and I've also written several plays" ("Preface," x–xi). LaBute posits what seems to be a proportional relationship between "creativity" and "personal unhappiness" (xi; i.e., eating junk food and gaining weight), though for the rest of the Preface he almost doth protest too much regarding how happy he is to be back to his baggy-sweater weight.

For LaBute, the creativity of playwriting allows him to disregard his physical imperfections; he specifically instances writing about a "visit [to] the beach" and a "delightful romance" (xi), two real-life situations in which an overweight body might cause dismay. Instead, LaBute claims, "Writers, for better or worse, are gods of their own universe … and while it might be a little lonely in this particular heaven, I've got a terrific view" (xi). With this sort of cheeky defensive comment linking artistic success to the curtailing of a distracting obsession with weight loss, LaBute makes his own case for why overweight people should not care about public opinion. If they can back up their size with professional accomplishment—and if accomplishment in fact wanes when suffering an obsession with thinness—they have every right to figuratively flip the bird to weightist onlookers. Lahr observed a connection between LaBute's adopted (now former) Mormon faith and his style as a playwright and filmmaker: "The Mormon obsession with moral improvement, and with 'pretending nothing bad ever happens,' as he says, accounts in large part for LaBute's relish of transgression" ("A Touch," 44). Evidently, LaBute's personal relationship to food, and the less than ideal body that results, are equally formative impulses in his work.

And yet LaBute is somewhat disingenuous when he equates his own situation with that of his heroine Helen in *Fat Pig*, as LaBute (and his avatar Adam in *The Shape of Things*) may be characterized as somewhat overweight, while he explicitly calls for an "obese" actor to play the title role in *Fat Pig*. LaBute is also surely aware of, and ultimately a beneficiary of, the somewhat forgiving standard applied to men's physical appearance and the much more stringent standard applied to women. In fact, his comments in the Preface implicitly forge his own connection to Tom and Carter, the men in his play who enjoy the latitude with respect to physical size—and even physical attractiveness— that plus-size Helen and pencil-thin Jeannie never do. Notably, the last scene in *Fat Pig* takes place on a beach, with all characters conforming to gender-specific rules regarding beach costume: the men in comfortable, concealing knee-length trunks and the women overexposed in the outdoor equivalent of panties and bra. LaBute's excess weight has never prevented marriage in his own life, whereas Helen is persistently, tragically single in *Fat Pig*. Although LaBute congratulates Helen for her healthy, well-adjusted relationship to her body, he also dimensionalizes her in moments of vulnerability and self-loathing (e.g., when she offers to have lap-band surgery to lose weight and keep Tom) and humiliates her by positioning her behind large amounts of unhealthy food that she eats with abandon in the first scene and with mortification in the last. Per the playwright's directions for the first scene, Helen is to appear with "a bunch of food in front of her" (5), which would indicate more than the two slices of pizza in view in most stagings of that scene.[1]

---

[1] Meanwhile, director Jo Bonney of the New York premiere positioned Helen onstage "eating, and necessarily, at length" as the audience entered the theater. With this staging, Tom's "reaction can thus be judged against [the audience's] own. They are already implicated in the aesthetic, moral questions raised by the relationship which now unfolds" (Bigsby, *Neil LaBute*, 167).

Finally, most of LaBute's audience would depart from his defense of binging on Cheetos and Doritos as a healthy and productive relationship to one's physical and emotional reality, even if they themselves are guilty of the same penchants, use the same modes of defense, or appreciate the creative results of LaBute's dietary indulgences.

Thus one of the remarkable features of *Fat Pig* is its tracing of the playwright's own marked ambivalence regarding his and his nation's love affair with addictive, unhealthy foods. Against whom does the audience direct its judgment, for instance, in the final scene, when Helen is "*slowly* devouring a hot dog. Bit by bit" and Tom, seemingly disgusted by the display, interrupts, "Come on, *slow down* a little bit, honey" (80, emphasis added). Is Helen to be exonerated from her offenses because she devours a hot dog slowly and in small, ladylike bites? Is it even physically possible to "devour" in this manner? And if her style of eating represents such admirable self-control, why does the playwright enable Tom to rewrite it as shameful and thus deserving of the rejection he will shortly inflict? Why does he excuse the weightism of Tom's obnoxious coworker Carter as the result of traumatizing shame at the hands of his 350-pound mother, so unattractive that she drove his father from the home and so obsessed with choosing candy bars at the grocery store that she makes her son late for his basketball game (48)? In fact, Carter needs no such sympathy-inducing backstory to utter his regrettably universal truths: "People are not comfortable with difference. You know? Fags, retards, cripples. Fat people. Old folks, even. They scare us or something.... The thing they represent that's so scary is what we *could* be, how vulnerable we all are" (71). Bigsby remarks that "not infrequently, LaBute's more obnoxious characters display an honestly lacking in those who seem less brutal ...[Carter] does not deal in euphemism or liberal sentiment. For him, the world is as it is" (*Neil LaBute*, 171).

Although writers such as David Mamet and Neil LaBute may seem holdovers from an earlier, less sensitive, more misogynist era, both writers in fact critically dissect the assumptions often motivating the privileged, articulate white middle-class (most often its men), as well as implicate playgoers usually from the same demographic in the behavior they spend much of a Mamet or LaBute play putting up rationalizing defenses against. As Bigsby remarks, "[LaBute's] characters ... lack concern for the consequences of their actions, treat life as a game in which their own needs take precedence." And "more often [than outright violence, LaBute] catalogues the small betrayals, casual deceits, instinctive cruelties which characterize daily experience" (*Neil LaBute*, 8).

Drama in Dialogue: *Oleanna* and *Fat Pig*

Neil LaBute once remarked to the *New Yorker*'s theater critic John Lahr that his admiration for playwright David Mamet was "beyond fan—stalker perhaps. Psychological stalker" (45). Lahr and others have discerned in LaBute's work "the same linguistic cunning as Mamet" (Lahr, "A Touch," 45); as Christopher Bigsby adds, both writers are "fascinate[ed] with characters for whom communication implies vulnerability, who deliberately hold each other at arm's length" (*Neil LaBute*, 14–15). And both writers focus on "solitary individuals … [who elevate] their predatory or simply self-serving instincts to the level of moral principle" (15). Both Mamet and LaBute are interested in power relations between individuals roughly matched in their amount of social cachet; just as often, however, LaBute ups the ante by dissecting the deliberate cruelty of those with a clear social or physical advantage going after weaker prey for the sheer Nietzschean pleasure of doing so. Bigsby argues in his comparison of Mamet's *Oleanna* to LaBute's *The Shape of Things* that "sympathies shift in the course of [*Oleanna*]" while LaBute "seems to create a more one-sided drama" (15). The same applies to many of LaBute's plays and screenplays: the victim, be this a person with a disability; a racial minority; or, as in *Fat Pig*, a woman with an unacceptable appearance, never has a chance, and audiences are simultaneously horrified and—the most controversial aspect of LaBute's work—often persuaded as to the logic (or at least the inevitability) of and thrilled by the evisceration performed.

Both Carol in *Oleanna* and Helen, the title character in *Fat Pig*, present images of abjection. Carol, with her average to limited intellectual ability is out of her depth in John's classroom and may be simply demanding too much when she insists early in the play, "*Teach* me. *Teach* me" (11), as if intelligence or aptitude were a wrapped package that can be handed across a desk. Toby Zinman calls Carol "exasperatingly dense, and her seemingly willfully irrational arguments infuriate [John] (and us)" (158). LaBute's Helen may also be out of her depth when she undertakes a relationship with Tom. As she is portrayed as witty and intelligent, she is certainly wise enough to know how important looks are, especially for women, in contemporary US culture. As with Mamet's Carol, the audience may view LaBute's Helen as in serious need of a reality check.

Both women are depicted as going too far in their demands for equality in a man's world. Carol is vilified by the audience for successfully imposing her will on John; Helen literally wants her cake and to eat it, too—to feast on tables full of junk food yet still be loved by a trim, handsome man. And although there is certainly sympathy for Helen when she is rejected by Tom in the final scene, there is a sense of society correcting itself, restoring a conventional, even moral order in the leave-taking, just as in a more tragic register Mamet saw society correcting itself in the Oedipal-like ousting of John. The audience both seeks a critical distance from LaBute's title—a slur that only infantile men like Tom and especially his coworker Carter are likely to use out loud—and finds itself silently embracing the sentiment behind it: if Helen insists on making "a pig" of herself in the first and last scene of the play, it is no wonder she winds up alone. In David Amsden's more puckish assessment, "You read those two toothy words and you wince, then you grin, then wince at yourself grinning" (115).

Both plays shift the balance of power, and inversely the vectors of audience sympathy, from men to women and back to men. Because in both plays the male characters—as often with men in general—have so much more at stake in their interactions with the women than the women have themselves, the audience cannot but feel for the loss risked or incurred by this male lead and hope for its recovery. What John, in *Oleanna*, sees slipping over the precipice by the end of the play—marriage, home, career—does indeed assume tragic, even epic proportions in a modern context. In *Fat Pig* we are asked to understand Tom's dilemma and sympathize with his own sadness at the end of the play. In fact, as we recall Tom's typical role in relationships, that per his friend Carter, "[Y]ou get bored or cornered or feel a touch nervous, and you drop 'em like they were old produce" (52), we may regard Tom's tearful final scene with Helen as a laudable mark of emotional maturation. He will genuinely mourn the loss of this relationship, and his tears are a gesture of atonement and a show of equal suffering. Helen is certainly victimized by the weightism of Tom's friends, but he shares her victim status. When earlier in the play Tom harshly insists to Jeannie that "[w]e don't *have* a relationship!" (46), he echoes LaBute's many cruel men from other plays and films, such as *In the Company of Men* and *The Distance from Here*. Yet Tom's blatant rejection of Jeannie also seems to indicate emotional growth: all of society drives him away from dating a fat woman like Helen, but at this point in the play he is bravely following his heart. In addition, Jeannie's also harsh and vindictive qualities make it difficult to feel sympathy for this character, and we know that as a thin, professionally successful woman, she will likely rebound in due time. To be sure, she is dating Carter by the end of the play and much less accusatory of Tom after that.

Both plays are set largely in a workplace, and John and Carol, as well as Tom and Jeannie, fall out over the differences of opinion regarding workplace rules and protocols. Pushed to her limit, Jeannie seems very much disposed to picturing her suffering at the hands of Tom as a form of sexual harassment; like Carol, Jeannie uses what power she has (through her position in the accounting sector) to control Tom's actions and expose his committing the kind of infraction (misusing company funds for nonbusiness expenses) that could get him fired. Just as Carol is readable as defensively accusing John of sexual harassment because she is ultimately unable to perform successfully in his class, so Jeannie wields her authority from the accounting office simply to lash back at Tom for refusing to continue seeing her. Finally Jeannie is only distracted in her agenda against Tom—petty threats about his record keeping and frequent stops by his office to vilify him on personal grounds— when she wins for herself another boyfriend; as Carol has no sexual interest in John and no other remedy for her complaint, she remains John's adversary. In *Oleanna*, standard protocol regarding professorial power is radically disrupted, whereas in *Fat Pig* the rules regarding personal appearance that govern corporate society are finally reinforced.

Doubt: A Parable (2004)

John Patrick Shanley (1950–)

Although his lead character, Sister Aloysius, is a cold, hard, and seemingly vindictive spoiler of innocence, joy, and fellow-feeling, John Patrick Shanley, a product of Catholic schooling in his native Bronx and later at a prep school in New Hampshire, dedicates his Tony- and Pulitzer Prize-winning *Doubt: A Parable* to "the many orders of Catholic nuns who have dedicated their lives to serving others ... Though they have been much maligned and ridiculed, who among us has been so generous?" Shanley is even on record as defending the priests—gay, straight, or otherwise—who took his part when he was struggling to buckle down into productive adulthood at the private school. Like *Doubt*'s 12-year-old Donald Muller, who does not appear onstage but is the object of Father Flynn's special attentions, "I was championed by homosexual teachers who were the only people watching out for me. And why were they doing it? They were really into boys.... Did they do anything to me? No. Did they want to? I don't know" (Coe; see also Witchel, 35). Alongside this ultimately beneficial experience, Shanley had a family member who was indeed molested by Father John Geoghan, whose exposure famously led to the resignation of Boston's Archbishop Bernard Francis Law in the early 2000s. Before Geoghan was caught and expelled, however, Shanley's family attempted redress at the parish level and were mortified—to the point of leaving the church— when Geoghan was transferred and promoted. In *Doubt*, the same happens at the end of the story to Father Flynn; although charges against him are never proven, his removal from St. Nicholas School is, for better or worse, its own proof; as Sister Aloysius tells young and guileless Sister James, "His resignation was his confession. He was what I thought he was. And he's gone" (58).

In interviews, Shanley also takes the unusual stance of blaming Vatican II's opening of church doors in the mid-1960s—the play is set in 1964—for facing men who may have joined the priesthood to suppress their pathological tendencies with overwhelming temptation: "I saw the dark side of the Second Vatican Council's message of 'go out into the community. When I was a kid, priests ... were priests. They were in the rectory. And so I think that this explosive combination of celibacy and 'go out into the community and make believe you're just one of the other folks' had a lot to do with the problems that followed" (Coe). In *Doubt*, Father Flynn and Sister Aloysius conflict over whether "we should sing a song from the radio [during the Christmas pageant] now and then. Take the kids out for ice cream."

SISTER ALOYSIUS:	Ice cream.
FLYNN:	Maybe take the boys on a camping trip. We should be friendlier. The children and their parents should see us as members of their family rather than emissaries from Rome....
SISTER ALOYSIUS:	But we're not members of their family. We're different. (30)

This debate, with its element of truth on both sides, is one of several in the play that leave the audience in as much doubt as the characters themselves. Throughout the story, an irresolvable contest takes place between doubt and "certainty," another word for faith, but one that Sister Aloysius wields like a bludgeon—with no solid evidence—when she realizes her limited ability to affect change in the male-dominated Church. Within the character of Sister James, an "innocence" that Sister Aloysius criticizes as "lazy" and irresponsible gullibility wars with suspicion, the seeds of reserve and uncertainty that Sister Aloysius plants in the younger woman's soul, ruining her love of teaching and throwing her calling into question. In the Preface, Shanley warns, "You may come out of my play uncertain. You may want to be sure. Look down on that feeling. We've got to learn to live with a full measure of uncertainty. There is no last word. That's the silence under the chatter of our time" (ix-x).

To maximize this crisis of indeterminacy, Shanley adds in the prospect that young Donald, the only African American boy at the school, is himself likely "that way" (48) and is thus suffering regular beatings at the hands of a homophobic father. In a key scene, Donald's mother confesses this family backstory to Sister Aloysius and pragmatically asks that the nun stay out of the matter regardless of its particulars, because of the nurturing attention Father Flynn has paid to Donald as well as the fact that her son is about to graduate anyway: "Let him take the good and leave the rest when he leaves this place in June. He knows how to do that. I taught him how to do that" (48). Once again, both Mrs. Muller and Sister Aloysius have their points, yet again Sister Aloysius resorts to threats when she feels fenced in by Mrs. Muller's position. Although Sister Aloysius is such a critical, mean-spirited figure that it is hard to sympathize with whatever she suffers in the throes of misogynist church hierarchy, one definitely spends the duration of *Doubt* shifting back and forth between support and suspicion with regard to Father Flynn. As Shanley suggests in his critique of Vatican II, it is all the qualities that make him so "of the people" and "of the flesh"—his coaching of the basketball team, his talk with the boys about the facts of life—that place him inappropriately in the vicinity of his youthful charges, at which point any "innocent" gesture, be this a touch on the wrist or a private talk, will take on unseemly connotations.

Although there is ultimately nothing so condemnatory about Father Flynn enjoying three lumps of sugar in his tea, his fingernails, which without any self-evident necessity he "wears a little long" (27), imbue his character with a diabolical touch. Because there is no "innocent" explanation for this grooming choice in a working-class man such as himself—if anything, they'd get in the way of his skills on the basketball court—they are plainly akin to the pointing finger in Father Flynn's parable of the gossiping woman visited in a dream by a heavenly rebuke. They, along with his caving in to Sister Aloysius's ruse—she falsely claims to have contacted a sister at his last parish with an incriminating story to tell, and he takes no stand against her—certainly point toward Father Flynn's guilt. Although Sister Aloysius seems at last to have triumphed in her convictions, she ends the play "bent with emotion" and confessing to Sister James, "I have doubts! I have such doubts!" (58). Elizabeth Cullingford argues that "Shanley maintains ambiguity to the last: she does not reveal what they are. Was she wrong to equate homosexuality with pedophilia, and to conflate orientation … with action … ? Was Father Flynn innocent after all? Or was she wrong to drive him away from St. Nicholas into a school perhaps less well equipped with suspicious sisters?" (262). In Annette J. Saddik's apt estimation, "The philosophical themes in this play revolve around the power of language and its role in constructing the truth; issues of interpretation and understanding; the epistemological questions concerning the meaning of knowledge; and the relationship between power and truth" (290).

In addition to its Pulitzer Prize and Tony for Best Play, *Doubt* won the 2005 Drama Desk Award for Best New Play, the Lucille Lortel Award for Outstanding Play and a Circle Award for best play. In 2007, it was adapted for the screen and nominated for several Oscars; in Hollywood, Shanley is also famed for his screenplay for the blockbuster *Moonstruck* (1987), for which he won an Academy Award, and somewhat infamous for having written and directed the ultimately disastrous *Joe Versus the Volcano* (1990), though now for some a "cult favorite" (Saddik, 279). Shanley continues to write for the screen and stage; his Irish-themed play *Outside Mullingar* (2014) was nominated for two Tony Awards.

Dead Man's Cell Phone (2007)

Sarah Ruhl (1974–)

As its title implies, Sarah Ruhl's marvelously smart and meaningful, critically acclaimed story begins when Jean approaches a man whose cell phone persistently rings in a café, only to discover that he will not pick up because he has passed away. Immediately, this significant aspect of modern life—recent technologies from VHS tape to answering machines, to myriad features of the cellular phone preserving (or enforcing) connections to the dearly departed (and even to perfect strangers)—presents as a prevailing theme. Falling sincerely for a beatific look on the man's face as he died—as we will learn in Act II, he, Gordon, was looking at Jean, who looked like "an angel" as she finished the café's last bowl of lobster bisque—Jean impulsively claims the phone as her personal responsibility: though Gordon has died, his phone rings on, and as she answers calls from his various survivors, including his mistress and his mother, she does her part to keep his memory alive, to maintain the illusion that he is "still there." The ruse works so well, Ruhl shows, because for all of us now, relationships are largely if not wholly constructed via such mediating technologies, such that Gordon was rarely more present to those he loved and worked with than as an answering voice or even just a message received. Like David Mamet, Ruhl is interested in modes of communication ancient and modern, used and abused, coming through loud and clear or lost to perdition. When she informs the dead man's various callers that he is simply "not here," she is both lying and telling an obvious truth; her polite inquiry, whether she can "take a message" (9), has profound implications: can one's meaning, one's unique truth, ever be successfully relayed and received in the modern age? Ruhl's epigraph from Dickens, that "[i]t was appointed that the book [the other's self] should shut with a spring, forever and ever, when I had read but a page," suggests that the tragic barriers between self and loved one are in fact age-old.

When various of the voices on the other end of Gordon's phone materialize, Jean attends the funeral where Gordon's mother, Harriet, gives a comically foul-mouthed eulogy; a meeting with the Other Woman who emotes jealousy over Jean's knowing him better; and a dinner hosted by his mother and also attended by his wife, Hermia, and brother, Dwight. Posing as a workplace associate who was with Gordon when he died (this is true in only the most superficial sense), Jean fabricates stories of his devotion to them all; as we get to know Gordon, it is clear that not only the stories but likely the devotions are utter falsehoods, and it is clear that Jean, like everyone else in Gordon's life, has come to love him best only now that he is gone. Later in the story, Jean learns what an unsavory character Gordon was (including illegally dealing in human organ trading) and feels uniquely called upon to atone for his misdeeds. Amy Strahler Holzapfel observes that "Ruhl emphasizes the body itself as a medium of communications" (119) with a running joke regarding Jean's supposed role in Gordon's operation in "in-coming" instead of "out-going." Though Gordon justifies his business as people being "floating receptacles waiting to be filled—with meaning—which [Jean] and I provide" (83), in fact, the analogy of humans to cell phones (just as good, even better) is challenged throughout the story.

While Hermia and Harriet (who triangulated over Gordon while he was alive) come together over Gordon's loss, Jean forms a bond with Dwight, although as with so many modern couples, the ringing cell phone—Gordon's own—intrudes upon their moments of soul-baring and lovemaking, calling their sincerity into question. Falling in love in the closet of the stationery store where Dwight works, the dead man comes between the two when Jean feels obliged to take a call on his behalf—she will "leave his cell phone on as long as I live…. Just in case someone calls. An old childhood friend. You never know" (53)—but is also simply irresistibly drawn to the lure of handheld technology. But as has been implied throughout the story, taking calls for Gordon comes with special risk; his illegal organ trading involves wealthy, desperate, violent people, and when Jean jets off to Johannesburg to call a halt to his transactions once and for all, she is gunned down—conked on the head with a gun—by an angry kidney seeker (played by the same actor playing the Other Woman). At death's door, Jean finds herself in the afterlife with Gordon, of all people, in, as Gordon explains, "a hell reserved for people who sell organs on the black market and the people who loved them" (80). She has been pipelined to his side at the moment of her own death, but because Jean has already switched her affections to Dwight, she contemplates the existential crisis of being trapped in eternity with the wrong man. Moments later, Gordon realizes that he himself has been pipelined to his mother, who loved him best after all, and disappears; Jean, "*alone in the afterlife, an Edward Hopper painting*" (89), places a frantic call to Dwight on the phone that has gone as dead as its first and second owners. In a fit of despair, she destroys the phone and, shedding redemptive tears, receives a second chance. She awakes on the floor of the Johannesburg airport and is whisked back to New York in Dwight's arms. The couple pledge to "love each other right now … not a mediocre love, but the strongest love in the world" (98). They share an unabashedly romantic kiss and a "lights out"; Ruhl regards herself as "very medieval about love … as opposed to modern and neurotic" (Lahr, "Surreal Life," 82), and the happy ending is an island of mutual rescue in a sea of individuals cocooned (if not entombed) in their devices. Per Julia M. Klein, "like *Waiting for Godot*, Ruhl's play teeters on the line between tragedy and comedy. But she rejects despair, choosing instead the possibility of communion" (B12).

Dead Man's Cell Phone is splendidly theatrical, ignoring the dictates of realism as it suits the playwright to do so and returning to their stabilizing elements—the café, the subway, the lobster bisque—in timely fashion. The structural and thematic refractions inaugurated by Beckett, Albee, and Shepard are on display in Ruhl's work, including this play: Jean both enjoys soup and visits the afterlife; Gordon is dead, then alive, then Jean's usher to the next world. As Jean and Dwight fall in love via their shared love of embossed invitations—"creamy, and thick, and you can close your eyes and *feel* the words" (48)—"*embossed stationery moves through the air slowly/like a snow parade./Lanterns made of embossed paper,/houses made of embossed paper*" (56). And in the afterlife Jean and Gordon watch a "*cell phone ballet./Beautiful music./People moving through the rain/with umbrellas, talking into their cellphones; fragments of lost conversation float up*" (87). In a note at the end of the script, Ruhl advises the production staff that these fragments of lost conversation might most effectively be "found text … that has already been left on your phone" (101) and even suggests "translating some or all of it into Japanese and various other languages" (102). Calling the cell phone in this play a "sonic medium for communication with the realms of the dead," Holzapfel remarked that the original New York production "blur[red] the realms of the living and the dead; all that separates the figures who inhabit the space are a series of colored flats … and a dark-toned lighting scheme" (118).

In an interview with John Lahr, Ruhl commented that "Aristotle has held sway for many centuries, but I feel our culture is hungry for Ovid's way of telling stories [with] … one thing transforming into another…. His is not the neat, Aristotelian arc but, instead, small transformations that are delightful and tragic" ("Surreal Life, " 81). In Klein's estimation, "*Cell Phone* goes off, like a small, brilliant fireworks display, in myriad directions" (B13). Having started out as a poet, and having enjoyed publication of her collection *Death in Another Country* at the age of 20, Ruhl also accounts for her plays' fugue-like structures (and even the stanzaic form taken by her stage directions) by seeing them "as three-dimensional poems" (qtd. in Lahr, "Surreal Life," 78). Even this play's prosaic elements, meanwhile, shimmer in an aura of other-worldliness: though stated only in the stage directions (as much of the play's meaning is, dismantling as it goes the final "fourth wall," between script and performance), Ruhl refers repeatedly to "an empty bowl of soup" and leaves it to the director, actors, and audience to wrestle with the enigma of that image. The cell phone, of course, is the most enigmatic absent presence in the story, if not in all modern life: the glowing, ringing, immortal (or at least endlessly rechargeable) indicator of both our limitless and drastically curtailed "thereness" to each other and a substitute so enthralling—we'd rather call than meet, text than talk, and play with the phone than be with each other—that it is the "Other Woman" in all our lives. In a thesis moment, Jean realizes, "it's like—when everyone has their cell phone on, no one is there. It's like we're all disappearing, the more we're there" (52–53).

From the play's title to the recurring character of the femme fatale (both the Other Woman and the Johannesburg woman, and even John's mother is a "lady in red" at John's funeral dinner), to the Hopperesque mood of loneliness and waiting suffusing the story, film noir is a situating context. Its most famous forebear, *Double Indemnity*, disrupts realistic narrative and time-framing as *Dead Man's Cell Phone* does; the entire film is a narrative given by the dying Walter Neff, opening with him wounded and staggering into his office to record a confession into a Dictaphone, enabling the flash-backs that are the main narrative. In the last moment, he dies in the arms of his partner, Barton Keyes, instrumental in exposing the crime Neff has spent the entire film confessing. Similarly, Ruhl's Gordon dies as the story begins, then revives at the beginning of Act II to narrate his final day, touching upon his ruined marriage, his lonely travels through the streets and subways of New York, his cynical attitude toward his line of work, and his final moment of spiritual communion with Jean, the angel in the café that afternoon who got the last bowl of lobster bisque. As a worldly, ruthless man used to getting his own way, Gordon is first angered by Jean's coup—in fact, the affront may have been so shocking as to do him in—but in his dying moment sees her goodness and realness and is "glad she had the last bite—I'm glad" (61). As Jean fell in love with Gordon at the moment of his death, so in a much more cynical register, having dealt the death blow herself, *Double Indemnity*'s femme fatale Phyllis Dietrichson informs Neff that she "never loved him til a second ago, when I couldn't fire the second shot." Gordon's resemblance to Walter Neff ends there, however, as it is actually Jean who is on a quest to solve a mystery, expose a criminal, and find love and affirmation on the lonely streets of the large, impersonal city; as the noir film tracked the alienation (verging on madness) of the brooding, damaged World War II veteran, so Jean navigates a city of isolation and sadness (53) but finds love in the nick of time.

Hamilton (2015)

Lin-Manuel Miranda (1980–)

Lin-Manuel Miranda is the Tony Award-winning lyricist/composer and lead performer of *In the Heights* (2005), an ensemble story of New York's Dominican-American community set in Washington Heights. As lore has already set it down, Miranda was on vacation in 2008, in the midst of *Heights*'s continued success onstage, when he picked up Ron Chernow's 800-page history of Alexander Hamilton at the airport. He became fascinated by the life of this immigrant from the West Indies who would serve his adopted country so vigorously and so variously during the American Revolution and its infant years; Miranda wrote the opening number as part of a planned "concept album" for the White House's Evening of Poetry, Music, and the Spoken Word event in May 2009; as recorded in Miranda and Jeremy McCarter's memoir of the musical's inception, President Obama was the first on his feet following Miranda's performance of "Alexander Hamilton." The one song grew into the 46 original and reprised numbers making up the record-breaking Broadway musical and cast album that have received in the popular press universal acclaim as "game-changing" and "revolutionary." As Miranda and McCarter write, "sometimes the right person tells the right story at the right moment…. That night [at the White House], Lin reintroduced people to the poor kid from the Caribbean who made the country rich and strong, an immigrant who came here to build a life for himself and ended up helping to build the nation instead. He is the prototype for the millions of men and women who have followed him to this day."

Hamilton is almost entirely sung in a score predominated by hip-hop and well intermixed with pop, R&B, and even traditional Broadway styles, such that all character development and plot exposition occurs via the lyrics and their diverse stylings. Writing for the *Hollywood Reporter*, David Rooney remarks, "[R]ap becomes a natural storytelling vernacular. The syncopated cadences and declamatory bluster of hip-hop seem tailor-made to depict the story of Hamilton a man who lived, worked, and fought like he was 'running out of time.'" Not only are Hamilton and his fated assassin, Aaron Burr, delineated in their respective strengths and weakness, but Thomas Jefferson, James Madison, and General Washington are fleshed out in song as well. *Hamilton* also introduces key subplots regarding the hero's personal life— his marriage to Eliza Schuyler, threatened by the affair with Maria Reynolds then restored through the tragic loss of their son Phillip in a duel, and his passionate alliance with Eliza's older sister, Angelica, who was as drawn to Hamilton's intelligence, courage, and ambition as her younger sister was but who sacrificed much happiness out of love for her. Critics give special com- mendation to the opening number, "Alexander Hamilton," which introduces the lead character through his first 20 years, from starving, bastard orphan- hood in the Caribbean to his hopeful arrival on US shores; "Cabinet Battle #1 and #2," which convey much intricate policy matter in the course of short but engaging raps; "The Room where it Happens," Aaron Burr's solilo- quy, during which the envy, resentment, and legitimate grievance against his strong-willed rival is worked through; and the women's several ballads includ- ing "Helpless," "Satisfied," "That Would be Enough," and "Burn." *Hamilton*'s signature song is "My Shot," a celebration of immigrant moxie that showcases the spirit, self-assurance, and optimism of the young Hamilton. Reprised in lyric and theme throughout the production—for example, when Hamilton realizes that "my shot" is best taken not in heroism in battle but as a player in Washington's military and presidency—the original rendition foreshad- ows "the shot" that will end Hamilton's life at the hands of Burr. Burr in turn expresses his resentment of Hamilton's heedless but ultimately winning ten- dency to "shoot off his mouth," to ignore his advice to "talk less and smile more," and to criticize Burr's more measured and dignified but less courageous and admirable course of watchful "waiting for it." Though a firm contrast is established between Hamilton's commitment to principle and Burr's willing- ness to side with any party in order to advance, at a key moment toward the end of both men's lives—as Burr notes in his closing, he lives on after assassi- nating Hamilton but has been dead to posterity ever since—they find them- selves reversing roles:

HAMILTON:	Is there anything you wouldn't do?
BURR:	No, I'm chasing what I want.
	And you know what?

HAMILTON: What?
BURR: I learned that from you. ("The Election of 1800," from
                    Miranda, *Hamilton*)

As noted above, popular and critical reception of this work has been unan-
imously ecstatic. It sold out through its off-Broadway run at the Public
Theater between February and May 2015, and seats for the Broadway run
at the Richard Rodgers Theater were rare to nonexistent into 2017. With
tickets selling as high as $475 apiece, the show regularly grosses more than a
million dollars a week, though true to its roots in Hamilton's (and Miranda's
own) humble urban background, *Hamilton* stages a daily lottery—originally
this was literally staged in the street outside the theater, now online—for
21 average theatergoers per show who are awarded entrance for the ridic-
ulously affordable price of "one Hamilton" ($10 US). Ben Brantley began
his review in the *New York Times* by admitting, "It really is that good" and
went on to praise the show's ensemble cast of "fully rendered individuals" and
its placement of history itself as "the star …, the evening's DJ, making sure
there's always something to dance to." In the *Hollywood Reporter*, Rooney
observed, "in terms of lyrical density, *Hamilton* possibly packs in more words
per minute than any musical in Broadway history…. You find yourself savor-
ing the wit and agility of one ingenious rhyming loop while another and then
another keep unfurling." Off-Broadway, *Hamilton* received 12 Lucille Lortel
nominations (winning 10), five Outer Critics Circle Nominations (winning
three), 14 Drama Desk nominations (winning eight), and the Obie for Best
New Theater Work of 2015. It won the 2016 Pulitzer Prize in drama and was
nominated for a record-breaking 16 Tony Awards, winning 11, including Best
Book and Original Score, Best Actor, Featured Actor, Featured Actress, Best
Choreography, Costumes (Musical), Direction (Musical), and Best Musical.
Miranda himself received a McArthur "Genius" grant in 2015.

Clearly this story, with its predominantly hip-hop score and actors of color
in all founding-father roles, continues up the path originated by playwrights
throughout the contemporary period. Athol Fugard set the stage by rewrit-
ing the rules regarding race and character, whereas August Wilson and Suzan-
Lori Parks are two American forebears who remarkably interweave stories of
America's minority communities into narratives of received (wealthy, white,
hegemonic) history. *Hamilton* is especially readable as a "rep 'n' rev" of Parks's
Topdog/Underdog, which traces the provenance of the Lincoln legend with
respect to the African American experience. As argued in discussion of this
play above, Parks steps into the tradition originated by Langston Hughes, as
he questioned Walt Whitman's claim to a democratic vision of America that

nevertheless assumed a white actor center-stage. Both Hughes and Parks remind their black and white audiences that "I, Too, Sing America," and in the opening number of *Hamilton*, this refrain is echoed when the chorus sings to Hamilton, "America sings for you." Whereas Parks uses irony, dark comedy, and post-modern play to situate her white-face Lincoln impersonator in a familial and national tragedy, Miranda draws no attention to the cross-racial casting in lyric or action per se; it is enough that Hamilton and his confrere Lafayette are immigrants who "get the job done," that Hamilton and his mentor-turned-assassin, Aaron Burr, are disadvantaged orphans, and that questions of freedom, slavery, and all men's equality resonate throughout the story.

As Miranda has acknowledged, modern musicals dealing in memorable ways with complicated historical or serious topical themes form another line of inspiration; the 1980 adaptation of Victor Hugo's novel of the French Revolution, *Les Misérables*, is an obvious intertext, as are breakthrough pop-musicals such as *Rent* (1993) and *Spring Awakening* (2006), as is the 1969 historical musical *1776*. *Hamilton* quotes the opening number of *1776* "The Adams Administration," when it calls out, "Sit down, John!," and Rebecca Mead records Miranda's comment with respect to his search for emotional impact in his composition process: "I really got my 'Les Miz' on in this score…. In terms of how it accesses your tear ducts, nothing does it better than that show." *Hamilton* is enjoyed for it citations of numerous precursors, from Gilbert and Sullivan's *Pirates of Penzance* to Rodgers and Hammerstein's *South Pacific*, to the current-day styles and stories of Tupac Shakur (regarded by Miranda as a modern rendering of the brash, outspoken, assassinated founding father; see Mead), Beyoncé, Destiny's Child, and Biggie Smalls (whose famed "Ten Crack Commandments" from the late 1990s is reworked here into "Ten Duel Commandments"). In *Slate*, Forrest Wickman filed a "track-by-track guide" to "All the Hip-Hop references in *Hamilton*," and in his review, Rooney placed *Hamilton* in a line of revolutionary musicals throughout the twentieth century, from *Showboat*, *Oklahoma!*, and *West Side Story* to *Hair*, the first rock musical, to magnificent upgrades to the tradition by Stephen Sondheim in *Company* and *Sweeney Todd*.

A just-as-riveting topic for *Hamilton* fans is the show's use of historical omission and distortion in order smooth out, streamline, and intensify the dramatic impact of an in-fact chaotic and crowded historical narrative, and in order to set its eponymous character in the best possible light. Yale historian Joanne B. Freeman wrote in *Slate* that Miranda's Hamilton is more "loveable" than his historical counterpart: "The real Hamilton was a mass of contradictions: an immigrant who sometimes distrusted immigrants, a revolutionary who placed a supreme value on law and order, a man who distrusted the rumblings of the masses yet preached his politics to them more frequently and passionately than many of his more democracy-friendly fellows." Though *Hamilton* lays such moving emphasis on its hero's immigrant identity and the essential role played by immigrants at each stage of the American enterprise, ironically, says Freeman, "when newly installed President Jefferson proposed opening the doors of citizenship, Hamilton protested, fretting about the corruption of national character and (revealingly) claiming that if only 'native citizens' had voted in 1800, Jefferson wouldn't be president." In his analysis of the controversy surrounding William Dunlap's early drama *André* (1798; see discussion in Section I), Norman Philbrick even points out that "those [progressive-minded] Republicans who saw or read *André* would not have forgotten that one of the principle defenders of the spy was [the conservative, English-identified Federalist] Hamilton" (116). Despite such departures from the record, however, Freeman praises *Hamilton*'s "blend of an inclusive present with a historical past that is rooted in fact.… The past isn't an exact fit for the present. But *Hamilton* isn't about an exact fit. It's about making that past inclusive and empowering, [about] humanizing and energizing a subject—the nation's founding—that all too often seems carved in stone." Also defending the final product, historian Chernow, who consulted on *Hamilton* in its early stages, declared, "I think [Miranda] has plucked out the dramatic essence of the character—his vaulting ambition, his obsession with his legacy, his driven nature, his roving eye, his brilliant mind, his faulty judgment" (qtd. in Piepenburg).

Per the textbook concluding here, *Hamilton* is the ideal lens through which to cast a final look back upon centuries of American identity formation via its stories told on the popular stage. Since the moment of original works such as Hunter's *Androboros*, Burgoyne's *Blockade of Boston*, Tyler's *The Contrast*, and Dunlap's *André*, American dramatists have plied their craft to demonstrate—and instigate—the particularities of the national character in all its noble, regrettable, hypocritical, and tragic aspects. With his multiple gifts as a lyricist, composer, and lead actor, Miranda is easily this century's answer to Broadway's original wunderkind, Major John André, who as we recall was at once an accomplished British soldier/spy and a handsome, talented stage presence who could "act, produce, even paint scenery" (J. Richards, 60). As James Nelson Barker's Captain Smith connected nation-building to play-making when he bid his followers, "We have a noble stage, on which to act/A noble drama; let us sustain/Our sev'ral parts with credit and with honor" (580), so Lin-Manuel Miranda's Hamilton is told by his chorus that "history has its eyes on you"; in the show's finale, the chorus asks the difficult question of "Who Lives, Who Dies, Who Tells Your Story."

Hamilton itself is a story about storytelling, about drama's ability not only to reflect and revive but when necessary to renovate and rewrite the historical record for modern audiences. As Hamilton attempted so fervently in his own life to always set the record straight, Miranda seemed drawn not only to this founding father's immigrant status and his "young, scrappy, and hungry" identification with Revolutionary-era America but also to his exceptional talents and equal ambitions in the direction of "fighting" and "writing." As a young man dreaming of greatness, Miranda's Hamilton desires only a regiment of his own to command during the war. Washington—the perennial wise and measured father-figure from Tyler's and Dunlap's early plays—reprises this role in *Hamilton*, recognizing his protégé's strengths as a communicator and assigning him key secretarial duties during the war, then the role of treasury secretary in his presidential administration. Following the end of war, Hamilton indeed "writes his way out" of embroilments with his fellow cabinet secretaries, challenges to the Constitution as lead author of the *Federalist Papers*, aspersions on his loyalty by confessing to an affair in "The Reynolds Pamphlet," and ultimately into posterity's better informed and much more appreciative estimation.

Together with Chernow's biography, Miranda's play deserves as much or even more credit for rescuing Hamilton from general modern obscurity and the chopping block of the $10 bill. With recent growing national interest to diversify the faces of US currency, it was decided by the Treasury Department in June 2015 that Alexander Hamilton would be the "dead white male" to be sacrificed, since at that time his national reputation was minimally known and indifferently regarded. Shortly after this announcement, Chernow and Miranda's work provided vital lost information regarding Hamilton's accomplishments, especially his genius with respect to establishing a national bank, the US mint, and related financial instruments, all of which stabilized the postwar economy, enabled the states to pay their debts, and provided the necessary guarantees to international trading and lending partners. As a result, the tide has now turned in the currency debate against Andrew Jackson, the first regular-man's president now mainly notorious for slave owning and the Indian Removal Act of 1830. Per Treasury Secretary Jack Lew's announcement in April 2016, Jackson's face on the $20 bill will be replaced with that of the Moses of her People, Harriet Tubman, revered to this day for leading hundreds out of slavery via the Underground Railroad in the 1850s. *Hamilton* is thus our final, remarkable contribution to the ongoing dialogue between American drama and the American populace, who may yet look to the stage for lessons forgotten, for the means by which to improve their present-day profiles—in the mirror and internationally—and for the roads best taken to enter illuminating communion with their fellow dramatists and fellow playgoers the world over.

Bibliography

2nd Marquess of Dufferin and Ava (Terence Hamilton-Temple-Blackwood). "Introduction." *Sheridan's Plays: Now Printed as He Wrote Them*. Ed. W. Fraser Rae. London: David Nutt, 1902. vii–xii.

Achilles, Jochen. "Does Reshuffling the Cards Change the Game?: Structures of Play in Parks's *Topdog/Underdog*." *Suzan-Lori Parks: Essays on the Plays and Other Works*. Ed. Philip C. Kolin. Jefferson, NC: McFarland, 2010. 103–23.

Achilles, Jochen and Ina Bergmann. "Richard Greenberg." *The Methuen Guide to Contemporary American Playwrights*. Eds. Martin Middeke, Peter Paul Schnierer, Christopher Innes, and Matthew C. Roudané. London: Bloomsbury Methuen Drama, 2014. 39–57.

Adler, Jacob H. *Lillian Hellman*. Austin, TX: Steck-Vaugh, 1969.

Adler, Thomas P. *American Drama, 1940–1960: A Critical History*. New York: Twayne, 1994.

———. "Fissures beneath the Surface: Drama in the 1940s and 1950s." *A Companion to Twentieth-Century Drama*. Ed. David Krasner. Malden, MA: Blackwell, 2006. 159–74.

———. "Lillian Hellman: Feminism, Formalism, and Politics." *Cambridge Companion to American Women Playwrights*. Ed. Brenda Murphy. Cambridge: Cambridge University Press, 1999. 118–33.

———. "Repetition and Regression in *Curse of the Starving Class* and *Buried Child*." *The Cambridge Companion to Sam Shepard*. Ed. Matthew C. Roudané. Cambridge: Cambridge University Press, 2002. 111–22.

Albee, Edward. "Which Theater is the Absurd One?" *New York Times Magazine*, February 25, 1962: 30+.

———. *The Zoo Story*. 1958. The American Dream *and* The Zoo Story: *Two Plays by Edward Albee*. New York: Plume, 1997. 5–49.

Allen, Robert C. *Horrible Prettiness: Burlesque and American Culture*. Chapel Hill: University of North Carolina Press, 1991.

Amsden, David. "Up with People." *New York*, November 29, 2004, 115–16.

Archer, William. "Introduction." *The Works of Henrik Ibsen*, Vol. 2. Trans. William Archer. Boston: Scribner's/Jefferson Press, 1911. 3–21.

"Archivist's Mailbag." "The Vestment Scandal of 1714." Trinity Wall Street.org. https://www.trinitywallstreet.org/blogs/archivists-mailbag/vestment-scandal-1714.

Aronson, Arnold. "American Theater in Context: 1945–Present." *The Cambridge History of American Theater, Vol. III: Post-World War II to the 1990s*. Eds. Don B. Wilmeth and Christopher Bigsby. Cambridge: Cambridge University Press, 2000. 87–162.

Atkinson, Brooks. "At the Theater." *New York Times*, February 11, 1949: 27.

———. *Broadway.* 1970. New York: Limelight, 1990.

———. "The Theater: *A Raisin in the Sun.*" *New York Times*, March 13, 1959: 24.

Badenhausen, Richard. "The Modern Academy Raging in the Dark: Misreading Mamet's Political Incorrectness in *Oleanna.*" *College Literature*, 25.3 (1998): 1–19.

Baker, Christopher. "A Trip with the Strange Woman: Amiri Baraka's *Dutchman* and the Book of Proverbs." *South Atlantic Review*, 78.3–4 (2013): 110–28.

Baraka, Amiri (LeRoi Jones). *Dutchman.* 1964. *The Kenning Anthology of Poets Theater, 1945–1985.* Eds. Kevin Killian and David Brazil. Chicago: Kenning Editions, 2010. 202–20.

Barker, James Nelson. *The Indian Princess* (1808). *Representative Plays by American Dramatists, Vol. 1, 1765–1819.* Ed. Montrose J. Moses. New York: Benjamin Blom, 1964. 565–628.

Barlow, Judith E. "Introduction." *Machinal.* 1928. London: Nick Herne Books, 1993, 2003.

Barnes, Clive. "Theater: Arthur Miller's 'The Price.'" *New York Times*, February 8, 1968: 37.

Bean, Annemarie. "Plays and Playwrights of the Harlem Renaissance." *A Companion to Twentieth-Century Drama.* Ed. David Krasner. Malden, MA: Blackwell, 2006. 91–105.

Beard, DeAnna M. Toten. "American Experimentalism, American Expressionism, and Early O'Neill." *A Companion to Twentieth-Century Drama.* Ed. David Krasner. Malden, MA: Blackwell, 2006. 53–68.

Bechtel, Roger. *Past Performance: American Theater and the Historical Imagination.* Lewisburg, PA: Bucknell University Press, 2007.

Beckett, Samuel. *Endgame.* 1957. New York: Grove/Weidenfeld, 1958.

Beete, Paulette. "Art Talk with William S. Yellow Robe, Jr." *Art Works/National Endowment for the Arts*, April 8, 2014.

Benston, Kimberly W. "Introduction." *Imamu Amiri Baraka (LeRoi Jones): A Collection of Critical Essays.* Edgewood Cliffs, NJ: Prentice-Hall, 1978. 1–20.

Ben-Zvi, Linda. "Murder, She Wrote: The Genesis of Susan Glaspell's *Trifles.*" *Theater Journal*, 44.2 (1992): 141–62.

———. *Susan Glaspell: Her Life and Times.* New York: Oxford University Press, 2005.

Bertolini, Diana. "A Disturbed Genius Seen Through the Eyes of an Intimate Friend: William Inge and Barbara Baxley." *New York Public Library Archives*, June 28, 2013.

Bigsby, Christopher (aka C.W.E.). *Albee.* 1969. Chip's Bookshop, 1978.

——— *Arthur Miller: 1915–1962.* Cambridge: Harvard University Press, 2009.

——— "Born Injured: The Theater of Sam Shepard." *The Cambridge Companion to Sam Shepard.* Ed. Matthew C. Roudané. Cambridge: Cambridge University Press, 2002. 7–33.

——— *Contemporary American Playwrights.* Cambridge: Cambridge University Press, 1999.

—— *A Critical Introduction to Twentieth-Century American Drama, Volume One: 1900–1940*. Cambridge: Cambridge University Press, 1982.

—— *David Mamet*. London: Methuen, 1985.

—— *Modern American Drama, 1945–2000*. Cambridge: Cambridge University Press, 2000.

—— *Neil LaBute: Stage and Cinema*. Cambridge: Cambridge University Press, 2007.

Birdoff, Harry. *World's Greatest Hit:* Uncle Tom's Cabin. New York: S.F. Vanni, 1947.

Bottoms, Stephen. "Christopher Shinn." *The Methuen Guide to Contemporary American Playwrights*. Eds. Martin Middeke, Peter Paul Schnierer, Christopher Innes, and Matthew C. Roudané. London: Bloomsbury Methuen Drama, 2014. 336–53.

Boucicault, Dion. *The Octoroon; Or, Life in Louisiana: A Play in Five Acts*. Printed, not Published, 1859.

Brandon, Henry. "The State of the Theater." 1960. *Conversations with Arthur Miller*. Ed. Matthew C. Roudané. Jackson: University of Mississippi Press, 1987. 56–67.

Brandt, Maria F. "'The Man in the Family': Staging Gender in *Waiting for Lefty* and American Social Protest Theater." *Critical Approaches to American Working Class Literature*. Ed. Michelle M. Tokarczyk. London: Routledge, 2011. 204–18.

Brantley, Ben. "*Hamilton*, Young Rebels Changing History and Theater." *New York Times*, August 6, 2015.

——. "In Shepard's *Buried Child*, a Father and Family Dissolve into Darkness." *New York Times*, February 17, 2016.

——. "A Sam Shepard Revival Gets Him to Broadway." *New York Times*, May 1, 1996: C15.

Brater, Enoch. *Arthur Miller: A Playwright's Life and Works*. New York: Thames and Hudson, 2005.

——. *The Essential Samuel Beckett: An Illustrated Biography*. 1989. London: Thames and Hudson, 2003.

"*Breaking a Butterfly* at Prince's Theater." *The Times*, March 6, 1884. *All about Henrik Ibsen*. National Library of Norway. ibsen.nb.no.

Broun, Heywood. "'The Emperor Jones' by O'Neill Gives Chance for Cheers." *New York Tribune*, November 4, 1920: 8.

Brown, Russell E. "Names and Numbers in *The Adding Machine*." *Names*, 34.3 (1986): 266–74.

Brun, M.V. "The Royal Theater." *Folkets Avis*, December 24, 1879. *All about Henrik Ibsen*. National Library of Norway. ibsen.nb.no.

Brustein, Robert. "The Men-Taming Women of William Inge." *Harper's*. November 1958: 52–57.

Bryan, Mark Evans. "American Drama, 1900–1915." *A Companion to Twentieth-Century American Drama*. Ed. David Krasner. Malden, MA: Blackwell, 2005. 3–17.

Canary, Robert H. *William Dunlap*. New York: Twayne, 1970.

Cantor, Harold. *Clifford Odets: Playwright and Poet*. Metuchen, NJ: Scarecrow Press, 1978.

Cardullo, Robert J. (aka Bert). "Appearance and Essence in Georg Kaiser's *From Morn to Midnight*." *Explicator*, 70.3 (2012): 170–74.

———— "Birth and Death in *A Streetcar Named Desire*." *Confronting Tennessee Williams's* A Streetcar Named Desire: *Essays in Critical Pluralism*. Ed. Philip C. Kolin. Westport, CT: Greenwood Press, 1993. 167–80.

———— "Names and Titles in Amiri Baraka's *Dutchman*." *ANQ* 22.3 (2009): 51–56.

Carson, Ada Lou and Herbert L. Carson. *Royall Tyler*. Boston: Twayne, 1979.

Carter, Steven R. *Hansberry's Drama: Commitment and Complexity*. Urbana: University of Illinois Press, 1991.

Centola, Steven R. "Compromise as Bad Faith: Arthur Miller's *A View from the Bridge* and William Inge's *Come Back, Little Sheba*." *Midwest Quarterly*, 28.1 (1986): 100–13.

Chinn, Sarah E. "Masculinity and National Identity on the Early American Stage." *Literature Compass*, 9.2 (2012): 106–17.

A Cinema History: A Chronological Review of the Best Films Worldwide from 1895–1922. acinemahistory.com. [Last accessed: 30th November 2016]

Clark, Barrett H. *The British and American Drama of To-day: Outlines for Their Study*. New York: Henry Holt, 1915.

Cliff, Nigel. *The Shakespeare Riots: Revenge, Drama, and Death in Nineteenth-Century America*. New York: Random House, 2007.

Coe, Robert. "The Evolution of John Patrick Shanley." Theatre Communications Group 4 November 2006. tcg.org. [Last accessed: 30th November 2016]

Cohen, Derek. "A South African Drama: Athol Fugard's *The Blood Knot*." *Modern Language Studies*, 7.1 (1977): 74–81.

Cohn, Ruby. *Edward Albee*. Minneapolis: University of Minnesota Press, 1969.

————. *Just Play: Beckett's Theater*. Princeton: Princeton University Press, 1980.

Crowley, John W. "James Nelson Barker in Perspective." *Educational Theatre Journal*, 24.4 (1972): 363–69.

Crowther, Bosley, "New *Children's Hour*: Another Film Version of Play Arrives, Shirley MacLaine and Audrey Hepburn Star." *New York Times*, March 15, 1962: 28.

Cruse, Harold. *The Crisis of the Negro Intellectual*. New York: New York Review of Books, 1967.

Cruz, Nilo. *Anna in the Tropics*. New York: Theatre Communications Group, 2003.

Cullen, Frank, Florence Hackman, and Donald McNeilly. *Vaudeville Old and New: An Encyclopedia of Variety Performers in America*, Vol. 1. New York: Routledge, 2006.

Cullingford, Elizabeth. "Evil, Sin, or Doubt?: The Dramas of Clerical Child Abuse." *Theatre Journal*, 62.2 (2010): 245–63.

Cummings, Scott T. *Maria Irene Fornés*. New York: Routledge, 2013.

————. "Maria Irene Fornés." *The Methuen Guide to Contemporary American Playwrights*. Eds. Martin Middeke, Peter Paul Schnierer, Christopher Innes, and Matthew C. Roudané. London: Bloomsbury Methuen Drama, 2014. 20–38.

Curry, Jane Kathleen. *John Guare: A Research and Production Sourcebook*. Westport, CT: Greenwood Press, 2002.

Davis, Peter A. *From* Androboros *to the First Amendment: A History of America's First Play*. Iowa City: University of Iowa Press, 2015.

————. "Plays and Playwrights to 1800." *The Cambridge History of American Theater: Volume One, Beginnings to 1870*. Eds. Don B. Wilmeth and Christopher Bigsby. Cambridge: Cambridge University Press, 1998. 216–49.

Däwes, Birgit. "William S. Yellow Robe, Jr." *The Methuen Drama Guide to Contemporary American Playwrights*. Eds. Martin Middeke et al. London: Bloomsbury, 2014. 447–66.

DesRochers, Rick. "The Mythology of History, Family, and Performance." Interview with Suzan-Lori Parks and George C. Wolfe. *Suzan-Lori Parks in Person: Interviews and Commentaries*. Eds. Philip C. Kolin and Harvey Young. London: Routledge, 2014. 107–9.

Dickey, Jerry. "The Expressionist Moment: Sophie Treadwell." *Cambridge Companion to American Women Playwrights*. Ed. Brenda Murphy. Cambridge: Cambridge University Press, 1999. 66–81.

————. "The 'Real Lives' of Sophie Treadwell: Expressionism and the Feminist Aesthetic in *Machinal* and *For Saxophone*." *Speaking the Other Self: American Women Writers*. Ed. Jeanne Campbell Reesman. Athens: University of Georgia Press, 1997. 176–84.

Dietrick, John. "Making it Real: Money and Mimesis in Suzan-Lori Parks's *Topdog/ Underdog*." *American Drama*, 16.1 (2007): 47–74.

Dorwick, Keith. "Stanley Kowalski's Not So Secret Sorrow: Queering, De-Queering, and Re-Queering *A Streetcar Named Desire* as Drama, Script, Film, and Opera." *Interdisciplinary Humanities*, 20.2 (2003): 80–94.

Downer, Alan S. *Fifty Years of American Drama, 1900–1950*. Chicago: Henry Regnery Company, 1951.

Dozier, Richard J. "Odets and Little Lefty." *American Literature*, 48.4 (1977): 597–98.

"Drumsheugh: Lesbian Sex Row Rocked Society." *Edinburgh Evening News*, February 25, 2009. edinburghnews.scotsman.com.

Dukore, Bernard F. *American Dramatists, 1918–1945*. New York: Grove, 1984.

Dunlap, William. *André: A Tragedy in Five Acts*. 1798. *Representative Plays by American Dramatists, 1765–1819*. Ed. Montrose J. Moses. New York: Benjamin Blom, 1938. 499–564.

————. *History of the American Theater*. New York: J&J Harper, 1832.

Durham, Frank. *Elmer Rice*. New York: Twayne, 1970.

"'The Easiest Way': Eugene Walter's Moving Portrayal of a Woman's Frailty." *Current Opinion* (Ed. Edward J. Wheeler), 51 (July 1911): 73–81.

Ebert, Roger. "On *Oleanna*: The Play's the Thing – The Film Can't Cut It." *Chicago Sun-Times*, November 4, 1994: 26.

Edwards, Herbert J. and Julie A. Herne. *James A. Herne: Rise of Realism in the American Drama*. Orono: University of Maine Press, 1964.

Elam Jr., Harry J. "August Wilson." *A Companion to Twentieth-Century Drama*. Ed. David Krasner. Malden, MA: Blackwell, 2006. 318–33.

———. *The Past as Present in the Drama of August Wilson*. Ann Arbor: University of Michigan Press, 2004.

Esslin, Martin. "The Theater of the Absurd." *Tulane Drama Review*, 4.4 (1960): 3–15.

Evelev, John. "*The Contrast*: The Problem of Theatricality and Political and Social Crisis in Post-Revolutionary America." *Early American Literature*, 31.3 (1996): 74–97.

Farfan, Penny. "Feminism, Meta-Theatricality, and Mise-en-scène in Maria Irene Fornés's *Fefu and her Friends*." *Modern Drama*, 40 (1997): 442–53.

Fawkes, Richard. *Dion Boucicault: A Biography*. London: Quartet Books, 1979.

Fearnow, Mark. "Theater Groups and Their Playwrights." *The Cambridge History of American Theater, Volume Two: 1970–1945*. Eds. Don B. Wilmeth and Christopher Bigsby. Cambridge: Cambridge University Press, 1999. 343–77.

Fishman, Joan. "Romare Bearden, August Wilson, and the Traditions of African Performance." *May All Your Fences Have Gates: Essays on the Drama of August Wilson*. Ed. Alan Nadel. Iowa City: University of Iowa Press, 1994. 133–49.

Fletcher, Anne. "Reading Across the 1930s." *A Companion to Twentieth-Century Drama*. Ed. David Krasner. Malden, MA: Blackwell, 2006. 106–26.

Fornés, Maria Irene. "Fefu and Her Friends." *Performing Arts Journal*, 2.3 (1978): 112–40.

Foster, Verna. "Suzan-Lori Parks's Staging of the Lincoln Myth in *The America Play* and Topdog/*Underdog*." *Journal of American Drama and Theater*, 17.3 (2005): 24–35.

Freedman, Jonathan. "Angels, Monsters, and Jews: Intersections of Queer and Jewish Identity in Kushner's *Angels in America*." *PMLA*, 113.1 (1998): 90–102.

Freedman, Samuel G. "Foreword." *Fences* by August Wilson. New York: Theatre Communications Group, 2007. vii–xiii.

Freeman, Joanne B. "How *Hamilton* Uses History." *Slate* (November 11, 2015).

Frick, John W. *Theater, Culture, and Temperance Reform in Nineteenth-Century America*. Cambridge: Cambridge University Press, 2003.

Fuchs, Elinor. "*Fefu and her Friends*: The View from the Stone." *The Theater of Maria Irene Fornés*. Ed. Marc Robinson. Baltimore: Johns Hopkins University Press, 1999. 85–108.

Fugard, Athol. *Blood Knot: A Play in Three Acts*. New York: Samuel French, 1964.

Gainor, J. Ellen and Jerry Dickey. "Susan Glaspell and Sophie Treadwell: Staging Feminism and Modernism, 1915–1941." *A Companion to Twentieth-Century Drama*. Ed. David Krasner. Malden, MA: Blackwell, 2006. 34–52.

Garland, Hamlin. "Mr. and Mrs. Herne." *Arena*, 4 (1891): 543–60.

Garner Jr., Stanton B. "Framing the Classroom: Pedagogy, Power, *Oleanna*." *Theater Topics*, 10.1. (2000): 39–52.

Gerould, Daniel and Marvin Carlson, eds. and trans. *Pixérécourt: Four Melodramas*. New York: Martin E. Segal Theater Center Publications, 2002.

Gilman, Richard. "Introduction." *Seven Plays*. By Sam Shepard. New York: Bantam, 1984. xi–xvii.

Gilroy, Harry. "The Bigger the Lie." *New York Times*, December 14, 1952. Rpt. *Conversations with Lillian Hellman*. Ed. Jackson R. Bryer. Jackson: University of Mississippi Press, 1986. 24–26.

Glaspell, Susan. "Allege Haines Was Murderer." *Des Moines Daily News*, April 9, 1901. MidnightAssassin.com. [Last accessed: 30th November 2016]

———. "Hossack Begged Wife to Aid Him." *Des Moines Daily News*, April 3, 1901. MidnightAssassin.com. [Last accessed: 30th November 2016]

———. "Now Before Grand Jury." *Des Moines Daily News*, December 11, 1900. Midnight Assassin.com. [Last accessed: 30th November 2016]

———. "She Prepares to Fight." *Des Moines Daily News*, December 6, 1900. MidnightAssassin.com. [Last accessed: 30th November 2016]

———. *Trifles*. New York: Frank Shay/Washington Square, 1916.

Gordon, Jane. "An Albee Revival (and a Premiere)." *New York Times*, June 6, 2004: CT5.

Gossett, Thomas F. Uncle Tom's Cabin *and American Culture*. Dallas: Southern Methodist University Press, 1985.

Goto, Andrea J. "Digging out of the Pigeonhole: African American Representation in the Plays of Suzan-Lori Parks." *Suzan-Lori Parks: A Casebook*. Eds. Kevin J. Wetmore Jr. and Alycia Smith-Howard. New York: Routledge, 2007. 106–23.

Gottlieb, Lois C. "The Perils of Freedom: The New Woman in Three American Plays of the 1900s." *Canadian Review of American Studies*, 6.1 (1975): 84–98.

Griffin, Alice and Geraldine Thorsten. *Understanding Lillian Hellman*. Columbia: University of South Carolina Press, 1999.

Grimstead, David. *Melodrama Unveiled: American Theater and Culture, 1800–1850*. Chicago: University of Chicago Press, 1968.

Gronbeck-Tedesco, John. "*A Streetcar Named Desire*: In Light of the New Stagecraft." *Valley Voices: A Literary Review*, 10.1 (2010): 100–11.

Grose, B. Donald. "Edwin Forrest, *Metamora*, and the Indian Removal Question of 1830." *Theatre Journal*, 37.2 (1985): 181–91.

Guare, John. "*The House of Blue Leaves*." 1971. The House of Blue Leaves *and Two Other Plays*. New York: NAL, 1987. 3–87.

———. "Preface to the Plume Edition." The House of Blue Leaves *and Two Other Plays*. New York: NAL, 1987. vii–xii.

Gussow, Mel. "Nilo Cruz's 'Anna Karenina' Lights the Cubans' Cigars." *New York Times*, September 14, 2003: B5.

———. "Off and Off-Off-Broadway." *The Cambridge History of American Theater, Vol. III: Post-World War II to the 1990s*. Eds. Don B. Wilmeth and Christopher Bigsby. Cambridge: Cambridge University Press, 2000. 196–223.

Haedicke, Janet V. "David Mamet: America on the American Stage." *A Companion to Twentieth-Century Drama*. Ed. David Krasner. Malden, MA: Blackwell, 2006. 406–22.

Hansberry, Lorraine. "The Negro Writer and His Roots." 1959. *The Black Scholar*, 12 (1981): 2–12.

———. "On Arthur Miller, Marilyn Monroe, and Guilt." 1964. *Women in Theater: Compassion and Hope*. Ed. Karen Malpede. New York: Drama Book Publishers, 1983. 173–76.

———. *"To Be Young, Gifted, and Black:* Lorraine Hansberry *in Her Own Words*. 1969. Ed. Robert Nemiroff. Englewood Cliffs, NJ: Prentice-Hall, 1970.

———. "Willy Loman, Walter Younger, and He Who Must Live." *Village Voice*, August 12, 1959: 7–8.

Hartnoll, Phyllis and Peter Found. "Pixérécourt, (René-Charles) Guilbert de." *The Concise Oxford Companion to the Theater*, 2nd ed. Eds. Phyllis Hartnol and Peter Found. Oxford: Oxford University Press, 1996. Oxford Reference, 2003.

Haugo, Ann. "Native American Drama: A Historical Survey." *Indigenous North American Drama: A Multivocal History*. Ed. Birgit Däwes. Albany: SUNY University Press, 2013. 39–62.

Havens, Daniel F. *The Columbian Muse of Comedy: The Development of a Native Tradition in Early American Social Comedy, 1787–1845*. Carbondale: Southern Illinois University Press, 1973.

Herne, James A. "Art for Truth's Sake." *The Arena*, February 1897: 361–70.

———. *Margaret Fleming*. 1890. *Nineteenth Century American Plays: Seven Plays Including* The Black Crook. Ed. Myron Matlaw. New York: Applause, 1967, 2001. 455–510.

Herne, Julie A. "Biographical Note." Shore Acers *and Other Plays*. New York: Samuel French, 1928/Wildside Press, 2010. ix–xxix.

Herren, Graley. "Narrating, Witnessing, and Healing Trauma in Paula Vogel's *How I Learned to Drive*." *Modern Drama*, 53.1 (2010): 103–14.

Hill, Errol G. "The African Theater to *Uncle Tom's Cabin*." *A History of African American Theater*. By Errol G. Hill and James V. Hatch. Cambridge: Cambridge University Press, 2003. 24–60.

———. "The Civil War to *The Creole Show*." *A History of African American Theater*. By Errol G. Hill and James V. Hatch. Cambridge: Cambridge University Press, 2003. 61–92.

———. "The Hyers Sisters: Pioneers in Black Musical Comedy." *The American Stage: Social and Economic Issues from the Colonial Period to the Present*. Eds. Ron Engle and Tice L. Miller. Cambridge: Cambridge University Press, 1993. 115–30.

Hitchcock, H. Wiley. "An Early American Melodrama: *The Indian Princess* of J.N. Barker and John Bray." *Notes*, 12.3 (1955): 375–88.

Hogan, Robert. *Dion Boucicault*. New York: Twayne, 1969.

———. *The Independence of Elmer Rice*. Carbondale: Southern Illinois University Press, 1965.

Holcroft, Thomas. *A Tale of Mystery, a Melodrama*. London: Richard Phillips, 1802.

Holditch, W. Kenneth. "The Broken World: Romanticism, Realism, Naturalism in *A Streetcar Named Desire*." *Confronting Tennessee Williams's* A Streetcar Named Desire: *Essays in Critical Pluralism*. Ed. Philip C. Kolin. Westport, CT: Greenwood Press, 1993. 147–66.

Holmes, Rachel. *African Queen: The Real Life of the Hottentot Venus*. New York: Random House, 2007.

Holzapfel, Amy Strahler. "Auditory Traces: The Medium of the Telephone in Ariana Reines's *Telephone* and Sarah Ruhl's *Dead Man's Cell Phone*." *Contemporary Theatre Review*, 21.2 (2011): 112–25.

Hornblow, Arthur. *A History of the Theater in America from Its Beginnings to the Present Time*, Vol. 1. Philadelphia: Lippincott, 1919.

Hunt, Lynn. *The Family Romance of the French Revolution*. Berkeley: University of California Press, 1992.

Hunter, Robert, with Lewis Morris. *Androboros: A Bographical* [*sic*] *Farce in Three Acts*. c. 1714. archive.org. [Last accessed: 30th November 2016]

Hutchisson, James M. "Poe, Anna Cora Mowatt, and T. Tennyson Twinkle." *Studies in the American Renaissance* (1993): 245–54.

Hwang, David Henry. *FOB*. 1980. *Trying to Find Chinatown: Selected Plays*. New York: Theatre Communications Group, 2000.

Ibsen, Henrik. *A Doll's House*. 1879. *The Works of Henrik Ibsen*, Vol. 2. Trans. William Archer. Boston: Scribner's/Jefferson Press, 1911. 22–191.

———. "Alternative Ending to *A Doll's House*." *Nationaltidende* (February 17, 1880): n.p. *All about Henrik Ibsen*. National Library of Norway. ibsen.nb.no. [Last accessed: 30th November 2016]

Inge, Williams. "Foreword." *Four Plays by William Inge*. New York: Random House, 1958. v–x.

Innes, Christopher. "Neil LaBute." *The Methuen Guide to Contemporary American Playwrights*. Eds. Martin Middeke, Peter Paul Schnierer, Christopher Innes, and Matthew C. Roudané. London: Bloomsbury Methuen Drama, 2014. 131–48.

Innes, Christopher et al. "Introduction." *The Methuen Guide to Contemporary American Playwrights*. Eds. Martin Middeke, Peter Paul Schnierer, Christopher Innes, and Matthew C. Roudané. London: Bloomsbury Methuen Drama, 2014. vii–xxiv.

Isherwood, Charles. "A Nagging Call to Tidy up an Unfinished Line." *New York Times*, March 5, 2008: E1+.

Jack, Sam T. *Beauty in Dreamland, or the Pearls of the Orient*. 1889. MS. Library of Congress.

Jacobus, Lee A. *Bedford Introduction to American Drama*, 2nd ed. New York/Boston: Bedford-St. Martin's 1993.

Jaroff, Rebecca. "Opposing Forces: (Re)Playing Pocahontas and the Politics of Indian Removal on the Antebellum Stage." *Comparative Drama*, 40.4 (2006): 483–504.

Johnson, Katie. *Sisters in Sin: Brothel Drama in America, 1900–1920*. Cambridge: Cambridge University Press, 2006.

Jones, Eugene H. *Native Americans as Shown on the Stage, 1753–1916*. Metuchen, NJ: Scarecrow Press, 1988.

Jones, Sally L. "The First but Not the Last of the 'Vanishing Indians': Edwin Forrest and Mythic Re-creations of the Native Population." *Dressing in Feathers: The Construction of the Indian in American Popular Culture*. Ed. S. Elizabeth Bird. Boulder: Westview Press, 1996. 13–27.

Jordan, Pat. "Neil LaBute Has a Thing about Beauty." *New York Times Magazine*, March 25, 2009: 28–31.

Kabatchnik, Amnon. *Blood on the Stage: Milestone Plays of Crime, Mystery, and Detection, 1925–1950*. Lanham, MD: Scarecrow Press, 2010.

Kaiser, Georg. *From Morn to Midnight*. 1912. Trans. Ashley Dukes. 1922. *Dramas of Modernism and Their Forerunners*. Ed. Montrose J. Moses with Oscar James Campbell. Boston: DC Heath, 1931, 1941. 139–65.

Keyssar, Helene. "Feminist Theater of the Seventies in the United States." *Cambridge Companion to American Women Playwrights*. Ed. Brenda Murphy. Cambridge: Cambridge University Press, 1999. 173–94.

Kimbrough, Andrew. "The Pedophile in Me: The Ethics of *How I Learned to Drive*." *Journal of Dramatic Theory and Criticism*, 17.1 (2002): 47–67.

King, Robert L. "The Rhetoric of Dramatic Technique in *Blood Knot*." *South African Theatre Journal*, 7.1 (May 1993): 40–49.

Kippola, Karl M. *Acts of Manhood: The Performance of Masculinity on the American Stage, 1828–1865*. Gordonsville, VA: Palgrave, 2012.

Klaver, Elizabeth. "The Cemetery as Public Space: *Spoon River Anthology* and Act 3 of *Our Town*." *Genre*, 48.1 (2015): 99–118.

Klein, Julia M. "Sarah Ruhl's Whimsical Hauntings." *Chronicle of Higher Education*, July 20, 2007: B12–13.

Knowlson, James. *Damned to Fame: The Life of Samuel Beckett*. New York: Simon and Schuster, 1996.

Kolin, Philip C. "Puck's Magic Mojo: The Achievements of Suzan-Lori Parks." *Suzan-Lori Parks: Essays on the Plays and Other Works*. Ed. Philip C. Kolin. Jefferson, NC: McFarland, 2010. 7–19.

———. *Williams: A Streetcar Named Desire*. Cambridge: Cambridge University Press, 2000.

———. and Harvey Young. "'Watch Me Work': Reflections on Suzan-Lori Parks and Her Canon." *Suzan-Lori Parks in Person: Interviews and Commentaries*. Eds. Philip C. Kolin and Harvey Young. London: Routledge, 2014. 1–25.

Koprince, Susan. "Baseball as History and Myth in August Wilson's *Fences*." *African American Review*, 40.2 (2006): 349–58.

Kornhaber, David. "Kushner at Colonus: Tragedy, Politics, and Citizenship." *PMLA*, 129.4 (2014): 727–41.

Krasner, David. *America Drama, 1945–2000: An Introduction*. Malden, MA: Blackwell, 2006.

———. "Coming of Age on the Rez: William S. Yellow Robe's *The Independence of Eddie Rose* as Native American Bildungsdrama." *Native American Performance and Representation*. Ed. S. E. Wilmer. Tucson: University of Arizona Press, 2009. 171–81.

———. "Eugene O'Neill: American Drama and Modernism." *A Companion to Twentieth-Century American Drama*. Ed. David Krasner. Malden, MA: Blackwell, 2006. 142–58.

Kumar, Nita N. "The Logic of Retribution: Amiri Baraka's *Dutchman*." *African American Review*, 37.2–3 (2003): 271–79.

Kushner, Tony. *Angels in America: Part One: Millennium Approaches*. New York: Theatre Communications Group, 1992.

———. *Angels in America: Part Two: Perestroika*. New York: Theatre Communications Group, 1992.

———. "The Secrets of *Angels*." Interview. *New York Times*, March 27, 1994: 44.

LaBute, Neil. *Fat Pig*. New York: Faber and Faber, 2005.

———. "Preface: The Weight of the World." *Fat Pig*. New York: Faber and Faber, 2005. ix–xii.

Lahr, John. "Been Here and Gone." *The Cambridge Companion to August Wilson*. Ed. Christopher Bigsby. Cambridge: Cambridge University Press, 2007. 28–51.

———. "Surreal Life: The Plays of Sarah Ruhl." *New Yorker*, March 17, 2008: 78–83.

———. "A Touch of Bad." *The New Yorker*, July 5, 1999: 42–49.

———. "Walking with Arthur Miller." *The New Yorker*, March 1, 2012.

Larson, Jennifer. "Folding and Unfolding History: Identity Fabrication in Suzan-Lori Parks's *Topdog/Underdog*." *Reading Contemporary African American Drama: Fragments of History, Fragments of Self*. Eds. Trudier Harris and Jennifer Larson. New York: Peter Lang, 2007. 183–202.

Lederer, Katherine. *Lillian Hellman*. Boston: Twayne, 1979.

Lee, Esther Kim. *A History of Asian American Theater*. Cambridge: Cambridge University Press, 2006.

———. *The Theater of David Henry Hwang*. London: Bloomsbury/Methuen, 2015.

Lee, Josephine. *Performing Asian Identity: Race and Ethnicity on the Contemporary Stage*. Philadelphia: Temple University Press, 1997.

LeMahieu, Michael. "The Theater of the Hustle and the Hustle of the Theater: Play, Player, and Played in Suzan-Lori Parks's *Topdog/Underdog*." *African American Review*, 45.1–2 (2012): 33–47.

Lepore, Jill. *The Name of War: King Philip's War and the Origins of American Identity*. New York: Vintage, 1999.

Lewis, Pericles. "Anton Chekhov." *Modernist Lab at Yale University*. modernism. research.yale.edu. [Last accessed: 30th November 2016]

Longmore, Paul K. "Screening Stereotypes: Images of Disabled People." *Social Policy*, 16.1 (1985): 31–37.

Looby, Christopher. Introduction. *Sheppard Lee, Written by Himself.* Robert Montgomery Bird. 1836. New York: New York Review Books Classics, 2008.

Lott, Eric. *Love and Theft: Blackface Minstrelsy and the American Working Class.* New York: Oxford University Press, 1993.

Ludwig, Sämi. "Realist Melodrama: Innovations on the Premodernist American Stage and Eugene Walter's *The Easiest Way.*" *Passionate Politics: The Cultural Work of American Melodrama from the Early Republic to the Present.* Eds. Ralph J. Poole and Ilka Saal. Newcastle, UK: Cambridge Scholars. 2008. 109–42.

"Magical Negro," *Wikipedia, The Free Encyclopedia*, December 7, 2016, https://en.wikipedia.org/w/index.php?title=Magical_Negro&oldid=753469843. [Last accessed: 30th November 2016]

Mallett, Mark E. "'The Game of Politics': Edwin Forrest and the Jacksonian Democrats." *Journal of American Drama and Theater*, 5.2 (1993): 31–46.

Malley, Patrick. "What Is and What Aint: *Topdog/Underdog* and the American Hustle." *Modern Drama*, 56.2 (2013): 186–205.

Mamet, David. *Oleanna.* New York: Pantheon, 1992.

Mann, Emily. "Nilo Cruz." *BOMB*, 86 (Winter 2004).

Mansbridge, Johanna. "Paula Vogel." *The Methuen Guide to Contemporary American Playwrights.* Eds. Martin Middeke, Peter Paul Schnierer, Christopher Innes, and Matthew C. Roudané. London: Bloomsbury Methuen Drama, 2014. 372–90.

Maslon, Laurence. "Broadway." *The Cambridge History of American Theater, Vol. III: PostWorld War II to the 1990s.* Eds. Don B. Wilmeth and Christopher Bigsby. Cambridge: Cambridge University Press, 2000. 163–95.

Mason, Jeffrey D. *Melodrama and the Myth of America.* Bloomington: Indiana University Press, 1993.

Matlaw, Myron, ed. *Nineteenth-Century American Plays: Seven Plays, Including* The Black Crook. New York: Applause, 1967, 2001.

Matthews, Kristin L. "The Politics of 'Home' in Lorraine Hansberry's *A Raisin in the Sun.*" *Modern Drama*, 51.4 (2008): 556–78.

McConachie, Bruce. "American Theater in Context, from Beginnings to 1870." *The Cambridge History of American Theater, Vol. I: Beginnings to 1870.* Eds. Don B. Wilmeth and Christopher Bigsby. Cambridge: Cambridge University Press, 1998. 111–81.

McKelly, James C. "Hymns of Sedition: Portraits of the Artist in African American Drama." *Arizona Quarterly*, 48.1 (1992): 87–107.

McNulty, Charles. "*Angels in America*: Tony Kushner's Theses on the Philosophy of History." *Modern Drama*, 39.1 (1996): 84–96.

Mead, Rebecca. "All About the Hamiltons." *New Yorker*, February 9, 2015: 48+.

Meserve, Walter J. *An Emerging Entertainment: The Drama of the American People to 1828.* Bloomington: Indiana University Press, 1977.

Meyer, Michael. *Ibsen.* 1967. Strupp (UK): Sutton, 2004.

Miller, Arthur. *Death of a Salesman*. 1949. New York: Penguin, 1976, 1998.

———. "The Family in Modern Drama." 1956. *The Theater Essays of Arthur Miller*. Eds. Robert A. Martin and Steven R. Centola. Revised and expanded edition. Boston: Da Capo, 1996. 69–85.

———. *Timebends*. New York: Grove, 1987.

———. "Tragedy and the Common Man." *New York Times*, February 27, 1949: X1+.

Miller, Gabriel. *Clifford Odets*. New York: Ungar, 1989.

Miranda, Lin-Manuel. *Hamilton*. Original cast recording. Atlantic: 2015.

———. and Jeremy McCarter. *Hamilton: The Revolution*. New York: Grand Central Publishing, 2016.

Mitchell, Loften. *Black Drama: The Story of the American Negro in the Theater*. New York: Hawthorn Books, 1967.

Moeller, Philip. "A Foreword." *The Adding Machine*. Elmer Rice. 1922. New York: Samuel French, 1956.

Mojica, Monica and Ric Knowles. "Introduction to the *Independence of Eddie Rose*." *Staging Coyote's Dream: An Anthology of First Nations Drama in English*. Eds. Monica Mojica and Ric Knowles. Toronto: Playwrights' Canada Press, 2003. 3–5.

Moody, Richard. "Lost and Found: The Fourth Act of *Metamora*." Metamora *and Other Plays*. *America's Lost Plays*, Vol. XIV. Ed. Eugene R. Page. Bloomington: Indiana University Press, 1940, 1965. 401–13.

Mordden, Ethan. *Anything Goes: A History of American Musical Theatre*. Oxford: Oxford University Press, 2013.

Morgenstern, Naomi. "The University in Crisis: Teaching, Tenure, and Transference in David Mamet's *Oleanna*." *Cultural Critique*, 82 (2012): 1–33.

Moses, Montrose J. "Anton Chekhov." *Dramas of Modernism and their Forerunners*. Boston: DC Heath, 1941. 3–5.

———. "Eugene Walter." *Representative Plays by American Dramatists, 1865–1911*. Ed. Montrose J. Moses. New York: Benjamin Blom, 1964. 707–10.

———. "Expressionism: Kaiser and Toller." *Dramas of Modernism and their Forerunners*. Eds. Montrose J. Moses with Oscar James Campbell. Boston: DC Heath, 1931, 1941. 133–37.

———. "James Nelson Barker." *Representative Plays by American Dramatists, 1765–1819*. New York: Benjamin Blom, 1964. 567–71.

Mowatt, Anna Cora Ogden. *Fashion*. 1845. London: Newberry, 1850.

———. *Autobiography of an Actress, or: Eight Years on the Stage*. Boston: Ticknor and Fields, 1854.

Muhammad, Elijah. *Fall of America*. Chicago: Muhammad's Temple of Islam No. 2, 1973.

Murphy, Brenda. *American Realism and American Drama, 1880–1940*. Cambridge: Cambridge University Press, 1987.

———. "*Oleanna*: Language and Power." *The Cambridge Companion to David Mamet*. Ed. Christopher Bigsby. Cambridge: Cambridge University Press, 2004. 124–37.

———. "Plays and Playwrights: 1915–1945." *The Cambridge History of American Theater, Volume Two: 1870–1945*. Eds. Don B. Wilmeth and Christopher Bigsby. Cambridge: Cambridge University Press, 1999. 289–342.

———. "Tennessee Williams." *A Companion to Twentieth-Century American Drama*. Ed. David Krasner. Malden, MA: Blackwell, 2006. 175–91.

Murray, Piper. "'They Are Well Together. Women Are Not': Productive Ambivalence and Female Hom(m)osociality in *Fefu and Her Friends*." *Modern Drama*, 44.4 (2001): 398–415.

Naden, Corinne J. *The Golden Age of American Musical Theater, 1943–1965*. Lanham, MD: Scarecrow Press, 2011.

Nethercot, Arthur H. "The Dramatic Background of Royall Tyler's *The Contrast*." *American Literature*, 12.4 (1941): 435–46.

Nodier, Charles. "'Introduction' to Pixérécourt's Théâtre Choisi." 1843. *Pixérécourt: Four Melodramas*. Eds. and trans. Daniel Gerould and Marvin Carlson. New York: Martin E. Segal Theater Center Publications, 2002. ix–xix.

North, Joseph. "Taxi Strike." *New Masses*, April 3, 1934: 9–11.

Ochsner, David. "They Call It Burlesque." Rev. by Gilbert W. Gabriel. *New Yorker*, August 22, 1925. *A New Yorker State of Mind*. Wordpress.com.

Odets, Clifford. *Waiting for Lefty*. 1935. *Six Plays of Clifford Odets*. New York: Grove, 1979. 1–39.

Olsen, Christopher. "Drama of the 1960s." *A Companion to Twentieth-Century American Drama*. Ed. David Krasner. Malden, MA: Blackwell, 2006. 229–46.

O'Neill, M. J. *How He Does It: Sam T. Jack: Twenty Years a King in the Realm of Burlesque*. Chicago: 1895.

Orbison, Tucker. "Authorization and Subversion of Myth in Shepard's *Buried Child*." *Modern Drama*, 37.3 (1994): 509–20.

Page, Eugene R. "Introduction to *Metamora*" In Metamora *and Other Plays. America's Lost Plays*, Vol. XIV. Ed. Eugene R. Page. Bloomington: Indiana University Press, 1940. 3–6.

Paran, Janice. "A Little Bit of Magic: The World of Nilo Cruz." Anna in the Tropics/ *McCarter Theater Education Forum*, September–October 2003.

Parker, Mary-Louise. "Paula Vogel." BOMB, 61 (Fall 1997).

Parks, Suzan-Lori. *Topdog/Underdog*. New York: Dramatists Play Services, 2002.

———. *Venus: A Play*. New York: Theatre Communications Group, 1997.

Peirce, Francis Lament. "Eugene Walter: An American Realist." *Drama*, 6 (February 1916): 110–21.

Pereira, Kim. "Music and Mythology in August Wilson's Plays." *The Cambridge Companion to August Wilson*. Ed. Christopher Bigsby. Cambridge: Cambridge University Press, 2007. 65–74.

Pérez, Henry. "Book Review: *Anna in the Tropics*." Henderson SU *Academic Forum*, 21 (2003–04).

Perry, John. *James A. Herne: The American Ibsen*. Chicago: Nelson-Hall, 1978.

Pettit, Alexander. "Published Native American Drama, 1970–2011." *The Oxford Handbook of Indigenous American Literature.* Eds. James H. Cox and Daniel Heath Justice. New York: Oxford, 2014. 266–83.

Philbrick, Norman. "The Spy as Hero: An Examination of *André* by William Dunlap." *Studies in Theater and Drama: Essays in Honor of Hubert C. Heffner.* Ed. Oscar G. Brockett. The Hague: Mouton, 1972. 97–119.

Piepenburg, Erik. "Why *Hamilton* Has Heat." *New York Times*, May 3, 2016.

Piggford, George. "Looking into Black Skulls: American Gothic, the Revolutionary Theater, and Amiri Baraka's *Dutchman.*" *American Gothic: New Interventions in a National Narrative.* Eds. Robert K. Martin and Eric Savoy. Iowa City: University of Iowa Press, 1998. 143–60.

Pixérécourt, René-Charles Guilbertde. *Coelina, ou L'Enfant du mystère.* 1800.

———. "Final Reflections on Melodrama." 1843. *Pixérécourt: Four Melodramas.* Eds. and trans. Daniel Gerould and Marvin Carlson. New York: Martin E. Segal Theater Center Publications, 2002. 315–18.

———."Melodrama." 1832. *Pixérécourt: Four Melodramas.* Eds. and trans. Daniel Gerould and Marvin Carlson. New York: Martin E. Segal Theater Center Publications, 2002. 311–14.

Plunka, Gene. *The Black Comedy of John Guare.* Newark: University of Delaware Press, 2002.

———. "John Guare and the Popular Culture Hype of Celebrity Status." *A Companion to Twentieth-Century American Drama.* Ed. David Krasner. Malden, MA: Blackwell, 2005. 352–69.

Porter, Laurin. "Teaching *Long Day's Journey* and *Buried Child.*" *Eugene O'Neill Review*, 25.1–2 (2001): 80–84.

Porter, Thomas E. "Acres of Diamonds: *Death of a Salesman.*" 1969. *Critical Essays on Arthur Miller.* Ed. James J. Martin. Boston: G. K. Hall, 1979. 24–43.

Postlewait, Thomas. "The Hieroglyphic Stage: American Theatre and Society, Post-Civil War to 1945." *The Cambridge History of American Theater, Vol. II: 1870–1945.* Eds. Don B. Wilmeth and Christopher Bigsby. Cambridge: Cambridge University Press, 1999. 107–95.

Pressman, Richard S. "Class Positioning and Shays Rebellion: Resolving the Contradictions of *The Contrast.*" *Early American Literature*, 21.2 (1986): 87–102.

Price, Steven. "Fifteen-Love, Thirty-Love: Edward Albee." *A Companion to Twentieth-Century American Drama.* Ed. David Krasner. Malden, MA: Blackwell, 2005. 247–62.

Queen, Frank. "Amusements/The National." *New York Clipper*, August 27, 1853.

———. "City Summary." *New York Clipper*, November 10, 1860. 238.

———. "City Summary." *New York Clipper*, March 28, 1868. 406.

———. "Introductory." *New York Clipper*, November 23, 1878. 278.

Quigley, Austin E. *The Modern Stage and Other Worlds.* London: Methuen/Routledge, 1985.

Rathbun, Paul. "Native Playwrights Newsletter Interview: William Yellow Robe, Jr." *American Indian Theater and Performance: A Reader*. Eds. Hanay Geiogamah and Jaye T. Darby. Los Angeles: UCLA American Indian Studies Center, 2000. 342–58.

Rebhorn, Matthew. "Flaying Dutchman: Masochism, Minstrelsy, and the Gender Politics of Amiri Baraka's *Dutchman*." *Callaloo*, 26.3 (2003): 796–812.

Rice, Elmer, *The Adding Machine*. 1922. New York: Samuel French, 1956.

Rich, Frank. "A Nightmarish Vision of Urban America as Assembly Line." *New York Times*, October 16, 1990: C13.

Richards, Jeffrey H., ed. *Early American Drama*. New York: Penguin, 1997.

Richards, Lloyd. "Athol Fugard, the Art of Theater no. 8." *The Paris Review*, 111 (Summer 1989).

Richardson, Gary A. *American Drama: From the Colonial Period through World War I*. New York: Twayne, 1993.

———. "Plays and Playwrights: 1800–1865." *The Cambridge History of American Theater: Volume One, Beginnings to 1870*. Eds. Don B. Wilmeth and Christopher Bigsby. Cambridge: Cambridge University Press, 1998. 250–302.

Rinehart, Lucy. "A Nation's 'Noble Spectacle': Royall Tyler's *The Contrast* and Metatheatrical Commentary." *American Drama*, 3.2 (1994): 24–52.

Rodríguez, Miriam López. "New Critical Approaches to *Machinal*: Sophie Treadwell's Response to Structural Violence." *Violence in American Drama: Essays on Its Staging, Meanings, and Effects*. Eds. Alfonso Caballos Muñoz, Ramón Espejo Romero, and Bernardo Muñoz Martinez. Jefferson, NC: McFarland, 2011. 72–84.

Rooks, David. "The Real Thing." *TCG/American Theater* (July/August 2005).

Rooney, David. "Critic's Notebook: Why *Hamilton* Counts as a Game-Changer." *Hollywood Reporter* (August 31, 2015).

Rorabaugh, W. J. *The Alcoholic Nation: An American Tradition*. New York: Oxford University Press, 1979.

Rose, Charlie. "The Gelbs on O'Neill." *Charlie Rose*. PBS (October 16, 2000). eoneill.org. [Last accessed: 30th November 2016]

Roudané, Matthew C. "Introduction." *The Cambridge Companion to Sam Shepard*. Ed. Matthew C. Roudané. Cambridge: Cambridge University Press, 2002. 1–6.

———. "Plays and Playwrights Since 1970." *The Cambridge History of American Theater, Vol. III: Post-World War II to the 1990s*. Eds. Don B. Wilmeth and Christopher Bigsby. Cambridge: Cambridge University Press, 2000. 331–418.

———. "Safe at Home?: August Wilson's *Fences*." *The Cambridge Companion to August Wilson*. Ed. Christopher Bigsby. Cambridge: Cambridge University Press, 2007. 135–44.

———. *Understanding Edward Albee*. Columbia: University of South Carolina Press, 1987.

Ruhl, Sarah. *Dead Man's Cell Phone*. New York: Theatre Communications Group, 2008.

Saal, Ilka. "Suzan-Lori Parks." *The Methuen Guide to Contemporary American Playwrights*. Eds. Martin Middeke, Peter Paul Schnierer, Christopher Innes, and Mathew C. Roudané. London: Bloomsbury Methuen Drama, 2014. 243–60.

Saddik, Annette J. "John Patrick Shanley." *The Methuen Guide to Contemporary American Playwrights*. Eds. Martin Middeke, Peter Paul Schnierer, Christopher Innes, and Matthew C. Roudané. London: Bloomsbury Methuen Drama, 2014. 279–96.

"Sam T. Jack's Widow to Marry." *New York Times*, February 28, 1901: 9.

"Sam T. Jack's Will Probated." *New York Times*, December 24, 1899: 14.

Saunders, James Robert. "'I done seen a hundred niggers play baseball better than Jackie Robinson': Troy Maxson's Plea in August Wilson's *Fences*." *Baseball/Literature/Culture: Essays, 2004–2005*. Ed. Peter Carino. Jefferson, NC: McFarland, 2006. 46–52.

Savran, David. "Ambivalence, Utopia, and a Queer Sort of Materialism: How *Angels in America* Reconstructs the Nation." *Theatre Journal*, 47.2 (1995): 207–27.

Savran, David. "The Haunted Houses of Modernity." *Modern Drama: Defining the Field*. Eds. Ric Knowles, Joanne Tompkins, and W. B. Worthen. Toronto: University of Toronto Press, 2003. 117–27.

———. *In Their Own Words: Contemporary American Playwrights*. New York: Theatre Communications Group, 1988.

———. "Making Middlebrow Theater in America." *Codifying the National Self: Spectators, Actors, and the American Dramatic Text*. Brussels: Peter Lang, 2006. 21–38.

———. "Tony Kushner." *Speaking on Stage: Interviews with Contemporary American Playwrights*. Eds. Philip C. Kolin and Colby H. Kullman. Tuscaloosa: University of Alabama Press, 1996. 290–313.

Schillinger, Liesl. "Is Neil LaBute Getting… Nice?" *New York Times*, May 2, 2004. http://www.nytimes.com/2004/05/02/theater/theater-is-neil-labute-getting-nice.html?_r=0. [Last accessed: 18th December 2016]

Schlueter, June. "Plays and Playwrights, 1945–1970." *The Cambridge History of American Theater, Vol. III: Post-World War II to the 1990s*. Eds. Don B. Wilmeth and Christopher Bigsby. Cambridge: Cambridge University Press, 2000. 294–330.

Scott, Clement. "Novelty Theater." *The Daily Telegraph*, June 8, 1889. *All about Henrik Ibsen*. National Library of Norway. ibsen.nb.no. [Last accessed: 30th November 2016]

Seibert Jr., Donald T. "Royall Tyler's 'Bold Example': *The Contrast* and the English Comedy of Manners." *Early American Literature*, 13.1 (1978): 3–11.

Seward, Lori and David Barbour. "Waiting for Lefty." *TDR*, 28.4 (1984): 38–48.

Shafer, Yvonne. *American Women Playwrights, 1900–1950*. New York: Peter Lang, 1995.

Shainberg, Lawrence. "Exorcising Beckett." *Paris Review*, 104 (Fall 1987).

Shanley, John Patrick. *Doubt: A Parable*. New York: Theatre Communications Group, 2005.

Shaw, John. "*The Drunkard.*" *The Chicago Reader*, January 4, 1990. chicagoreader. com. [Last accessed: 30th November 2016]

Shedd, Sally. "'There is no Keyhole on my Door': Musings Visibility and the Power of the 'Unmarked' in *The Children's Hour.*" *Journal of Dramatic Theory and Criticism*, 21.2 (2007): 139–42.

Shepard, Sam. *Buried Child.* 1978. *Seven Plays.* New York: Bantam, 1984. 61–132.

Sheridan, Richard Brinsley. *The School for Scandal: A Comedy in Five Acts.* 1777. *Sheridan's Plays: Now Printed as He Wrote Them.* Ed. W. Fraser Rae. London: David Nutt, 1902. 147–221.

Shuman, R. Baird. *William Inge*, rev. ed. Boston: Twayne, 1989.

Siegel, Lee. "Angles in America." *The New Republic*, December 29, 2003–January 12, 2004: 27–30.

Silverstein, Marc. "'We're Just Human': *Oleanna* and Cultural Crisis." *South Atlantic Review*, 60.2 (1995): 103–120.

Smith, William Henry. *The Drunkard.* 1844. New York: Samuel French, 1850.

Sobel, Bernard. *A Pictorial History of Burlesque.* New York: G.P. Putnam's Sons, 1956.

Sofer, Andrew. "Maria Irene Fornés: Acts of Translation." *A Companion to Twentieth-Century American Drama.* Ed. David Krasner. Malden, MA: Blackwell, 2005. 440–55.

Spencer, Jenny S. "Sex, Lies, and Revision: Historicizing Hellman's *The Children's Hour.*" *Modern Drama*, 47.1 (2004): 44–65.

Stewart, D. Travis (a.k.a. Trav S.D.). "Barons of Burlesque: Sam T. Jack." *Travalanche.* https://travsd.wordpress.com/2012/09/25/barons-of-burlesque-sam-t-jack/ [Last accessed: 15th February 2017]

Stierstorfer, Klaus. "Introduction." London Assurance *and Other Victorian Comedies.* Ed. Klaus Stierstorfer. Oxford: Oxford University Press, 2001. ix–xlvii.

Stone, John Augustus. *Metamora; or, The Last of the Wampanoags.* 1829. Metamora *and Other Plays. America's Lost Plays*, Vol. XIV. Ed. Eugene R. Page. Bloomington: Indiana University Press, 1940, 1965. 7–40.

Strand, Ginger. "Treadwell's Neologism: *Machinal.*" *Theatre Journal* 44.2 (1992): 163–75.

Suthern II, Orrin Clayton. "Minstrelsy and Popular Culture." *American Popular Music: Readings from the Popular Press, Volume I: The Nineteenth Century and Tin Pan Alley.* Ed. Timothy E. Scheurer. Bowling Green, OH: Bowling Green SU Popular Press, 1989. 75–85.

Tancheva, Kornelia. "Sophie Treadwell's Play *Machinal*: Strategies of Reception and Interpretation." *Experimenters, Rebels, and Disparate Voices: The Theater of the 1920s Celebrates American Diversity.* Eds. Arthur Gewirtz and James Kolb. Westport, CT: Praeger, 2003. 101–10.

Teachout, Terry. "Come Back, William Inge." *Commentary*, 127.4 (1986): 71–4.

Thacher, James. *Military Journal of the American Revolution.* Hartford, CT: Herlburt, Kellogg, and Co., 1862.

Toll, Robert C. *Blacking Up: The Minstrel Show in Nineteenth-Century America.* London: Oxford University Press, 1974.

Treadwell, Sophie. *Machinal.* 1928. London: Nick Herne Books, 1993, 2003.

Tucker-Abramson, Myka. "The Money Shot: Economics of Sex, Gun, and Language in *Topdog/Underdog.*" *Modern Drama*, 50.1 (2007): 77–97.

Tufts, Carol Strongin. "Who's Lying?: The Issue of Lesbianism in Lillian Hellman's *The Children's Hour.*" *The Minnesota Review*, 33 (1989): 63–78.

Tyler, Royall. *The Contrast.* 1787. *Representative Plays by American Dramatists, 1765–1819.* Ed. Montrose J. Moses. New York: Benjamin Blom, 1938. 431–98.

Uno, Roberta. "Interview: William Yellow Robe." *MELUS*, 16.3 (1989–90): 83–90.

Urban, Ken. "John Guare." *The Methuen Guide to Contemporary American Playwrights.* Eds. Martin Middeke, Peter Paul Schnierer, Christopher Innes, and Matthew C. Roudané. London: Bloomsbury Methuen Drama, 2014. 58–75.

Vogel, Paula. *How I Learned to Drive.* 1998. *The Mammary Plays.* New York: Theater Communications Group, 1998.

Voss, Ralph F. *A Life of William Inge: The Strains of Triumph.* Lawrence: University of Kansas Press, 1989.

Wade, Leslie A. "Sam Shepard and the American Sunset: Enchantment of the Mythic West." *A Companion to Twentieth-Century American Drama.* Ed. David Krasner. Malden, MA: Blackwell, 2005. 285–300.

Wainscott, Ronald. "Plays and Playwrights: 1896–1915. *Cambridge History of American Theater, Volume Two: 1870–1945.* Eds. Don B. Wilmeth and Christopher Bigsby. Cambridge: Cambridge University Press, 1999. 262–88.

Walder, Dennis. "Crossing the Boundaries: The Genesis of the Township Plays." *Twentieth Century Literature*, 39.4 (1993): 409–22.

Walter, Eugene. *The Easiest Way.* 1909. *Representative Plays by American Dramatists, 1856–1911.* 1921. Ed. Montrose J. Moses. New York: Benjamin Blom, 1964. 710–814.

Wattley, Ama. "Father-Son Conflict and the American Dream in Arthur Miller's *Death of a Salesman* and August Wilson's *Fences.*" *The Arthur Miller Journal*, 5.2 (2010): 1–19.

Weales, Gerald. *American Drama since World War II.* New York: Harcourt, Brace, 1962.

———. *Odets: The Playwright.* London: Methuen, 1985.

———. "On the Horizon: Thoughts on 'A Raisin in the Sun.'" *Commentary* (June 1, 1959): 527–30.

Weaver, Jace. *Other Words: American Indian Literature, Law, and Culture.* Norman: University of Oklahoma Press, 2001.

Wemyss, Francis C. *Chronology of the American Stage, 1752–1852.* New York: Benjamin Blom, 1852.

Weinert-Kendt, Rob. "Christopher Shinn's Plays Explore What Victims Do Next." *Los Angeles Times*, May 11, 2013.

Wertheim, Albert. "American Theater in the 1950s and Inge's Plays." *William Inge: Essays and Reminiscences on the Plays and the Man.* Eds. Jackson R. Bryer and Mary C. Hartig. Jefferson, NC: McFarland, 2014. 13–24.

———. "Dorothy's Friend in Kansas: The Gay Inflections of Williams Inge." *Staging Desire: Queer Readings of American Theater History.* Eds. Kim Marra and Robert A. Schanke. Ann Arbor: University of Michigan Press, 2002. 194–217.

———. *The Dramatic Art of Athol Fugard: From South Africa to the World.* Bloomington: Indiana University Press, 2000.

Wetmore Jr., Kevin J. "Introduction: *Perceptible Mutabilities.*" *Suzan-Lori Parks: A Casebook.* Eds. Kevin J. Wetmore Jr. and Alycia Smith-Howard. New York: Routledge, 2007. xvii–xx.

Wickman, Forrest. "All the Hip-Hop References in *Hamilton*: A Track-by-Track Guide." *Slate*, September 24, 2015.

Wilder, Thornton. *Our Town: A Play in Three Acts.* 1938. New York: Harper & Row, 1957.

Williams, Simon. "European Actors and the Star System, 1752–1870." *The Cambridge History of American Theater: Volume One, Beginnings to 1870.* Eds. Don B. Wilmeth and Christopher Bigsby. Cambridge: Cambridge University Press, 1998. 303–37.

Williams, Tennessee. *A Streetcar Named Desire.* 1947. *Plays, 1937–1955.* New York: Library of America, 2000. 467–564.

Wilson, August. *Fences.* 1985. New York: Theater Communications Group, 2007.

Winter, William. "A Few Remarks on the *School for Scandal.*" *The School for Scandal: A Comedy in Five Acts by Richard Brinsley Sheridan, Remodeled and Arranged by Augustin Daly.* Printed from the Prompter's Copy for Mr. Daly, 1874.

Winterson, Jeannette. "Essay on Lillian Hellman's Play, *The Children's Hour.*" *Jeanette Winterson.* jeanettewinterson.com

Witchel, Alex. "The Confessions of John Patrick Shanley." *New York Times Magazine* 7 November 2004: 32–37.

Wollencott, Eric Barnes. *The Lady of Fashion: The Life and the Theater of Anna Cora Mowatt.* New York: Scribner's, 1954.

Woollcott, Alexander. "Second Thoughts on First Nights: The New O'Neill Play." *New York Times*, November 7, 1920: 88.

Worthen, W. B. "Still Playing Games: Ideology and Performance in the Theater of Maria Irene Fornés." *The Theater of Maria Irene Fornés.* Ed. Marc Robinson. Baltimore: Johns Hopkins University Press, 1999. 61–75.

Wright, William. *Lillian Hellman: The Woman, The Image.* New York: Simon and Schuster, 1986.

Yellow Robe Jr., William S. *The Independence of Eddie Rose.* 1986. *Staging Coyote's Dream: An Anthology of First Nations Drama in English.* Eds. Monica Mojica and Ric Knowles. Toronto: Playwrights' Canada Press, 2003. 6–73.

Zack, Jessica Werner. "My Brother's Keeper: An Interview with Athol Fugard." *Words on Plays: Insights into the Play, the Playwright, the Production:* The Blood Knot. San Francisco: American Conservative Theater, 2008. 6–12.

Zinman, Toby. "David Mamet." *The Methuen Drama Guide to Contemporary American Playwrights.* Eds. Martin Middeke et al. London: Bloomsbury, 2014. 149–67.

Index

Printed by Printforce, the Netherlands